D1447269

POLITICAL PARTIES

MAURICE DUVERGER
Institut d'Etudes Politiques de l'Université de Paris

POLITICAL PARTIES

THEIR ORGANIZATION AND ACTIVITY IN THE MODERN STATE

translated by

BARBARA and ROBERT NORTH

with a Foreword by

D. W. BROGAN

METHUEN & CO LTD
11 NEW FETTER LANE E.C.4

Les Partis Politiques was first published in Paris in 1951, by Armond Colin. The present translation incorporates revisions subsequently made by the author.

First English language edition published July 15th, 1954
Reprinted twice in 1955

Second English Edition revised, 1959
Reprinted twice
Third Edition 1964
Reprinted 1967

First published as a University Paperback 1964
Reprinted four times
Reprinted 1976
ISBN 0 416 68320 7

Printed in Great Britain
at the
University Printing House, Cambridge
(Euan Phillips, University Printer)

Distributed in the USA by
HARPER AND ROW PUBLISHERS, INC.
BARNES AND NOBLE IMPORT DIVISION

CONTENTS

BOOK I

PARTY STRUCTURE

BOOK II

PARTY SYSTEMS

FOREWORD

'PARTY is organized opinion', said Disraeli, a judgment very like that of Benjamin Constant quoted by M. Duverger. But Disraeli knew that party, even a hundred years ago, was more than that. He had not described Tadpole and Taper for nothing, nor did he undertake to organize the amorphous Tory interest into a new party, without reflecting that more than a community of opinion was required. But his emphasis, like that of Benjamin Constant, was on opinion and we start on our reflections on our party system, or that of any other country, with the simple and erroneous assumption that parties are and must be primarily doctrinal bodies. This is not so and M. Duverger shows us not only that this is not so, that the doctrinal unity of a party may be only one of the factors that accounts for its existence and efficacy, but that it may be largely fictitious and accidental or, at best, rest on a historical tradition that may not have any great relevance to the problems facing the party or the country in which the party exists and works.

It is important to emphasize this truth, for we fall, too easily, into the trap of identifying parties with the same label, the same formal doctrine with one another and are surprised when we find that, for reasons that we fail to grasp, two 'Socialist' parties react in very different ways and find it difficult to collaborate because their fundamental unity of doctrine, assuming that there is one, is not, in itself, an adequate foundation on which to build a common programme and a common plan of immediate action, much less to put that plan of action into effect.

It is the first of the many merits of this pioneering book that, by his wealth of illustration and documentation, M. Duverger makes plain to us the great variations in party organization, in social composition, in the kind of aims and interests that the party professes to serve (and perhaps, does serve) that are possible. Because it is roughly true to say that modern parties have the longest continuous history in Britain, we fall into the naïve assumption that British parties are model parties and that countries like France, or Germany, or the United States which do not have neat two-party systems of the British type are wrong, that the multiplicity of parties (as in France), the absence of doctrinal division (as in the United States), is an anomaly that history *must* be in the process of rectifying. It need not be and that is one of the first lessons that we can learn here from the great range and appositeness of M. Duverger's illustrations. We do learn a necessary humility from the very varied experiences of countries like Sweden, Belgium, the Netherlands, even from the only South American state in which democracy (in our sense) can be said to be deeply rooted. And the highly idiosyncratic character of the party system of Uruguay, with its century-old *colorados* and *blancos* is of value to us, if only by reinforcing the lesson that there are more things in the political heaven and earth than we dream of when contemplating, with excessive satisfaction, the perfection of our own party system, and the parliamentary system of which it is both a product and an essential element.

For M. Duverger will have none of the fashionable denigration of parties; they are a necessity of the democratic system and never more than today. Never more than today, because the modern party system is modern. It is a twentieth-century mechanism designed to solve the problem of how to bring 'the people', the new mass voters, into the political community. Here, again, M. Duverger's outside point of view is of especial value to us. Because, in a narrow sense, our party system is old, because party names and party affiliations are still, in some regions, traditional, we are inclined to ignore the novelty of much or most of our party habits and so fail to see what are the true novelties, the true possibilities and the true dangers of our present party system.

We have known since the pioneer work of Sir Lewis Namier how rash it is to interpret the party system of the eighteenth century in our terms. We have learned from Dr. Gash how rash it is to interpret the early nineteenth century in our terms. We have more recently learned from Dr. Pelling how ambiguous a term is 'the rise of the Labour party' and from Mr. Ivor Bulmer-Thomas how novel, in many ways, are our current party practices. But we are still victims of bad linguistic habits and misunderstood history. It is refreshing to look at our system without importing into our field of vision memories of the Long Parliament and the quarrels over the Exclusion Bill.

In Britain, as in all other countries, we are seeing a growth in party power and discipline that comes from what the French call the 'decline of the notables'. When, as in England until quite recently and in France in a somewhat more remote period of time, there were in most regions, 'natural leaders', usually members of traditionally respected and powerful families, the party system was bound to be weak. A Russell, a Cavendish, a Hobhouse did not need the approbation of party headquarters to be the natural representative of the Whig or Liberal interest. A Stanley in Lancashire had an important political position even if the record of the dynasty was not one of absolute fidelity to either of the great 'parties'. It is still true that a conservative party, in all countries, has a larger number of 'notables' in its ranks than has a party of the left (if it is really, not merely verbally, a party of the left). It is recruited, in its upper ranks that is, from men with weight independent of their mere place in the party hierarchy and they often owe their place in that party hierarchy to their own social and professional position. This is true not only of the British Conservative party, but of the Radicals in France for they are 'notables' in their own way, prominent local lawyers, doctors, 'intellectuals', prosperous bourgeois. It is natural, as M. Duverger points out, that a party like this should want single-member constituencies where the personal weight of its leaders can count and should resent joint-lists and proportional representation and all the modern mechanics of elections that make the party investiture so overwhelmingly important. Here France is only following on a road that Britain has already trodden.

For to bring the masses into the political system means to encourage parties that are not mere aggregates of local and personal interests, but parties that give or profess to give to the man in the street a voice in politics that he cannot have if all he is given as a political choice is between one group of notables and another.

It is here that M. Duverger makes one of his most useful distinctions, between the 'interior' and 'exterior' parties. The old parties were really parliamentary groupings; their justification, theoretical in the time of Burke, theoretical and practical in the era after the first Reform Act, was to get a working parliamentary majority together. The party, outside parliament, had a mainly fictitious existence. But the new parties representing the masses had to have a party life outside parliament. Parliamentary politics might be only one of the objects, one of the instruments of the party and of the groups it professed to represent. The non-parliamentary section of the party might be profoundly suspicious of the parliamentary forces as they always had to compromise, to accept deals, to suppress or ignore party doctrines. And all these, however necessary, were, at best, odious necessities to the class that the French call the 'militants' the convinced and active party members. In France, these militants took with a bad grace the truth in Robert de Jouvenel's dictum, 'there is more in common between two deputies, one of whom is revolutionary, than between two revolutionaries, one of whom is a deputy'. And one reason why the French Communist party has kept its hold on the workers, despite attempts to set up rival revolutionary parties, has been that it has made it evident that the parliamentary party is *not* the boss of the Party. It may be obscure who is, but the deputies are deputies, not masters. In Britain, it is only necessary to point to the repeated clashes between the rank and file, as represented in the party Conference, and the party, as represented in Parliament. The party 'militants' may elect their favourites to the executive, but they cannot, simply by doing that, make them leaders of the parliamentary party. That after all represents, not merely the party members, but those who vote the party ticket.

One of the most fascinating analyses of this book is the examination of the meaning to be attached to being a 'member' of the party. The members may be (as in American states with closed primaries) simply those who voted or will vote for the party ticket, but who do no more than that. If membership is no more than that, then the party is the ruling élite, the oligarchy that Robert Michels thought it must be, in any case. But it can be and usually is more than that. The member may be identified by the fact that he pays his subscription more or less regularly (although figures based on contributions are often very misleading as M. Duverger points out). But in what form does he pay a subscription? Does the member of a British trade union who does not 'contract out' of the political levy, by that act (possibly one of mere idleness or timidity) thereby become, in any serious sense, a member of the Labour party? Not, M. Duverger holds, in the sense that a member joining the Labour party in his own private capacity, is. But the fact that the Labour party is a federation of unions, societies, individuals, though not unique, does mark it off from those continental socialist parties that are simple parties, without group membership or even group allies, if only because their most natural allies, the trade unions, have passed under Communist control.

It is invidious to select one section of this book rather than another for special praise, but it is, perhaps, permissible to suggest that the most valuable section for us (apart from those which enable us to understand our own system better) is the description and discussion of the character of the Communist parties. For we, with our tiny Communist party, have very little understanding of the strength and character of Communist parties in countries like France and Italy. For a Communist party is a development of the 'popular' parties that M. Duverger sees as a necessity of the modern democratic state. But it is a variant so extreme as to be a type by itself. This is not due to its being in aim, even in western countries, a one-party party, or to its being totalitarian in its view of society. It is due to its discipline, its organization and to the degree to which the party takes over *all* of the lives of its militants. A Communist militant is not able to answer as vaguely as did some of those in the very interesting poll taken at Auxerre. His militancy is what the party defines, not what he defines. But M. Duverger suggests that, even in a Communist party, as in France, the party has not an absolutely free hand in deciding how its militants will do their party work. Ideally, the model unit may be and is the 'cell', but as M. Duverger shows, in France, the tendency is for the local territorially based 'section' to replace the 'cell', as it would do but for constant vigilance from above. As M. Duverger insists, we are at a disadvantage in discussing Communist practices because the real working of the inner party machine is hidden from us and the evidence of public statements by party leaders and of refugees from the party is to be taken with caution. But what can be learned by an outsider, is set forth with clarity and objectivity here.

The Communist parties carry to an extreme that intensification of party discipline and that extension of the range of party activities that marks off the new, mass parties, from the bourgeois parties that, slowly and reluctantly, follow in their footsteps. It is natural for the Communists to have taken under party control, sport, art, science, to have undertaken to give to party members a full life lived inside the party organization and under party discipline. It is inevitable, as M. Duverger points out, that there should be purges. There *must* be purges. And it is inevitable, too, that discipline must apply to aspects of life that are not, in other parties, under party control. M. Aragon must keep his enthusiasm for Picasso under control and men of science and doctors must accept official doctrine in genetics and in medical practice, as they accept it in the 'ordinary' areas of party life. There are, in fact, no non-party areas. It might be said that the idea of enlisting sport and art is not new and not specifically Communist, but the old Clarion cycling clubs and the old William Morris choirs were pale prefigurations of the elaborate social system that a Communist party, in a country where it has mass support, can build up.

M. Duverger's business is not to distribute good conduct prizes and so he notes, with scientific objectivity, the advantages that totalitarian parties (not merely Communist parties) have over the old, loosely articulated, badly disciplined and merely 'political' parties. As a democracy fighting a dictatorship inevitably takes on the colour of its opponent, so must a democratic party system take on the colour, imitate the methods of its enemies. And in France, especially, it is idle to lament the old days of a rudimentary system with no more serious object than to send groups to the Chamber and in some cases, with no more serious object, once the groups got there, than to get ministerial portfolios for the members. The existence of the Communists (and of mass parties or leagues called into existence by the power of the Communists), makes the days of the old parliamentary groups, loosely called parties, as remote as the factions of 1789. For, in party organization, 1880 was nearer 1789 than 1954 is near 1880 or even 1900.

There are countries of which this is not yet true. M. Duverger recognizes the unique character of the American party system and does not, as is too often done in England, dismiss it as a mere aberration. It is there and it is historically explicable. But he notes how ominous and how dangerous, in a free world dependent on American power, is the existence of a party system so badly articulated and so localized. The weakness of the American party system may be, he suggests, the greatest obstacle to the success of American policy.

There is so much richness in this book that it is possible to go on picking out plums for a very long time. We are invited to contemplate the reasons why, even in a left party, young 'bourgeois' are likely to become leaders sooner than members of working-class origin. It may be just a question of education, but even so, the phenomenon deserves notice, for a democratization of the educational system means, in effect, the drawing into the middle classes of the intellectually brightest of the children of the working class. The problem will remain even if its economic cause is altered. We are given sagacious reflections on how important is the public house or saloon or bistro in the formation of political currents of opinion. We are asked to reflect on what light a reading of the party press casts on the degree of 'militancy'. (Are all readers of the *Daily Herald* more militant than all readers of the London *Daily Mirror* or are all readers of the New York *Post* more militant than the readers of the New York *Daily News*?)

We are warned, too about misunderstanding the effect of electoral law on party methods, against exaggerating the importance of proportional representation. We are warned against seeing, in the granting of a real power of dissolution to the French government, an answer to the instability of French ministries. We are asked to notice the exaltation of the party as a sacred thing that marks all totalitarian parties. (I can remember the passionate sincerity with which an orator at the first post-war Congress of the French Communist party talked of 'notre beau parti'.) We are reminded of the variety of parties and institutions summed up, too generally, under the head of 'one-party states'. There was Ataturk's Turkey, as well as Hitler's Germany and Stalin's Russia. And if we wish to preserve what we are accustomed to call liberty, the first necessity is to clear our minds of cant, to look at the modern party system as it is and, above all, accept the fact that it is new, that it must be studied in its own terms, not in terms of nostalgia for the past. We must not hanker after (to quote from F. D. Roosevelt) 'horse-and-buggy' parties in an age when they are as obsolete as the horse-and-buggy. It is easier said than done, but the first step to doing it is to know what we are discussing, what instruments we are attempting to improve. For that task this book is most timely and most useful.

D. W. Brogan

PREFACE

THIS work starts from a basic contradiction: it is at the present time impossible to give a valid description of the comparative functioning of political parties; yet it is essential to do so. We find ourselves in a vicious circle: a general theory of parties will eventually be constructed only upon the preliminary work of many profound studies; but these studies cannot be truly profound so long as there exists no general theory of parties. For Nature answers only when questioned and we do not yet know what questions this subject demands. The example of America is cogent: studies of political parties abound; they are based upon considerable and serious observation; they are often of great value; not one, however, throws any light upon problems like the evolution of party structures, the number and reciprocal relations of parties, the part they play in the State, for all these studies are conceived within the framework of America alone, they deal with problems that are specifically American and do not refer to general questions. Yet how can one refer to general questions when for the most part they are still undefined?

The aim of this book is to break out of the circle and to sketch a preliminary general theory of parties, vague, conjectural, and of necessity approximate, which may yet serve as a basis and guide for detailed studies. First, it defines practical methods of investigation: some offer no originality since they are but the adaptation to political parties of techniques that are known and tried; others are more novel; all seek to introduce objectivity into a field where high feeling and special pleading are the general rule; many presuppose that the leaders of parties will realize the value of such studies and will make available the abundant evidence so far denied to us. Secondly, it seeks to draw up a general plan of the field of study by compiling a balance sheet of all the essential questions and by coordinating them one with another so as to bring out their interdependence and their individual importance. This attempt at methodical classification is primordial: political science will make no true progress so long as its investigations are scattered and individual, empirical rather than scientific. Finally, this book attempts, on the basis of preliminary evidence as complete, varied, and extensive as possible, but still of necessity fragmentary and inadequate, to formulate hypotheses capable of guiding the future research which will one day permit the formulation of authentic sociological laws.

The constant endeavour to classify and systematize which is evident in this book should not therefore cause astonishment. It is the result of a deliberate attempt to transpose into political science the technique of the 'working model' that is, fundamentally, to restore to favour, in a new guise, the methodical use of hypothesis in science. In consequence, by the use of every possible means of investigation, not solely mathematical and statistical techniques, the usefulness of which is limited in this case, an attempt has been made to construct 'models'—they might better be termed 'patterns' or 'schemas'—that is to say, coherent aggregates, more or less approximate in character, whose sole value is to inspire and to guide further detailed studies aimed at verifying them or, more probably, at destroying them. In either case they will have sufficiently served the cause of truth. According to the amount of evidence on which each is based the schemas offer varying degrees of approximation to the truth, but, in each case, an attempt has been made to determine precisely the degree.

The reader is therefore asked never to forget the highly conjectural nature of most of the conclusions formulated in this book—a point of which he will constantly be reminded. In fifty years' time perhaps it will be possible to describe the real working of political parties. For the time being we are in the age of 'cosmogonies'. Science judges them severely once it has arrived at maturity—without them, however, there would be no science, or at least it would take longer to develop.

The majority of studies of political parties are most concerned with analysing their doctrines. This tendency is due to the Liberal conception, which views the party primarily as an ideological group. 'A party is a group of men professing the same political doctrine', wrote Benjamin Constant in 1816. This conception has given rise to many interesting works which belong rather to the history of political ideas than to sociological analysis. The comparative study of parties limits the investigation almost entirely to a description of the influence of doctrines on structure, which is moreover much less important than might be expected. In his 'Essay on Parties' (1760) David Hume made the shrewd observation that the programme plays an essential part in the initial phase, when it serves to bring together scattered individuals, but later on organization comes to the fore, the 'platform' becoming subordinate. Nothing could be truer. Nevertheless, the statement does not apply to certain contemporary political parties in which doctrine has taken on a religious character that gives the parties a totalitarian hold over the life of their members.

In recent years the Marxist conception of party as class, taking the place of the Liberal idea of the party as doctrine, has given a new direction to research. The relation of the individual's standard of living, his profession and his education to his political affiliation has been studied. These analyses are essential, and elsewhere in this book attempts will be made to define strict methods of measuring the social composition of parties. The elementary Marxist opposition of middle class to working class will also often be used in a wide sense (the terms 'proletariat', 'masses', etc., are used). Certainly this dualism is very approximate, and Marxist sociologists are as aware of this as their adversaries. There are many more shades of social stratification than this rough manicheism suggests. None the less this schema is true in one respect: the 'bourgeoisie' and 'proletariat' do not perhaps constitute two classes, defined in strictly economic terms, but they characterize two states of mind, two social attitudes and two ways of life, the distinction between which throws light on certain problems concerned with the structure of parties.

However, the principal object of this work is not to study the social composition of parties any more than their doctrines. It is essentially the study of party institutions and their place in the State. For present-day parties are distinguished far less by their programme or the class of their members than by the nature of their organization. A party is a community with a particular structure. Modern parties are characterized primarily by their anatomy. The protozoa of former periods have been succeeded by the twentieth-century party with its complicated and differentiated organism.[1]

[1] It is a fact that the orginality of twentieth-century parties lies in their organization. It is also a fact that this organization is tending to become an essential factor in the activity of the party, in its influence and its function. These facts explain the general tenor of this book. This does not mean that the author considers party organization a more important factor than the doctrine or the social basis of the party. In fact, he is more inclined to the view that the last is the most important. On this point, he would, with some modifications, almost be prepared to accept the Marxist theory of *substructure* and *superstructure*. To some extent, therefore, this work may be said to deal with superstructure. But the relations between this and substructure are not one-way only. In fact, for some types of contemporary party, organization tends to be determined from above, the superstructure affecting the substructure. Such, at least, seems to be the inner significance of contemporary party evolution.

This evolution can be seen in speech. The Americans refer to certain forms sometimes assumed by their parties as 'the machine'. The Communists call the hierarchical structure of their party the 'machinery' (*appareil*), and generally use the expressive term Organization (with a symptomatic capital letter) to refer to it. Ostrogorski[1] was the first to clear the way to this engrossing analysis. His detailed study, essentially analytical, has had a great many admirers but few imitators. Moreover it is concerned with two countries only, and only with middle-class parties. Later, prompted by the development of Socialism, Roberto Michels wrote an excellent little book[2] in which he describes in terms still appropriate today the oligarchic tendencies of mass organizations. Apart from these two works there is in existence no comparative study of the structure of parties. There is also Hartmann's[3] book, in which he analyses the constitutions of twelve of the principal parties in Central Europe, but this work is merely descriptive and thus limited in scope.

The author is thus venturing into virgin territory, and into especially difficult territory. The organization of parties depends essentially on unwritten practice and habit. It is almost entirely a matter of custom. Constitutions and rules never give more than a partial idea of what happens, if indeed they describe reality at all, for they are rarely strictly applied. Moreover party life is deliberately shrouded in mystery. It is not easy to obtain precise information about parties, even on elementary points. We find ourselves in a primitive juridical system, where the laws and rites are secret and the initiated keep them closely hidden from the sight of the uninitiated. It is only the old guard of the party that knows much about the ins and outs of its organization and the subtle intrigues that take place. These people, however, rarely possess a scientific mind which allows them to retain the necessary objectivity, and they do not talk willingly.

In spite of years of investigation the documentation the author has been able to collect is incomplete, and there are many omissions and points of uncertainty. He therefore craves the reader's very special indulgence for errors which are often inevitable, and would be pleased to have them brought to his notice, so that efforts at research, doomed to failure without the greatest possible number of collaborators, may be completed. He expresses his thanks to all

[1] *Democracy and the Organization of Political Parties*, 2 vols., London, 1902.
[2] *Political Parties*, London, 1915, 2nd ed., Leipzig, 1925.
[3] *Die Politische Partei*, Brünn, 1931.

those who have helped him to collect the information without which this book would not have been possible, notably to Professor James K. Pollock; M. Jean Meynaud, the International and the French Associations of Political Science; Professor Barents and M. de Jong; Professor Castberg, M. Einar Löchen and the Political Science students of Oslo University; Dr. J. Goormaghtigh, M. Heuse, and M. Van Houte; M. Nilson and the *Chr. Michelsen Institute*; the Swiss Federal Statistics Bureau; Dr. Tarik Z. Tunaya and M. Ilhan Arsel; the secretariats and information bureaux of the different political parties, etc., not forgetting his own students at the *Instituts d'Etudes politiques* in Paris and Bordeaux.

For this first edition in English I have completely revised and, where possible, brought up to date the text and figures of the original edition published in France in 1951.

In this connection I wish to record my gratitude to Professor S. E. Finer for many helpful suggestions.

M. D.

NOTE TO THE THIRD EDITION

Since the First Edition was published in 1951 there have been numerous studies of political parties written in many countries. This trend owes something no doubt to the present work which in fact aimed at encouraging such research.

It is as yet too soon to attempt a synthesis of the results obtained in this way for inclusion in a complete recasting of the present work. For this reason, I have confined my revision to points of detail bearing on the facts rather than the theories put forward. Indeed the latter seem scarcely to have been questioned. The space devoted to the influence of electoral systems may perhaps seem somewhat excessive but, on the whole, the most recent work confirms the general direction of this influence and the working hypothesis formulated seven years ago.

1st *March*, 1957

FIGURES

INTRODUCTION

THE ORIGIN OF PARTIES

We must not be misled by the analogy of words. We use the word 'parties' to describe the factions which divided the Republics of antiquity, the troops which formed round a condottiere in Renaissance Italy, the clubs where the members of the Revolutionary assemblies met, and the committees which prepared the elections under the property franchise of the constitutional monarchies as well as the vast popular organizations which give shape to public opinion in modern democracies. There is some justification for this identity of name, for there is a certain underlying relationship—the role of all these institutions is to win political power and exercise it. Obviously, however, they are not the same thing. In fact it is hardly a century since parties, in the true sense of the word, came into being. In 1850 no country in the world (except the United States) knew political parties in the modern sense of the word. There were trends of opinion, popular clubs, philosophical societies, and parliamentary groups, but no real parties. In 1950 parties function in most civilized nations, and in others there is an attempt to imitate them.

How did we pass from the system of 1850 to that of 1950? The question is not prompted solely by pure historical curiosity. Just as men bear all their lives the mark of their childhood, so parties are profoundly influenced by their origins. It is impossible, for example, to understand the structural difference between the British Labour party and the French Socialist party without knowing the different circumstances of their origin. It is impossible to make a serious analysis of the multi-party system in France or Holland, or the two-party system in America, without referring to the origins of parties in each of these countries, which explain their proliferation in the first two and their restriction in the last-named. On the whole the development of parties seems bound up with that of democracy, that is to say with the extension of popular suffrage and parliamentary prerogatives. The more political assemblies see their functions and independence grow, the more their members feel the need to group themselves according to what they have in common, so as to act in concert. The more the right to vote is extended and multiplied, the more necessary it becomes to organize the electors by means of committees capable of making the candidates known and of canalizing the votes in their direction. The rise of parties is thus bound up with the rise of parliamentary groups and electoral committees. Nevertheless some deviate more or less from this general scheme. They originate outside the electoral and parliamentary cycle, and this fact is their most outstanding common characteristic.

The Electoral and Parliamentary Origin of Parties. The general mechanism of this genesis is simple. First there is the creation of parliamentary groups, then the appearance of electoral committees, and finally the establishment of a permanent connection between these two elements. In practice there are various departures from this strict theoretical scheme. There have usually been parliamentary groups before electoral committees. Indeed there were political assemblies before there were elections. Parliamentary groups can be formed in an autocratic chamber just as well as in an elected chamber. In fact the struggle of 'factions' is generally to be seen in all hereditary or co-opted assemblies, whether it be the Senate of classical Rome or the Diet of Poland. Certainly 'faction' is not the same thing as 'parliamentary group'. Between the two there is all the difference which exists between the inorganic and the organized. But the second evolved from the first more or less gradually.

A priori it would seem that community of political doctrine has constituted the essential impulse in the formation of parliamentary groups. Yet facts do not always confirm this hypothesis. Often geographical proximity or the desire to defend one's profession seems to have given the first impulse. Doctrine only came afterwards. Thus in certain countries the first parliamentary groups were local groups which eventually became ideological groups. The rise of parties in the French Constituent Assembly of 1789 is a good example of this kind of development. In April 1789 the provincial representatives to the Estates General began to arrive at Versailles, where they felt rather bewildered. Quite naturally the representatives of the same region tended to meet together so as to escape from the feeling of isolation which assailed them, and at the same time to make preparations for the defence of their local interests. The initiative was taken by the Breton deputies, who hired a room in a café and organized regular meetings among themselves. They then perceived that they shared certain ideas not only on regional matters, but also on the fundamental problems of national policy. So they tried to enrol the deputies from other provinces who shared their views, and in this way the 'Breton club' became an ideological group. When the Assembly was transferred from Versailles to Paris the meetings of the club were at first interrupted and a new meeting-place had to be found. This time, no room in a café being available, the leading spirits hired the refectory of a convent, and it was under the name of this convent that they were to become famous in history. Almost everybody has forgotten the 'Breton club', but who does not know of the Jacobins? An analogous process, transforming a local group into the nucleus of an ideological faction, was later to give rise to the Girondin club.

There should be no confusion between such local groups and those whose name is derived from their meeting-place. The example of the Jacobins is worth quoting here too, since it seems to be typical of a whole phase of the very beginnings of party development. Similarly, in the French Constituent Assembly of 1848, there were the groups of the Palais National, the Institut (Moderate Republicans), the Rue de Poitiers (Catholic Monarchists), the Rue de Castiglione and the Rue des Pyramides (Left). In the Frankfurt Parliament there were the parties of the Café Milani (Extreme Right), the Casino (Right Centre), the Hotel de Wurtemberg (Left Centre, from which the party of Westendhal and that of the Hotel d'Augsburg broke away), the Hotel d'Allemagne (Left), and the Hotel du Mont-Tonnère (Extreme Left). We have here a very different phenomenon from that of the Breton club or the Girondin club. The deputies meet in the same place because they have ideas in common, instead of becoming aware of their community of ideas after meeting as a result of their common origins. This is an ideological group and not a local group, but the fact that the name is derived from the meeting-place shows that the doctrines are still too vague to be used to define the party.

Next to local and ideological factors personal interest finds a place. For example certain groups are more or less obviously parliamentary unions for common defence. The desire for re-election has naturally played a great part: it never completely disappears from parliamentary groups, even when they have reached maturity. Obviously, voting techniques which require a collective effort, for example voting by list (*scrutin de liste*) and proportional representation, strengthen this general tendency: in some countries (e.g. Switzerland and Sweden) the formation of the first really organized parliamentary groups coincided with the adoption of the proportional system. Hope of a ministerial post is also an important factor leading to the coagulation of parliamentary energies: several Centre groups in the French Assemblies are nothing but coalitions of candidates for office (*ministrables*). Nor do they succeed in passing beyond this stage to become real parties. If we are to believe Ostrogorski,[1] corruption has played quite a large part in the development of British parliamentary groups. Over a long period, English ministers made sure of substantial majorities by buying the votes, if not the consciences, of Members of Parliament. The procedure was semi-official: in the House itself there was a desk where members came to receive the price of their vote on a division. In 1714 the post of Political Secretary of the Treasury was set up to take charge of these financial operations; the secretary in question soon became known as the 'Patronage Secretary' because for purposes of corruption he had at his disposition the nominations to government posts. Responsible for distributing the government's largesse to the members of the majority party, the Patronage Secretary kept a close watch on their votes and their speeches. He thus became in their eyes the man with a whip, 'the Whip', just as in hunting the 'whips' gather hounds into a pack. Strict discipline was in this way gradually instituted in the majority party. It was in the nature of things that the minority should adopt in self-defence a similar discipline—although it was based on different methods. Later, when parliamentary morality had been gradually improved, the structure of the groups in Parliament, including their strong organization and the authority of the whip, outlived the causes which had given it birth.

It would be interesting to discover whether the British system has been used in other countries and whether parliamentary corruption produced, either by action or in reaction, a strengthening of the internal organization of the groups of members. It has been recognized that phenomena like corruption have been important, in a certain phase of the development of democracies, as a means whereby the government could resist growing pressure within the assembly: the examples furnished by Guizot in France and Giolitti in Italy are well known. But have they had everywhere else the

[1] But this interpretation is far from commanding general assent amongst English scholars.

same effect on the development of parties as in England? Any hasty generalization on the question would be best avoided. In Italy, the Giolitti system seems on the contrary to have broken up parliamentary groups that were coalescing and increased the personal nature of political struggles.

The emergence of local electoral committees is directly linked with the extension of popular suffrage; this makes it necessary to bring the new electors into the party. For example, the adoption of universal suffrage brought about the expansion of the Socialist parties that occurred in most European countries as the twentieth century opened. However, such mechanical extension of the suffrage is not the only factor in the birth of local committees: the development of egalitarian feelings and the desire to oust traditional social elites is another without which the first would have had no effect. Consider a political system of very limited suffrage as in France from 1815 to 1830 or in England before 1832. Here no committees were needed to bring together the electors; they were both sufficiently evolved socially and sufficiently few in numbers to be able to make a direct choice between candidates without these being presented by a party: the election took place, so to speak, amongst gentlemen, amongst people of the same world, who were acquainted with one another, or almost. Electoral committees do indeed exist sometimes under such a system of limited suffrage, but they play a very minor part. Imagine however the sudden extension of the suffrage: if, at the same time, no one creates or develops active committees capable of securing the confidence of the new electors, these will inevitably tend to vote for the only candidates of whom they have any knowledge, namely the traditional social elites. Thus, at the elections to the French National Assembly in 1871 the suffrage suddenly became free after twenty years of official candidatures, but there were no parties, and so the great mass of voters in country areas turned to the local landlord. The result was the *Republic of Dukes*. The creation of electoral committees tends therefore to be a left-wing effort because fundamentally it is advantageous to the Left: the task is, by means of these committees, to make known new elites which will be able to compete in the minds of the electorate with the prestige of the old elites. But the Right is obliged to follow the example in order to retain its influence: this phenomenon of contagion from the Left will be seen again and again as we analyse the structure of the parties.

The precise way in which an electoral committee is created is difficult to describe in terms of general principles alone, for local conditions here assume a major role. Sometimes it is the candidate himself who gathers around him a few faithful friends in order to ensure his election or his re-election: such a committee is somewhat artificial in character. In some countries, as for example in England, it was not considered right for a candidate to stand for election without backing; he was therefore obliged to persuade a few friends to stand surety for him. Many committees formed in the nineteenth century owed their origin solely to this fact. Sometimes, on the other hand, a few men form a group to launch a candidate and help him in his campaign: take for example the committee formed in 1876 in the 6th *Arrondissement* of Paris by a group of students and a few workmen to support the candidature of Emile Acollas, Professor of Law at the Sorbonne, who was the first Socialist candidate under the Third Republic. Very often some previously existing society gives rise to the creation of a committee: during the French Revolution 'philosophical societies' played an active part in elections; in the United States local clubs exercised considerable electoral influence in the early days of the Union. Frequently too newspapers bring about the creation of electoral committees, as witness the well-known cases of the influence exerted by *Le National* and *La Réforme* in France in 1848.

Sometimes particular circumstances have favoured the birth of committees. An example is to be found in the electoral registration system set up by the English Act of 1832 which entrusted the establishment of electoral lists to parish overseers of the poor who were fiscal officers ill-equipped for such tasks; but appeals by individuals were allowed on many counts, with the result that private initiative played a considerable part. It was however slow to act, all the more so because the law had fixed a registration fee of one shilling that many people were reluctant to pay. In consequence Registration Societies rapidly sprang up in association with the candidates to facilitate the procedure of registration and to urge electors to submit to it. The movement was begun by the Liberals, but the Conservatives soon followed suit. At first the Registration Societies did not concern themselves with the nomination of candidates, who retained their freedom entire, but as the Societies grew they entered this field as well.

In the United States electoral committees have similarly benefited from special conditions. Since a large number of public posts are elective, the mass of voters would find themselves at a loss were they not guided by some selecting organization. Moreover, since the Presidential election was based on a single ballot, the intervention of well-organized committees was essential to avoid any splitting of votes. Furthermore the constant stream of immigrants was perpetually introducing into the voting body a mass of newcomers completely ignorant of American politics: their votes had to be directed towards candidates of whom they knew nothing apart from the fact that they were recommended by the Committee. Finally the establishment from the time of Jackson onwards of the Spoils system, which allotted to the victorious party all the Civil Service posts, placed at the disposal of the committees powerful material means: just as corruption strengthened the structure of parliamentary groups in England, so in America it consolidated that of the electoral committees.

Once these mother-cells, parliamentary groups and electoral committees, have come into being, it is enough that some permanent co-ordination be established between them and that regular connections unite them, for us to find ourselves faced with a true political party. In general the parliamentary group has played the essential role in this particular phase. From above, the group coordinated the activity of parliamentary representatives, but each of these, on the other hand, was eager to develop his connections with his own electoral committee, on which would depend at some time in the future the renewal of his mandate. The result was that the different committees found themselves federated indirectly because their nominees collaborated within the parliamentary group. It only needed these relationships to become institutional instead of personal for the birth certificate of a party to be officially delivered. However, the legal registration of the facts is less important than their sequence in practice. To complete the description we must add that the first effort of a party after its creation normally consists in sponsoring the creation of electoral committees in constituencies where it still has none. In contrast with the earlier ones, these are created as a result of an impulse from the centre. The mechanism of party evolution is thus reversed. The full importance of this observation will become apparent when we attempt to determine how far any party is centralized or decentralized, or the respective influence of parliamentarians and 'inner leaders' in its direction. In the second stage the creation of committees in constituencies not represented in parliament usually leads to the setting up of a party administration distinct from the parliamentary group: the party grows away from its origins (although it remains strongly marked by them). It then tends to resemble parties of the second type which are by their structure at several removes from this electoral and parliamentary mechanism, having been created outside it: these are the externally created parties.

Extra-Parliamentary Origins of Parties. In the course of our examination of the genesis of parties within the electoral and parliamentary framework we have noted the intervention of outside organizations: philosophical societies, working-men's clubs, newspapers, and so on. The distinction between externally created parties and parties created within the electoral and parliamentary framework is not rigorous: it denotes general tendencies rather than clearly differentiated types, with the result that it is often difficult to apply in practice. In a fairly large number of cases, however, the shape of a party is essentially established by a pre-existing institution of which the true activities lie outside elections and parliament: it is then accurate to speak of creation from without.

The groups and associations which may thus bring about the birth of a political party are very numerous and most varied. It is out of the question to draw up an all-embracing list: we shall limit ourselves to a few examples. The activity of the Trade Unions is best known: many Socialist parties have been directly created by them and have moreover retained for varying periods the character of 'secular arm' of the Trade Unions in electoral and parliamentary matters. The British Labour party is the most typical example: its birth was the result of a decision taken by the Trades Union Congress in 1899 to create a parliamentary and electoral organization (Holmes' motion, passed on a card vote by 548,000 to 434,000). Undoubtedly there already existed the Independent Labour party (I.L.P.), led by Keir Hardie, and especially the Fabian Society: both played a very important part in securing the adoption of Holmes' motion (he was in fact a member of the I.L.P.). But the decisive factor was the action of the Trade Unions: the consequence is that the party remains closely dependent upon them. Here is a measure of the influence exerted on structure by origins. James Bryce rightly proposed a distinction between two categories of Socialist parties: Workers' parties, created by Trade Unions, and Socialist parties proper, created by parliamentarians and intellectuals, the second being much more doctrinaire and much less realist than the first.

With the influence of Trade Unions in the creation of parties must be compared that exercised by Agricultural Co-operatives and by Peasants' Associations. Although fewer Agrarian than Labour parties have developed, they have none the less displayed great activity in certain countries, particularly in the Scandinavian democracies, Central Europe, Switzerland, Australia, Canada, and even in the United States. Sometimes they are but simple electoral and parliamentary organizations conforming to the first type described (e.g. France). Elsewhere, on the contrary, they resemble in the circumstances of their creation the British Labour party: agrarian Trade Unions and groups decide on the creation of an electoral organization or else transform themselves directly into a party.

The activity of the Fabian Society in the creation of the Labour party illustrates the influence of philosophical societies, as they were called in the eighteenth century, and of groups of intellectuals on the genesis of political parties. The part played by students' associations and university groups in nineteenth-century European popular movements and in the emergence of the first left-wing political parties is well known. A similar phenomenon is at work today in some Latin-American states. In the same way Freemasonry seems to have played a part in the genesis of the Radical party in France and of various Liberal parties in Europe. In Belgium, there is clear evidence of the nature of its action: the Grand Master of Belgian Freemasonry, Defacqz, had in 1841 founded a political association, the *Alliance*, which set up local societies throughout the country. In 1846 the Alliance called a congress of all these provincial societies in the Hôtel de Ville at Brussels; there were 320 delegates. Under the presidency of Defacqz the Congress decided to set up permanent Liberal associations in the cantons. Similarly there must be a fairly large number of cases of political parties created by groups of intellectuals: it is, however, very rare for such a party to enlist sufficient popular support for it to be successful in countries with universal suffrage. The recent failure in France of the attempt by Jean-Paul Sartre and a few left-wing writers to found the *Rassemblement démocratique révolutionnaire* (R.D.R., Revolutionary Democratic party), is a good example. This method of creating parties would appear more suited to a system of limited suffrage.

On the other hand the influence of the Churches and of religious sects is always considerable. For example in the Netherlands the Anti-Revolutionary party was set up by the Calvinists in opposition to the Catholic Conservative party; in 1897, even more intransigent Protestants created the Christian Historical party to protest against the collaboration of the Catholics and the Anti-Revolutionaries. Catholic organizations, if not the clergy itself, played a direct part in the creation of the right-wing Christian parties that emerged before 1914, and in the contemporary rise of Christian-Democratic parties. In Belgium, the action of the religious authorities was a decisive factor in the development of the Catholic Conservative party. In order to campaign against the 'calamitous' laws of 1879 concerning secular teaching and to protect religious education, the clergy brought about the creation of 'Catholic school committees' throughout the country. They led to the withdrawal of children from the State schools and an increase in the number of confessional schools. In 1884, these committees transformed themselves into local sections of the Catholic party, which thus became one of the most highly organized in Europe. The influence of the Church in the creation of Christian-Democratic parties in 1945 seems to have been less direct. In France, for instance, the ecclesiastical authorities took no initiative in the matter (emphasis must however be laid upon the catalysing action of the *Association catholique de la jeunesse française* (A.C.J.F. Catholic Association of French Youth) and of its various specialized branches: Young Christian Workers, J.O.C.; Young Christian Students, J.E.C.; Young Christian Farmers, J.A.C.). Although the A.C.J.F. did not intervene as an organization, it supplied the party leaders and workers, both at the national and at the local level. In Italy, Catholic Action seems to have played a similar role, the intervention of the clergy being often more direct; so, too, in Germany.

To the list of organizations such as Trade Unions, Philosophical Societies and Churches, which are capable of giving birth to parties, must be added Ex-Servicemen's Associations. On the morrow of the 1914 war they played a great part in the creation of Fascist or pseudo-Fascist parties. Well-known examples are the influence exerted by the former Baltic *freikorps* on the origins of National Socialism and the role of Italian Ex-Servicemen's Associations in Fascism. A yet more definite example occurred in France in 1936 when an association of ex-servicemen—the *Croix de Feu*—transformed itself openly and directly into a political party, the *Parti social français* (P.S.F., French Social party). It is true that some two years previously the Croix de Feu had in part lost its character of Old Comrades' Association to take on that of a 'league' in the special sense of the word in French politics. Like parties, 'leagues' are associations set up with political aims, in contradistinction to the other 'external organizations' studied so far, but they do not employ the same means to attain their ends. Party action is always exerted on the electoral and parliamentary plane, if not exclusively, at least to a very great extent; on the contrary, 'leagues' do not put forward candidates at elections and make no attempt to group parliamentary representatives; they are solely organizations for propaganda and agitation. Consequently, by their very nature, leagues are violently anti-parliamentary: they refuse to play the parliamentary game, differing in this from Fascist and Communist parties which are equally hostile to parliament in doctrine but make use of parliament to conquer power. The league phenomenon corresponds to a politically primitive method, for in a democracy it is obviously more efficacious to use electoral and parliamentary methods to destroy the system than to act from without. The line of development natural to the league is thus a transformation into an extremist party and it is a fact that some such parties, notably the Italian Fascist party, were leaguist in character before becoming true parties.

With the influence of leagues on the formation of parties may be compared that of secret societies and clandestine groups. In both cases in fact we are concerned with organizations having a political aim but which do not function on the electoral and parliamentary plane, the former because they do not wish to, the latter because they cannot, since they are banned by law. (This definition of secret societies, it will be noted, excludes Freemasonry which properly speaking is not secret but discreet.) When the legal ban disappears the clandestine groups tend to be transformed into parties. Thus in 1945 Resistance movements in many formerly occupied countries were to be seen attempting to change themselves into parties, generally without succeeding. However the French *Mouvement républicain populaire* (M.R.P., People's Republican party), and even more the Italian Christian Democratic party can be considered very largely to have issued from former clandestine organizations. Such too were the origins of the Russian Communist party which in 1917 passed direct from illegality to power, retaining moreover certain notable features of its former organization (subsequently introduced into all the Communist parties throughout the world which were reorganized after the pattern of the first one). Here again we note the influence exerted by genesis upon permanent structure. In the case of Communism it is true that the retention of the organization due to clandestinity was also justified by the possible need to reassume speedily the structure of a secret group should governmental persecution make it necessary.

Finally, this enumeration of the different 'external organizations' which may bring about the creation of a political party would not be complete without mention of the action of industrial and commercial groups: banks, big companies, industrial combines, employers' federations, and so on. Unfortunately here it is extremely difficult to pass beyond the bounds of generalizations and hypotheses, for such action is always cloaked in great discretion. In the *Encyclopaedia of Social Sciences*, E. H. Underhill demonstrates the part played in the birth of the Canadian Conservative party in 1854 by the Bank of Montreal, the Grand Trunk Railway, and by Montreal 'big business' generally. Similar influences could no doubt be discovered at work in the formation of almost all right-wing parties; but on this point we have for the most part at our disposal only presumptions (well-founded, it is true) but not evidence: very tactful investigations would be required to make clear the forms and degrees of influence exerted by capitalist groups on the genesis of political parties.

Whatever their origin parties which have come into being outside parliament offer a marked contrast with parties arising within the electoral and parliamentary cycle. To begin with they are generally more centralized than the latter. In fact, their development begins at the top whereas that of the others starts at the base. Their committees and local groups are set up through the drive from a pre-existent centre, which can therefore restrict their liberty of action as it pleases; but in the case of parties of parliamentary or electoral origin it is the local committees which are in existence first and which create a central organism to co-ordinate their activity and consequently limit its powers so as to preserve the greatest possible amount of autonomy. The extent to which the extra-parliamentary institution creating the party is decentralized obviously has an influence on the degree of decentralization of the latter: for example Labour parties are less centralized than Communist parties; parties created by capitalist groups are less centralized than Labour parties, and so on. None the less there is a certain correlation between extra-parliamentary origin and centralization. For analogous reasons, parties arising outside the cycle are generally more coherent and more disciplined than parties of electoral and parliamentary origin. The former have at their disposal an organization already in existence which binds together naturally all the cells at their base; the latter have all these bonds to create with no other starting-point than the coexistence of a few representatives within the one parliament.

Similarly the influence of the parliamentary group is very different in the two types of parties. It is immense in the case of parties of parliamentary or electoral origin. The parliamentary representatives play an essential part whether they as a body constitute the directing organization of the party or whether as individuals many of them are members of a controlling committee theoretically distinct from the parliamentary group. This preponderance of the elected representatives is easily explained by the mechanism of the party's development in which the greatest part was played by the members of parliament. On the other hand parties of extra-parliamentary origin were set up without their intervention, so it is easy to understand that their influence is always less there. In fact in such parties there is a certain more or less open mistrust of the parliamentary group, and a more or less definite desire to subject it to the authority of an independent controlling committee. Certainly many other factors enter into the explanation of this phenomenon. For example it happens in all Socialist parties, whether of parliamentary origin, as in France, or of extra-parliamentary origin, as in England. This example, however, does not invalidate the preceding statement. On the contrary, is it not striking to note that the practical influence of the parliamentary group is much more developed in the French Socialist party than in the Labour party? And have not all Socialist parties, even those closest to the electoral and parliamentary cycle, been more or less subjected to the influence of extra-parliamentary elements? Among the factors determining the influence of parliamentary representatives on a party the origin of that party remains a fundamental one.

The scope of the discussion needs to be enlarged. It is the whole life of the party which bears the mark of its origin, and its attitude with regard to the elected representatives is only one particular manifestation of the general importance accorded to electoral and parliamentary activities in relation to the others. Parties of extra-parliamentary origin show a much greater independence of them than those born and bred in the shade of the Chamber. For the latter the winning of seats in political assemblies is the essence of the life of the party, the very reason for its existence and the supreme purpose of its life. On the other hand, for the former, the electoral and parliamentary struggle remains very important, but it is only one of the elements in the general activity of the party, one of the means, among others, that it uses to realize its political ends. For example, for the Radical party in France the main question is the winning of the greatest possible number of seats in parliament; for the M.R.P. the essential is, on the other hand, the promotion of certain spiritual and moral values in political life, and this lays as much stress on educational work as on electoral campaigns: finally, for the Communist party, the electoral campaigns are only one element, and that often a very secondary one, of an all-embracing strategy aiming at the complete seizure of power and the exercising of it in totalitarian form. Certainly these differences cannot be explained entirely by dissimilar origins, but their influence is incontestable. The result is that parties of extra-parliamentary origin, even when attached by their doctrine to the parliamentary system, never allot to it the same value as do parties of the first type. Their development therefore entails a certain independence in fact (often unconscious and repressed) with regard to parliaments and elections.

This point gains in seriousness from the fact that electoral and parliamentary creation seems to correspond to an old type and extra-parliamentary creation to a modern type. Up to 1900 the greater number of political parties arose in the first way: apart from the influence of the Church on certain Catholic parties (notably the Belgian Conservative party), that of industrial and financial groups on the parties of the Right, and that of intellectual circles (and Freemasonry) on some Liberal parties, we find very few extra-parliamentary interventions before the birth of Socialist parties at the beginning of the century. From that time on, however, creation outside parliament becomes the rule and creation within parliament becomes the exception: the recent example of the *Parti Républicain de la Liberté* (P.R.L., Republican party of Liberty) in France, and its failure, is a good illustration of the unwonted nature of such a procedure at the present time. Nevertheless exception must be made of countries new to democracy, that is to say, countries where political assemblies and universal suffrage have scarcely begun to function properly: here the development of parties conforms to the first type described. This does not contradict the preceding affirmation—on the contrary it emphasizes its truth by showing that the electoral and parliamentary creation of parties corresponds to a certain phase of democratic evolution, that of the progressive establishment of universal suffrage (in practice, and not only in legal texts, the latter usually preceding the former). The question is then to organize progressively a mass of new electors, by passing from a personal vote to a collective vote: the development of local committees is the natural answer to this. But once this first phase is passed, once parties are firmly constituted, fresh parties as they appear beat against the barrier of the old ones: separate local movements no longer suffice to break down this barrier; these movements cannot pass beyond their birthplace, and remain incapable of giving rise to a truly national party. In other words, the first type described corresponds to the creation of political parties in a country where no system of organized parties yet exists. As soon as such a system is at work, the second type of creation becomes the more usual.

BOOK I

PARTY STRUCTURE

ONE of the most marked features of party structure is its heterogeneity. The same name is used for three or four sociological types which differ in their basic elements, in their general framework, in their bonds of membership, and in their governing bodies.

The first such type corresponds approximately to the 'middle-class' parties of the nineteenth century, which still survive in the shape of Conservative and Liberal parties; in the United States, they continue to occupy the political stage (the American parties retain, however, certain markedly original traits). They are based upon caucuses which are narrowly recruited, rather independent of one another and generally decentralized; their aim is not so much to increase their membership or to enlist the masses as to recruit outstanding people. Since their activity is entirely directed towards elections and parliamentary alliances it has in consequence a somewhat seasonal character; the framework of their administration is embryonic; on the whole, their leadership is in the hands of their parliamentary representatives and is very markedly individual in form: real power in them belongs to a particular group revolving round a parliamentary leader and the life of the party stems from rivalry amongst such small groups. The party is concerned only with political questions; doctrine and ideological problems play a very small part in its life and membership is generally based upon interest or habit.

The structure of the Socialist parties of continental Europe is different, being directed to organizing as large a proportion of the masses as possible. It therefore involves a definite scheme of affiliation complemented by a very strict system of individual subscriptions; on these the party is dependent for its finances. (This is the technique of public finance based upon taxation, whereas parties of the first type adhere to the technique of private finance: their funds come from donations and subsidies provided by a few backers—merchants, industrial undertakings, banks, and so on.) The caucuses of the first type are here replaced by 'branches'. These are working units, wider-based and less exclusive, in which the political education of members assumes considerable importance alongside the purely electoral activity. The number of members and the collection of subscriptions entail the setting up of a considerable administrative organization. Consequently within the party there is to be found an ever-growing number of permanent officials who naturally tend to form a class and to assume a certain authority: the seeds of bureaucracy begin to develop. The personal aspect in leadership becomes less important: a system of complicated institutions grows up (Congresses, National Committees, Councils, Executives, Secretariats) with an authentic 'separation of powers'. In theory, election is the rule at all levels; in practice, powerful oligarchic tendencies manifest themselves. Doctrine plays a much more important part within the party: rivalries, instead of being struggles between personalities, take on the character of conflicts between opinion. The party moreover steps outside the purely political domain to invade the fields of economics, society, the family, and so on.

In more recent times, Communism and Fascism have created a still more novel sociological type. In contrast with the semi-decentralization of Socialist parties they have in common a very strict centralization, a system of vertical links ensuring that the elements at the base are strictly divided into cells, this being a protection against any attempt at schism and division, and ensuring very strict discipline; leadership based on autocratic methods (nomination from above and co-option) in which the influence of parliamentary representatives is practically non-existent. Neither of them pays more than secondary attention to electoral struggles; their real field of action lies elsewhere—in unceasing propaganda and agitation, using direct and sometimes violent methods, strikes, sabotage, incidents, etc. Both try to adapt themselves equally for conditions of open struggle and clandestine combat in case the State should react against them with prohibitions and proscriptions. Both are equally based on a strict totalitarian doctrine, which requires not only political adhesion, but an absolute pledging of the whole human being, which admits of no distinction between public and private life, but claims the same right to direct the latter as the former. The most important point is that both parties develop in their members an irrational attachment, founded on myths and beliefs of a religious nature, and thus the faith of a Church is combined with the discipline of an army. Nevertheless, there remain profound differences between Communist and Fascist parties. The first is their structure: Communist parties are based on a system of workplace cells, Fascist parties on some kind of private army. Next their social composition: Communism claims to be the political expression of the working class, the advance guard of the proletariat fighting for its liberation; Fascism constitutes the defensive army of the upper and lower middle classes aiming at preventing both their elimination and the seizure of political power by the working class. The final difference is one of doctrine and inner philosophy: Communism believes in the masses, Fascism in the 'elite'; Communism is egalitarian, Fascism is aristocratic. Communism is based on an optimistic metaphysical system, on a belief in progress, on a profound faith in the civilizing virtues of technical progress. Fascism retains a pessimistic view of humanity; it rejects the nineteenth-century respect for science as well as the rationalism of the eighteenth century; it places great emphasis on traditional primitive values—the community of race, blood, and soil. In the Fascist subconscious it is not the workman but the peasant who is the incarnation of the supreme values.

Several types of parties remain outside this general schema; first of all the Catholic and Christian Democrat parties, which occupy a position more or less midway between the old parties and the Socialist parties; next the Labour parties, constituted on a basis of Trade Unions and Co-operative Societies, according to a pattern of 'indirect structure' which will require special analyses; the Agrarian parties, whose diversity of organization is very great and whose role remains limited to a few countries; and lastly, the archaic and prehistoric types of party that will not be discussed here, and that are to be met with in certain countries in the East, in the Middle East, in Africa, and in Latin America, or in pre-1939 Central Europe: these are but followers grouped around an influential protector, clans formed round a feudal family, camarillas united by a military leader.

Our schema remains moreover, very approximate and vague: it describes tendencies rather than any clear-cut distinction. More exactly, it is based upon a coincidence between several categories of individual differences, relating to the basic party elements, their general articulation, the organization of membership, the degrees and kind of participation, the nomination of leaders, the part played by parliamentary representatives, and so on. The essential aim of the investigation that follows lies in defining these basic distinctions with the maximum precision. So far we have only considered the geometrical point on which they converge.

CHAPTER I

PARTY ORGANIZATION

To recognize two elements within a group of human beings, the members and the leaders, those who obey and those who command, those who govern and those who are governed—the 'gouvernants' and the 'gouvernés', as Duguit would say—is to see truly but not to see enough. On the one hand a crowd of individuals bound by a certain solidarity, on the other a few leaders—such a description befits a crowd on the day of a rising, or a children's gathering in a recreation ground, or a band of robbers led by a chief; it is appropriate for small or unstable communities, for prehistoric parties which still remain personal clans, followers grouped round a protector. It does not suffice for large, enduring communities; in these the members fit into an institutional framework of a more or less complex character; the total community is a collection of small basic communities, bound to each other by co-ordinating machinery. In modern parties this organization assumes great importance: it constitutes the general setting for the activity of members, the form imposed on their solidarity: it determines the machinery for the selection of leaders, and decides their powers. It often explains the strength and efficiency of certain parties, the weakness and inefficiency of others.

Important changes in this respect have taken place in the last fifty years. While, within the great nations of the West, the general structure of the State remained unchanged in its general lines, the structure of parties has been completely transformed at least twice. Two revolutions have taken place—and even three in some countries—the result of which has been to modify the general conditions of political life and to upset the substructure of democracy. Between 1890 and 1900 the Socialist parties replaced the old structure of restricted caucuses, fairly independent of one another, by a system of local branches, unreservedly open to all members and firmly linked one with another. Between 1925 and 1930 the Communist parties developed an even more novel structure which was based on quite small workplace groups, strongly bound together by the procedure of 'democratic centralism', and yet compartmentalized thanks to the technique of vertical links: this admirable system of organization of the masses has done even more for the success of Communism than Marxist doctrine or the low standard of living of the working classes. Finally, at about the same time, the Fascist parties were creating veritable political armies, private militia capable of taking possession of the State by force and thereafter acting as its Praetorian guard.

However, not all Western nations have known such transformations. They have not taken place in America, where the parties still retain their ancient and traditional organization: the most modern material techniques coexist there alongside an out-of-date political technique. England and the Dominions have experienced no important Communist or Fascist movements; as for the Socialist parties there, they have taken on a very novel pattern, being constructed upon a Trade Union basis: this 'indirect' form (which is only exceptionally met with in other countries) will moreover repay special attention before we analyse on the one hand the basic elements in political parties and on the other the general articulation which unites and co-ordinates the component cells.

I. DIRECT AND INDIRECT STRUCTURE

Let us compare the present French Socialist party with the British Labour party of 1900. The first is composed of individuals who have signed a membership form, who pay a monthly subscription, and who attend the local branch meetings more or less regularly. The second was made up of Trade Unions, Co-operative Societies, Friendly Societies, and groups of intellectuals who had united to establish a common organization: there were no party supporters or members, only members of the component groups, the Trade Unions, Co-operative Societies, Friendly Societies, and so on. The French Socialist party is an example of a 'direct' party: the Labour party of 1900 an example of an 'indirect' party.

This distinction corresponds, for political parties, with that between the unitary and the confederate state at the national level. In the unitary state there is a direct link between the citizen and the national community: in the same way, in the 'direct' party the members themselves form the party community without the help of other social groupings. On the other hand, in a Confederation, the citizens are joined to the nation through the intermediary of the member states; similarly the 'indirect' party is made up of the union of the component social groups (professional or otherwise). This comparison is, however, not very satisfactory, as state federalism imposes an all-embracing community on each one of the particular communities constituted by its members: there is a Swiss nation, Swiss patriotism, a real Swiss community over and above the community and the patriotism of the canton. On the other hand the idea of 'indirect' party supposes that there is no party community really distinct from the component social groups. Properly speaking one is not a member of a party but of a social group which belongs as a body to the party. Nevertheless, this theoretical pattern is often modified in practical application.

Forms of Indirect Party. Generally speaking, there are two categories of parties with an indirect form: Socialist parties and Catholic parties. In the first, the raw material of the party is made up of workers' Unions, Co-operatives, and Friendly Societies: the party is a community based on a single social class. In the second, the party appears as a federation of workers' Unions and Co-operatives combined with Peasants' Associations, Chambers of Commerce, Associations of Industrialists, and so on: the party unites different social classes, each of which retains its own organization. In both categories, there is a great variation of form: each party has its own originality. Only a few concrete examples will therefore be given, and their relation to general tendencies shown. The British Labour party and the Belgian Workers' party will serve for the Socialist parties, the Belgian Catholic Bloc and the Austrian People's party for Catholic parties.

There is a third category of indirect parties: Agrarian parties, within which agricultural Unions and Co-operatives have played the same part as the workers' Unions and Co-operatives within Socialist parties. Nevertheless, none of them has reached as high a degree of organization as the latter: in their case the indirect form constitutes a fundamental tendency which has nowhere been fully realized and which has even often remained very embryonic in character. However, one might give as examples the Agrarian parties of Balkan Europe, notably the Bulgarian Agrarian party; the Australian Country party, based in fact on the pattern of the Labour party; the Flemish *Boerenbond*, a branch of the Catholic Bloc between 1921 and 1939, which will be described later. On the other hand, we might distinguish between the indirect parties whose initial political group is formed by the meeting at local level of all the members of the constituent groups and those whose basic elements are made up solely of the delegates of such groups. The British Labour party is an example of the first type; the Belgian Workers' party and the Swedish Social Democratic party are examples of the second. The first alone conforms fully with the conception of a mediated party.

The British Labour party has developed a great deal since its creation in 1900. Several stages can be distinguished in its long history, of which the landmarks are the Trade Union Act of 1913, the reform of its constitution in 1918, the 1927 Trade Union Act, and its repeal in 1946. The general picture is of a purely indirect party being transformed into a mixed party in which individual members are found side by side with affiliated members. The first system lasted till 1918, with a first adulteration in 1913 as a result of the well-known Osborne case. No private membership was possible outside the ranks of the Trade Unions and the other Socialist groups: within these there was no distinction made between members who agreed to support the party and other members. The different organs of the party at the various levels were made up of delegates from the component groups, representing the group. Nevertheless, the existence of permanent posts within these organs, in particular the post of secretary (entrusted to Ramsay MacDonald) played a large part in the formation of 'a party spirit': in this way a truly party community was quite soon born at the leadership level.

But the reform imposed on the Labour party by the Act of 1913 and the reform decided upon by the party itself in 1918 brought about a lessening of its indirect character. Before 1913, the Trade Unions affiliated to the Labour party paid the latter a subscription out of the total of the dues they themselves obtained from their members without asking these members for any special sum for political purposes. But in 1908 a railway-worker, W. V. Osborne, brought an action against his Union with the aim of preventing it from using its funds for political purposes. After several appeals the case was finally brought before the House of Lords, which found for the defendant (1909): the very existence of the Labour party was at stake. Finally the Trade Union Act of 1913 adopted a conciliatory solution based on two principles: (1) the Unions had the right to decide by a secret ballot on membership of a political association (in practice the Labour party) and on payment of funds to it; (2) if this decision were taken the funds paid by the

Union to the Labour party were to correspond to a special addition to the individual subscription paid by each member of the Union, anyone of them always having the right to refuse this 'political levy' on condition that he signed an express declaration ('contracting out').

The first provision made no change in the organization of the Labour party except that a secret ballot was required before a Trade Union could belong to the party. On the other hand the second provision profoundly modified its form. Before 1913 there was not a trace of a 'direct' party: there was no individual link between the members of the Union and the party. Henceforth, on the other hand, the 'political levy' constituted a link of this nature: within the Union it was possible to distinguish between the members of the party (those who paid the political levy) and the others (those who refused to pay it). However, this membership was almost automatic in character: silence meant consent; any new member of a Union who did not protest was included in the party. A reform of enormous importance in this respect was brought about by the Trade Union Act of 1927, passed by the Conservatives after an unsuccessful attempt at a General Strike. The rule established in 1913 was reversed; now, silence meant refusal; only those members of the Unions who formally accepted the political levy were obliged to pay it. Under this system, the party becomes really 'direct' in character: the act of the new member of the Trade Union who declares in writing that he is willing to pay the political levy is equivalent to individual membership of the party. It is even clearer and more precise than the undertaking required by many parties on the enrolment of a new member. At this stage, the Labour party might be considered as being much more like a party of the traditional type than like the purely federative party it had been originally. But in 1946 the Labour Government repealed the Act of 1927 and reverted to the old system—the procedure known as 'contracting out' came into force again: if the Union member says nothing he pays the political levy and an express declaration is necessary to free him from this liability. This is a return towards the indirect pattern.

The reform brought about in 1918 in the constitution of the party made it less indirect from another point of view, and this was a lasting change. Side by side with the collective membership of Trade Unions, Co-operatives, and other Socialist groups the Labour party from then on allowed the individual membership of men and

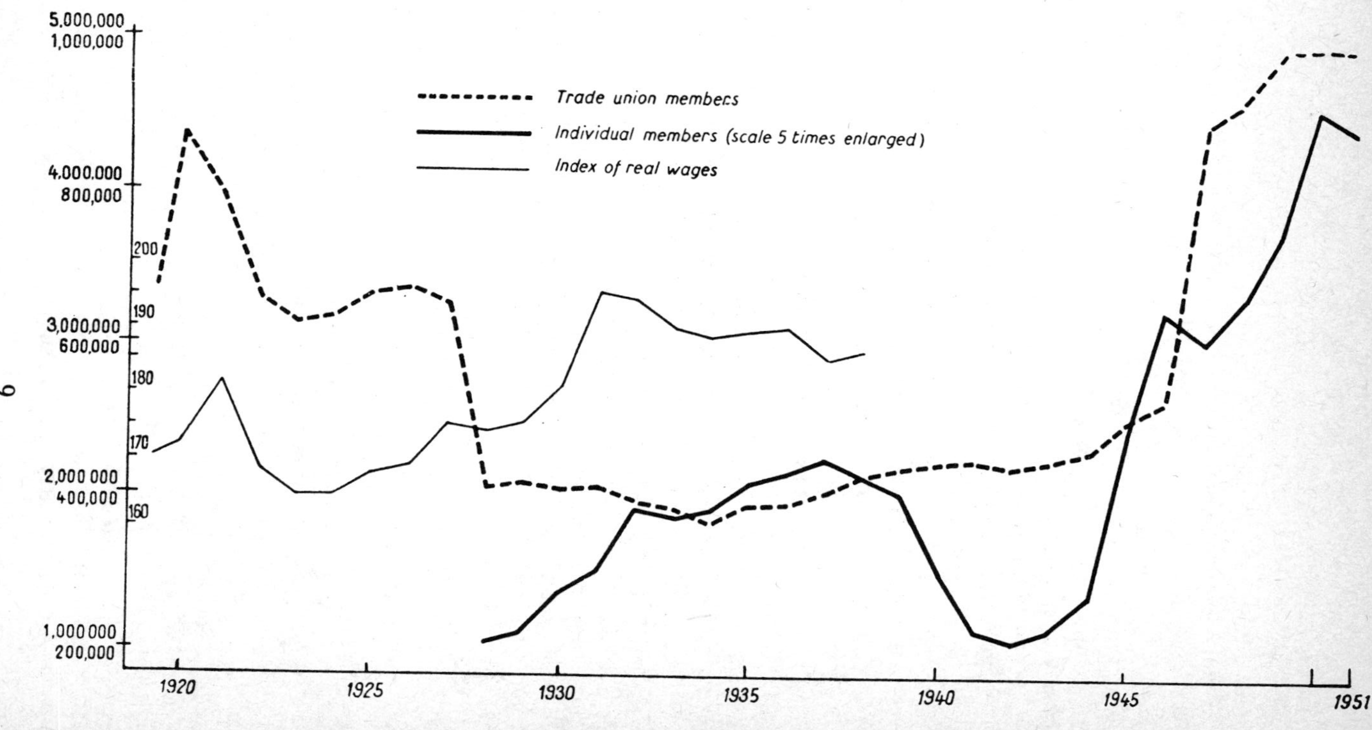

Fig. 1. Individual membership in the Labour Party

women not belonging to the organizations mentioned. Thus a real 'direct' party community was established alongside the Trade Unions and other corporate communities united with the party by federation. The party has continued to grow in importance; with its 729,624 individual members the Labour party was in 1949 the most powerful Socialist party in Europe, even without taking into account the support of the Trade Unions (Fig. 1). Nevertheless the latter continue to wield a large majority in the directing bodies of the party at all levels.

This development from an 'indirect' form to a 'direct' form occurs again in a much more marked form in the Belgian Socialist party which underwent a profound change in 1945. A change in structure led furthermore to a change in title, the old P.O.B. (Belgian Workers' Party) being called thereafter P.S.B. (Belgian Socialist Party). In its first form it was a federation of Co-operative Societies, Trade Unions, Friendly Societies, and Socialist Leagues (Young Socialists, cultural organizations, and so on), somewhat similar to the Labour party in spite of some marked differences. The leading part was taken by the Co-operatives and not by the Trade Unions. Before the creation of the party the latter had had at their disposition no powerful organization; this had been created by the party instead of itself creating the party. The development of the party, supported by the Co-operatives, had energized the Trade Union movement. In consequence the Trade Unions had no strong central organization outside the party, unless it were their 'General Committee', of which the secondary role is clearly indicated by the modesty of its name. In theory, all Trade Union members were members of the party, and vice versa. This dual affiliation tended moreover to lead to triple and even quadruple affiliation, since the Trade Union party member had to join the party Co-operative Associations and the party Friendly Societies. However, there was no exact coincidence between these different groups. All Co-operators were not Trade Unionists, nor were all Trade Unionists members of the Friendly Societies: furthermore, the members of the Socialist Leagues sometimes remained outside the Trade Unions.

On the other hand, the basic cells of the party were not made up of the delegates of the component groups (Trade Unions, Co-operatives, and Friendly Societies) but of the actual members of these groups; the local working-class league brought together all the members of the party. A comparison can be made between this formation and that of the Swedish Social Democratic Workers' party: membership of the local branch (*arbetarekommun*) is open either to individuals or to groups—in practice Trade Unions, Co-operatives, etc. The branch officers are elected by a general meeting of all the members, whatever the nature of their membership, and without the various component groups being separately represented; the organization is far less indirect than that of the Labour party. Since 1945, the Belgian Workers' party has been even less so: the Trade Unions having broken away from it (under Communist pressure), it was reorganized with individual memberships, on the model of other continental Socialist parties. Nevertheless its new constitution allows for the collective membership of 'economic, social, and cultural groups determined to associate their efforts with those of the party'; the liaison between them and the party organizations at different levels is ensured by committees drawn equally from both. It so happened that the struggle against Leopold III gave the opportunity for fresh co-operation between the party and the Trade Unions, which came together with the Co-operatives and Friendly Societies within the framework of the 'National Committee for Common Action'. There is a very marked tendency towards a return to the earlier set-up.

The Belgian Catholic party between 1921 and 1945 offered an example of indirect formation different both from that of the Labour party and that of the Belgian Workers' party. After the 1914 War, the development of Christian Democratic tendencies had weakened the old Federation of Catholic groups, which had remained very middle class and conservative, and made a profound division in the party. In order to recover its unity, at least relatively, and to give more place to Social Catholics and their organizations, a fundamental reform in structure was brought about in 1921. The party became based on *standen*, that is to say on the social 'estates' (in the sense in which this word was understood under the Old Regime, for example in the term 'Estates General'). Under the name of Catholic Union four basic associations were now united: the former Federation of Catholic groups, representing the Conservative middle class; the *Boerenbond*, a league of Flemish peasants (joined in 1931 by the Walloon Agricultural Alliance); the National League of Christian Workers, consisting of Trade Unions, Co-operatives, and Friendly Societies; and lastly the Federation of Middle Classes, uniting artisans and shopkeepers. Each of these groups sent six representatives to the General Council of Catholic

Union, over which each presided in turn. The influence of the General Council was small: its powers were practically limited to arbitration and making proposals. Its essential function was to arrive at an agreement between the *standen* for the setting-up of unified Catholic lists at the elections. Thus no real party community existed either at the membership level or at the officer level. Direct membership of the party was not possible, only membership of one or other of the *standen*. The General Council of the party, at least in its primitive form, was only a kind of Diet formed by representatives of the *standen*. Nevertheless, it gradually took on a more autonomous character through the creation of a permanent President, through the introduction of persons other than representatives of the *standen* and by the grant of a real power of decision: it was a first step, though a small one, towards the establishment at the higher level of a direct party community.

A comparison can be made between the Belgian Catholic Bloc of 1921–39 and the present Austrian People's party. The latter is composed of three professionally based groups, one for the peasants (*Bauernbund*), the second for manual and white-collar workers (*Arbeiter und angstellten bund*), the third for the middle classes (*Wirtschaftbund*). Other associations are federated with these, notably the *Jugendbewegung*, cultural and sporting groups, and so on. Nevertheless, the *Bünde* of the Austrian People's party are much less autonomous than the *standen* of the Belgian Catholic Bloc. The latter were only related at the top by a common direction with little power and with a federal structure. Among the former there was co-ordination at all levels, by means of complex hierarchical organizations, with very considerable prerogatives, whose members are not solely the representatives of each *Bund*. It might well be asked whether this is not the subdivision into corporate sections of one political community rather than the juxtaposition for political reasons of independent communities: in this case it would be more like a direct party than an indirect party. But this is not a correct interpretation: each *Bund* is independent from the economic and financial point of view, like the *standen*; like them, too, it has its own legal personality. Within the People's parliamentary group the deputies from each *Bund* can be clearly distinguished. (This was not always the case in the Belgian Catholic Bloc.) It is indeed an indirect party, but it is more completely and perfectly organized.

* * *

Factors in Indirect Structure. Direct parties are the rule, indirect parties the exception: that is to say the former are far more widespread than the latter. It is therefore of interest to investigate the factors which cause a party to adopt an indirect form, instead of following the well-worn path of direct organization. But it is difficult here to define general patterns. Very often special political circumstances play an essential part. For example, the split between the Trade Unions and the Socialist party in Belgium, limiting its indirect character, was the consequence of the influence of the Communists in the Trade Unions in 1945, which led them to create an autonomous organization (the F.G.T.B.). In France, on the other hand, this influence brought about a cleavage within the Trade Union movement and the new non-Communist Central Office (the C.G.T.-F.O.) was much more bound up with the Socialist party than the old one. Similarly the coming together of the Trade Unions and the Belgian Socialist party in 1950 was the result of a local political crisis: the controversy over the King; the Committee of Common Action, originally created for the struggle against Leopold III, having survived it to become an instrument of permanent collaboration. It should be obvious that great difficulties stand in the way of formulating general laws.

No doubt, doctrinal influences have probably played a part in the adoption of an indirect form. It is tempting to relate the indirect character of certain Catholic parties with the corporate doctrines of Christian democracy, inspired by the Encyclicals *Rerum Novarum* and *Quadragesimo Anno.* The relationship is all the more apparent for the Austrian People's party since these corporative doctrines had in fact a profound influence before the *Anschluss* in Austria where they served as a basis for the official organization of the State. Yet hasty conclusions would be premature, here as elsewhere. Most of the present large Christian-Social parties, notably in France, in Germany, and in Italy, have a direct form. It is probable that the desire to imitate the Socialist parties and to borrow their methods has played a greater part than the corporative doctrines; all the contemporary Catholic parties are more or less connected with organizations of Christian Trade Unions, just as the Socialist parties are with lay Trade Unions.

In the case of the latter, it would be even more tempting to relate the indirect structure with party doctrines. Does the Marxist conception of party as the political expression of a class not define exactly the formation of the Labour party? But the fact that of all

Socialist parties the Labour party is precisely the one that is the least attached to the teachings of Marx suffices to invalidate this explanation. On the whole, indirect participation is found especially in the Nordic Socialist parties, where Marxist doctrines play a rather small part, whereas the Latin Socialist parties (notably the French Socialist party), dominated by more ideological preoccupations, are organized on a direct basis. The explanation must no doubt be reversed; the Trade Union formation of the Labour and similar parties explains their interest in concrete reforms and their lack of enthusiasm for doctrine, whereas the direct political form of the French Socialist party and its emulators has turned them towards theoretical questions. It is not Marxism which has led to a Trade Union formation but the Trade Union formation which has drawn away from Marxism, by giving precedence to preoccupation with immediately effective reforms over the desire for a complete transformation of society.

National temperament has no doubt had a greater influence on the adoption of an indirect form than have doctrines. There are hardly any indirect parties to be met with in Latin countries, but only in Nordic, Anglo-Saxon, and Germanic countries. In Belgium, where the two principal parties simultaneously adopted indirect organization at one period of their history, it seems to have been stronger in Flanders than in the Walloon states: can one not see here the influence of a rather powerful corporate instinct of which there are quite a few traces in the history of Flanders? The electoral system also seems to have played a part in this matter. It will be seen that the absence of universal suffrage, by restricting the development of Socialist parties, to the resultant advantage of Trade Unions or Co-operatives, has no doubt favoured the intervention of the latter in the formation of the former. On the other hand, voting for a list of candidates has perhaps favoured in Belgium and in Austria the federal organization of Catholic parties on the basis of the *standen* and the *bund* by allowing each of these the choice of its own delegates on the common list: a single-member system would have obliged them to agree in every constituency on a single candidate and would have encouraged fusion. Unfortunately all these explanations remain partial, superficial, and largely hypothetical.

The analysis may be carried further provided it is confined to the domain of Socialist parties alone. At the beginning of the century there was quite a keen struggle between the 'Labour' parties (of indirect structure) and the really 'Socialist' parties (of direct structure). Often the two types existed at the same time in the same country (for example in Australia, in New Zealand, in Belgium, and in England): but generally in the end the Socialist parties disappeared in favour of the Labour parties. In other places purely Socialist parties, with direct structure, were the only ones to develop, while the Trade Unions retained an autonomous organization, unconnected with political action. Here indirect structure seems to be the result of the Trade Unions developing before the party, the opposite situation entailing on the other hand direct structure. In certain countries, through the absence of universal suffrage (Belgium and the Scandinavian countries) or special conditions of the electoral struggle (the two-party system in England), there was no possibility at the end of the nineteenth and beginning of the twentieth centuries of any parliamentary representation of the proletariat nor of any influence on the elections other than locally. Consequently working-class action developed first of all in the occupational sphere by means of Trade Unions or Co-operatives which became powerful and organized *before* the existence of Socialist parties. When political and electoral evolution allowed the development of the latter the trade organization already in existence provided them with a ready-made framework as well as with solid support: whence the tendency to indirect structure. Here England provides a striking example, for Trade Unions had acquired considerable power by the end of the nineteenth century: in 1895 there were 1,500,000 Trade Union members, a fifth of the total number of adult workers. At the same period the Independent Labour party, founded by Keir Hardie, gained only 45,000 votes and not a single seat in Parliament because of the two-party system. The Trade Union organization alone made it possible to form a powerful political party capable of taking its place between the Liberal and Conservative giants.

In Sweden and in Belgium the absence of universal suffrage prevented the working class from finding political expression through a party. On the other hand Trade Union and Co-operative action could bring about improvements in the conditions of the workers. Hence the development of Trade Union action in Sweden and of Co-operative action in Belgium. In both countries the political fight for universal suffrage was conducted with an industrial weapon: the strike (General Strikes of 1891 and 1893 in Belgium; of 1902 and 1908 in Sweden). Thus the Socialist party was naturally obliged to take shape on the basis of the existing class organizations, and to take on an indirect structure. That of the Belgian Workers' party, based on the Co-operatives, has already been defined; in Sweden the Trade Unions decided to join the Social Democratic party in 1898; at first compulsory for all Trade Union members, affiliation became optional in 1900; then in 1908 a clause was introduced allowing individual Union members to withdraw after presenting a declaration in writing; this gave the party a form akin to that of the Labour party.

In France, on the other hand, universal suffrage allowed the working class to take part in politics at a time when the development of Trade Unionism was impeded by obstacles, legal or otherwise, due to memories of the *Commune*. The French Workers' party of Jules Guesde was founded in 1879; the Federation of Trade Unions (C.G.T.) only in 1902: it was not possible for the party to be based on the Trade Unions because the organization of the party preceded that of the Trade Unions. When the Trade Union organization grew stronger it was confronted with a Socialist party that was already powerful, that it considered too parliamentary, too doctrinaire, and too 'bourgeois' but with which it could not compete without dividing the working class. This naturally made it turn towards purely industrial action. In other countries, for example Germany, the party reached such a degree of development compared with the Trade Unions that the latter became clearly subordinate in character, and almost the instrument of the party: this is the opposite of the situation in England, where the party is the instrument of the Trade Unions. In Belgium the situation was more or less the same until 1945: the Trade Unions developed within the party, like a kind of ancillary organization, the Co-operatives having furnished the first basic elements of the indirect structure.

It would be tempting to generalize from these observations and present a general sociological schema: when the Trade Unions or Co-operatives developed before the Socialist party the natural tendency of the latter was to become organized within their framework, on the basis of indirect participation: on the contrary, if the party developed before the Trade Unions it followed the classical method of direct participation (the Trade Unions tending either towards autonomy or towards dependence on the party according to the power of the latter at the time of their appearance). In the absolute form of a sociological law, these conclusions are false. Taken on the other hand to be the expression of a basic tendency, combining with many other factors liable to attenuate or invalidate the results, they seem capable of providing an explanatory principle.

II. THE BASIC ELEMENTS

A party is not a community but a collection of communities, a union of small groups dispersed throughout the country (branches, caucuses, local associations, etc.) and linked by co-ordinating institutions. The term 'basic elements' is used for these component units of the party organization. The contrasting of direct and indirect parties was in a 'horizontal' plane; the idea of basic elements refers to a 'vertical' plane. Each of the corporate or professional groups which compose an indirect party is itself a union of 'basic elements': Trade Unions, Co-operatives, Guilds of the Boerenbond, local middle-class Leagues, etc.; but these are not political by nature: the party only appears through their agglomeration, either at the summit alone, or at the different levels. Moreover there should be no confusion between the 'basic elements', the units from which the party springs, and the 'ancillary organizations', institutions which centre upon it, either to bring together supporters, or to strengthen the bonds of membership: youth movements, women's organizations, sports clubs, cultural organizations, etc. As a matter of fact it is not always easy to distinguish between them and the professional or corporate communities whose union forms the indirect parties: the Trade Unions, for example, are sometimes ancillary organizations of a direct party, sometimes a branch of an indirect party. Only a general analysis of the structure of a party makes it possible to distinguish between the two.

The basic elements of each party have their own particular form. The French Radical Socialist caucus, the branch of the French Socialist party, the caucuses and electoral agents of the American parties, the cells of the Communist parties, the 'fasces' of the Italian Fascist party: all these institutions are profoundly different one from the other. Each party has its own structure which bears little resemblance to that of other parties. In spite of everything four main types of basic element may be distinguished and most of the existing parties can be related to one of them. These elements are the caucus, the branch, the cell, and the militia.

The Caucus. Though this unit might equally well be called a committee, a clique, or a coterie, the English political term 'caucus' will be used here. The first characteristic of the caucus is its limited nature. It consists of a small number of members, and seeks no expansion. It does not indulge in any propaganda with a view to extending its recruitment. Moreover, it does not really admit members, for this limited group is also a closed group; you do not get into it simply because you desire to do so: membership is achieved only by a kind of tacit co-option or by formal nomination. In spite of this numerical weakness the caucus nevertheless wields great power. Its strength does not depend on the number of its members but on their quality. It is a group of notabilities, chosen because of their influence.

The caucus functions in a rather large geographical area, usually corresponding to the chief electoral division. In France the caucuses work really within the framework of the arrondissement, which was the basic political division under the Third Republic. In America they are especially important in the counties and municipalities within which take place the elections for the principal administrative posts available as 'spoils'. Moreover the activity of the caucus is seasonal: it reaches its peak at election times and is considerably reduced in the intervals between the ballots. In short the caucus is semi-permanent by nature: we no longer have an ephemeral institution, created for a single electoral campaign and destined to end with it: neither do we yet have a completely permanent institution, like the modern parties for whom agitation and propaganda never cease.

Underlying these general characteristics, several types of caucus can be distinguished. First, there is the distinction between the 'direct' caucus and the 'indirect' caucus. The French Radical Socialist caucuses are a good example of the first. They are composed of notabilities chosen for their individual qualities and their personal influence: influential tradesmen, small country landowners, notaries or doctors in the country or in small towns, civil servants, teachers, lawyers, etc. None of them formally represents a class or a group: they are not delegates but individuals. Moreover their selection does not depend on any precise rule: it is the result of a kind of tacit co-option. Let us consider on the other hand a Labour party caucus in an electoral constituency before there were individual members: it was composed of members elected respectively by the local branches of the Trade Unions, the Trades Councils, the Socialist societies, the Co-operative organizations, and so on.

This basic element of the Labour party consisted in the meetings of the delegates of the local basic elements of each of the communities which collectively constituted the party: here was an 'indirect' caucus. However different it is from the French Radical caucus, a typical 'direct' caucus, it has in common with it the general elements just defined. Each of its members can be considered as a 'notability', no longer because of his own personal characteristics, but because of his special position as a delegate. This represents an abandonment of the idea of a traditional elite, outstanding through birth or natural selection, in favour of the idea of an 'institutional' elite, owing its position to the confidence of the organized masses.

With these caucuses of notabilities can be compared the caucuses of 'experts', composed of people chosen less for their personal influence than for their acquaintance with the methods of fighting an electoral campaign: American party caucuses for example. Nevertheless, the experts are met with less within the caucus itself than at the level of electoral agents, the representatives of the caucus in smaller local divisions, in which through them its influence permeates to the very foundations of the country. In France, the caucuses formed at the arrondissement level try to have an agent in each commune. In the United States the caucuses formed at the county or city level co-ordinate the action of the *precinct-captains* (there are about 3,000 counties and 140,000 precincts). These electoral agents must be distinguished from the voluntary propagandists who help the party caucuses during the electoral campaigns, for example the canvassers in England: the latter correspond to the idea of 'supporter' which will be defined later: the former constitute an element in the very framework of the party.

A detailed analysis of the position of electoral agents and the part they play would be very useful. They are rarely true employees of the caucus, paid by it and working full time for it. Neither are they purely voluntary assistants, like the supporters just mentioned. Generally they occupy an intermediate position, drawing certain material advantages from the party, but also having a private profession which gives them a certain independence. Nevertheless, in the United States the captains are sometimes supported entirely by the party, either directly or indirectly (the party giving them a more or less fictitious post which allows them to work for it). The important place held by liquor retailers in the cohort of electoral agents has often been remarked upon. What place could be more propitious for political propaganda than the bar, the tavern, or the pub, where people come to relax as well as to have a drink, and where people can meet in groups and have a free discussion? Who could be better placed than the manager to lead this discussion and to spread his ideas? With a little understanding of human nature he can exercise a great deal of influence: the parties know it and try to attract him. The bar tends to become the Agora of modern democracies.

Caucuses are an archaic type of political party structure. They form the normal organization of parties under a property qualification franchise, or in a system of universal suffrage that is still in its beginnings. If we except the indirect caucuses, the others do indeed group the traditional social elites. In their composition as well as in their structure (weak collective organization, predominance of individual considerations) they represent the influence of the upper and lower middle class. In Marxist terms they are the normal political expression of the middle class. An attempt to discern pattern would lead one to distinguish two types of caucus in late nineteenth-century Europe: the one, corresponding to the Conservative parties, grouping aristocrats, industrial magnates, bankers, even influential churchmen; the other corresponding to the Liberal or Radical (in the French meaning of the word) parties, being composed of tradespeople and lesser industrialists, civil servants, teachers, lawyers, journalists, and writers.

Normally (under the nineteenth-century property franchise) parties were nothing but federations of caucuses. Further, it is easy to see the relationship between these caucuses and the electoral committees of the period before there were any parties. When these committees were no longer set up *ad hoc* for each contest, but survived the election and acquired a relatively permanent character, they became real party caucuses. It is not always easy to say where the one begins and the other ends.

The coming of universal suffrage did not entail the immediate disappearance of the caucus system in every country. As long as the masses had not been able to form their own Trade Union or political organizations they acted within the framework already in existence. The caucuses therefore sought a way of influencing them, notably by increasing the number of electoral agents. This represents an effort, sometimes unconscious, to impose old forms on the masses, so as to keep them in a passive role in spite of universal suffrage, in order to limit the political consequences of the latter. Nevertheless, the greater efficiency of recruiting techniques directly adapted to the masses (for example the system of branches) has usually brought about the decline of the caucus.

But this decline is not general. In the first place the system of the 'indirect caucus' has revitalized the old organization of parties and has made possible its satisfactory adaptation to the new social structure. By replacing middle-class members, outstanding for their birth or their wealth, by representatives delegated by working-class Trade Union or Co-operative organizations, it has rendered possible the organization, within the framework of the caucus, of authentic people's parties, really based upon the masses, like the British Labour party. It must also be recognized, however, that the framework has in the process been profoundly transformed. There is a vast difference in structure between the old nineteenth-century English caucuses of the Conservative or Liberal parties and the caucuses of the Labour party. The indirect caucus is clearly abnormal in comparison with the classic type of caucus which, in spite of the advance of democracy, still occupies at the present day a very important place in the structure of parties. In this connection we might quote the case of parties of the Right in most countries in the world, and the special case of American parties. It is all quite natural in the first case. The middle class represented by these parties of the Right does not like the organization and collective action which accompany branches and cells. The existence of this class is based on the recognition of a traditional 'elite' which is the result either of birth or of free competition. It is therefore natural that it should always find its political expression within the framework of the caucus. Moreover, this is an attitude shared by both upper and lower middle class. The latter was Liberal and progressive at the beginning of the century but is gradually tending to follow in the footsteps of the former. The fact is that the English Conservative party, the North-European Liberal and Conservative parties, the French parties of the Right, and the French Radical party (in spite of the attempted reform of 1955–57) are still organized on the basis of the caucus. Some of them have tried to adopt the branch system, but in vain. It does not correspond to their social substructure.

In the United States, the two great parties are both in the same position, although there are many points of difference. American parties are first of all electoral machines, which ensure the nomination of candidates in what might be termed pre-elections officially organized by the state laws relating to *conventions* or *primaries*: in this respect they are quite original organizations (see below, p. 362). Furthermore, they are not ideological groups nor class communities: throughout the huge territory of the Union each of them unites people of very different opinions and very diverse social positions. Fundamentally they are but teams of men expert in the winning of votes and the administrative posts which are available under the spoils system: experts who are moreover often interchangeable (the captains sometimes offer their services to the rival party, just as a technician might change his employer). But these preoccupations and characteristics are not absent from European parties: the difference lies in the methods rather than in the goal. On the other hand, we find in American parties traces of the political and parliamentary organization which is a characteristic of their opposite numbers in the Old World: here again the contrast is not absolute. Comparison remains possible therefore to some extent.

With these reserves, American parties can be considered as formed on the basis of the caucus: moreover, a distinction should be made between the hierarchy of official caucuses, rising from the caucuses of counties, wards, or cities to the national caucus, and the unofficial caucuses constituted by the *bosses* and the *machines*. In every case we have small groups of well-known people whose personal influence counts more than their number; and of notabilities recruited by a sort of co-option within the *machine*, in conformity with the classic system of direct caucuses. The fact that these notabilities often belong to one particular species, that of the professional politician, makes no difference. Thus American parties have a very archaic general structure. Even though they have developed electoral agents and accentuated the technical character of the caucus they have kept the old political framework of bourgeois democracy. The explanation of this phenomenon would be a rewarding subject for research. The problem is not to inquire why the American parties have not replaced the caucuses by branches or cells, for experience shows that very few parties in the world have changed their organization in this domain: the old European parties remain faithful to the caucus like their opposite numbers on the other side of the Atlantic. The real problem is to find out why universal suffrage and the entry of the masses into the political life of the United States have not given rise to a party of the Left with a modern organization. It is the problem of the non-existence in America of a large Socialist party, and it seems to be connected with the absence of class-consciousness in the American worker, and with his deep individualism—Lenin would say with his lower middle-class (*petit-bourgeois*) character. The archaic organization of American parties thus seems the consequence of the essential conservatism of American politics, in the European sense of the term. The two great American parties would sit on the Right or in the Centre in the parliamentary geography of Europe: the fact that they are still based on caucuses is thus in conformity with the general tendency already described.

The Branch. In itself, the term 'branch' designates a basic element which is less decentralized than the caucus: a branch is only part of the whole, and its separate existence is inconceivable: on the other hand the word caucus evokes an autonomous reality, capable of living on its own. As a matter of fact, it will be seen that parties founded on branches are more centralized than those founded on caucuses. But the profound originality of the branch lies in its organization, and not in its connection with the other branches. In this respect, the branch can be described by contrasting each of its characteristics in turn with those of the caucus. The latter is restricted in nature, the branch is extensive and tries to enrol members, to multiply their number, and to increase its total strength. It does not despise quality, but quantity is the most important of considerations. The caucus formed a closed circle into which you could enter only by co-option or as a delegate; the branch is wide open. In practice you only need to wish to belong to be able to do so. Certainly most parties make rules of membership and define entrance requirements, as will be seen later; but these generally remain theoretical, at least in the branch system (this is less true for the cell system). The caucus is a union of notabilities chosen only because of their influence: the branch appeals to the masses.

Moreover it tries to keep in touch with them: which is the reason for its geographical basis being less extensive than that of the caucus. In France, for example, the caucuses function chiefly at arrondissement level: the branches are built up within the framework of the *commune*. In the large towns they even tend to multiply and to be based on the *quartier* or ward. Certain parties (but not all) also admit within the branch smaller subdivisions which make possible a closer-knit organization of members: German and

Austrian 'block' and tenement units; French Socialist party 'groups'. Nevertheless, a certain mistrust of excessively small subdivisions, as leading to rivalry and disorder, can be seen: thus the constitution of the French Socialist party, when it was united in 1905, affirmed the precedence of the branch over the group by refusing the latter any kind of autonomy. This was a reaction provoked by the disputes between small groups which had weakened the earlier Socialist parties. Finally the permanence of the branch contrasts with the semi-permanent nature of the caucus. Outside the election period the latter lives through a period of hibernation in which its meetings are neither frequent nor regular. On the contrary the activity of the branches, obviously very great at election times, remains important, and above all regular, in the intervals between ballots. Socialist branches generally meet every month or every fortnight. Moreover the character of the meeting is not the same as that of the caucus: it deals not only with election tactics, but also with political education. Party speakers come to talk of problems to the branch members; their lecture is usually followed by a discussion. It is true that experience has shown that meetings have a strong tendency to wander on to petty local and electoral matters; but usually the parties make praiseworthy efforts to counter this tendency and to ensure an adequate place for discussions of doctrine and of general questions.

As the branch is a more numerous group than the caucus it possesses a more perfected internal organization. The caucus has a hierarchy of a very simple kind: usually the personal influence of a leader can be seen at work and that is all. It is sometimes predominant: in the United States the caucus often consists of none but the followers of the 'boss'. Sometimes there are offices and official titles: president, vice-president, treasurer, secretary, recorder. But they do not correspond to a very strict division of work; rather are they honorary distinctions (that of 'president' enjoys particular prestige). On the contrary the hierarchy of the branch is more definite and the division of duties more precise. An organized committee is necessary to direct the mass of members, and it must comprise at the very least a secretary to call meetings and draw up the agenda and a treasurer to collect individual subscriptions. Whence the setting up of a regular procedure for appointing the committee, generally by election, as will be seen later.

The branch is a Socialist invention. The Socialist parties which became organized on a purely political basis and direct structure naturally chose it as the fundamental unit in their activities. Certain Socialist indirect parties adopted it too: for example the initial group of the Belgian Workers' party was the local 'Workers' Guild', which brought together the members of Trade Unions, Co-operatives, and Friendly Societies, a great number of members belonging simultaneously to several organizations: such an organization makes the party less indirect in character, and more like a direct party having many 'ancillary organizations' aimed at strengthening the bonds of membership. The choice of the branch by Socialist parties was perfectly natural. They were the first to try and organize the masses, to give them a political education, and to recruit from them the working-class elites. The branch corresponded to this triple requirement. In contrast to the caucus, the middle-class organ of political expression, it seemed the normal organ of political expression for the masses. But these masses did not all accept Socialism: consequently, various middle-class parties tried to attract them in their direction by the very methods that were making the working-class parties so successful. In many countries the parties of the Centre and even of the Right changed their organization and replaced the caucus by the branch as a basic element. Almost all the new parties have followed these tactics, but many old parties as well: this is an interesting example of contagious organization.

Nevertheless, the effects of this contagion are limited. In most of the Conservative or Centre parties that have adopted it the branch system exists more in theory than in practice. Generally meetings are not very frequent (one General Meeting every year, according to the constitution of the Belgian Christian Social party; nevertheless, out of 677 branches existing in the Walloon provinces in 1948, 233 met at least once a month). Moreover, there is very little control over the enrolment of members, and no regular collection of subscriptions:[1] so that there is no longer any certainty about who is a member of any particular branch, apart from its committee and a small nucleus of the faithful. This nucleus is often very small, for absenteeism flourishes on a grand scale: in fact a branch meeting is sometimes not very different from a caucus meeting, as far as the number of people present goes. Fundamentally the real basic element of the party is here the branch committee, which meets regularly and ensures the day-to-day functioning of the organization. The committee in question is

[1] *Bulletin of the Christian Social Party*, 1948, p. 429.

nothing but a caucus of a rather special type: it is the old caucus continuing, slightly transformed and slightly rejuvenated, in the guise of a branch. Party leaders generally deplore this state of affairs, without fully realizing that it is inevitable because it is inherent in the substructure of their groups. The middle class, whether it be upper, lower, or intermediate, is not fond of collective action; moreover it thinks (and here it is wrong) that its political education is adequate, and that it does not need the teaching given at branch meetings; it finds difficulty in recruiting from itself the devoted and lively spirits who might make meetings interesting: its customs and habits provide it with other distractions than these little political groups, which are on the other hand rather appreciated by the working class; it has other opportunities of affirming its social importance, and still retains a certain disdain of politics, whereas the mass of the people sees in politics a means of bettering its position. Rather different motives have similar results in the peasant classes, so that the branch system corresponds primarily to the working-class mentality. Naturally these remarks on social psychology are general and superficial in character; beh piour varies according to countries, races, and traditions. Neverthless, it seems that traces of this general tendency can be found everywhere.

All the same the borrowing of the branch system by the Conservative and Centre parties has an interesting sociological significance. Putting aside the motives of efficiency which inspired it, and the hope of enrolling in this way the working classes, in greater or less numbers, its underlying motive seems to be the desire to 'democratize' the party, to give to it a structure more in accordance with the political doctrines of the period. For there is no doubt that the caucus is undemocratic (except in its indirect form, which remains exceptional); this small closed group, composed of semi-co-opted, well-known figures, is obviously oligarchic in character. The branch, on the other hand, which is open to all, and in which the leaders are elected by the members (at least in theory), corresponds to the requirements of political democracy. Thus the branch constitutes the 'legitimate' structure of parties, in the sociological sense of the term: an institution is legitimate when it corresponds to the dominant doctrines of a period, to the most widely held beliefs on the nature and the form of power. The adoption of the branch by Conservative parties has the same significance as the adoption of universal suffrage and the parliamentary regime by illiterate and feudal nations: it is a sacrifice to the ideas of the times, a homage paid by vice to virtue (if you call virtue orthodoxy and vice heterodoxy). It is no more efficient in practice; for doctrines do not suffice to guarantee the functioning of institutions, if the latter are not adapted to the social substructure on which they are based.

Apart from the Socialists, the only parties that have been able to make the branch really live are Catholic parties or parties with Fascist tendencies, which confirms our earlier analysis. Religious faith in the first case, the Nationalist mystique in the second, have led the middle classes towards a political set-up which is naturally repugnant to them. These two types of party, moreover, through their very doctrines, override class distinctions, and generally succeed in attracting to themselves some proportion of the working-class masses. No doubt detailed research would show that predominantly working-class branches function better than those which are predominantly middle-class or peasant in character. An analysis of the Socialist parties would probably confirm these results. With them there can be observed a progressive decline of the branch system which seems correlated to their gradually becoming more middle-class. It would be interesting to undertake a series of monographs on the life of a Socialist branch from its origins to the present day (unfortunately, records are rarely kept, and even more rarely are they adequate). It would no doubt be established that its activity is much less today than in the heroic days of 1900–14. This diminution of energy would probably correspond to an evolution in the social structure of the branch, as its purely working-class character gradually diminishes. At the present time, in most Socialist parties, the 'proletarian' branches seem to be more alive than the 'middle-class' or mixed branches.

The Cell. Two fundamental features distinguish the cell from the branch: the basis of the group and the number of members. The branch, like the caucus, has a local basis, narrower than that of the caucus, but still geographical. On the contrary, the cell has an occupational basis; it unites all party members who work at the same place. There are factory, workshop, shop, office, and administration cells. The home of the members matters little: in the large towns, where many companies employ salaried workers who live in the suburbs, it is possible to find members of one cell who live quite a considerable way from one another. This dispersion is even greater in certain particular cases, notably that of 'shipboard cells', which unite the sailors of one ship. Nevertheless, area cells must of necessity exist side by side with workplace cells, either to unite isolated workers (in Communist parties you must have at least three members in a factory to form a cell) or to group the members of the party who do not work in a large undertaking: artisans, doctors, lawyers, tradespeople, industrialists, and landworkers. The area cell resembles the branch because of its geographical basis. It generally differs from it in the narrower character of the latter: instead of a branch for each *commune* we find district cells, a cell for each village and hamlet, street cells, and 'block' cells (in towns where there are large residential units). But area cells never have the same importance: the real cell is the workplace cell which unites party members working in the same place.

With regard to the number of its members, too, the cell is a much smaller group than the branch. In an average district a branch normally has more than a hundred members. Frequently there are branches with several hundred members, and even with several thousand. Cell membership on the contrary must never reach a hundred. 'It was not without surprise that we learnt that certain of our cells had more than a hundred members; there is no need to emphasize how impossible it is for such cells to exert effective action', said M. Léon Mauvais in his report on the problems of organization to the French Communist party Congress in 1945.[1] Later he made a more precise statement: 'There are cells of between fifteen and twenty members which achieve three times as much work as cells with fifty or sixty members.' So the optimum number of members is between fifteen and twenty. Nevertheless, the constitution of the Communist party does not fix any definite ceiling because the number of members is not the only thing that matters. There is also the question of finding additional leaders. Dividing up an excessively large cell necessitates finding a second secretary capable of carrying out the duties involved. M. Léon Mauvais explains this very well when he declares in the same report: 'As soon as circumstances allow us to appoint a second secretary we must decentralize [that is divide] the cells with too large a membership.'

The nature and size of the cell give it a much greater hold on its members than has the branch. In the first place, we are dealing with a group that is absolutely permanent since it is set up at the

[1] *Le Parti communiste français, puissant facteur de l'union et la renaissance de la France*, brochure, Editions du Parti communiste, 1945, p. 10.

very place where the party members meet daily in their work. Apart from meetings proper, there is constant contact between members. At the beginning or end of the working day the secretary can easily circulate orders, share out the work, and control the activity of each member. Action is all the more effective for the average number of members being low: in a branch of several hundred members the leaders can neither know each one personally nor keep in continuous contact with them all. In a cell of between fifteen and twenty members this presents no particular difficulties. The result is too that the members of the cells know each other well and that party solidarity is stronger.

It is increased by the occupational nature of the cell which gives it a concrete direct basis: factory problems, conditions of work and salaries are an excellent point of departure for a sound political education. Certainly there is a danger here that the cell might become entirely taken up with vocational claims, to the exclusion of purely political questions, that is to say that it should do the usual work of a Trade Union. This 'economic' deviation is the permanent temptation of cells; on reading the reports on organization to the Communist party Congresses it can be seen that much effort is necessary to avoid succumbing to it.[1] But provided this can be avoided, what an admirable basis for the political formation of the masses! The major difficulty here is the inevitable divergence between principles and their daily application. The mass of the people soon loses interest in general ideas, even very attractive ones, unless the direct consequences are pointed out. For the masses politics are not a luxury. It is different in a large middle-class party, especially in Latin countries where ideas are cherished in their own right. Now, when the local group consists of a branch, this connection between principles and the realities of daily life is not encouraged. General politics have little direct connection with sewerage, the upkeep of local roads, or personal quarrels. On the other hand they have a close connection with wage increases, security of employment, conditions of work and business organization. These links are even closer if the party professes the Marxist doctrine which considers politics as but a superstructure of economics. If the party makes a constant effort to relate each particular claim to a general principle, to link each special problem to its policy as a whole and to give each question of detail a place in

[1] Cf. the interesting statements of M. A. Lecœur, in his report to the Twelfth Congress (1950), pp. 13 and 14.

the pattern of its doctrine it will give its members a formation that is sound and unequalled; it will have an incomparable hold over them.

Certainly the bearing of this analysis is limited. It is especially valid for working-class parties: in the case of the others the cell pattern would weaken the political education and loyalty to the party rather than strengthen it. Working-class mentality in Europe considers the conditions of work and professional life to be the result of collective action of a political nature because it is only by collective action, usually political in nature, that it has ever effectively succeeded in bettering them. On the other hand the upper and lower middle classes and the peasants tend to consider work and professional life as private matters because their progress is essentially the result of an individual personal effort (the American working class shares the same point of view); economic evolution, which is clearly heading for a planned economy, has not yet brought about any profound change in this attitude, precisely because the middle classes and the peasants refuse to acknowledge it. For the working-class parties themselves labour problems are not the only basis of political life. Many other factors come into play, notably passion, mysticism, and faith. None the less, the cell system remains very strong, all the more so as it makes it possible to link with the work of the factory political problems apparently far removed from working life: for example it makes possible the political strike either directly or through control of the Trade Unions.

Finally it should be noted that the cell is perfectly suited to clandestine action. The branch is ill-suited to it, for it is confronted with the major difficulties of secret action: the convocation of each member and the choice of a meeting-place. In the cell these difficulties can easily be avoided: the members meet every day at their place of work, it is easy to 'contact' them at any time and it is almost never necessary to call them together as a group. It is easy to pass the word on, and to organize small meetings before and after working hours: all that is needed is to multiply the cells, making each one very small. This adaptation of the cell to clandestine action is quite natural, for the cell was in fact created for clandestine action. Cells existed in Russian factories before 1917. Miniature clubs, hunted by the police, they spread revolutionary propaganda in the face of the greatest dangers. Together with the secret intellectual clubs they formed the very basis of the Russian Social Democratic party. When the most powerful section of the latter arrived in power, and was transformed into the Communist party, it retained this organization which provided an excellent basis for the education and enrolment of the masses.

Branches were a Socialist invention: cells are a Communist invention. More precisely they are an invention of the Russian Communist party, and their adoption was imposed on all Communist parties throughout the world by the Third International in its resolution of 21 January 1924: 'The centre of gravity of the work of political organization must be transferred to the cell.' This uniformity was not achieved without difficulty. In France, where the Communist party, the result of a cleavage in the Socialist party in 1920, had retained the latter's form of organization, that is to say the branch, the militant members manifested a certain opposition to the new system. It must be recognized that the division of existing branches, the regrouping of their members by factories, and the choosing of a great many responsible officials for the new bodies set enormous problems which, considering the speed of the transformation (which had to be completed by April 1925), it was difficult to solve without making errors of detail. In the report of M. Maurice Thorez to the Lille Congress in 1926 there are some interesting statements on this subject.

In contrast with the branch, the cell has not been the subject of imitation, at least of successful imitation. Several non-Socialist parties have succeeded in organizing themselves on the basis of the branch: Communist parties alone have the cell as their basis.[1] The phenomenon deserves some explanation. It is easy to understand that the 'middle-class' parties have difficulty in adopting the cell system: shopkeepers, industrialists, doctors, and country landowners cannot be grouped on the basis of workplace cells. The cells could only unite clerks, civil servants, and engineers, and would never form more than a very small section of the whole of the party. But this argument does not hold for the Socialist parties. Why did they not adopt for the organization of their members a structure that was much more efficient than their branch system? No doubt the opposition of the Trade Unions was a determining factor: they saw in the workplace cell a dangerous rival. In the indirect Socialist parties there could never be any question of cells. In the others the existing links with Trade Unionism led to a negative answer. It must not be forgotten that round about 1930,

[1] Nevertheless, the development of cells in certain Fascist parties should be noted; see below, p. 39.

when the efficiency of the cell system began to be obvious, the Socialists had in most countries the support of the majority of the members of the great confederations of Labour. For the Communists the Trade Unions were a fortress to be besieged, against which the cells furnished a good weapon of war. For the Socialists they were a fortress to be defended; their desire was therefore to avoid anything that might possibly weaken them.

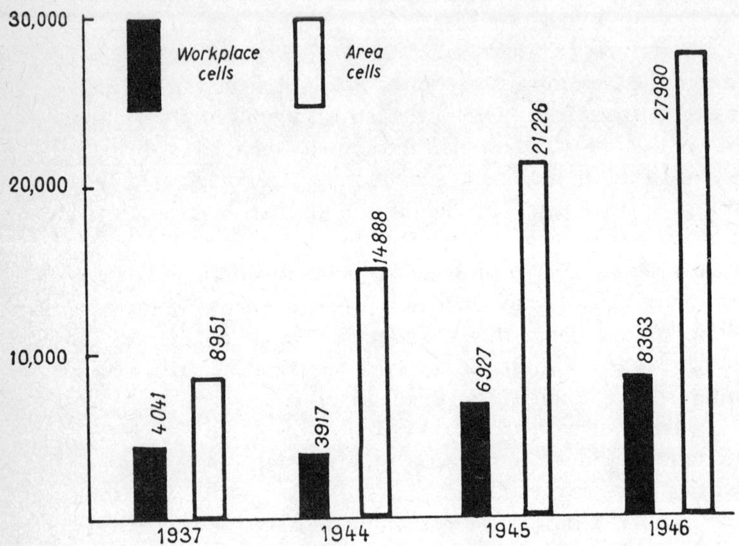

Fig. 2. Workplace and Area cells in French Communist Party.[1]

On the other hand the will of party members certainly played an important part. The resistance to the reorganization of the Communist party in 1924–5 seems to prove that members preferred the old system of branches to the new system. Acquired habits and a love of traditions have evidently to be taken into account. Nevertheless resistance to the cell goes deeper than mere resistance to innovations: at the present time, when the system has been in existence in Communist parties for twenty-five years, members tend to prefer area cells to workplace cells. At the most recent Congresses of the party held in France, notably in 1950, this phenomenon was stressed several times, and the Communist party leaders insisted at length on the fundamental nature of the work-

[1] From figures quoted in report of M. Léon Mauvais to the Paris Congress, 1945, pp. 6 et seq., and the reports of the Strasbourg Congress, 1947, pp. 230–3.

place cell. 'It is a political question of the highest importance, concerning the fundamental idea of our party', said M. Maurice Thorez.[1] In his report on organization, M. A. Lecœur considers that this dissatisfaction with the workplace cell is the result of the latter having taken the wrong direction, by concerning itself overmuch with labour disputes and neglecting political questions. We may well wonder if this is sufficient explanation, and if the preference for the local group (that is to say the branch) does not depend on deeper causes. It cannot be doubted that the work of the branches (or area cells) is less effective. But many people do not belong to a party for the work alone: they seek in it a distraction from their daily anxieties, a widening of their horizons, a 'diversion', as Pascal would say. From this point of view branch meetings, with their larger attendance, the possibility of meeting people from other walks of life, the lectures, the discussions and debates on matters of local interest, offer more possibilities of being diverting than cell meetings. The cell system can therefore only be set up and maintained by a constant effort from the centre. This effort is possible in a Communist party, where the leaders of the party have a great deal of authority. It is not so in a Socialist party, which is more decentralized and less disciplined.

One would be tempted to say that the branch system is 'natural' in a party which is composed of the masses of the people, that is to say that it corresponds to the most obvious tendency, to the law of least effort, whereas the cell system is 'artificial', that is to say that

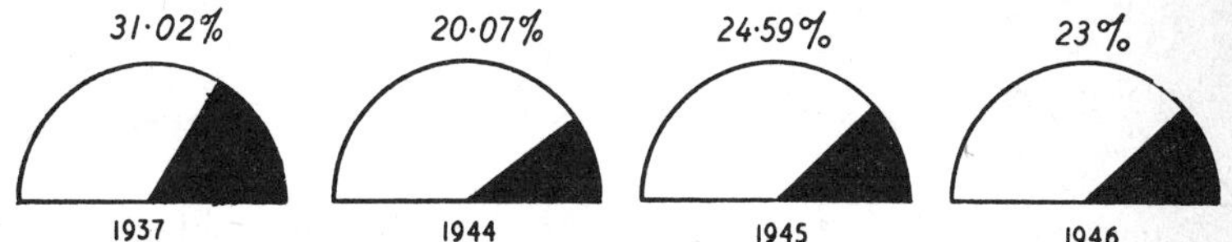

Fig. 3. Percentage of Workplace cells in French Communist Party.[2]

constant tension is necessary to maintain it. Nevertheless this difference must not be exaggerated, nor the difficulty of keeping a party alive on the basis of cells. The latter difficulty is perhaps accentuated today in the French Communist party, by the fact that the most powerful confederation of Trade Unions, the C.G.T., is directly affiliated to the party. When the principal Trade Unions

[1] *La lutte pour l'indépendance nationale et la paix*, Editions du Parti communiste, 1950, p. 91.

[2] See p. 32 n. 1.

are Socialist, the Communist cell has an important and precise basis of action, the struggle against them, the spreading of slogans making for exacting demands, the 'infiltration' of the Unions themselves. On the other hand, when the Trade Unions are Communist, there is a risk of the activity of the cell infringing upon the action which rightly belongs to the Trade Union. In any case it will be seen that workplace cells noticeably diminished in numbers in the French Communist party in 1945, compared with pre-war figures (see Figs. 2 and 3). This phenomenon is partly explained by the change in its social structure, the increase in membership being proportionately larger in the middle and agricultural classes than in the working class (see Fig. 4). But this is not the only

Year	*Industrial Areas*		*Semi-Industrial Areas*		*Agricultural Areas*	
	No. of Members	*% of Pop.*	*No. of Members*	*% of Pop.*	*No. of Members*	*% of Pop.*
1937	144,383	1·02	93,926	0·646	54,392	0·284
1944	153,000	1·08	120,634	0·83	97,834	0·512
1945	222,323	1·57	202,018	1·389	192,014	1·6
% increase n 1945 compared with 1937	53·9%		115%		253%	

Fig. 4. Membership of French Communist party before and after 1939 War.[1]

factor: in 1944, the number of workplace cells was smaller than in 1937, whereas working-class membership had increased. Since 1946 it seems that the proportion of working-class membership of the party is increasing whereas the number of workplace cells has decreased: the report presented by M. A. Lecœur to the 1950 Congress, without giving the total figures, quotes several typical examples and adds: 'These are not isolated cases, but examples

[1] Table based on figures quoted by M. Léon Mauvais in report to 1945 Congress, op. cit., pp. 4–5. The author does not indicate which regions he considers as 'industrial' or 'agricultural'. Further, the figures he gives for the population of these regions in 1937 total 47,744,500 inhabitants, which is more than the population of France at that date (41 millions): the figures must therefore include overseas territories.

illustrating the general tendency.'[1] The maintenance of the work-place cell as the fundamental element of the party seems therefore to be hedged about with difficulties, but the leaders are trying to surmount them because they think the system much more effective than the branch system.

This certainly does apply in the case of a working-class party. The branch allows of only a slack, superficial, intermittent discipline; the cell, on the contrary, because of its size and its permanence, ensures a regular, tight, and sound discipline. It is certain that the work of the cells deters many from becoming members. They prefer the branch debates. But these are precisely the less good, the less sincere, the less dependable members. The others on the contrary find in the cell a means of immediate, precise, serious action as well as a means of education. The cell system certainly constitutes one element in the strength of the Communist parties. But it will be seen that because of it the centre of gravity of political action is changed. The caucus is essentially an electoral and parliamentary organization, an instrument suited for winning over electors and bringing pressure to bear on those elected: it makes it possible to organize an election and to put citizens in touch with their representative. In the branch there is already a definite change in character: the branch meetings make the education of members possible. The branch is not only working for success in the elections, but to give its members a political education, and thus to form an elite proceeding directly from the masses and capable of acting in their name. Nevertheless, concern with electoral and parliamentary matters remains predominant. On the contrary, in the cell these preoccupations become quite secondary. Its nature and size do not make the cell a suitable weapon for fighting an election: it no longer coincides with an electoral division or subdivision; it is designed for action at the workplace and not for participation in a political election. Certainly agitation within the cells can be of use in electoral campaigns, but in an indirect and roundabout way: the campaigns must be conducted by other bodies.

Thus the choice of the cell as the basis of organization entails a profound change in the very concept of a political party. Instead of a body intended for the winning of votes, for grouping the representatives, and for maintaining contact between them and their electors, the political party becomes an instrument of agitation, of propaganda, of discipline, and, if necessary, of clandestine

[1] Op. cit., p. 14.

action, for which elections and parliamentary debates are only one of several means of action, and a secondary means at that. The importance of this change cannot be overemphasized. It marks a breach between the political regime and the organizations it has produced to ensure its working. The coming of universal suffrage and parliamentary democracy brought about the rise of political parties; but the very development of parties has given some of them a structure which alienates them from elections and parliament. The cell system is only one minor aspect of this phenomenon: we shall meet more serious ones.

Militia. The breach between political parties and electoral and parliamentary action is even more definite in the case of those parties that have taken a militia as their basis. The militia is a kind of private army whose members are enrolled on military lines, are subjected to the same discipline and the same training as soldiers, like them wearing uniforms and badges, ready like them to march in step preceded by a band and flags, and like them ready to meet the enemy with weapons in physical combat. But these members remain civilians; in general, they are not permanently mobilized nor maintained by the organization: they are simply obliged to meet and drill frequently. They must always be ready to hold themselves at the disposition of their leaders. Moreover there are usually two categories to be distinguished among them: some constitute a kind of active army, and the others simply a 'reserve'. For example, within Hitler's body of Storm Troops there were active members who were summoned three or four times a week and almost every Sunday for propaganda marches or for the protection of political meetings; on the other hand militia-men more than thirty-five years old, or reserved because of their occupation, were grouped in separate regiments, and called upon for much less exacting duties. Similarly when an organization of Italian shock troops was set up in 1921 a distinction was made between the *principii*, who were active elements, and the *triari*, a kind of territorial army to which were assigned duties of secondary importance.

The military character of the militia appears not only in its composition but in its structure. The latter is based on very small groups which build up into pyramids to form larger and larger units. In the case of the National Socialist Storm Troops the initial element was the squad (*schar*), composed of between four and twelve men; a group of from three to six squads formed the section (*trupp*); four sections constituted a company (*sturm*); two companies a battalion (*sturmbaum*); three to five battalions a regiment (*standarte*), which would thus consist of between one thousand and three thousand men; three regiments constituted a brigade (*untergruppe*); four to seven brigades, a division (*gruppe*), each division corresponding to one of the twenty-one German regions. The Union of the Soldiers of the Red Front, the militia of the German Communist party (dissolved in 1929 and reconstituted in the shape of the Fighting Anti-Fascist League), was based on groups of eight (then five) men living in the same district, and as far as possible in the same block of houses, so that they could be easily mobilized. Four groups constituted a section (*abteilung*), and three sections a company (*kamaradschaft*). The organization of Mussolini's *Fascii* followed the same model, the basis being the combat squads (*squadri di combatimento*), grouped into sections, centuries, cohorts, and legions, according to terminology borrowed from Roman history.

No political party has ever been exclusively formed on the basis of the militia. There were in the German National Socialist party, side by side with the Storm Troopers, workplace cells and branches of the classical type. So it was in the Italian Fascist party, even at the time of the punitive expeditions and squadrism; even more so in the Communist party of the Weimar Republic, where the Red Front militia played merely a protective role. On the other hand almost all parties are driven to form some kind of militia, more or less embryonic, when they wish to maintain order at their meetings and protect their speakers and supporters. This does not prevent the militia being considered as the basic fundamental element of certain parties, whereas in others it plays a very secondary and unobtrusive role. It is rare that a party is based exclusively on one only of the four 'basic elements'—except perhaps the old nineteenth-century parties based on caucuses. In the parties composed of branches there are usually individual correspondents in those communes where there are as yet no branches, and they are in touch with the arrondissement committee: they are very like the electoral agents of the parties based on caucuses (for example, in the Walloon states the Christian Social party in 1948 possessed 677 local branches, but 1,847 correspondents in districts where there were no branches). The parties based on cells are obliged to develop area cells—which are very like branches—to unite their members who cannot be grouped within the occupational set-up.

Similarly a party based on a militia can also include a network of branches and cells without losing its individuality. The distinction made between parties based on caucuses, parties based on branches, parties based on cells, and parties based on a militia, depends on the constituent element that is fundamental but not necessarily exclusive. It is not even necessary that this element should group the numerical majority of the members of the party. In the French Communist party the workplace cells are far less numerous than the area cells; in the German National Socialist party it seems that the total membership of the Storm Troops was very little more than a third of the total membership of the party (in 1922, 6,000 members of the S.A. to 15,000 members of the party; in 1929, 60,000 to 175,000; in 1932, 350,000 to 1,200,000).[1] Nevertheless the workplace cell remains the essential basis of the Communist party, just as the militia remained that of the Nazi party. Each respectively gives to its party its general direction, its tactics, its individuality, and its style.

Just as the cell is a Communist invention, so the militia is a Fascist creation. In the first place it corresponds to the doctrine of Fascism, to that mixture of Sorel, Maurras, and Pareto, which affirms the predominance of the elites, of the activist minorities, and the necessity of violence to allow them to conquer and to retain power: the militia organizes these minorities and gives them the means of violent action. It is also explained by thesocial structure of Fascism, which is an instrument of the middle classes for preventing the domination of the working classes by opposing with force of arms the strength of the masses. It is also a result of the historical context of Fascism; in 1920, in the midst of the disorder and anarchy in Italy, the *Fascii* re-established an order which was brutal but immediate and visible, thus making good the deficiencies of the government; similarly the Storm Troops wrested from the Communist and Socialist crowds their dominance of the street, while at the same time arousing the hope of a rebuilt army in the Germany of Weimar, defeated but militaristic.

It is clear that the militia is even further removed from electoral and parliamentary action than are the cells. It is an instrument for overthrowing a democratic regime and not for organizing it. This is more obvious than with the cells, but it is not necessarily more efficient than they are. The Fascist militia bore Mussolini to

[1] Figures taken from J. Benoist-Méchin, *Histoire de l'Armée allemande*, Paris, 1938. (To be treated with caution.)

power by the march on Rome; the Nazi militia kept Hitler in power by making possible the scenario of the Reichstag fire and the subsequent dissolution of the Communist party, which made sure of a parliamentary majority for the Nazis without a popular revolt. None the less, militia parties do not disdain elections and parliaments in the power-winning period, as do the cell parties. Hitler reacted violently against the tendencies of Roehm, Mussolini against the excesses of squadrism. Both take part in elections, organize intense electoral propaganda, and weave complicated parliamentary intrigues. But that is only one aspect of their action, and not the essential one. The important thing is that they employ electoral and parliamentary machinery in order to destroy it, and not so as to act within its framework. Cell parties do the same thing.

Further it is worth considering whether the two systems of the cell and the militia do not in fact tend to overlap and complete each other. It is a curious fact that parties based principally on the militia are also very interested in cells and try to give them considerable importance in their organization. Workplace cells were well developed in the National Socialist party; within the 'first section for organization' placed at the head of the party, the direction of workplace cells formed one of the three essential divisions (under the control of W. Schumann).[1] If the Fascist party had given them no place before it came to power, that is because they were not yet in existence (the non-Russian Communist parties were not to adopt them till 1924). But the small Fascist parties that existed in various European countries on the eve of the 1939 War tried—not without difficulty—to establish some. On the other hand parties based on the cell are the only ones that have on occasion given great scope to the militia system (outside the Fascist parties). Certainly many others have employed it; the German Social Democrats had the 'Empire Banner', the Austrian Social Democrats their working-class militia; even the Belgian Workers' party founded a Youth Militia in 1920. But these efforts were never developed very far. The only German political party besides the Nazis which had established a strong militia in opposition to the Hitler Storm Troops was the Communist party. The development of Communist militia in 1945 in Europe is still more symptomatic: other parties had struggled in the Resistance movement and fought the enemy; the Communist parties were the only ones who managed to form an autonomous military organization during the

[1] *Dokumente der Zeitgeschichte*, Munich, 1941.

occupation, and to make it the backbone of powerful popular militia forces after the Liberation. The role that these forces have played in certain Eastern European countries, notably in Czechoslovakia, is well known.

This tendency for the militia and cell to be used together could be explained by the fact that they both depart from electoral and parliamentary methods: so a party based on the first has no scruple about using the second, and vice versa. Further investigation might discover some relationship between the structures of these two systems: the smallness of the groups at the base, the close contact between their members and the frequency of their action. Does not the cell ensure a kind of 'civil mobilization' of the member, just as the militia ensures a kind of military mobilization? Above all the general articulation which joins these small groups—squads and cells—into one body presents the same general design.

III. GENERAL ARTICULATION

How are the small basic communities—caucuses, branches, cells, militia—which agglomerate to constitute the party, linked one with another? This is the problem of the general articulation of the party; superficially it is a purely technical and consequently a secondary question; in reality, it is essentially a political question and therefore of prime importance. For the arrangements for linking and relating the primary groups of the party have a profound influence upon its militants, upon its ideological unity, and the efficacy of its action, and even upon its methods and principles.

In general, political articulation tends to model itself upon the articulation of administration in the state: the grouping of the 'basic elements' assumes therefore the pattern of a hierarchical pyramid coinciding with the official territorial divisions. One level often seems preponderant in character, and generally corresponds to the basic administrative area. In France, cells and branches are organized into federations by 'departments', the 'arrondissement' and 'canton' groupings being subordinate and secondary in importance. In Belgium, the unit of articulation is the 'arrondissement', the committees at canton and province level being much less important. In the Netherlands, the unit is chiefly the district, in Switzerland the canton, and so on. Nevertheless, some parties show a tendency to dissociate their articulation from the administrative set-up: the French Communist party has for some time now made use of the 'circle' (*rayon*) and the 'region', which are purely party units having no administrative counterpart; the different levels in the articulation of the Fascist militia show very marked originality; the German Social-Democratic party's districts do not coincide with the limits of the *Länder* (Fig. 7), and so on. Furthermore, the tendency to make one of the levels of articulation outstanding in importance is not general: parties are to be found which multiply such levels, giving to all an almost equivalent importance. Structure in this sense has a great bearing upon the degree of centralization in the party.

Weak Articulation and Strong Articulation. Let us compare the French Radical Socialist party with the Belgian Christian Social party, each of them being a typical representative of one category of party organization. The articulation of the former is very weak. Essentially the party is made up of local associations, federations, and newspapers collectively affiliated. As a general rule, only departmental federations can be directly affiliated since the constitution only permits the affiliation of an association if it figures on the rolls of a federation, when one exists. But nothing is laid down concerning the internal structure of these federations and the integration within them of the local associations. The result is that each is free to organize itself as it wishes. The articulation of the federations within the body of the party is scarcely more precise. It is true that the constitution lays down a system of representation for the party Congress and for the Executive Committee, but this is not strict. Before the 1914 War, Congress was made up of the parliamentary representatives belonging to the party and of delegates from the newspapers, associations, and federations without the number of such delegates and the method of their nomination being defined; at the present moment, members of the local associations and of the federations, who have paid their subscriptions, can take a 'Congress ticket' (on payment) and attend; anyone—or almost anyone—can thus be a member of Congress.

The composition of the Executive Committee, the most important central body, is no more clearly prescribed. It includes *ex-officio* members and members elected by the Congress. The *ex-officio* members are the party's senators and deputies, general councillors and municipal councillors (of towns with more than 50,000 inhabitants), honorary presidents and vice-presidents, chairmen or former chairmen, general secretaries and former general secretaries, chairmen and secretaries of departmental federations. Before 1914 the members elected by Congress comprised two delegates for each department and for every 200,000 inhabitants. Afterwards, the Congress elected for each department: (1) one member per 100,000 inhabitants or fraction of 100,000 inhabitants; (2) one member per 200 paid-up members or fraction of 200. Since 1945, this latter category alone exists but it represents scarcely a quarter of the Executive, the remainder being made up of *ex-officio* members. The weakness of articulation here is evident.

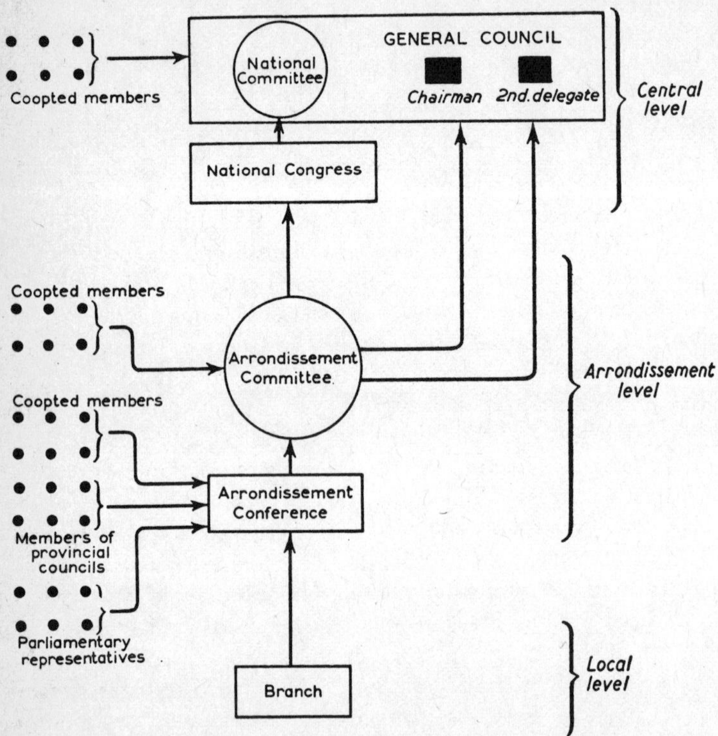

Fig. 5. Articulation of Belgian Christian Social Party.

Instead of being a grouping of basic communities in which each is allowed expression proportionate to its numbers, the Radical party resembles an incoherent agglomeration of associations linked by vague and variable bonds, resultant upon hidden intrigues, rivalries between cliques, struggles amongst factions and personalities. A large number of moderate and Conservative parties throughout the world show the same type of structure. It does not attain the same degree of vagueness in all cases, but some have an even weaker and vaguer system of articulation, as witness the American parties.

A comparison with the Belgian Christian Social party affords a striking contrast. There, regulations prescribe the articulation in minute detail, in such a way as to guarantee that each basic element plays its part in the total life of the party. (Fig. 5.) Every year the local branches elect delegates, in the proportion of one for every 100 members (with a minimum of two delegates); these, joined by the parliamentary representatives and provincial councillors, form the Conference of the arrondissement and elect a chairman and at least twelve members; they themselves in turn co-opt members to the number of one-half of the elected members: the group thus formed is the Committee for the arrondissement and is charged with the local direction of the party. Each Committee elects from the Conference its own delegates to the national Congress, in the proportion of one delegate per 250 members duly enrolled in the group of branches in its area. The Congress is the supreme tribunal of the party and chooses the majority of the members of the National Committee (others being co-opted) which is charged with the permanent management of the party. It may constitute itself a General Council by adding to itself the chairmen of the arrondissement committees, together with a second representative for each arrondissement and two members co-opted by itself. The General Council is a body intermediate between the Congress and the National Committee and makes it possible to consult local groups directly and rapidly on important questions.

The system of articulation of the Belgian Christian Social party is not original; it is largely inspired by the structure of the Belgian Socialist party. It has been taken as an example because it is recent and detailed in character, but it does no more than apply a system which, in broad outline, is to be found in almost all the Socialist parties of the world, in most Catholic and Christian Democratic parties, and in a large number of parties of other tendencies. In Communist and Fascist parties (and in many others which are neither Communist nor Fascist) the pattern of articulation is rather different, because the hierarchical levels are more numerous and the geographical framework is not the same; but the basic features remain the same. In all these there is the same strong articulation as compared with the weak articulation of the French Radical Socialist party. The party appears as an organized community, in which all the basic elements have a definite place which determines their respective importance. In actual fact, intrigue and factions remain possible, but only in so far as they find support within the party community and its component groups. A 'tendency'—such as is found in the French Socialist party—must strive to gain a certain number of supporters in each branch, a certain number of branches in each federation, a certain number of federations in congress, before it can exert an influence upon the party.

Strong articulation must not be confused with democratic structure. It is, of course, true that weak articulation is not democratic: the whole organization of the Radical party is conceived with a view to stifling the member's voice and to giving the power in the party to small oligarchic groups. But the contrary is not true: a rigid system of articulation may or may not be democratic. In Socialist parties a high degree of democracy is assured by election at all levels strict voting procedure and verification of delegates' credentials. In the Christian Democratic parties various devices (e.g. co-option as in the Belgian Christian Social party) tend to diminish this democratic character. In Communist parties the nomination of local leaders by the central body leads to a *de facto* oligarchy: rigidity of articulation becomes in this case a factor contributory to oligarchy, a means of strengthening the leaders' domination of the members of the party.

What are the factors which determine weakness or strength in a party's system of articulation? The traditional differences in national temperament may be invoked here. However vague and dangerous such notions may be, they are not entirely devoid of interest: for example, it is rather striking that Latin Socialist parties should be less strongly articulated than Scandinavian Socialist parties, and the Italian less strongly articulated than the French (in fact, if not according to the texts of the constitutions). But this does not take us very far: for the French Communist party is more rigid than the German Socialist party, the French Socialist party more rigid than the English Conservative party, and so on. Special historical circumstances may equally be invoked in explanation: the needs of the underground movement between 1940 and 1945 led European political parties to strengthen their system of articulation, and traces remained long after the Liberation. Such factors are however quite secondary.

The electoral system seems to be more important. The list vote (*scrutin de liste*), operating within the framework of a large constituency, obliges the caucuses or local branches of the party to establish amongst themselves a strong system of articulation within the constituency, so that they can agree upon the composition of the lists. On the other hand, the single-member system (*scrutin uninominal*), operating in a small constituency, tends to make each small local group of the party into an independent entity, and consequently to weaken the articulation of the party. If the list-vote coincides with proportional representation, with the practical absence of cross-voting (*panachage*) and with the establishment of a strict rank-order amongst the candidates which predetermines their chances of election, then the necessity for strong articulation is even greater. With or without P.R. the list-vote tends towards a system of articulation which goes beyond the local level: it diminishes the influence of men and increases that of ideas, it makes general programmes override parish-pump considerations and therefore acts in the direction of the national organization of the party. Moreover P.R. necessarily implies such an organization in some systems, e.g. if the distribution of remainders is effected on a national basis.

These conclusions do not emerge from *a priori* reasoning, but from a considerable number of practical observations. In chronological order we can cite first the example of Belgium, where at the end of the nineteenth century party structure was amongst the strongest in Europe: it coincided with list-voting. It will be noticed next that the adoption of P.R. strengthened articulation everywhere: it is striking that only at that moment did official statistics in many countries begin to classify deputies by party; it had not been possible earlier because of the weakness in organization of the parties. Finally, there is the specially impressive case of France, in which the weakly articulated parties of the Third Republic were replaced by the strongly articulated parties of the Fourth while single-member constituencies (*scrutin d'arrondissement*) were replaced by P.R. The Radical party was born of the arrondissement and still hankers after it. Similarly, the single-member constituency system coincides with very weak party articulation in America. However, the influence of the electoral system does not seem to be decisive: within the same country, marked variations can be observed in the strength or weakness of party articulation. Socialist parties everywhere are more strongly articulated than Conservative parties, whatever the electoral system. In France itself it may well be asked whether the greater rigidity of parties under the Fourth Republic as compared with those of the Third does not arise from the effacing of the weakly organized parties (Radicals and Moderates) in 1945–6, and from the growth of strongly organized ones (Socialists and Communists) to whose number a newcomer, the M.R.P., was added.

In point of fact, the essential factor seems to be the nature of the basic elements which compose the party. Analysis shows that there is a correlation between them and the strength or weakness of party articulation. In the nineteenth century parties were based upon the caucus and weak articulation; today most Conservative, Moderate, and 'Liberal' parties in Europe still display these two essential characteristics; the American parties are in like case. On the other hand the Socialist parties and most Catholic parties, which are based upon the branch, display at the same time strong articulation; and it is generally stronger in Socialist parties, where the branch is better established and more widespread than in the Christian-Democratic parties, where the branch functions less regularly. Finally, in Communist parties, built up on the basis of cells, and in Fascist parties, where the basic unit is the militia, the articulation is even more precise, rigid, and strong. Furthermore, it would be possible to note similar differences in questions of detail: the Italian Fascist party, in which the militia was less well-organized, displayed a weaker system of articulation than the German National Socialist party, in which the Assault Branches or Storm Troops had attained a very high degree of organization. However, national temperament too is not unconnected with these differences.

Explanations might be sought for this phenomenon. One might say that the caucus system is a product of profound individualism, that it corresponds to the political influence of outstanding men, and that weakness in articulation is consequently a natural phenomenon in such a system. Conversely, the cell system demands the very strict and detailed co-ordination of the efforts of these small units, scattered in different firms, if they are not to spend themselves in purely bargaining activities that are very limited in aim. This necessity is even more imperative in the system based on militia: the very nature of a military organization implies constant co-operation between the various basic units and very precise liaison on hierarchical principles between them. As for the branch, its name implies its integration within a wider community, while the democratic structure of the party, which it aims to bring about, calls for each basic group to play a part proportional to its real importance in the control of the party, and this in turn produces a fairly rigid and fairly strong system of articulation.

These *a posteriori* explanations are however of little importance: the essential fact is the general coincidence in practice of the caucus system with weak articulation, of the branch system with strong articulation, and of the cell and militia systems with very strong articulation. Other facts of this kind can be picked out. They show that we are here faced with a fundamental dividing line, with a basic distinction between two types of parties. For example, it is observable that strong articulation corresponds with complex organization, weak articulation with simple organization. The more precise the connection the party seeks to maintain between the different basic elements, the more is it led into multiplying co-ordinating bodies, developing their function, defining the distribution of work amongst them, and, in this way, creating, instead of a weakly organized embryonic authority, a veritable machinery of government, including a separation of powers: legislative power devolving upon the 'Congress' (or, in its absence, on the 'General Council' or 'National Council'), executive power residing in an Executive Committee ('National Committee', 'Central office', etc.), juridical power being entrusted to Committees of 'Arbitration', or 'Control' or settlement of 'Disputes'. This growing complexity of the machinery of party government is obviously favoured by the fact that the parties with a strong system of articulation are also those which aim at enrolling members in greater numbers (in branches, cells or militia) than do the parties of weak articulation (in the caucus). Here then we have a correspondence with another distinction: that between cadre parties and mass parties. These different points will be considered in more detail below.

Vertical Links and Horizontal Links. Important though it may be, the distinction between strong articulation and weak articulation does not go far enough. It provides us only with the first elements of classification, with our first bearings, and these only very approximate. In order to make it more precise, we must determine the direction of the system of articulation. This leads us to establish, firstly the distinction between vertical and horizontal links, secondly that between centralization and decentralization.

The idea of vertical links is not new. The Communist party may have carried it to a point of great perfection, but it did not invent it.

In a general sense, one may define the vertical link as that which joins two bodies subordinate the one to the other: for example, the branch in a commune and the arrondissement committee, an arrondissement committee and a provincial federation, a provincial federation and the central committee. On the other hand, the horizontal link is that which joins two bodies on the same level, the link between Neuilly branch and Passy branch, between the committees of Libourne and La Réole, between the federations of Dordogne and Lot-et-Garonne. A system of vertical links consists in allowing only the first type and not the second within the party. In this fashion a rigid compartmentalism is finally achieved: groups at the same level cannot communicate with one another except through the medium of the apex. This presupposes two things: the absence of all direct horizontal connections and the use of delegation to form the superior bodies. Let us suppose that two village branches have not the right to establish direct contact horizontally; if the federal Congress is composed of all the members of the local branches the two village branches in question could make contact at the Congress; an indirect horizontal link would come into being. On the other hand, if only the delegates of the branches, duly empowered, are admitted to the Congress, no contact will take place between the two branches proper.

The Communist party provides the best example of a coherent and strict system of vertical linkage. The cells do not communicate with one another directly but through the medium of the *section* which is the next level. The section is composed of delegates from the cells; the delegates elect a committee which nominates its officers. The sections themselves do not communicate with one another, but through the medium of the next level, the *federation*, made up of delegates from the sections meeting in conference every six months; the conference elects a federal committee which nominates its officers. Finally, the federations do not intercommunicate except through the medium of the apex, the National Congress, a meeting every two years of delegates from the federations; it elects a Central Committee which in turn nominates the Political Bureau, the Secretariat, and the Political Control Committee. This system completely prevents any development within the party of schisms, fractions or opposition. Dissidence springing up in one cell cannot directly contaminate neighbouring cells. It can reach the section level only by way of the cell delegates, but here each one has already been selected and proved his reliability.

The same obstacles are to be encountered at each of the higher levels, more overwhelming each time because the material is better-trained and more tried. It is significant that freedom of discussion is considerable within the cells themselves (all evidence agrees on this point) but that it decreases the higher one goes in the hierarchy.

The risks of contagion are further diminished by centralization, which reinforces the vertical effect of the links. Each delegate of a lower body is not responsible to his mandators but to the higher body: his duty is therefore to keep the latter informed of any likelihood of disaffection showing itself within the group which is entrusted to him, not in order to defend that group's point of view, but to induce the central body to intervene and save the situation. These different safeguards are all the stronger because the centre plays a considerable part in the nomination of the various officers, it is in permanent contact with them, they warn it of any suspicious tendency, and because, so it appears, some secret machinery is set up by it to keep a check on the official machinery.[1] The centre can therefore intervene with great energy and effectiveness as soon as any weakness is apparent in any part of the organization. The system is very reminiscent of the safety precautions used in ships, with their division into watertight compartments, hermetically sealed off from one another.[2]

The system of vertical links is not only an admirable way of maintaining the unity and homogeneity of the party, it also enables it to transform itself very easily into a secret movement. For the vertical links and the watertight compartments are in fact fundamental necessities for an underground movement: the effect of police action is thus limited to a very narrow sector of the organization. The way in which this transfer from open action to secret action is effected is very simple. The party first jettisons the less faithful members, who leave it as a result of the ban or from fear of persecution. It makes its basic groups a little smaller: in 1940, for example, groups of five, then of only three members. But it retains its general organization, simply applying more strictly the permanent rules forbidding horizontal liaison. The possibility of clandestine activity was very influential in securing the adoption of the vertical link system by the International in 1924: those were the

[1] Cf., for example, the evidence of Ruth Fischer, *Stalin and the German Communist Party*, New York, 1948. All this evidence comes from ex-members of the party and so is to be treated with caution.

[2] The analogy is used by the party itself. Cf. *Vie du parti*, clandestine publ., 1941, 2e trimestre, No. 3, pp. 9, 11–12.

heroic days when the party had to act half in broad daylight, half in secret. The 1939 War and the Occupation on the one hand, recent bannings and persecutions on the other, have restored the full force of the original motive. However, too many people today judge the Communist system of vertical linking solely from the point of view of its adaptability to secret action: its value as a unifying measure is undoubtedly greater.

The Communist party has no monopoly of vertical links. Generally Fascist parties adopt a similar system: the National Socialist party, for example, was in essence based upon vertical links. Direct nomination by the central body of all leaders, at all levels, makes watertight division much easier. Before the 1908 law on associations the German Socialist party had been led by the restrictive measures taken by Bismarck to adopt a very original system of vertical linking: the Socialists in each locality elected, at an open meeting, one man as 'trustee'; the 'trustees' alone made up the legal organization of Social Democracy. Thus the branches did not communicate directly with one another but only through the medium of their 'trustees'. However, this compartmentalism had juridical rather than political force; it was used to get round the law much more than to secure political homogeneity. In fact, a tendency towards vertical links can be observed in almost all parties, that is, at least, in all that possess relatively strong articulation. The branches hardly ever communicate directly with one another, nor do the federations, and the fundamental articulation of the party runs from below upwards, using the system of delegation. It is a false opposition to contrast horizontally linked parties with vertically linked parties: one can only contrast parties with solely vertical links and parties with mixed links, both vertical and horizontal, it being fully understood that the former generally outnumber the latter. In parties of weak articulation, horizontal links reach their maximum: they are operative on the two levels of leaders and of members. Thus there is horizontal linking when there are direct contacts between the members of basic party units, or between the leaders of two neighbouring local caucuses, or two neighbouring federations, and so on. Within the Radical Socialist party such contacts can be carried on in almost complete liberty, since the party constitution lays down no ban and gives no ruling on the matter.

In parties of strong articulation horizontal links are exceptional in character. They still provide, however, the essential system of articulation in indirect parties, taking the form of contacts between the leaders of the basic units. In the Belgian Catholic Bloc between 1921 and 1936 the managing committee acted as a horizontal link between the Boerenbond, the Middle-Class League, the Federation of Catholic Associations, and the Christian Trade Unions. In the same way, the committees of the Labour party are made up of a system of horizontal links between delegates of the Trade Unions, the Co-operative Societies, the Friendly Societies, and the Socialist Leagues.

In the direct parties themselves horizontal links still retain a considerable degree of importance, not nowadays as a system of internal articulation, but as an instrument of party imperialism. They are, in this sense, used to secure control of organizations ancillary to the party or to infiltrate opposition parties or parallel organizations. In the first case, use is made of horizontal links with the leaders, in the second, members of the basic groups form the horizontal links. A party may develop Trade Unions, cultural and sports societies, political associations with a restricted objective (National Front, Peace Movement, and so on): all these associations having as their aim to win over sympathizers and through them to increase the party's influence. The party will retain control of them by establishing horizontal links between their controlling bodies and its own, at the various levels: the leaders of the ancillary organizations will be the same as those of the party or will be nominated by the party and controlled by it.

Often these links remain occult: officially the Trade Unions, cultural and sports societies, Fronts and other alliances are distinct from and independent of the party, but in fact all the key positions remain in the hands of the party. To this end, several devices may be employed. The former German Social Democratic party had developed the technique of 'dual status': all the leaders and officials of the Trade Unions, theoretically independent, had to be chosen amongst party members. The Communist party has perfected the system by adding to it the technique of camouflage: the controlling bodies of the ancillary organizations include a considerable number of independent people, as illustrious as possible, who simply act as a 'façade'. Behind them, all the posts of effective control are manned by members of the party: the French National Front of 1945, with its headquarters bedecked with generals, bishops, academicians, artists and professors, is the best example of this technique.

Infiltration is applied not to organizations ancillary to the party but to parallel institutions: independent Trade Unions, rival parties, and so on. The infiltrating party sets up groups for common action between these institutions and itself at the basic unit level. Through them the infiltrators exercise an influence on the infiltrated: they may succeed in either securing control or the partial disintegration of the victim. Obviously, the technique presupposes that the attacker is much better organized than the attacked: it is a case of the weakest going to the wall. For this reason infiltration is chiefly used by the parties built up on the basis of the cell or the militia. The Communist party has very often used it: the infiltration of the C.G.T. before the 1939 War, the committees for common action with the Socialist party in France and in other countries, the system of alliances and Fronts which broke up opposition parties in the People's Democracies, and so on.

Centralization and Decentralization. There is frequent confusion between vertical linkage and centralization, and between horizontal linkage and decentralization. Although these notional categories overlap at many points, they are none the less based upon entirely different foundations. Vertical links and horizontal links define ways of co-ordinating the basic elements of which the party is made up; centralization and decentralization define the way in which power is distributed amongst the different levels of leadership.

Let us take two parties, A and B. In the first, A, the local branches may establish close relationships amongst themselves; the effective authority at the local level belongs to the Departmental Conference to which all members of the branches are freely admitted and in which all tendencies can find expression; this is a case of horizontal linking. In the second, B, the branches are strictly separated from one another; authority at the local level is in the hands of a managing committee elected by a Conference, itself made up of delegates nominated by the branches; this is a case of vertical linking. But let us suppose that the local Executive Committee of party B possesses exactly the same powers as the local Conference of party A, that these are very considerable relative to the prerogatives conferred upon the central bodies of A and B, and that the fundamental decisions of the party are thus taken at local level: then here we have two decentralized parties. In contrast, let us suppose that the local bodies of A and of B have no real prerogatives, that everything is decided by the central bodies:

then we have two centralized parties. In theory, therefore, decentralization cannot be assimilated to horizontal linking, nor centralization to vertical linking. In practice, there is an undeniable tendency towards assimilation, but it is neither general nor absolute: in the French Socialist party, for example, linkage is predominantly vertical, in spite of very considerable decentralization. There is even greater need to guard against any confusion between weak articulation and decentralization, between strong articulation and centralization: the French Socialist party is decentralized but strongly articulated, the British Conservative party centralized but weakly articulated, and so on.

Centralization and decentralization take on many different guises. Four general types of decentralization might be distinguished: local, ideological, social, and federal. The first corresponds to the generally accepted notion of decentralization; it is characterized by the following factors: the local leaders of the party come from the bottom; they enjoy wide powers; the centre has little control over them; the fundamental decisions are taken by them. This local decentralization sometimes coincides with a weak system of articulation, as is to be seen in the French Radical Socialist party or in American parties; it can also be found in association with strong articulation, as is evidenced by the French Socialist party. It has an important influence on the political attitude of the party; it makes for parochialism, that is to say, it directs the party's energies towards questions of purely local interest at the expense of great national and international questions. There exists no party policy in the true sense, only local counterbalancing and contradictory policies, inspired by special interests but giving rise to no general interest and no overriding view of the problems. The narrowness of French politics during the period of the Radical Republic is to be explained in large measure by the decentralization of the party in power; the same is true of the political uncertainties in the American Congress. It is a serious matter that the greatest nation in the world, which is assuming responsibilities on a world-wide scale, should be based on a party system entirely directed towards very narrow local horizons.

Ideological decentralization is quite different in nature: it consists in granting a certain autonomy to the different 'wings' or 'tendencies' to be found within the party by giving some weight to each in the ruling bodies, by granting recognition to separate organizations, and so on. The French Socialist party developed this system a good deal: tendencies were often strongly organized within it and until 1945 they were represented on the Executive Committee proportionately to their strength; the new constitution formally abolished this rule, but in fact it is still applied to some extent. Almost all direct Socialist parties have had more or less experience of ideological decentralization and of 'wings'. The *Bolsheviks* were nothing but a majority wing inside the clandestine Russian Socialist party, whilst the *Mensheviks* represented a minority wing. The Slav mentality had moreover multiplied these groups and sub-groups whose proliferation was favoured by the conditions of clandestine struggle. Within the Russian Communist party, after the seizure of power, different wings long continued to exist: the struggle for ideological centralization was long protracted and it may be considered to have really come to an end only in 1936. Sometimes ideological decentralization is favoured by the variety of organizations within the party: thus autonomous youth organizations very often become the seat of dissent. (In this connection, it would be most interesting to study the history of the Socialist Leagues of Youth in France and other countries.) In Germany, the leaders of the Storm Troops tried at one period to set themselves up as an independent group within the Nazi party: the terrible massacre of June 1934 was required to put an end to it. The danger of ideological decentralization is obviously that it may lead to schism: the Socialist parties have had many bitter experiences of this kind. But it has the advantage of maintaining an atmosphere of discussion, of intellectual rivalry, of freedom. At the same time it gives general questions precedence over parochial questions, in this respect differing radically in its effects from local decentralization.

Social decentralization is characteristic of indirect parties of the Catholic type. It consists in organizing into an autonomous group, inside the party, each economic class: middle-class, agriculturists, salaried workers, etc., and in giving important powers to these corporative branches. Such a structure was described in the opening pages of this chapter. From a certain point of view, it would be tempting to compare it with local decentralization. It is in fact just as much a system for the organization of particular interests. The framework is not the same nor are the interests of the same kind, but their particularism subsists. Social decentralization may moreover be considered to be the more effective of the two: for the division of labour, the progress of commerce and technical developments engender differences in individual interests often more considerable than geographical parochialism; social contrasts are more definite nowadays than local contrasts. It has also the merit of making clear the general lines of economic and social problems, but it does not allow of their solution since it tends to the juxtaposition of contradictory solutions, each *stand* or group seeking to make its own point of view prevail, and arbitration between them being difficult. Like ideological decentralization, it introduces a deep division into the party: in this connection it is interesting to consider the experience of the Belgian Catholic Bloc in which indirect structure seems to have increased divisions instead of diminishing them.

The federal structure of the state is sometimes reflected in that of the parties: for example, in Switzerland they are primarily organized on the basis of the canton. But this coincidence is not general. In the first place, since national groups form the basis of the political and administrative divisions of the federal state their independence inside the party assumes rather the form of local decentralization. More fundamentally, because the federal structure of the state has allowed each of these groups to express its individuality directly in the machinery of government, their autonomy within the party is not justified. In consequence, many federal states have parties of the classic type, with little extra local decentralization. On the other hand, in a nation where distinct groups have not been able to find expression for their individuality in the federal structure of the state, it becomes important to give it expression within the parties. In this way, a certain element of federalism can be introduced into the machinery of government of a unitary state. Such, for example, was the case in Austro-Hungary before 1914 where the Socialist party was obliged to divide into seven almost autonomous bodies: German, Hungarian, Czech, Polish, Ruthenian, Slovene, and Italian. The case of present-day Belgium is comparable. In 1936 the Belgian Catholic Bloc was reorganized on a federal basis. Henceforward it was to be composed of two sections: the Catholic Social party for Brussels and the Walloon and the *Katholieke Vlaamschë Volkspartig*, represented as bodies in a common directorate. The war prevented the operation of this organization and the new political tendencies to which it gave birth led to the more unitary structure of the Christian Social party. None the less this organization shows a considerable degree of federal decentralization, the party is made up of two wings, one

Flemish, the other Walloon. Each wing is given an equal number of representatives in the National Committee and in the General Council. Each wing holds separate meetings during the National Congress except for certain ceremonial meetings in common. This structure gives the advantage to the Walloon wing, which enjoys equality with the Flemish wing inside the ruling bodies of the party although it comprises many fewer members: in 1947, the Walloon wing totalled 39,739 members against 84,779 in the Flemish wing, in 1948, 49,737 compared with 120,197, and in 1949, 65,888 against 160,077. The Belgian Socialist party has never been willing to adopt such a federal structure, proclaiming itself a unitary body. All the same great care is clearly taken by it to maintain between the two linguistic groups a certain equality inside its ruling bodies.

Many parties which claim to be decentralized are in reality centralized. We must therefore not allow ourselves to be misled by the letter of the constitution, but must analyse its application in practice before coming to a conclusion. Generally the local leaders are proud of their importance and like to persuade themselves that their role is essential, even when the reality is different. Other parties openly acknowledge that their structure is centralized but mitigate the effect of this term—which definitely conveys a pejorative flavour—by adding some popular epithet: thus the Communist party speaks of 'Democratic centralism'. The expression is worth remembering: two forms of centralization may be distinguished, one autocratic, the other democratic, if the latter term be taken as indicating a desire to keep in touch with the rank and file. In autocratic centralism all decisions come from above, and their application is controlled locally by representatives of the centre. Fascist parties are generally organized on this basis, although they have often to struggle against the tendency of certain subordinate leaders to show their independence: we have already referred to activities of this kind on the part of Roehm in the Nazi party. In this connection we may also mention the centrifugal movement which made its appearance in the Italian Fascist party immediately after the seizure of power, each local leader acting the tyrant in his own area; this was the period of the 'Ras', a term used for the feudal lords of Ethiopia. A very interesting example of autocratic centralization is offered in present-day France by the French People's Rally (*Rassemblement du peuple français*, R.P.F.): alongside each Departmental Council, elected but in fact only consultative in function, is to be found a delegate nominated by the central authority and exercising in practice the power of decision. During the 1948 elections to the Senate several disputes broke out between the Departmental Committees and the delegates from the centre concerning local nominations. Here we have a characteristic example of autocratic centralism in action: it aims at making the decision of the superior body prevail over the opinions of the local members.

Though more effective 'democratic centralism' is much more flexible. By this term, the Communist party understands a group of complex institutions having the following aims: first to make known to the centre with the greatest possible accuracy the point of view of the rank and file, so as to allow it to make valid decisions; second, to ensure that the decision taken by the centre is applied at all levels, strictly and exactly but with understanding, that is to say with the agreement of the rank and file. Thus, the system is centralized, since decisions are made at the top; it remains democratic, since they are arrived at in the light of opinions from below and since the agreement of the base is constantly sought in their application. In order to attain this result the local leaders, although elected by the base (with some intervention by the centre, which will be examined below), are responsible to the higher levels and not to their mandators. Their function is therefore to convey as accurately as possible to the higher levels the reactions and opinions of the base, and to explain patiently and carefully to the base the reasons motivating the decisions of the centre. They are not passive representatives who simply record the views of their electors and try to make them prevail, as in a decentralized system; but neither are they simply representatives of the centre charged with blindly imposing upon the base the will of the centre, as in autocratic centralism. Their function as both informants and educators is complex and furthermore most important.

Democratic centralism presupposes on the other hand that very free discussion takes place at the base *before* decisions are taken, in order to enlighten the centre, but that the strictest of discipline is observed by all *after* the decision has been reached. In fact, evihence seems to prove that there is real discussion within the cell: however, this 'discussion must be pursued within the framework of the party's principles, the principles of Marxism-Leninism',[1] which is natural. But discussions must cease after the decision: everything must then be done to apply it. In this connection demo-

[1] Maurice Thorez at the 1950 Congress; brochure, pp. 87–8.

D

cratic centralism provides for very careful control by the centre of the implementation of decisions: the party leaders at all levels must check the application of the orders by the units placed under their command. At the same time it is essential that the executants should always make the base understand the reasons for the decision carried out so that the fundamental contact shall never be lost.

A variety of opinions may be held about the Communist party: it must be acknowledged that the machinery it has set up is remarkably effective and that it cannot be denied a certain element of democracy because of its unremitting care to retain contact with the base, 'to listen-in to the masses'. Some electoral agents of the old parties (for example, some Radical 'caucus-men' under the Third Republic, some American 'bosses') were able in some intuitive and empirical way to understand the deeper feelings of the masses and to stay always in close touch with them. The strength of the Communist party lies in having constructed a scientific method capable of achieving these results, with the dual advantages of the scientific method: greater precision and possibility for all adequately trained personnel to practise it. More fundamentally still, the value of the method arises from the fact that it is not purely passive, that it is not limited to recording the reactions of the masses, but that it makes it possible to act upon them, to steer them gently, prudently but fundamentally. One may deplore the use made of the instrument, one cannot refuse admiration for its technical perfection.

It remains for us to define the factors which lead the parties to adopt centralized articulation or decentralized articulation apart from their deliberate desire to adopt either system because of its practical effectiveness or its connection with the doctrines of the party. In passing, we have already noted some of the individual reasons which may thus explain centralization or decentralization in certain countries. Alongside these special factors, we have to ask what general factors exist that act in combination with them. The influence of history may here be recalled: the way in which a party comes into being seems to exert some effect on the degree of centralization. It has already been pointed out that parties of parliamentary and electoral origin generally have a more decentralized structure than those of external origin which owe their creation to a drive from the centre and not from the base. Thus Labour parties are more centralized than parliamentary Socialist parties; Catholic parties are generally fairly centralized as a result of the part played in their creation by the clergy or by Catholic organizations (e.g. Catholic Action, Catholic Association of French Youth).

The method of financing is also very important. In middle-class parties, where election expenses are for the most part defrayed by the candidates or their local backers, the caucuses at the base are richer than the centre and therefore independent. On the other hand, if the financial backers have acquired the habit of directly subsidizing the centre, it can exercise greater pressure upon the local groups. In parties financed by large and regular subscriptions, collected by the sale of annual cards and monthly stamps, it is most important to know what is the distribution of resources between the centre and the local branches. In the French Socialist party, for example, the centre sells the monthly stamps to the federation for 16 francs each; they are then free to fix the price for sale to the members. In the Seine Federation, 40 francs are retained by the federal bodies (which sell the stamps to branches for 56 francs), and from 20 to 50 francs by the branches (which sell them to members for between 75 and 125 francs). It is clear that this system definitely favours the base, at the expense of the centre: in fact the French Socialist party is very decentralized. On the other hand, in the Communist party, each party unit (cell, section, federation, central committee) receives a flat 25% of the subscriptions.

The electoral system also seems to have some influence on this question. The single-member constituency where a simple majority suffices to elect obviously encourages decentralization by giving priority to narrow local opinions and to the personality of candidates who with their party caucuses may make themselves independent of the centre. But list-voting does not directly encourage centralization: it simply extends the field of decentralization. In France the single-member system makes the arrondissement committees very independent; the list system makes them dependent on the departmental federations but maintains the independence of the latter with regard to the centre: in fact, in the application of P.R. it has been observed that many Socialist federations resist claims by the centre to impose its candidates or to interfere with their order of ranking. On the whole, only P.R. systems working on the national level seem to encourage centralization: they are rarely applied. It may therefore be considered that the different electoral procedures generally encourage decentralization rather than centralization; in fact the most centralized parties are those which only attach secondary importance to elections and do not organize themselves in the light of them, namely parties of the Communist and Fascist types.

However, a difficult problem is raised by the situation in Great Britain: has the single-member single-ballot system not contributed towards the fairly considerable centralization of British parties? The tendency of small local groups to independence is in this case counteracted by another factor: the need to avoid the 'wasting' of votes and consequently to exercise strict discipline in the nomination of candidates, and this naturally leads to the establishment of two rather strongly centralized parties. But if the British parties are centralized the American parties are very decentralized, although they function in the same single-member single-ballot system. It is true that the very special machinery of elections in the United States, with the 'primary' nomination of candidates and with the number of administrative posts to be filled, makes any serious comparison impossible. Furthermore other factors have certainly contributed to the establishment of centralization in Britain, particularly the high degree of discipline in the parliamentary groups which has naturally spread outwards to the organization of the party, and the distribution of electoral funds from the centre, as James Bryce emphasized. In short, no precise conclusion can be formulated concerning the influence of the simple majority system with a single ballot upon the centralization of parties.

CHAPTER II

PARTY MEMBERSHIP

How do we define a party member? The reply varies according to the party: each holds to a concept of membership which is peculiar to it. The expression 'party member' does not mean the same thing to Communists and Radicals, to the French Socialist party and the British Labour party, to the Belgian Catholic Bloc of 1920–36 and the Christian Social party of 1945. For American parties, it even has no meaning at all; one can only enumerate the militants who are part of the 'machine', the supporters who reinforce it during election campaigns, the people who take part in 'primaries', and the citizens who vote for the party's candidates at elections.

Within each party, moreover, there are to be found several kinds of member. The Labour party, for example, has made the distinction, ever since 1918, between affiliated members and individual members. Though direct parties which include only individual members seem to show more homogeneity, this is more apparent than real. Supporters, adherents, militants, propagandists, form a series of concentric circles of ever-increasing party solidarity. Though they are generally unacknowledged, these distinctions are none the less real. There are degrees of 'participation'—if we can so speak of the link which binds the individual to the party. Can we even speak of degrees? Can X's participation be assessed as three or four times greater than Y's? Or are there really different kinds of participation? The question leads us to investigate the real nature of participation, to define the content of the sociological bond which unites the members of the community to which we give the name 'party'.

It is an absorbing study that reflects two essential characteristics of our time: the revival of groups, the rebirth of religions. The bonds of participation tend to grow even stronger; at the same time they tend to assume a truly religious form. The decline of official religions coincides with the rise of political religions. Today the term party includes veritable churches with their clergy, their faithful, their belief, their orthodoxy, their intolerance. However this is not a general phenomenon, with the result that in this domain, too, parties of very diverse natures can be seen existing side by side. All in all, these differences in nature approximately coincide with the differences in structure that have already been defined. Firstly, the old parties based on caucuses with their weak, decentralized organizations which retain the characteristics of the early *ad hoc* parties and in which members are neither very numerous nor very enthusiastic; secondly, the modern parties based on cells and militia, centralized and organized, with their fanatical mass membership, with a religious faith superimposed upon a semi-military discipline; finally, the parties based on branches, with their great number of members, which lie midway between the first two and represent a middle term in party solidarity, a lay membership. But perhaps these differences in participation are the result of a difference in age, for the first are the oldest, the second the youngest, while the third represent the mid-term in time as in organization.

I. THE CONCEPT OF MEMBERSHIP

In everyday language the concept 'member' of a party coincides with that of adherent—in Europe at least. The latter is distinguished from the 'supporter', who declares his agreement with the doctrines of the party and sometimes lends it his support but who remains outside its organization and the community it forms; the supporter is not, properly speaking, a member of the party. However, as soon as we attempt to examine the difference more closely, it blurs and at times disappears. There is no better criterion of its subtlety than the enormous differences that divide parties on the question of counting their membership. For some, the most serious research can produce only very approximate figures. In 1939, two articles, both objective and sincere, appeared in the same number of *Esprit*; one attributed to the French Radical Socialist party 80,000[1] members, the other 200,000.[2] On the other hand, other parties, such as the Socialist and Communist parties, are able to establish a count of their members almost as precise as a national census.

The difference does not arise solely from better organization, a stricter maintenance of registers and indexes: it arises out of the very nature of the party community. For these two types of party,

[1] *Esprit*, May 1939, p. 176. [2] Op. cit., p. 209.

the term member has neither the same meaning nor the same importance. As a matter of fact, it has scarcely any meaning or importance for the first type. The concept of member is linked with a particular notion of political party that was born at the beginning of the twentieth century along with Socialist parties and that has subsequently been imitated by others. It does not correspond to the old conception of party which flourished in the nineteenth century in parliamentary systems with a franchise based on a property qualification. The concept of membership is a result of the evolution which led from the cadre party to the mass party.

Cadre Parties and Mass Parties. The distinction between cadre and mass parties is not based upon their dimensions, upon the number of their members: the difference involved is not one of size but of structure. Consider, for example, the French Socialist party: in its eyes the recruiting of members is a fundamental activity, both from the political and the financial standpoints. In the first place, the party aims at the political education of the working class, at picking out from it an elite capable of taking over the government and the administration of the country: the members are therefore the very substance of the party, the stuff of its activity. Without members, the party would be like a teacher without pupils. Secondly, from the financial point of view, the party is essentially based upon the subscriptions paid by its members: the first duty of the branch is to ensure that they are regularly collected. In this way, the party gathers the funds required for its work of political education and for its day-to-day activity; in the same way it is enabled to finance electioneering: the financial and the political are here at one. This last point is fundamental: every electoral campaign represents considerable expense. The mass-party technique in effect replaces the capitalist financing of electioneering by democratic financing. Instead of appealing to a few big private donors, industrialists, bankers, or important merchants, for funds to meet campaign expenses—which makes the candidate (and the person elected) dependent on them—the mass party spreads the burden over the largest possible number of members, each of whom contributes a modest sum. This invention of the mass party is comparable with that of National Defence Bonds in 1914: before then Treasury Bonds were issued in large denominations and taken up by a few great banks which loaned to the state: in 1914 came the brilliant idea of issuing many more small bonds to be taken up by as many members of the public as possible. In the same way, it is characteristic of the mass party that it appeals to the public: to the paying public who make it possible for the electoral campaign to be free from capitalist pressures; to the listening, active public which receives a political education and learns how to intervene in the life of the State.

The cadre party corresponds to a different conception: the grouping of notabilities for the preparation of elections, conducting campaigns and maintaining contact with the candidates. Influential persons, in the first place, whose name, prestige, or connections can provide a backing for the candidate and secure him votes; experts, in the second place, who know how to handle the electors and how to organize a campaign; last of all financiers, who can bring the sinews of war. Quality is the most important factor: extent of prestige, skill in technique, size of fortune. What the mass party secures by numbers, the cadre party achieves by selection. Adherence to it has therefore quite a different meaning: it is a completely personal act, based upon the aptitudes or the peculiar circumstances of a man; it is determined strictly by individual qualities. It is an act that is restricted to a few; it is dependent upon rigid and exclusive selection. If we define a member as one who signs an undertaking to the party and thereafter regularly pays his subscription, then cadre parties have no members. Some do make a show of recruiting after the contagious pattern of mass parties, but this is not to be taken seriously. The problem of the number of members belonging to the French Radical Socialist party is susceptible of no precise answer, simply because the problem itself is meaningless. The members of the Radical party cannot be counted, because the Radical party recruits no members, strictly speaking: it is a cadre party. American parties and the majority of European moderate and Conservative parties belong to the same category.

This distinction, though clear in theory, is not always easy to make in practice. As we have just noted, cadre parties sometimes admit ordinary members in imitation of mass parties. In fact, the practice is fairly widespread: there are few purely cadre parties. The others are not in practice far removed from them, but their outward form is likely to mislead the observer who must look beyond the official clauses laid down in the constitution or the declarations of the leaders. The absence of any system of registration of members or of any regular collection of subscriptions is a fairly reliable criterion; no true membership is conceivable in their absence, as we shall see. The vagueness of the figures put out can also be considered presumptive evidence: in 1950, the Turkish Democratic party claimed before the elections that it had 'three or four million members'. Obviously, it was referring to supporters, in actual fact, it was essentially a cadre party. In the same way, the distinction seems contradicted by the existence of indirect parties: mass parties which have no personal members. Consider the example of the Labour party: it was founded in 1900 to make it financially possible for working-class candidates to contest elections; from the financial point of view, the system is a mass-party system, election costs being met by Trade Unions, collectively. But this collective membership remains quite different from individual membership: it involves no true political enrolment and no personal pledge to the party. This profoundly alters the nature of the party and of membership, as we shall attempt to show in detail later. On the other hand, let us take the example of American parties in States which operate the system of 'closed primaries' with registration of electors; they resemble mass parties from the political point of view. Participation in the primary, with the registration and pledges it involves, may be considered as an act of membership. Moreover, activity connected with the nomination of candidates presented at elections by a party constitutes one of the activities typical of party membership. But, in this particular instance, this is the sole activity: there is no activity which at all resembles the branch meetings of the mass parties. More particularly there is no regular system of subscription to provide for the financing of the party and of election campaigns: from the financial point of view these are clearly examples of the cadre party. All things considered, the indirect party and the American party with closed primaries should be classified as semi-mass parties, though these examples must not be held to constitute a third category distinct from the two others because of their heterogeneous nature.

The distinction between cadre and mass parties corresponds to a difference in social and political substructure. In the beginning, it coincided on the whole with the replacement of a limited franchise by universal suffrage. In electoral systems based on a property qualification, which were the rule in the nineteenth century, parties obviously took on the form of cadre parties: there could be no question of enrolling the masses at a time when they had no political influence. Moreover, capitalist financing of elections appeared natural. Indeed, it has survived the property franchise. In point of fact, the coming of universal suffrage did not immediately lead to the arrival of true mass parties. The cadre parties simply attempted to make their organization more flexible by pretending to open their ranks to the masses. The Birmingham caucus system in the British Liberal party, the Primrose League in the Conservative party, the institution of primaries in America, correspond to this first stage. The problem was how to give the masses some scope for political activity and how to confer on the notabilities composing the caucus the air of having been popularly invested. In the first two cases some approach was made towards the mass party: there existed a system of formal membership as well as a periodic subscription. But the real life of the party was lived independently of the members: the Primrose League, an organization distinct from the party proper, aimed at social mixing; the primaries are limited to the nomination of candidates; the Birmingham caucus alone with its local branch foreshadowed a true mass party, but it proved to be no more than a passing experiment. The political and financial bases of the mass party were lacking. There was no question of rescuing candidates and elections from the clutches of capitalist finance, nor of educating the masses and making direct use in political life of their activity. The question was rather how to use the political and financial strength of the masses as an ancillary force. The first step had been taken, but only the first step.

The introduction of universal suffrage led almost everywhere (the United States excepted) to the development of Socialist parties which made the decisive transition, not always, however, at once (cp. Fig. 6). In France, for example, the first Socialist groups were not very different from the middle-class parties; registration of members, collection of subscriptions, autonomous financing of elections, developed only slowly. Development was even slower in Italy and in politically less-developed countries. Yet, at the outbreak of the 1914–18 War, the European Socialist parties constituted great human communities profoundly different from the earlier cadre parties. A notable example is the German Social Democratic party which, with more than a million members and an annual budget of nearly two million marks, constituted a veritable state more powerful than some national states. It was the Marxist conception of the class party that led to such massive structures: if the party is the political expression of a class it must naturally seek to rally the whole of the class, to form it politically, to pick out the élites capable of leadership and administration.

This effort of organization also made it possible to free the working class from the tutelage of middle-class parties: in order to put up independent working-class candidates at elections it was necessary to become independent of capitalist financing (except perhaps as a makeweight, the roles being reversed) and this was possible only with collective finances. To establish, in opposition to the middle-class political press, a working-class political press, it was necessary to collect funds and organize the distribution of the newspaper. Only a mass party could make these things possible.

This explains why the distinction between cadre and mass parties also corresponds approximately with the distinction between Right and Left, Middle-class and Workers' parties. The middle-class Right had no need, financial or political, to seek the organized support of the masses: it already had its élites, its personages, and its financial backers. It considered its own political education to be adequate. For these reasons, until the coming of Fascism, attempts to create mass Conservative parties have generally failed. The instinctive repugnance felt by the middle class for regimentation and collective action also played some part in the failures, just as the opposite tendency amongst the working class favoured mass organization in Socialist parties. It would not be out of place to reiterate at this point some earlier observations. Nothing less than the development of Communism or of revolutionary tactics was required before the middle classes, realizing that cadre parties were inadequate, were to make serious attempts to create mass parties: in 1932, the National Socialist party had reached a membership of 800,000. This however really signified its breach with democracy. Under the electoral and parliamentary system cadre parties have generally been found sufficient by the Right; in the struggle against the electoral and parliamentary system mass parties of the Fascist type have rarely shown the balance and stability of proletarian parties. They tend, moreover, as we shall see, to lose their pure mass-party characteristics.

Finally this distinction between cadre parties and mass parties coincides with differences arising out of the various kinds of party organization. Cadre parties correspond to the caucus parties, decentralized and weakly knit; mass parties to parties based on branches, more centralized and more firmly knit. Differences in recruiting technique follow from the differences in the kind of community to be fashioned. As for parties based upon cells or upon militia, they too are mass parties, but less definitely so. It is true

	Germany	Austria	Denmark	France	Great Britain			Norway	Holland	Sweden	Switzerland
					Trade Union Members	Individual Members	Total				
1900					353,070		375,931		3,200	44,100	
1901					455,450		469,311		4,000	48,241	
1902					847,315		861,150		6,500	49,190	9,155
1903			22,061		956,025		969,800	17,000	5,600	54,552	8,912
1904					885,270		900,000		6,000	64,835	19,840
1905	400,000			34,688	904,496		921,280		6,816	67,325	20,337
1906	384,327		29,651	40,000	975,182		998,338	19,100	7,471	101,929	20,000
1907	530,466			52,913	1,049,673		1,072,418		8,423	133,388	
1908	587,338		34,078	56,963	1,127,035		1,158,565	27,838	8,748	112,693	20,439
1909	633,309			57,977	1,450,648		1,486,308	27,789	9,504	60,813	21,132
1910	720,038			69,085	1,394,402		1,430,539		9,980	55,248	20,671
1911	836,562			69,578	1,501,783		1,539,092		12,582	57,721	21,508
1912	970,112			72,692	1,858,178		1,895,498	43,557	15,667	61,000	27,500
1913	982,850	89,628	48,985	75,192					25,708	75,444	29,730
1914	1,085,905		57,115	93,218	1,572,391		1,612,147	53,866	25,609	84,410	29,585
1915	585,898		60,072	25,393	2,053,735		2.093,365	62,952	25,642	85,937	27,485
1916	432,618		67,724	25,879	2,170,782		2,219,764		24,018	105,275	31,307
1917	243,061		78,320	28,224	2,415,383		2,465,131		24,893	114,450	
1918	249,411		91,791	15,827	2,960,409		3,013,129	94,165	27,093	129,432	39,765
1919	1,012,299	332,391	115,900	133,277	3,464,020		3,511,290		37,628	151,364	52,163
1920	1,180,208	335,863	126,603	179,787	4,317,537		4,359,807		47,870	143,090	51,250
1921	1,028,574	491,160	129,756	50,449	3,973,558		4,010,361	45,946	37,412	134,753	40,483
1922	1,464,868	553,022	124,549	49,174	3,279,276		3,311,036		41,472	133,042	36,552
1923	1,261,072	514,273	130,371	50,496	3,120,149		3,155,911		42,047	138,510	34,000
1924	940,078	566,124	143,203	72,659	3,158,102		3,194,399	40,394	41,230	153,187	31,306
1925	844,495	576,107	146,496	111,276	3,337,635		3,373,870		37,894	167,843	31,788
1926	823,526	592,346	144,680	111,368	3,352,347		3,388,286		41,221	189,122	33,339
1927	867,671	669,586	148,472	98,034	3,238,939		3,293,615	68,016	43,196	203,338	36,727
1928	937,381	713,834	149,120	109,892	2,025,139	214,970	2,292,169		46,169	221,419	41,621
1929	1,021,777	718,056	163,193	119,519	2,044,279	227,897	2,330,845	76,579	53,395	234,962	43,867
1930	1,037,384	698,181	171,407	125,563	2,011,484	277,211	2,346,908	80,177	61,162	277,017	47,444

1931	1,008,953	653,605	173,890	130,864	2,024,216	297,003	2,358,066	83,071	69,263	296,507	50,722
1932		648,497	179,579	137,684	1,960,269	371,607	2,371,787	87,315	78,920	312,934	55,186
1933			190,070	131,044	1,899,007	366,013	2,305,030	95,327	81,914	326,734	57,227
1934			191,995	110,000	1,857,524	381,259	2,278,490	104,517	87,212	330,350	55,571
1935			195,142	120,083	1,912,924	419,311	2,377,515	122,007	84,269	346,786	52,881
1936			191,424	202,000	1,968,538	430,694	2,441,357	142,719	87,826	368,158	50,599
1937			199,283	286,604	2,037,071	447,150	2,527,672	160,245	87,312	398,625	45,039
1938			198,836	275,373	2,158,076	428,826	2,630,286	170,889	88,897	437,239	42,860
1939			206,995		2,214,070	408,844	2,663,067		82,145	458,831	37,129
1940			188,825		2,226,575	304,124	2,571,163			487,257	33,842
1941			193,599		2,230,728	226,622	2,485,458			498,209	31,742
1942			206,565		2,206,209	217,783	2,453,932			519,322	32,995
1943			216,816		2,237,307	235,501	2,503,240			538,747	34,606
1944			232,215		2,373,381	265,763	2,672,845			553,724	37,453
1945		357,818	243,532	335,705	2,510,369	487,047	3,038,697	191,045		563,981	40,956
1946	701,448	500,181	267,876	354,878	2,635,346	645,345	3,322,358	197,638	114,588	558,584	47,662
1947	875,479	570,768	287,736	296,314	4,386,074	608,487	5,040,299	202,043	108,813	588,004	51,342
1948	844,653	616,232	296,175	223,495	4,751,030	629,025	5,422,437	203,094	117,244	635,658	52,697
1949	736,218	614,366	294,969	157,897	4,946,207	729,624	5,716,947	204,055	109,608	668,817	52,983
1950	684,698	607,283	283,907	140,190	4,971,911	908,161	5,920,172	203,094	105,609	722,073	53,697
1951	649,529	621,074		126,858	4,937,427	876,275	5,849,002		112,000	739,474	53,852
1952	627,827	627,435		116,327	3,071,935	1,014,524	6,107,859		110,000	746,004	53,911
1953	607,456	657,042		113,455	5,056,912	1,004,685	6,096,022	178,004	111,000	753,785	54,346
1954	585,479	666,373	283,221	115,494			6,498,027		112,000	757,426	54,111
1955		689,040							125,000		

GERMANY: 1. Figures prior to 1919 from J. Longuet, *Le mouvement socialiste international* (Encyclopédie socialiste, syndicale et coopérative de l'Internationale ouvrière), Paris, 1913, pp. 231–2. Cf. also: *Yearbook of the International Labour Movement*, 1956–7, London, 1956.

2. 1946–50 figures relate to West Germany only (in the corresponding area, in 1931, the Socialist party numbered 610,212 members).

BELGIUM: The Belgian Socialist party claimed 150,000 members in 1951 (individual members) against 650,000 in 1931 (affiliated members: the two figures are not comparable because of dual or triple affiliations which magnify the real figures). In 1911 it claimed 222,669 (again affiliated members. Cf. J. Longuet, op. cit., pp. 115–6).

GREAT BRITAIN: The total includes not only Trade Union and individual members but also members affiliated through Co-operative, Friendly, and Socialist Societies.

HOLLAND: Figures from 1946 onwards are for 31 December each year, except in 1950 when figures are for 30 September. The December figures are generally about 2,000 below those for September.

Except where otherwise indicated all statistics are taken from the official party handbooks.

Fig. 6. Membership of European Socialist Parties, 1900–55.

that Communist and Fascist parties enrol the masses in as great numbers as do Socialist parties, even before their seizure of power and their transformation into the sole party: the German National Socialist party numbered 800,000 members in 1932, the French Communist party one million members in 1945, the Italian Communist party two million members in 1950. A development can however be traced. Periodically, Communist parties indulge in internal 'purges', with the aim of banishing the lukewarm, the passive, the suspect; in this way quality again becomes more important than quantity. They tend moreover to exercise strict supervision of recruitment: some Socialist parties similarly provide for this kind of supervision, but the system is little applied by them whereas the Communists seem to be stricter. In Fascist parties the emphasis on quality is even more marked, more perhaps in their doctrine, which is clearly aristocratic, than in their practice: the enormous growth in numbers of the National Socialist party in the last years before the seizure of power can scarcely have permitted any serious 'screening' of members.

In any case the general tendency is undeniable. It raises the problem of whether we are still dealing with true mass parties or whether there is a gradual evolution towards a new conception, a third category: devotee parties, more open than cadre parties, but more closed than mass parties. In the Leninist conception the party should not include the whole of the working class: it is only the advance guard, the fighting wing, the 'most enlightened' section of the working class. This represents a change from the conception of the party as class; it is the party conceived as the elite. Fascist doctrines are even more definite on this point; anti-egalitarian and Nietzschean, fundamentally aristocratic, they view the party as an 'Order', made up of the best, the most faithful, the most brave, the most suitable. The age of the masses is gone: we are in the age of elites. In consequence the meaning given to the term 'member' tends to vary. Even within the party there are to be found concentric circles corresponding to different degrees of loyalty and activity. In the National Socialist party there was first of all the Party, then the S.A., then the S.S. In the Communist party the official doctrine is egalitarian and therefore opposed to such a hierarchy; however, it is possible to discern an 'inner circle' that is reliable and permanent and around which is grouped the mass of ordinary members, often quite unreliable (the difference was very marked in the pre-war French Communist party).

The extent of such phenomena must not be exaggerated; they are as yet restricted. We may still classify the Communist and Fascist parties as mass parties so long as we remember their rather particular character, especially in view of the fact that the Socialist parties, in their early days, presented some characteristics analogous with those under discussion: they were then very strict about the members they recruited; before old age made them less exacting, they sought to be devotee parties. This last concept is clearly too vague to constitute a separate category, but it corresponds to an undoubted fact. In analysing what is meant by 'participation' we shall be led to consider it from another aspect.

Criteria of Membership. Only in mass parties is there any formal machinery of enrolment, comprising the signing of a definitive undertaking and the payment of an annual subscription. Cadre parties know neither the one nor the other; admission is accompanied by no official formalities, the periodic subscription is replaced by occasional donations; there are in consequence no precise criteria of membership and only the adherent's activity within the party can determine the degree of participation.

To join a mass party the most usual procedure is to fill in a membership form, a printed document which generally includes a passage declaring that the signatory undertakes to observe the rules of the party and to spread its doctrines, as well as blank spaces for filling in the name, address, date of birth, and various details of the kind. To join a party means in the first place completing and signing a membership form. This procedure has two great advantages. In the first place, it gives material form to the act of membership; all judicial systems accord to the written word particular importance, not only because of its evidential value (documents *endure*), but because of the psychological value attached to it. In our civilization a written undertaking is much more binding than a verbal one; the signature has taken on something of the magical character that primitive societies associate with particular gestures, particular formulae, particular rites. Some Fascist parties moreover go even further; they organize complicated and collective ceremonies in order to enhance the importance of the undertaking; this is simply an exaggeration of a tendency general amongst all mass parties. However, the membership form has a second advantage: it constitutes a file of information about the new member. The preciseness and extent of the information asked for vary from party to party.

In some cases, the information is not noted on the membership form itself but on a separate document sometimes completed by a veritable investigation concerning the new member.

In fact, two kinds of enrolment can be distinguished: open and restricted. The first includes no other conditions and formalities than the signature of a membership form (and the payment of a subscription); entry to the party is therefore unrestricted. The system of registration laid down for certain closed primaries in the United States presents points of similarity: enrolment on the primary lists corresponds somewhat to the signature on a membership form, although there is no question of true affiliation to the party, only of the simple right to vote in the nomination of its candidates. On the other hand, restricted enrolment is very different. It takes place in two distinct acts: an application for admission on the part of the signatory, a decision to admit taken by a responsible organ of the party. Power to admit is generally the prerogative of the local branch, with the possibility of appeal to higher authorities in cases of refusal; sometimes the application is considered by a special committee. Generally the system is completed by an obligatory sponsorship: one or two members of the party must stand warrant for the political and moral qualities of the applicant, accepting responsibility in a signed statement. This form of enrolment, with a decision of the party and with sponsors, is the usual procedure laid down in the constitutions of Socialist and Communist parties. The precautions taken are a result of the difficulties experienced by these parties in their early days and in particular of the efforts of the police to introduce spies into them: hence the supervision by sponsors, the preliminary investigation, and the final decision by the branch. However, as the activity of the parties gradually became less dangerous and less subject to surveillance, these precautions fell into disuse. Often they are now nothing but unimportant formalities and so restricted enrolment finally becomes open. The restrictions are only really applied in certain exceptional circumstances when screening once again becomes necessary. For example, after the Liberation the scrutiny of new members became much more thorough in many European parties to prevent 'collaborators' from taking refuge within them. In Germany, Austria, and Italy today new members are quite carefully checked on account of the former Fascist regimes: the attitude adopted by the applicant during those regimes is investigated.

Once accepted, the member receives a card made out in his name that gives concrete form to his status as a member of the party. The kind of card is moreover linked with the subscription system. By this criterion there are two distinct kinds of party. In one, the subscription is collected annually, in a single amount. The total figure is relatively small and involves no great financial sacrifice on the part of the member. Payment is certified by franking the card with a stamp showing the year. (The card is therefore permanent.) In the others, on the contrary, the subscription is made up of two elements: one annual, which corresponds to payment for the card itself (so that the card is renewed annually), the other monthly, for which stamps are affixed to the annual card (or to pages bound inside). Subscriptions of the second type are much higher: for example, in the Belgian Socialist party the minimum subscription varies between 6 and 100 Belgian francs per month; in the French Socialist party, between 75 and 200 French francs. However, the second type corresponds essentially to the Workers', Socialist, and Communist parties: it is a strange paradox that the parties based upon the poorest classes should have adopted the highest subscriptions. The explanation generally offered invokes psychological motives: it is true that devotion to the party is greater amongst the working classes than amongst the middle classes and this makes it easier to set the subscription high. But the financial explanation must also be mentioned: in Conservative parties, the subscription has not the same fundamental importance that it has in working-class parties; the members know that donations from financial backers will make good any deficit in the party chest and that these donations are the real source of party income. In working-class parties, on the contrary, the subscriptions are the prime method of financing the party and election campaigns: 'live on the subscriptions' is the aim proclaimed by the party and only the realization of this aim can guarantee its independence. The members understand this vital importance of the subscription and accept the sacrifice that it entails for them.

Furthermore, the parties have attempted to introduce some principle of justice into the levying of contributions. Instead of the system of uniform contributions—which corresponds to the most primitive of fiscal techniques, the poll tax—some of them have established a system of proportioning contribution to income (or even a system of family contributions, as is to be found particularly in the Austrian Socialist party). In the Belgian Socialist party, for example, there are seven different rates of contribution, which correspond to the payment of 6, 10, 15, 20, 25, 50, or 100 Belgian francs (with, in addition, a reduced rate of 3 francs per year for old-age pensioners or the unemployed man): the moral obligation is laid on the member himself to choose the rate of contribution which corresponds to his financial situation. In the German Social Democratic party there are twelve rates of contribution, ranging from a quarter-mark to thirty marks; the distribution of members amongst the different levels is, it should be noted, very uneven (Fig. 7). In the French Communist party the contributions have every appearance of being proportionate: members not gainfully employed pay 10 francs a month; those with a salary below 10,000 francs a month pay 30; those whose salary falls between 10,000 and 15,000 francs pay 40; those with a salary of over 15,000 francs pay 60. But the ceiling is so low (at minimum subsistence level) that this scale aims primarily at establishing a reduced contribution for members of very limited means, all the rest being for practical purposes on the same footing. In the French Socialist party, there has in recent years been considerable discussion of the problem of proportional contributions and a decision in favour was taken in 1950; many branches were already applying the system and were moreover profiting by it. It is a paradox that resistance to the change came from the very people that it was intended to benefit, the poorest members; they were anxious not to give the impression of being 'cut-price Socialists'.[1] This episode makes clear the true nature of the subscription; to take into account only its financial significance would be to miss the main point. It is a psychological factor in membership and participation. To pay your subscription regularly, to pay a high rate of contribution that entails some sacrifice, such acts bear witness to the strength of the bonds that unite the member to the party. But they also reinforce the bonds: one's devotion to a community, like one's devotion to a fellow creature, is proportional to the sacrifices one makes for it.

Viewed from the angle of whole-heartedness in participation the system of individual contributions, which obtains in the direct parties, has definite advantages; from the point of view of its purely financial return the Trade Union system of collective finance that is the rule in some indirect parties—notably the British Labour party—has undeniably greater advantages. The wealth of the Labour party is due essentially to the funds it receives from the Trade Unions. If it had to do without their support and seek

[1] From the speech of M. Staub to the National Council, 1947.

District	Total Membership	No. of Members at Each Rate of Subscription											
		·25 Mark	·30 Mark	·5 Mark	1 Mark	2 Marks	3 Marks	5 Marks	7 Marks	10 Marks	20 Marks	25 Marks	30 Marks
Schleswig-Holstein	67,765	18,207	—	13,220	20,813	2,093	373	269	—	27	2	—	—
N.W. Hamburg	71,648	—	12,064	14,502	33,725	1,759	636	226	—	98	54	—	—
Weser-Ems	20,502	716	1,148	4,891	8,165	631	174	45	—	11	1	—	—
Hanover	72,522	4,919	—	18,851	31,909	1,050	692	239	—	56	20	—	1
Brunswick	19,595	1,435	—	5,112	10,014	757	268	105	4	20	3	—	1
W. Westphalia	28,274	—	—	7,285	16,466	238	106	79	17	36	6	3	2
E. Westphalia	89,354	2,988	—	29,899	48,644	862	272	159	11	22	6	—	1
Lower Rhine	48,383	774	—	12,781	26,292	878	645	305	3	79	14	—	2
Middle Rhine	15,296	1	—	5,167	8,267	1,854	304	150	5	14	8	—	—
Rhine-Esse-Nassau	12,230	111	—	1,993	5,773	519	84	46	5	2	—	—	—
N. Hesse	21,395	—	754	5,408	11,793	122	56	14	—	15	—	—	—
S. Hesse	45,056	763	—	9,871	28,323	1,178	402	165	5	35	6	3	4
Hesse-Rhine	5,953	88	—	1,803	3,103	367	35	27	—	4	—	—	—
Wurtemberg-Baden	31,260	5,831	—	4,845	16,520	541	171	51	3	15	3	—	3
S. Wurtemberg	4,035	467	—	413	2,272	90	28	16	1	2	1	—	—
S. Baden	8,950	—	—	1,380	5,540	104	40	23	—	7	4	—	—
E. Bavaria	13,795	—	—	6,607	3,816	180	38	17	—	3	—	—	—
Franconia	53,645	—	3,368	15,949	25,281	1,196	225	147	—	17	6	—	—
S. Bavaria	35,588	4,698	—	11,753	15,762	192	70	54	25	1	4	3	—
Palatinate	23,024	346	—	6,769	14,017	550	163	42	1	12	5	—	2
Berlin	47,948	—	—	7,481	26,026	4,778	455	743	7	229	84	11	6
TOTAL	736,218	41,344	17,334	185,980	362,521	19,939	6,237	3,022	87	705	227	20	22

Fig. 7. Distribution of paid-up members in German Social Democratic party, 1949.

members and individual contributions from workers outside the Trade Union framework its resources would diminish very considerably. Even the 1927–46 system proves more favourable than extra-Trade Union membership: it is quite a different matter to be obliged, when one joins a Trade Union, to express one's acceptance of the political levy than to have to perform a separate and distinct act to join the party. The second procedure demands much more personal initiative and a much more deliberate act of will. From the point of view of party solidarity it is therefore less favourable than the act of joining a direct party; the signature of a formal application for admission to the party establishes a more intimate link than acceptance of the political levy. The latter procedure is however more efficient from the financial point of view: collection is much simpler since the political subscription is only an addition to the Trade Union subscription. Collected at the same time, it is not clearly felt to be distinct from it; in the contracting-out system it is in fact not distinct at all; hence the sacrifice is less painful, hence it is easier to obtain party funds. The party subscription here has every appearance of an indirect tax, incorporated in the charge for services rendered, and it is consequently less obvious and less onerous. This feature is even more marked in the financial help given to the party by the Co-operative and other similar organizations; this is in the ultimate resort financing by industrial and commercial undertakings, very like the system in use amongst Conservative parties. The system of collective and indirect contributions is then very advantageous from the point of view of finance, but it is no encouragement to participation; on this point contribution and membership are fundamentally distinct: the contribution is not a criterion of and an element in membership.

However, is it possible to speak in any valid sense of membership of an indirect party? At first sight, there seems to be no doubt. In fact, it appears that there is more intense participation in them than inside the direct parties. The English workman who is a member of a Trade Union, itself integrated within the Labour party, is surely bound to his party by a tie very much stronger than binds the French workman for whom Trade Union activity and political activity involve different organizations. It would seem that the superposition of loyalties brings about a reinforcement of each individual tie: there is multiplication as well as addition. An example that would seem to make this clear is that of the Flemish peasant who is an indirect member of the Belgian Catholic Bloc thanks to the intermediary of the Boerenbond. This admirable organization, which first took shape in 1887 on the initiative of a Campine priest, now embraces the whole religious, intellectual, professional, economic, and social life of farm-workers. Club, Evening Institute, Trade Union, Co-operative, Friendly Society—it is all of these and moreover aims at fortifying the religious convictions of its members, at completing their intellectual education, at developing their moral standards as well as at bettering their material conditions by the most varied means: collective buying and selling of produce and fertilizers, savings bank and agricultural loan corporation, collective insurance against cattle—diseases, fire, and agricultural risks, and so on. At the same time, from 1919 to 1940, it formed the framework of their political life, since it was one of the four *standen* of the Catholic party. It is easy to understand the enormous strength that the party drew from this backing.

But this is not the heart of the problem. The indirect structure of parties raises the question of what is really meant by the party community. There is no doubt that the bonds of party are strengthened by identity of class interests as they find expression in the groups on which the indirect party is based; but this is not truly a political bond, a true participation in the life of the party. Members of these basic groups cannot properly be considered to be true members of the party, since the links between these individuals and the party are, in spite of appearances, too tenuous. In considering this question we must beware of an error that is only too frequently made: when we emphasize the strength of the links that unite the Flemish peasant to the Boerenbond we are demonstrating the power of the Boerenbond, not that of the Catholic party. What did the Catholic party mean between 1921 and 1939 to the Flemish peasant who was a member of the Boerenbond? Very little; thanks to the Boerenbond, the peasant was certainly a *voter* for the party (and he has remained a party voter); but he cannot be considered to be a true *member* of the party. The fact that the Boerenbond had itself joined the Catholic Bloc in no way changes the facts: indirect membership is not true membership. No community in the sociological meaning of the term, no human group based upon ties of solidarity, was really created at individual member level by the coalition of the four *standen*. Only collaboration between the delegates of each *stand*, within the party organizations, could give birth to a community in the proper sense of the word, but this only at the higher level: the party existed only at the level of the leading strata, not at the level of the masses.

The experience of the Labour party makes it possible to verify experimentally these assertions and at the same time to temper their dogmatism. After the suppression of contracting-out in 1927 the number of Trade Unionists belonging to the party (that is to say, who agreed to pay the political levy) fell from 3,200,000 to 2,000,000, and remained stable about this figure for many years (cp. Fig. 15). After the restoration of contracting-out in 1946 this figure rose, however, from 2,600,000 to 4,000,000. Thus in 1928 1,200,000 Trade Union members refused to continue their membership of the party, solely because they were asked to make an express declaration instead of tacitly consenting. Before they had not dared to refuse, afterwards they did not dare to accept. On the other hand, in 1947 1,400,000 Union members entered the party solely for the lack of a deliberate act of refusal, although formerly they had not been willing to make a deliberate act of membership. Participation based upon such futile considerations is derisory. When the feeling of solidarity is so weak, can we properly speak of a true community? In the two cases quoted, a curious coincidence is to be noted between the proportion to the total Trade Union membership of membership resulting from the contracting-out procedure alone: 37·85% in 1927, 35% in 1947. It may therefore be claimed that more than a third of the Labour party members inside the Trade Unions feel no real attachment towards the party: their affiliation is a result of their weakness, not of their conviction. It remains true, however, that more than two-thirds are ready to give express confirmation of the tacit membership resultant upon their silence on the question of the political levy. Consequently, in the case of the Labour party, indirect participation is really half-hearted only for a minority of its members, approximately one in three. For the others, it is not inferior to a good many direct participations. In fine, one-third of the indirect members of the Labour party should not be considered as party members, in the strict sense of the term; only the remaining two-thirds can validly be compared with the members of the ordinary mass parties. No individual criterion however makes it possible to distinguish between the two categories: we can make an overall estimate, based upon two experiments, that is valid for the Labour party alone, for obviously there is no warrant for applying these findings to other indirect parties.[1]

[1] On the whole, very few Trade Union members avail themselves of the right of individual withdrawal by written declaration: in the Swedish Social Democratic party in 1938, for example, 4·5% of the members of affiliated Unions refused membership of the party in this way; in 1948, the proportion fell to 2·5%.

In short, the task of discovering a strict definition of member that will be valid for all parties seems vain. In the direct mass parties alone the act of joining and the regular payment of subscriptions may be accepted as criteria. But these formal and external notions are inadequate: to be a member of the Socialist party is quite different, in spite of the similarity of procedure involved, from being a member of the Communist party. How many degrees and shades of participation are to be found amongst the members of the same party? A quantitative analysis will afford us a first brief survey and will therefore complete our conception of the term member.

Membership Figures. The membership of a party can be the subject of interesting numerical analyses. Unfortunately these are confronted by two kinds of difficulty: parties do not always publish their membership figures; the figures that are available are not always based upon sound methods.

Some parties do not make available any figures for the total number of members: in some cases they themselves do not know them because of their slackness in keeping records and collecting subscriptions. Socialist, Communist, and Fascist parties alone (along with some Christian Democratic parties) make periodic counts when subscriptions are paid in. Very few of them, however, publish their results: some do no more than make them known at party congresses and in party circulars confined to the organization; others keep them completely secret, satisfying inquiries with approximate round figures. The collection of worthwhile material concerning this question is very difficult. What is obtained must moreover be used with care. In M. Léon Mauvais's report to the 1945 Congress of the French Communist party, he stated that the party numbered 'at the end of 1944, 385,000 members duly enrolled'.[1] If, however, we add together the figures for each region, given for the month of December 1944 a few lines further on in the same document, we can only reach a total of 371,468.[2] The difference here is not great; in the figures quoted for 1937 it is very much greater: 340,000 according to M. Maurice Thorez in his general report to the 1945 Congress,[3] 291,701 according to M. Léon Mauvais, at the same Congress, if we add together the regional figures that he gives.[4] The difference may be explained by dif-

[1] Léon Mauvais, *Rapport au Congrès de 1945*, Editions du Parti communiste, 1945, p. 4.

[2] Op. cit., p. 6. [3] Op. cit., p. 56. [4] Op. cit., p. 6.

ferent methods of enumeration; possibly M. Léon Mauvais based his figures on the number of duly registered members and M. Maurice Thorez based his on the number of cards and stamps bought by the cells.

There are in fact two kinds of statistics possible, the one based upon the number of cards bought from the Central Office by the branches, the other upon the number of cards really sold to members. Since branches and cells order their cards and stamps in advance, the first figures are generally higher than the second. This is particularly noticeable in the middle of the year, and most obvious just before a Congress or an electoral campaign: in preparation for new members, branches send in fairly big orders. In the report of M. Léon Mauvais it is made clear that at the end of April 1945 the party numbered 616,300 registered members; by 25 June 906,627 cards had been issued by the party's Central Office. It is quite obvious that the party did not gain 300,000 new members in less than two months (M. Léon Mauvais expressly says as much moreover); the disparity is due to the different method of counting. By the end of the year the two figures should coincide, all cards distributed having in theory been placed with members. In practice, of course, there are unsold cards, with the result that counts based upon the cards distributed and not upon the cards issued to members give inflated figures. That is why such counts find favour with the parties and why some of them attempt to confuse the two methods of enumeration. In 1945 the French Communist party made a clear distinction between the two sets of figures because it was then on the increase and the difference between the figures was a better means of assessing its success. In the period since 1947, when it has been losing members, the distinction has not been clearly made. The Labour party and most Socialist parties, however, draw up their figures correctly, counting only the cards really issued; for that reason they have often been used as examples.

The local branches and associations often try however to collect funds to buy and keep a number of cards greater than the real number of their members. In autocratic parties this is a way of finding favour with headquarters; in democratic parties it is a way of increasing the number of representatives sent to Congress and so of securing increased influence in the ruling bodies of the party. The number of delegates and votes granted to each local association is generally proportionate to the number of cards and stamps that it actually pays for; this gives the association a reason for buying as many as possible. Obviously financial resources impose some limitations and in consequence rich associations gain an advantage. For example, in the French Socialist party the Pas-de-Calais and the Senegal federations, to quote random examples, are over-represented in this way. Consequently statistics based upon the number of cards and stamps sold always produce figures higher than the actual: yet as a general rule no others are to be found. This does not mean that they are useless; the margin of error no doubt remains approximately constant for each party. In so far as we are comparing membership of the same party at different periods of its development statistics based upon finance are valid. They are less so for a comparison between similar parties in different countries (e.g. Socialist parties in Europe) for usage is not everywhere the same. They are in no way valid for a comparison between different parties within the same country; such a comparison would in any case have no meaning because the concept of membership is not identical in all parties.

With all due reserve as to their inner significance, figures of party membership can be used in two kinds of inquiry; research into the evolution of parties, research into their composition. The first category allows us, in the first place, to assess the connection between political and economic events and the size of the party communities. On this point one noteworthy conclusion seems to emerge from a few general observations: the connection is much less close than is generally believed. The party community is relatively insensitive to external events. It is true that the two world wars, for example, did generally bring in their train a variation in membership figures: the growth of Socialist parties in France and England in the periods 1919–20 and 1945–6 is very striking in this connection; in the Scandinavian countries, however, this influence is much less marked. But the clearest case of the insensitiveness of membership to external events is provided by the great economic crisis of 1929. On the whole, it does not seem to have brought about any notable variations in the number of members belonging to European parties. Here the example of the Socialist parties is particularly typical. In France the crisis was felt from 1931–2 onwards, attaining its peak in 1934; now the membership figures of the French Socialist party remained approximately stable throughout these years around 120,000–130,000 (Fig. 8). They do not tally with the generally accepted view that economic difficulties give increased strength to left-wing parties: this notion may be true of the electors, it is not so for party members. In actual fact, economic difficulties seem on the contrary to coincide with a slight decrease in membership, even although the party was in opposition. A certain correlation can from time to time be observed between the curve of real wages and the membership of Socialist parties; it is however

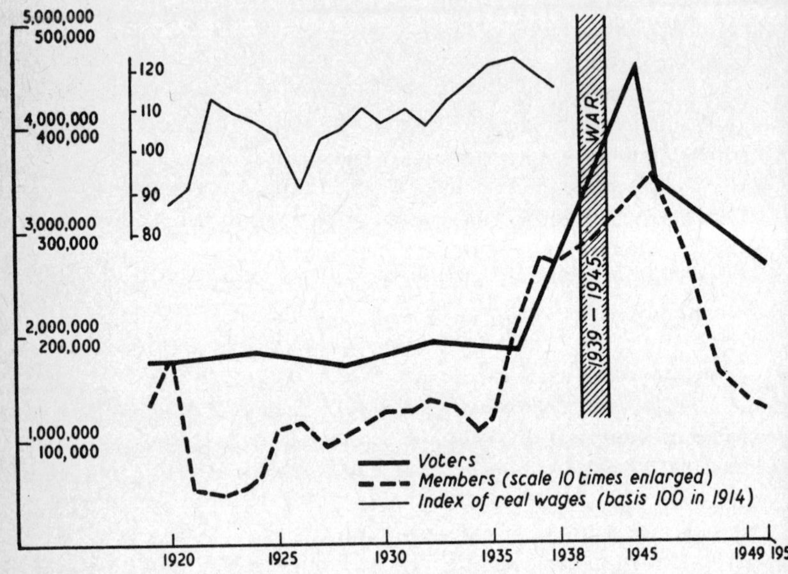

Fig. 8. Members and Voters: French Socialist Party.[1]

extremely vague. (Cp. Fig. 1 and Fig. 16.) In England the Trade Union members of the Labour party—who should however have been more sensitive to the crisis—displayed during this period an even more remarkable stability, around the two-million figure (cp. Figs. 1 and 15). The extent of the variation from one year to another is never higher than 3·2%: a loss of 1·7% in 1930, a gain of ·65% in 1931, losses of 3% in 1932, 3·2% in 1933, and 2·2% in 1934, a gain of 2·75% in 1935. Thus from 1932 to 1935 there is to be seen a

[1] For 1924, the total number of Socialist voters has been calculated by extrapolation from 1919 figures on the basis of the nineteen Departments in which the party put up separate lists; elsewhere it was allied with the Radicals and was included in the lists put up by the Left-wing Cartel. In these nineteen Departments it obtained 628,883 votes compared with 595,034 in 1919; this leads us to attribute to it a total of approximately 1,814,000 votes for the whole of France (as against 1,727,963 in 1919).

slight tendency to fall, but in three years it did not attain 10% of the membership. It is true that, during the same period, the number of individual members increased in very considerable proportions, passing from 227,877 in 1929 to 419,311 in 1935: the greatest increase took place in 1930 and in 1932 (25% in each year). But it is a curious fact that the variations in membership took place in opposite directions: the two groups of Labour members, individual and Trade Union, did not react in the same way to identical events. It would seem that the two communities are rather heterogeneous, which confirms our earlier remarks concerning the special nature of indirect or affiliated members.

Yet in Germany on the other hand, a very marked correlation may be observed between the development of the National Socialist party and that of the economic crisis. There is a certain parallelism between the unemployment figures and the membership figures of the N.S.D.A.P. (Fig. 9). Similar remarks might be made concerning the German Socialist party in which this phenomenon appears to be much more attenuated. But between 1930 and 1934 the French Communist party figures remained stable, rising from 40,000[1] to 45,000[2] members, that is to say a yearly increase barely higher than 1%: it is true that the economic crisis was in fact less severe in France than in Germany. Is there a case for distinguishing between two kinds of party, the traditional parties relatively insensitive to external events and the new parties, whose rise or decline is determined by them? The two categories would correspond to two different sociological types: the first, stable and stabilizing communities, playing some part as political shock-absorbers, the second, eager and fragile groups which on the contrary amplify the swings of opinion caused by external events. No hasty conclusions must be drawn: let us limit ourselves to drawing attention to the relative insensitiveness of the party community, to its partial isolation with respect to political and economic events. On the other hand the community appears very much more sensitive to problems that are truly party problems: internal crises and schisms, for example, cause considerable variations in the number of members. After the Tours Congress, the French Socialist party declined from 179,787 members in 1920 to 50,449 in 1921; it remained at that level for three years and recovered only with the 1924 electoral campaign. In the same way the split

[1] M. Thorez, *Rapport au Congrès de 1947*, p. 84.
[2] M. Thorez, *Rapport au Congrès de 1945*, p. 56.

in the Norwegian Labour party in 1920 caused its membership to diminish from 95,165 to 45,946. With these causes may be compared the fluctuations in membership of the English Labour party

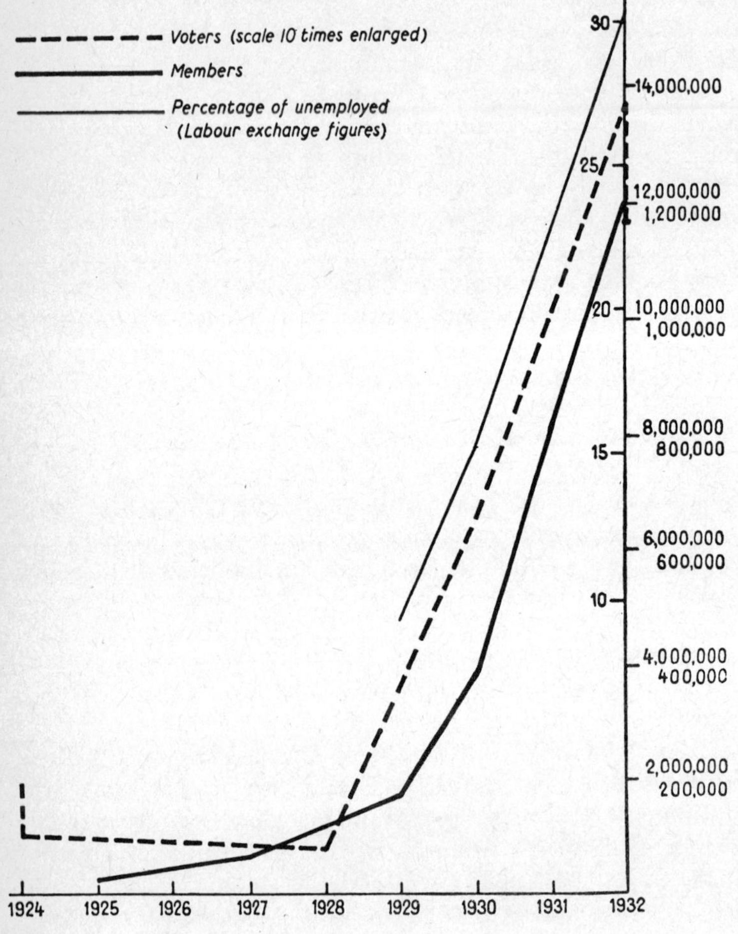

Fig. 9. Rise of Nazi Party, 1924–32.

and the Swedish Socialist party as a consequence of the reforms concerning the affiliation of Trade Union members. The party community shows undeniably one of the characteristics of a closed community: a community shut in upon itself, it seems to live according to its own laws, different from the laws of the national community in which it is included; it has a personal rhythm of development.

This rhythm depends closely upon that of elections: it has already been emphasized that the activity of some parties is scarcely more than seasonal: active at periods of electoral campaigning, they seem to go into hibernation in the intervals. It seems that these changes concern not only the propaganda of the party but its very composition. An analysis of the fluctuation in membership reveals on occasion traces of a regular variation linked with the ballot (primarily with general elections, the only ones that are truly political in character). For example, in the French Socialist party one can make out vaguely between 1919 and 1939 a kind of 'electoral cycle': the number of members increases in election year and generally in the year immediately following, but a stabilization or 'deflation' occurs subsequently. There would thus be two years of 'inflation' and two years of 'deflation'. The phenomenon is clearly perceptible for the 1924 Election (−2·5% in 1922, +2·7% in 1923, *+49%* in 1924, *+53·2%* in 1925, +·07% in 1926, −11·9% in 1927) as well as for the 1936 Election (−16·1% in 1934, +9·15% in 1935, *+68%* in 1936, *+41·5%* in 1937, −3·9% in 1938). It is less clearly marked for the 1928 Election (−12% in 1927, +12% in 1928, *+8·8%* in 1929, +5% in 1930, +4·2% in 1931) and even less clear for the 1932 Election (+4·2% in 1931, *+5·2%* in 1932, but *−4·7%* in 1933). It may be that we have here in fact some repercussion from the world economic crisis, just as the 1924 and 1936 increase due to the General Elections was magnified by the special conditions of the campaign and the heat engendered by the 'Cartel' and by the 'Popular Front' movements. A closer scrutiny of the membership figures, taking into consideration the yearly intake of new members and paying attention at the same time to the members lost (by exclusion, death, and especially overt or tacit resignation) gives some confirmation of these cyclical fluctuations: new names are generally more numerous in election year and the following year; names crossed off generally more numerous in the two following years. Nevertheless, the phenomenon is not at all absolute in character. Nor is it general in character: the variation is scarcely perceptible in the British, Swedish, and Norwegian Socialist parties, for example. No general conclusions can be drawn from an analysis based solely upon four elections and a single party.

It does however help to draw attention to a vital distinction, that between stable and unstable members. There are many people who one day sign an application for membership and take a party card but who do not renew their card the following year and forget

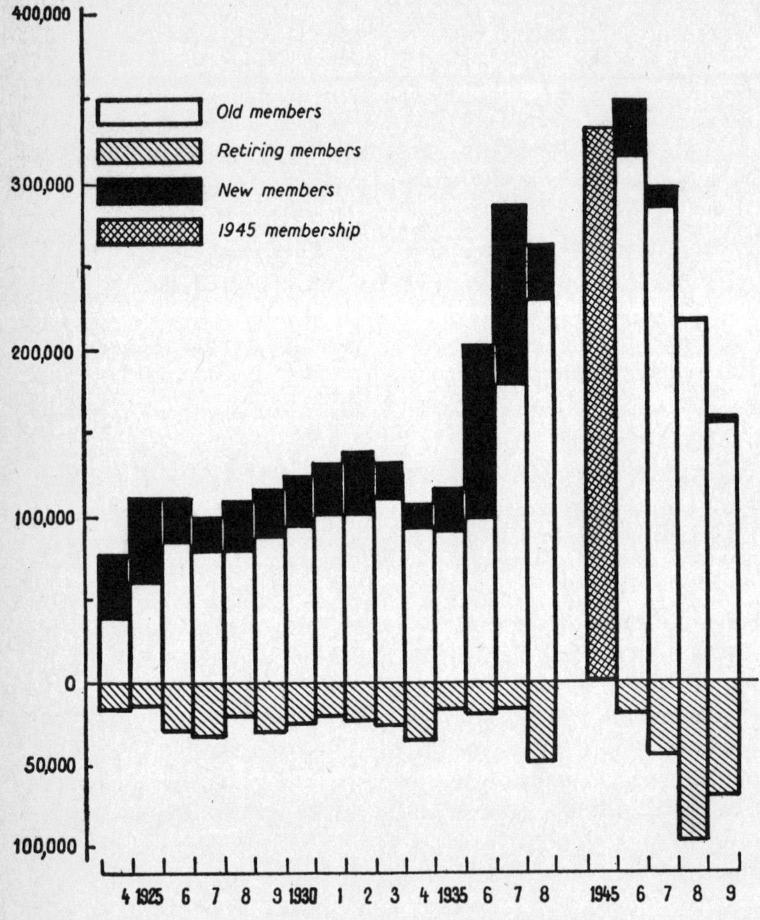

Fig. 10. Membership of French Socialist Party.

they are members: some of them do send in a formal resignation, most simply cease all contact with the party (they continue moreover to figure upon the lists in parties where the registration system is not strict, and to swell artificially the number of members).

Very frequently their period of membership is even briefer: the new member forgets his party after a few months, even at the end of a few days. Sometimes, on the contrary, he remains attached for two or three years. But, in any case, these are not stable members; the stable member remains firmly attached to his party throughout a long period, often throughout his whole life. It would be most advantageous to be able to isolate clearly these two categories. Unfortunately the statistics of the parties do not make any distinction, or any very clear distinction, between them. It is true that until 1950 the French Socialist party used to list separately each year 'new members', 'old members', and 'past members' (Fig. 10). But the next year the 'new members' had become 'old members', which introduced confusion into this latter category. In particular, in the enumeration of 'past members' no account was given of the 'seniority' of those who left the party. To be worth while the statistics should distinguish between: (1) new members who joined during the year, (2) members of a year's standing, two years', three years', and so on. In the same way, members crossed off should be separated into categories by length of membership. Then detailed research could be undertaken on stability of membership. But parties will never co-operate to this extent; they have only too obvious an interest in camouflaging the proportion of unstable to stable members: it might perhaps reveal a weakness.

In some parties indeed this proportion is high. Serious investigators estimate for example that one of the constant features of the French Communist party is its perpetual self-renewal; it has been said that in 1939 scarcely 3% to 4% of its members had belonged to it for more than six years.[1] Such statements are difficult to check. However, checks carried out in different cells suitably selected for sampling should make approximate verification possible. The official statistics of the party already make it possible to draw certain conclusions. In 1937, the party claimed 340,000 members as against 45,000 in February 1934. Consequently more than 87% of the members of the party in 1937 were of less than four years' standing. In December 1944, the party claimed 385,000 members, and in December 1945, 1,032,000 members: at the latter date nearly two out of three members were of less than one year's standing, but one in every four remained a member for only a short time, since in December 1949 the party claimed a membership of 786,000 (Fig. 11). The inflation in membership of the

[1] *Esprit*, May 1939, p. 157.

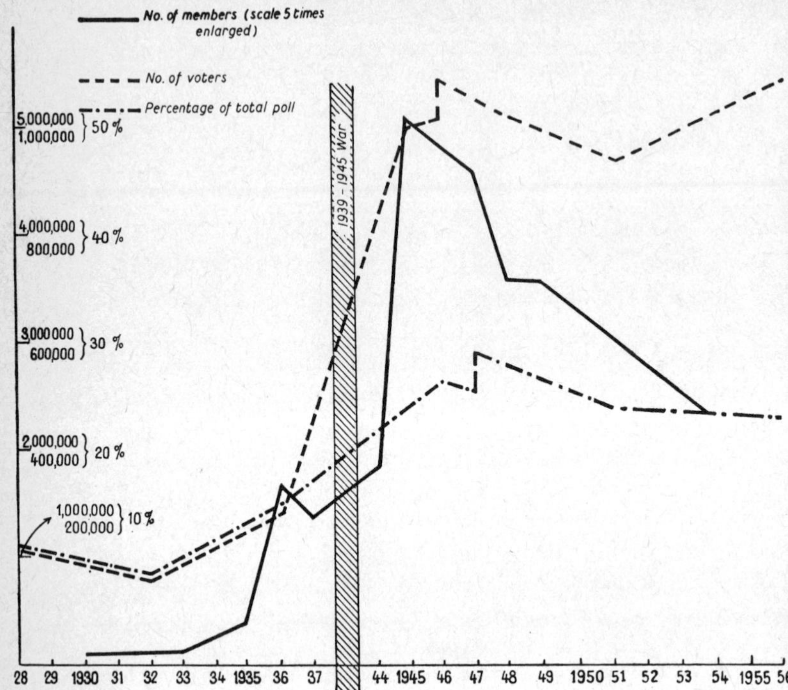

Fig. 11. Members and Voters: French Communist Party, 1928–56.[1]

[1] Membership figures:—1930, 40,000; 1933, 45,000; 1935, 80,000; 1936, 363,000; 1937, 340,000; 1944, 385,000; 1945, 1,032,000; 1947, 907,700; 1948, 798,400; 1949, 786,800; 1954, 500,000. These figures are drawn from the following sources:—

1930 M. Thorez, *Au service du peuple de France* (Speech to 1947 Congress), Paris, Ed., du parti communiste français, 1947, p. 85.

1933 M. Thorez, *Une politique française* (Speech to 1945 Congress), Paris, Ed., du parti communiste français, p. 56 (February, 1934, figures referred to 1933).

1935 *Loc. cit.* (Congress of Villeurbane, January, 1936).

1936 G. Walter, *Histoire du parti communiste français*, Paris, 1948, p. 380 (October, 1936 figures).

1937 M. Thorez, *op. cit.*, p. 56 (Congress of Arles, December, 1937).

1944 L. Mauvais, Report on Organization, 1945 Congress, p. 4.

1945 M. Thorez, *Au service du peuple de France*, p. 84.

1947–9 M. Thorez, *La lutte pour l'indépendance nationale et pour la paix* (Speech to 1950 Congress), Paris, Ed., du parti communiste français, 1950, p. 90 (Figure of annual cards distributed).

1954 Figures quoted at Party Congress (A. Lecoeur, *L'autocritique attendue*, 1955, p. 62, considers that there is considerable exaggeration, and that all post-1945 membership figures are similarly inflated. Some authorities estimate 1954 figures at 350,000.)

French Socialist party in 1924–5 showed no greater stability: in 1924, the party registered 34,668 new members as against 38,000 old members; in 1925, 50,537 new as against 60,939 old; but in 1926 28,031 members left the party, in 1927 31,522, compared with an average of 12,000 for the preceding years. In just the same way the Labour party spurt in 1920 seems to have been made up chiefly of unstable members: from 1918 to 1920, within two years, 1,353,126 new members joined the party, or an increase of 46·3%. But the figures decrease by 31·5% from 1920 to 1922, to remain fairly steady up to 1927. In two years 1,034,351 members left the party, that is 76·4% of the increase that had taken place during the preceding period. We may assume that more than three out of four of the recruits who entered the party between 1918 and 1920 were only unstable members. On the other hand, the increase registered in 1936–7 by the French Socialist party seems to have been more enduring: it took in 100,211 new members in 1936 and 101,332 more in 1937; but it registered only 16,728 withdrawals in 1937 and 49,338 in 1938.

Systematic analyses which enabled us to separate out the stable and unstable members would lead the way to a much more profound knowledge of the nature of the party community. Only then should we be able to distinguish the superficial variations, which affect only the unstable members, from the real transformations which affect the stable: the growth of the French Socialist party in 1936–7 would in this light assume quite a different meaning from that ascribed to its inflation in 1924–5. From this point of view the crisis that it is at present undergoing might be considered to be a falling back upon the stable members. But this falling back is accompanied by a very considerable decrease in the average figure of new memberships. Before the war the party never had fewer than 15% new members per year (by comparison with the number of old members); this proportion fell to less than 4% in 1947, to ·31% in 1948, and to 1·9% in 1949. Such a drying-up of new recruits is the symptom of a serious sclerosis.

The distinction between stable and unstable members has a bearing not only upon the development of the party community but also upon its composition. Further fundamental research ought to be undertaken in this field: it is at present rendered difficult by the lack of precision in the statistics. At the least we should need to know the composition of membership by age and by sexes, by social categories, by geographical distribution. In fact, present

E

enumerations often convey only the regional distribution as well as the distribution by sexes: even then both are not always given. It will therefore be necessary to make up for the deficiencies in the aggregate statistics by many field surveys: studying the life of one branch of the party over a fairly long period; extending such analyses to the greatest possible number of branches, in different milieux. Unfortunately each one of the surveys will encounter great obstacles: non-party members will have difficulty in gaining access to the essential documents; party members will run the risk of interpreting them one-sidedly. However, studies of this kind are the indispensable complement to research into electoral geography and sociology; the distribution of votes obviously depends upon the strength of the parties and upon their nature. And the latter cannot be appreciated solely by an external, general enumeration of the party's members: we must determine, as precisely as possible, their different categories, the respective sizes of these categories, and their evolution. At the same time we must compare with the members, who form the basic structure of the party community, those who gravitate around them or are outstanding amongst them: the supporters, the militants, the propagandists.

II. DEGREES OF PARTICIPATION

Within parties in which no system of formal membership exists three concentric circles of participation can be distinguished. The widest comprises the electors who vote for the candidates put forward by the parties at local and national elections (further distinctions could be drawn between these latter two types but this aspect of the problem will be neglected in order to simplify our exposition). The second circle is made up of supporters, a vague term for a vague concept corresponding none the less to a reality: the supporter is an elector, but more than an elector: he acknowleges that he favours the party; he defends it and sometimes he supports it financially; he even joins bodies ancillary to the party. The terms fellow-traveller and crypto-communist, often employed nowadays, designate supporters. Finally the third, the inmost circle, is composed of the militants; they consider themselves to be members of the party, elements in the party community; they see to its organization and its operation; they direct its propaganda and its general activities. The 'caucus-men' of the cadre parties are militants. In parties that have members, these constitute a fourth circle, intermediate between the last two: wider than the circle of militants, narrower than the circle of supporters: membership involves a greater degree of participation than the sympathy of the supporter, but less than militancy. Fruitful comparisons can be made between members on the one hand and each of the other three groups on the other: membership is a good criterion.

The fundamental problem consists in determining the relationships between the different circles. The attempt to solve it is not purely disinterested; it concerns much more than pure scientific curiosity. It involves the very nature of political parties and the democratic character of their organization. For the inmost circles animate and guide the outer circles: in so far as the first are representative of the second—that is to say where there is coincidence of general orientation—the system can be called democratic; otherwise this series of concentric circles is to be defined as an oligarchy.

Electors. The elector category has from the standpoint of political science one considerable advantage over all the others: it is easily measurable. There are usually fairly adequate electoral statistics available although these do not always show clearly the party affiliation of candidates: in this respect, there are serious gaps in some European statistics for the periods prior to the introduction of P.R. These gaps are even more serious for local elections, though the latter are less important for the matter at issue, because questions of personality and local interest affect support for the party more here than in general elections.

In cadre parties the counting of electors provides the only possible measure of the party community. The strength or weakness of a party may be assessed by the number of its voters. The evolution of a party may be traced through the fluctuations of its vote. It is even possible to assess the more or less democratic nature of its directing bodies by comparing their composition with the distribution of the party's electors. Thus American authors consider that the National Convention (entrusted with the selection of the party's candidate for the presidential election) is not representative in character because the delegates to it are not proportionate to the number of the party's electors, country voters being over-represented just as the Southern vote is over-represented in the Republican party (cf. Fig. 19). In mass parties, on the other hand, membership is taken as the basis of representation, but it then becomes essential to determine the relationships between the two categories. Electors and members compose two distinct categories, of which the second tends to lead the first, as we shall see: parliamentary representatives designated by the electors being more and more subjected to the authority of the directing committees that emanate from the members. It is therefore important to be sure whether the reactions of these two groups converge or diverge—statistical comparisons can in this respect provide useful information.

But such comparisons are not always easy. In the first place, they encounter the difficulty already discussed: the general lack of accuracy in the counting of figures for membership: one term of the comparison must therefore always be viewed with reserve. Again, they face the difficulty of comparing electoral statistics and party statistics. The correlation coefficient method cannot be used in this field because the points of comparison are too few in number: membership counts scarcely exist prior to 1905–10, so that figures for comparison are available for only a dozen general elections at most; even this number must be reduced in most countries, for it is impossible to make comparisons when parties are still too underdeveloped: the series are therefore too short for any worthwhile calculation to be carried out. Moreover correlation coefficients would make it possible to compare membership strength with electoral strength only at the moments of the general election; yet the variations in the total of members during the interval between two elections constitute one of the fundamental elements of the problem. The rhythms of the series are in fact different: an annual rhythm for membership statistics a quadrennial or quinquennial rhythm for election statistics, often altered by dissolutions or prorogations. Correlation coefficients would not give a sufficiently selective analysis. The best method consists in drawing comparative graphs of the curves for electors and the curves for members, based upon the fundamental statistics. The scales for these curves cannot be identical because of the great difference in numbers that separates electors and members. In consequence we must adopt scales that are related to one another in a way that corresponds approximately to the average relationship of the two groups over the whole period under consideration. Such curves can be usefully complemented by determining rates of increase for electors and members respectively, since these make more precise measurement possible.

It becomes possible to make comparisons between the respective situations of members and electors in a number of parties (dif-

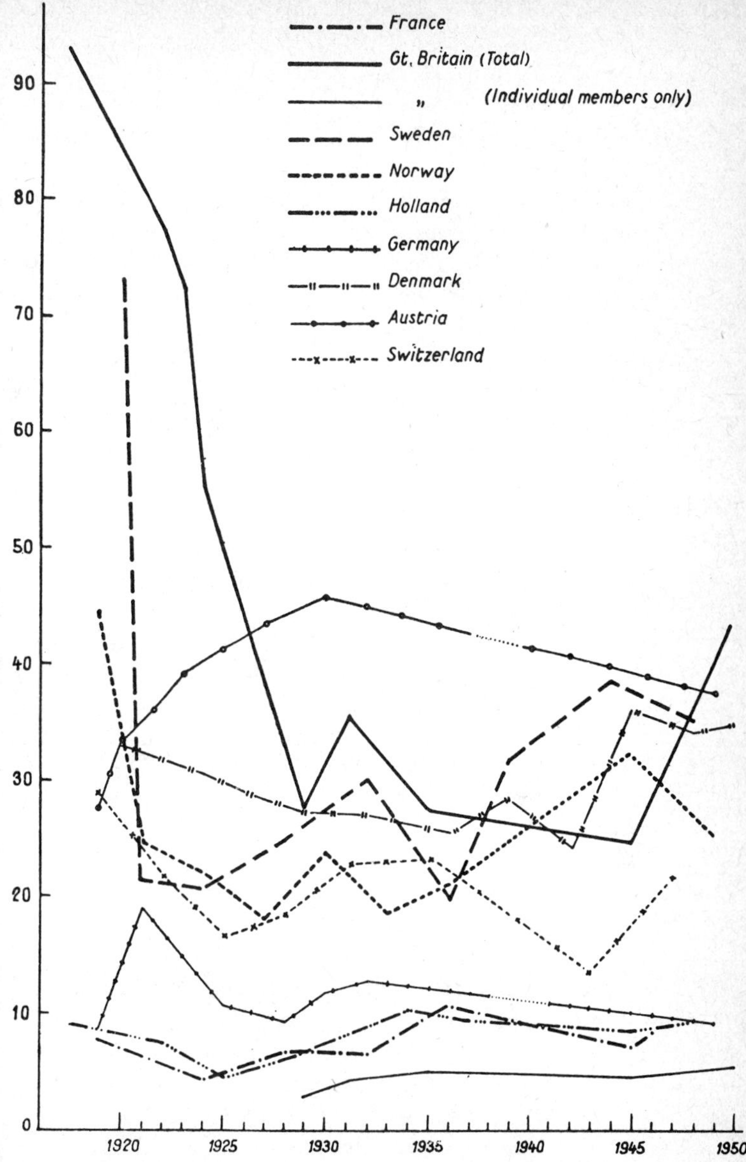

Fig. 12. Changes in membership ratios of European Socialist Parties (1918–50).

ferent parties in the same country, similar parties in different countries), if we determine for each party on the date under consideration the *membership ratio*, that is the relation of the number of members to the number of electors. By relating the membership ratios of one particular party for a succession of elections, we can draw membership curves which allow us to make comparisons both in time and in space (Fig. 12). The membership ratio must not be accorded more significance than it in fact possesses: it is a measuring tool and nothing more. Nor must it be forgotten that membership does not mean the same thing to all parties, that in practice it has no true meaning in cadre parties and that even the mass parties differ greatly in their system of registration and in the strictness of their enumeration. It would, for example, be quite meaningless to compare membership ratios as between the Radical Socialist and Communist parties, since the concept of membership is entirely different in the two cases. In the same way the membership ratio of the Labour party is not comparable with that of the French Socialist party because the former is indirect in structure and the latter direct. In short, three kinds of comparison remain possible: (1) comparison of the membership ratios of the same party at different periods of its development (this complements the comparative graphs already described); (2) comparison of the membership ratios of the same party in different areas of the country or in different social classes or age-groups (though the last is scarcely ever possible, because statistics give no word on the subject: the investigator would have to draw up his own statistics, either by sampling or by survey); (3) comparison of membership ratios of Socialist parties (Figs. 12 and 13), of Communist parties, of Christian Democratic parties, and so on (the more closely the parties resemble one another in structure, the more exact the comparison: it is more accurate for Communist than for Socialist parties, for Socialist than for Christian Democratic parties); (4) comparison within the same country of fairly similar parties: Communist and Socialist parties, for example, or Socialist and Christian Democratic parties—though this last comparison must always be treated with the strictest reserve.

In this way a vast field of study lies open for research and offers the possibility of useful discoveries. It would seem that investigations might well be orientated around a central theme: the systematic measurement of the disparity between the reactions of electors and the reactions of party members. Thus one could, taking either districts or countries, set the membership ratios alongside the votes polled by a party in order to discover whether there exists any relation between them, whether they vary directly or inversely, or whether their variations show no correlation. The same comparison could be made by professions, by social categories, and by age-groups. Naturally, such analyses would have to be made for the greatest possible number of parties and go as far back into the past as statistics permitted. No account would be taken of the

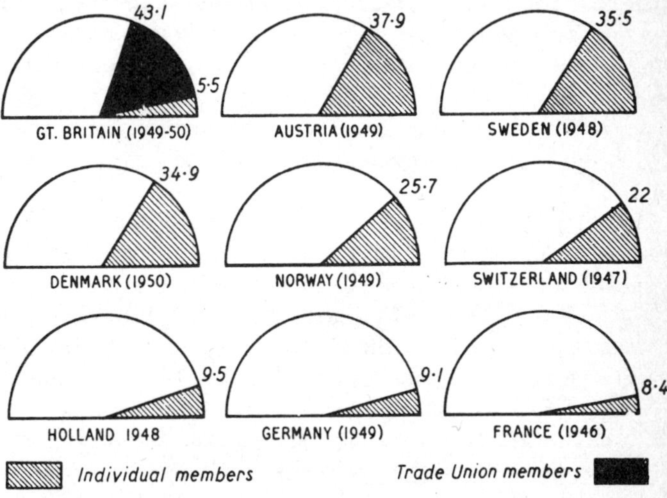

Fig. 13. Membership ratios in European Socialist Parties.

incubation period of parties, since the smallness of their membership and of their electoral vote at that time would allow of no valid comparison: during such a period they are able to put up only a few isolated candidates, which falsifies the figure of electors attributed to them in the national statistics; nor do they as yet possess branches or caucuses in every district in the country, which similarly falsifies the figures for membership in party censuses. Parties can be analysed only after they have reached a certain degree of development, only after they have reached the adult stage.

Only by searching and repeated investigations of this kind will it be possible to check the accuracy—or the degree of error—of a hypothesis suggested by a few preliminary inquiries that are in fact limited both in number and in scope: the relative independence of electors and members, the difference in the reactions displayed by the two groups in face of political events, the divergence of their respective development as groups. It is true that comparison and analysis reveal periods when members and electors develop on parallel lines: for example in the French Socialist party between 1906 and 1914, and between 1928 and 1932 (Fig. 8); in the Swedish Social Democratic party between 1924 and 1940, and so on. However such coincidences between the two groups are relatively rare. They seem to correspond to periods of party growth or of increasing ascendancy. It is frequently the case in fact that the rate of growth is not the same for membership as for the electorate, the latter generally increasing more rapidly than the former: indeed it is observable that the membership ratio tends to decrease as the number of electors rises and to increase as that number falls. An analysis of the data for Socialist parties, comprising sixty-three cases and spread over nine countries, reveals only twenty departures from this general tendency (Fig. 14); furthermore, five of the exceptions (e.g. France, 1919–28; Norway, 1918–24; Great Britain, 1945–50) can be explained as the result of an internal crisis in the party or of a modification in the system of membership, and this robs them of all significance. The membership group seems therefore to be more stable than the electoral group. These conclusions are however valid only for Socialist parties (we have noted the instability of Communist membership) and are only very approximate in character: in France, for example, the stability of electors during the period 1919–39 provides a striking contrast to the instability of members; in the case of electors the maximum variation is 14·7% compared with the average of the two extreme figures; in the case of members we reach a variation figure of 121·7%. In Switzerland the stability of the electors since 1930 is similarly very much greater than that of members: the variation is 1·4% for the former and 28·7% for the latter.

Differences in rapidity of development are moreover less important than the complete divergences which seem to be even more numerous: they reflect the disparity in the reactions of each group to political and economic events on the one hand, to internal party crises on the other. Two patterns seem to stand out fairly clearly: (1) the reaction of members to crises or to events within the party is more marked than that of electors; (2) but the reaction of both to political and social events is different without it being possible to determine whether it is either more or less marked. The reactions of Socialist parties to Communist schisms or 'left-wing'

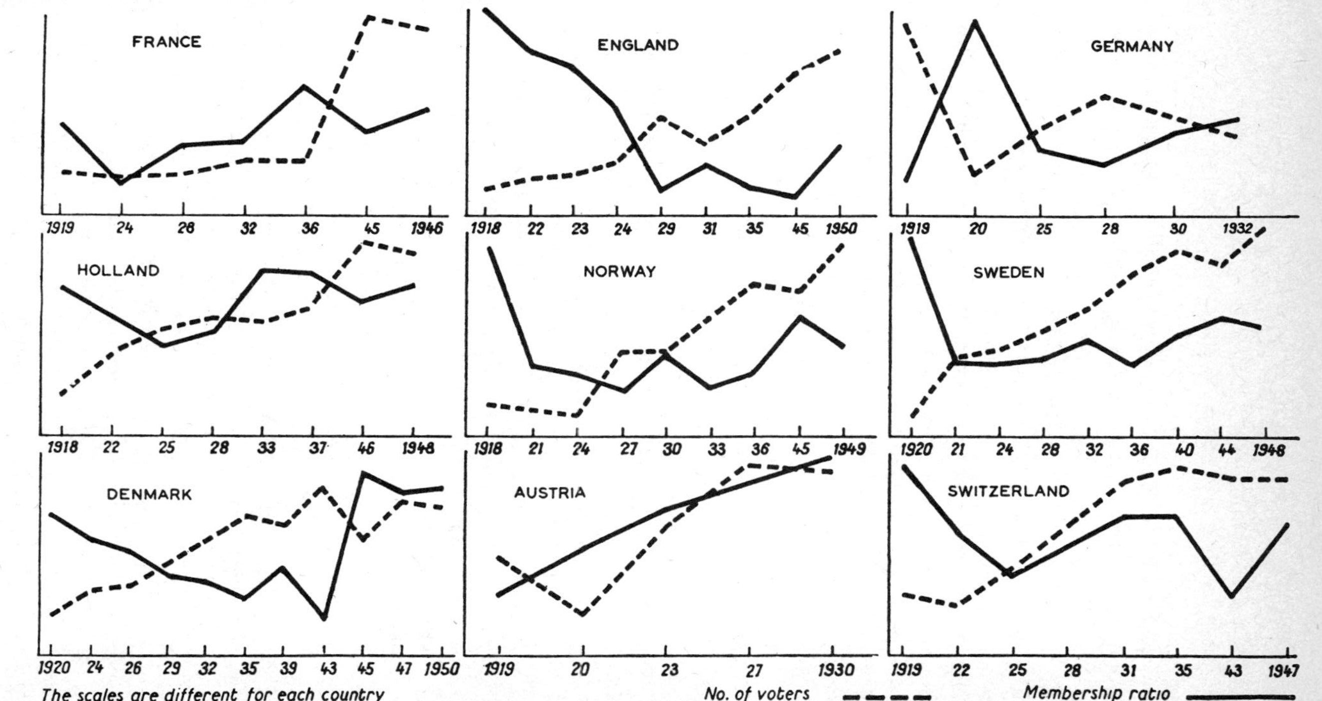

Fig. 14. Comparison of variations in membership figures and membership ratios in European Socialist Parties.

splits immediately after the 1914 War provide a good illustration of the first of these tendencies. In France the Socialist party lost 46·6% of its members between 1919 and 1924, but only 2·4% of its electors. In Norway the secession of the Social Democrats cost the Workers' party between 1918 and 1921 nearly 60% of its members whilst its electors diminished by only 8%. In Germany, on the other hand, the Independent Socialist party split was accompanied between 1919 and 1920 by a considerable fall in the number of electors voting for the Social Democrats (46·5% decrease), whilst the membership increased by 6·8% (Fig. 16). The reaction of Labour party members and electors to fluctuations in the contracting-in and contracting-out procedure was even more divergent: between 1924 and 1929 the adoption of the former at the expense of the latter caused a decrease in the number of affiliated Trade Union members of 35·3%; but none the less the number of electors rose by 51·5%; the disparity was not so great between 1945 and 1950 when contracting-out was reinstated and caused a rise in the number of Trade Union members equal to 96·3%,[1] whilst the figures for electors rose by 10·5%.

The difference in behaviour of electors and members towards political and social events has already been shown in their respective reactions to the 1914 and 1939 Wars. Both brought about a general expansion of Socialist parties in electors and members alike. But the increases are rarely parallel in the two groups, the disparity in rates being incidentally not very easy to measure because of electoral reforms which in many cases increased the total electorate: consequently, some correction must be introduced. This parallelism is noticeable as an exception in the case of the French Socialist party between 1914 and 1919: the figures for electors rose by 31·5% and those for members by 30%. In England, on the contrary, between 1910 and 1918, the Labour party electors (in relation to the total poll) increased by more than 200%; during the same period membership increased by only 100% (Fig. 15). Between 1935 and 1945 the Trade Union membership of the Labour party increased by 20·5% and individual membership by 16·2%, whereas the number of electors voting for the party rose by 43·7%. These examples suggest a reversal of the preceding pattern: in this case the reactions of the electors are more marked than those of the party members. However, such a conclusion would be premature: in France, for example, the percentage of

[1] Based upon the 1949 figure.

Socialist votes (relative to the total of votes cast) rose from 20% in 1936 to 25% in 1945, that is a rate of increase of 25%, whilst the membership figures rose by 65·8%. This simply means that there was a divergence in behaviour; it was much more considerable in some countries. In Switzerland, for example, the number of Socialist electors fell from 265,428 in 1914 to 195,121 in 1920,

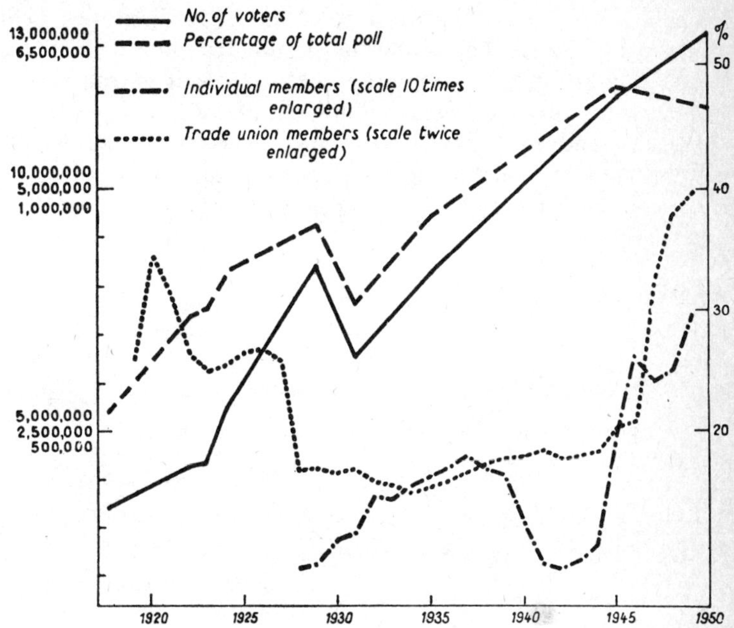

Fig. 15. Members and Voters: Labour Party.

whilst the number of members rose from 84,410 to 143,090; in just the same way, the number of electors fell from 1,546,804 in 1940 to 1,436,571 in 1944 whereas the membership figures rose from 487,257 to 553,724. In Norway Socialist electors decreased in number from 618,616 in 1936 to 609,348 in 1945, while the number of members rose from 142,719 to 197,683. Faced with the same event, which was nevertheless of considerable importance, the two communities reacted in diametrically opposed ways.

Other examples, equally typical, could be quoted. During the political crisis in England, brought on, between 1918 and 1935, by the breakdown of the two-party system, the behaviour of Labour electors was entirely different from that of Labour party members.

From 1918 to 1922 Labour electors and Labour party members increased, the first more rapidly than the second at a rate of 30% compared with an increase of 10% in the membership. Between 1922 and 1923 the electors increased slightly, by 2·6%, but the membership declined, by 4·7%. Between 1923 and 1924 the figures for electors increased more noticeably (approximately 26%), while those for membership remained almost unchanged (an increase of 1·2%). Between 1924 and 1929 there was a still more marked rise in the number of electors, reaching 51·5%, but membership fell off, decreasing by 26%, which, it is true, can be explained as a result of the abandonment of contracting-out. Between 1929 and 1931, on the contrary, the electors decreased in number whereas membership rose again slightly, by 1·16% (the rise in individual membership considered separately was much more marked: 38%).

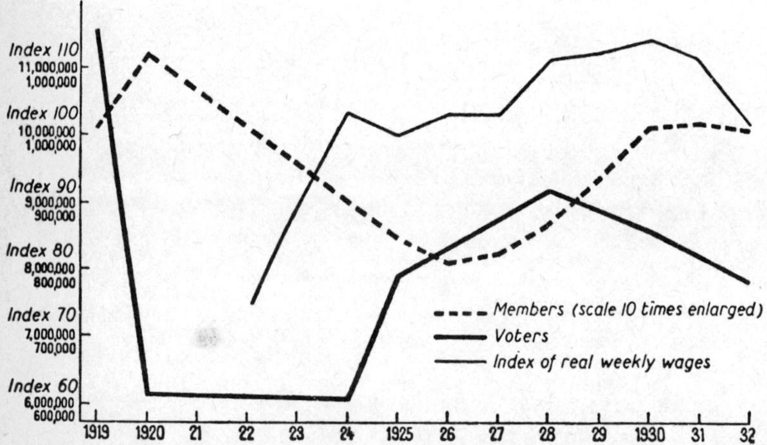

Fig. 16. Members and Voters: German Social Democratic Party.

In Germany, under the Weimar Republic, the reactions of Social Democrat electors and party members were generally divergent: from 1919 to 1920 electors decreased and members increased; from 1920 to 1925 members decreased and electors increased; from 1928 to 1930 members increased and electors decreased. The movement in the figures for the two groups coincided only between 1925 and 1928, and between 1930 and 1932: the variations in the number of electors were moreover more marked than the variations in membership (Fig. 16). In short the two groups followed entirely different patterns of behaviour. In France the victory of the Popular Front in 1936 produced a decrease of 1·7% in the Socialist party poll compared with 1932, but a considerable increase in membership, which rose by 45%. In the same way the falling away of Socialist electors from 1945 to 1946, when their members decreased from 4,561,000 to 3,432,000, representing a drop from 23·8% to 17·9% of the total poll, coincided with a rise in membership of 5·7%.

These observations are, of course, superficial and incomplete. None the less they make it possible to advance, solely as a working hypothesis, the idea that there is a disparity between the two groups: party electors and party members. It is just as if the latter group constituted, by comparison with the former, a closed circle, an exclusive world of which the reactions and the general behaviour obeyed its own laws, different from those which determine the changes amongst electors, that is the variations in public opinion. It seems unnecessary to emphasize the importance of such observations. In so far as they are verified, in so far as a 'law of disparity' can in fact be defined, the traditional conception of political democracy will be overthrown: for as we shall see later, the ruling bodies of the parties, stemming from the members, tend to control the parliamentary representatives chosen by the electors. This would be no more than a minor evil were the political attitudes of both electors and members roughly the same; the members could then be considered as the most conscious section, the vanguard, of the electors. But the law of disparity would destroy this illusion, by showing that the essential differences in behaviour of the two groups in no way permit one of them to claim that it reflects and represents the other. Measurement of the disparity between electors and members is thus equivalent to measuring the degree of oligarchy which impregnates the systems that we term democratic.

Supporters. The meaning of the term 'elector' was simple and clear, the meaning of 'supporter' is vague and complicated. The supporter is something more than an elector and something less than a member. Like the elector, he gives the party his vote, but he does not limit himself to that. He makes manifest his agreement with the party; he confesses his political preference. The elector votes in the secrecy of the polling-booth and does not reveal the choice he has made. The very precision and amplitude of the measures taken to ensure the secrecy of the ballot prove the importance of this secrecy. An elector who says how he has voted is no longer solely an elector: he is on the way to becoming a supporter. By that act he at the same time brings into operation certain phenomena of social contagion: his declaration carries with it an implicit element of propaganda; similarly, it brings him into fellowship with other supporters and creates the first bonds of a community. There is no true community of electors for they do not know one another, there exists only a group that can be classified, *in toto*, and measured statistically. There is a community of supporters, often embryonic, often amorphous, but real none the less.

The avowal of a political preference, the recognition of sympathy for a party, may assume many forms and many degrees. It is not sufficient to declare that one voted for a party once, especially if it be added that this vote was an exception, that it depended on special circumstances, and that one has no intention of repeating it: this would be less a demonstration of sympathy than of rancour. The situation is quite different if the vote is considered to be customary and normal—which is approximately the attitude of the American citizen in the closed primary. A further step is taken if the declaration of sympathy does not remain purely passive but is accompanied by some positive effort in favour of the party: regular reading of its newspapers, attendance at its rallies and public meetings, contributions to its funds, propagandist activities like canvassing and so on. Imperceptibly, unalloyed sympathy can be transformed into true membership and even into militancy.

If the supporter is something more than an elector he is something less than a member. His relationships with the party have not been consecrated by the official and formal bonds of a signed undertaking and a regular subscription. One might almost say that the relation of supporter to member resembles the relation of concubinage to marriage. Why is there this absence of formal membership? In cadre parties because formal membership does not exist. One cannot regularize the relationship by signing the register because there is no register; concubinage has to be endured because marriage is not possible. Members of the caucuses may be regarded as militants, in the sense that will be defined later; all those who gravitate around them are supporters. But this explanation is not valid for mass parties, for in them organized membership exists. Whence therefore this refusal to enter the ranks of the party, this desire to remain outside the real party community when agreement with the party is acknowledged? There are various motives. Sometimes the supporter is confronted by some material obstacle: his duties do not allow him to join formally. Some states for example withhold from their officials the right to join parties that are considered to be subversive; some employers impose the same rule, formally or tacitly, upon their employees. Or else the supporter himself may consider that his profession is incompatible with any over-rigorous commitment; it may be from lack of time (which would prevent him from carrying out his duties as a member) or for fear of embarrassment (the tradesman does not want to lose his customers, the clergyman does not want to dismay his flock, the officer does not want to compromise his authority). All these reasons are not to be despised: some betray a lack of courage and of disinterestedness, but others are based upon altruistic motives, even although these sometimes constitute more or less conscious excuses.

In other cases the obstacle is to be found elsewhere. It is not to be found outside the citizen, in the social pressures exerted upon him, but within him. The supporter may refuse to become a member because he dislikes regimentation, because he refuses to give up his personal independence: this feeling is very strong in some agricultural and middle-class circles and explains why membership is a less well-developed feature in right-wing parties and in agricultural areas. It is a strongly held view also amongst intellectuals and artists, except for those who, on the contrary, intoxicated as it were with the community spirit, throw themselves body and soul into collective action with a frenzied abandonment of individuality which itself is evidence both of a marked degree of mental instability and of a certain desire for moral masochism. (The attitude of intellectuals within the party always raises special problems, for they either experience great difficulty in staying in the ranks or on the other hand they exaggerate their surrender to the collectivity; whether individualist or mystic, they have a place apart, often unstable, which generally earns them the distrust of the other members of the party.) Often the refusal to join is the result of some ideological disagreement with the party: the supporter prefers this party to all others and consequently helps it, but he does not share all its views and therefore refuses to enter it completely. He makes common cause with it on particular issues, but recognizes no general overall agreement.

In this way, it is possible to reach, not without some difficulty, an approximate definition of the supporter. But what practical criteria can be used to recognize him? On what bases can we establish statistics for supporters such as could be compared with the figures for party electors and members, with a view to measuring the correlation between the respective behaviour of these different groups? Here we are in difficulties. It is possible to attempt to make a direct count of certain special kinds of supporter; for example, we can count the readers of the party newspaper. But this is not a determining factor: many parties have the greatest difficulty in getting even their members to read the party organ; this applies with even greater force to the supporter. Some readers are not supporters at all but are simply curious; some readers are even opponents who have discovered a means of rousing their anger: but neither category is very numerous and they are lost in the great mass of readers. Finally, there are also very delicate problems involved in choosing the newspaper which is to serve as a basis for taking a census of supporters. In any case, the fact of reading the party's Press (or journals sympathetic to the party) distinguishes only one category of supporters. Another (which often overlaps the first) is to be distinguished by the act of attendance at party meetings and rallies. This criterion is no more exact than the first: many come to public meetings out of curiosity or for amusement and are not true supporters. None the less the indication provided is not entirely valueless: in police reports it is felt to be of the greatest use in assessing variations in the influence of a party upon public opinion. In America participation in the primaries (where there are closed primaries)[1] constitutes an excellent standard for measuring support for the party: a comparison between the statistics for those taking part in primaries and the electoral statistics would permit of valuable comparisons between supporters and electors (cf. Figs. 42 and 43).

In most cases we can in the last resort find out who are the supporters only by organizing inquiries and Gallup polls. Even then the concept of 'supporter' is too vague for any simple direct question to produce adequate answers on this score. We should have to establish degrees of support objectively defined and at the same time ask the precise motives which prevent support from transforming itself into formal membership. But the reticence of people

[1] Except in the Southern states where the single-party system leads to mass abstention in the elections proper but to increased attendance at the primaries (cf. Fig. 42).

questioned by observers is nowhere greater than in this particular field, in France at least. Hence the difficulty of carrying out precise and detailed surveys.

As an example we can quote the questions asked in 1949 at Auxerre during the conduct of a general sociological inquiry into the structure of an average French town.[1] Question 136 read as follows: 'Have you any preference for any particular political party?' and Question 137 read: 'Do you belong to a political party?' No details were asked about the party for which preference was expressed or of which membership was declared, nor about the motives for preference or membership. This voluntary discretion on the part of the observers greatly limited the scope of their inquiry. Some of the results obtained are however worth quoting as examples.

On the whole, in Auxerre supporters outnumber members by 5 to 1, the proportion being higher for men (three supporters to one member) than for women (nine supporters to one member) as the following percentages show:

	Total	*Men*	*Women*
Supporters . . .	29	31	27
Members . . .	6	10	3

It is interesting to compare with these aggregate results the percentages of supporters and members within each social category and their proportion to one another:

	Supporters	*Members*	*Members expressed as % of Supporters*
Liberal and technical professions . . .	42	9	21·4
Managerial . . .	32	11	34·3
Small tradesmen . .	36	7	19·4
Clerks . . .	34	7	20·2
Workmen . . .	22	8	36·6
Artisans . . .	19	5	25·8
Manual and domestic workers	17	2	11·7
Not employed . .	34	4	11·7

[1] Ch. Bettelheim et S. Frère, *Auxerre en 1950*, Paris, 1950, Cahiers de la Fondation nationale des Sciences politiques, No. 17.

The distribution of members and supporters by social classes is as follows:

	Members	*Members and Supporters*
Liberal and technical professions .	9	9
Managerial	7	5
Small tradesmen . . .	7	7
Clerks	20	19
Workmen	31	20
Artisans	5	5
Manual workers . . .	3	6
Not employed	18	29

The table shows that subordinate employees—clerks and workmen—tend to provide the majority of members of political parties. However, one isolated and summary investigation gives no grounds for definite conclusions.

Finally we must consider separately the hypothesis of an *organized enrolment* of supporters, the latest stage in party technique. For a long time mass parties exhibited a certain contempt for supporters, likening them to the lukewarm, of whom the Bible says 'Because you are neither hot nor cold, I will spew you out of my mouth'. Gradually they have realized however that the lukewarm provide a natural source of future members, more responsive than others to the party's propaganda, that they could be used to enlarge the circle of party members proper, that they have qualities that could give the party an opportunity to penetrate into circles naturally hostile to it by using them as a protective smoke screen, attenuating the rigour of its doctrines, and adopting the disguise of the wolf turned shepherd. But these different tasks could only be satisfactorily accomplished if the supporters ceased to be an amorphous, indefinite, invisible mass and were organized into collective bodies like the members. Hence the idea of organizations ancillary to the party and open to supporters. The term 'ancillary organizations' is here used to describe the various bodies, created by the party and controlled by it constitutionally or in fact,[1] which make possible wider or greater participation: wider participation, by

[1] The technique used to secure control of ancillary organizations has already been defined. (Cf. p. 51.)

grouping around the nucleus of members proper, satellite organizations made up of supporters; greater participation, through completing the political organization of the member by organization on the family, social, and cultural planes. Two classes of ancillary organization might be discerned: those designed for supporters, those for members. In practice, most can be employed in both ways. Here we shall concern ourselves with the first aspect, leaving the second for later consideration.

Youth Associations, Women's Clubs, Sports Clubs; Old Soldiers' Clubs, Intellectual or Literary Clubs, Societies for amusement and leisure; Trade Unions, Friendly Societies, Co-operative Societies; Leagues of International Friendship, Taxpayers', Tenants', Housewives' Associations; Patriotic or Pacifist Movements, and so on: ancillary organizations can assume the most diverse shapes, take action in the most varied fields, group the most dissimilar people. Their very multiplicity and variety provide one element in their success: the whole technique of the ancillary organization is in fact based upon the specialized and limited nature of the aims it pursues. Political parties are communities with general aims: they provide complete and coherent systems of thought about society; they aim at a total organization of national and even international life. This breadth of aim drives away from them many people who agree with them about some particular aim but not about the whole. The brilliant idea that some modern parties have had is to set up alongside the party (the community with general aims) a series of 'doubles'—as many satellite communities with restricted aims as possible. Most tenants are dissatisfied with their landlord and can agree to unite against him in order to defend their personal interests as tenants; but the majority of them are not Communists and would not agree to joining the Communist party even to press their tenants' claims. However, if the party should create a Tenants' Association, officially self-governing, officially non-political, but of which in fact it controlled the activities, a large number of tenants would join: the party watchwords could be spread amongst them with some preliminary precautions; purely specialized manifestations on behalf of tenants' claims could then at the appropriate moment be used to support the party's general policy; discreet and intelligent propaganda would also make it possible to recruit new party members.

We have deliberately chosen as an example an ancillary organization far removed from the sphere of politics; it is a concrete and living example however: the Tenants' Association in France is linked with the Communist party. Some organizations are linked more closely: there are Communist Sports Clubs; there are Choral Societies, Athletic Associations, Societies for artists and intellectuals, and Recreational Clubs attached to parties: the French Federation of Film Societies was associated with the Communist party. There are other cases in which the ancillary organizations come closer to political action: the fundamental case is that of the Trade Union. The problem of the relationships between Trade Unions and Workers' parties has been answered very differently in different countries and for different Unions; the two extremes are fusion within the body of an indirect party (British system), or Trade Union independence of the parties (the French doctrine, expressed in the Amiens Charter). In fact, Trade Unions and political parties have always sought to influence one another. Even before 1914 the German Social Democratic party had made a systematic attempt to reduce Trade Unions to the status of ancillary organizations. The Communist parties have perfected the technique: in France, from 1936 onwards, they carried out a methodical colonization of the C.G.T. (made possible by the C.G.T.'s acceptance of fusion with the former C.G.T.U. created by the Communists after the Tours schism). This colonization reached its peak after the Liberation and led to the secession of the non-Communist unionists and to the creation of the C.G.T.-F.O.: today the French C.G.T. is nothing more than an ancillary organization of the Communist party. Through the Unions the party can organize a vast mass of workers that it groups around working-class bargaining points: this is in fact an example of the system of communities of limited aim, used by the party for its own general aims.

Finally, the system is used in ancillary organizations of a directly political nature, which aim at uniting those who share the party's opinion upon some precise issue, which is suitably selected and isolated from the remainder of the party's doctrine. Two examples of such use can be quoted: the 1945 National Front, the present-day Peace Campaign, both of them ancillary to the Communist party. In the first case, the aim was to unite those who felt some nostalgia for the days when all patriotic elements were united against the enemy in the Resistance. The spirit of political unity and national union against the divisions and struggles of the party has always evoked a deep response in public opinion, especially in the Latin countries in which the party system does not work well, and especially after a war which had strengthened the feeling of patriotic union; the original idea was to make use of this anti-party spirit in the service of one party. Communist tactics, which were at that period in favour of coalitions, made the realization of the Front possible. However, for lack of organization, the National Front met with little success; on the other hand, the Peace Campaign, being better-organized, seems to have achieved better results. Europe, ruined by the last war, convinced that a third would bring a repetition of the infernal cycle, Occupation—Destruction—Liberation, provides a splendidly fertile soil for the seeds of pacifist propaganda. A large number of Europeans, very far removed from Communism, are in consequence vulnerable to the attacks of the Peace Campaigners and provide an effective contribution to the general strategy of the party.

It may be questioned whether the technique of ancillary organizations of a political nature is not gradually evolving towards a transformation of the idea of party, which would accentuate its oligarchic character and would at the same time permit of the complete fusion of the two conceptions of the mass party and the devotee party. The general organization of the party would then consist of two concentric circles: the party, a closed and exclusive circle, made up solely of the purest, most ardent, and most convinced members: the 'front', a wider circle, open to all, of which the members would serve the party as a mass for manœuvre, as reserve troops, and a field for propaganda. In certain People's Democracies, particularly in Yugoslavia, the National or Patriotic Fronts are no longer used to coalesce opposition parties around the Communist party—which was their original function—but to group a kind of second-rank Communist, thought to be unworthy of admission to full membership of the party. In this case, we are no longer dealing with supporters proper but with true members; however, we must make a distinction, as the pre-1939 Russian Communist party did, between two classes of members: the faithful and the catechumen, the citizens and the subjects, the active and the reserve lists. Such an evolution would correspond very well with the general tendency towards oligarchy.

Militants. The meaning of the term militant is scarcely any easier to define than that of supporter. In this connection, we must recall the distinction made between cadre parties and mass parties.

In the latter, the term militant is used to describe a special class of member. The militant is an active member: the militants form the nucleus of each of the party's basic groups, on which its fundamental activities depend. Within the branch, for example, there is always to be found a small circle of members, markedly different from the mass, who regularly attend meetings, share in the spreading of the party's slogans, help to organize its propaganda, and prepare its electoral campaigns. These militants constitute a kind of caucus within the branch. They are not to be confused with the leaders: they are not directors but executives; without them it would not even be possible to carry out any activities. The other members do no more than provide a name for the register and a little money for the chest; the militants work effectively for the party. In cadre parties there is no difference between militancy and membership. The caucuses, characteristic of this type of party, are made up entirely of militants; around them gravitate supporters who are not included, properly speaking, within the party community.

It would be valuable to be able to measure the relative proportions of militants and members in any party. If it were possible in this way to compare the membership ratio, which allows of comparisons between the body of members and the body of electors, with a militancy ratio, expressing as a percentage the number of militants compared with the number of members, we should have a much sounder appreciation of the real strength of political parties. If moreover it were possible to work out these ratios by social classes, by age groups, and by regions, the position of the party communities within the national community could be defined more precisely. Unfortunately here we encounter the same difficulties as in the determination of the supporter: the lack of any enumeration, the very impossibility of an enumeration, because of the vagueness of the category which it is desired to enumerate. Furthermore, in this matter the parties are much more discreet than in others: they are very anxious to have it thought that all their members are militant, which increases their apparent strength. Studies and surveys alone will make it possible to achieve some results, except for those parties where the militants are organized separately, as for example in the Austrian Socialist party with its system of *Parteimitarbeiter* (cf. below, p. 156). But these are subordinate ranks rather than militants properly speaking.

In this connection, we may quote the replies secured by the

Auxerre investigators within the framework of the general survey already referred to. Item No. 139 of their questionnaire (complementing Questions 137 and 138 concerning support for a party or true membership) was couched as follows: 'Are you a militant member? If so, how much time do you give to political activities?' The extreme vagueness of the question may be regretted; it robs the replies of any real meaning. The investigators note that they did not consider as active militants those who said they gave no time to political activity;[1] of these some had replied in the affirmative to the question 'Are you a militant member?' It would have been interesting to know what conception of militancy they had in mind. At all events, the percentages amongst those who gave a reply are as follows:

	Total	*Men*	*Women*
Members . . .	6	10	3
Militants . . .	2	4	1
% of militants to members .	33	40	33

It is difficult to assess these results, since no distinction is made between the various parties. They should be considered with reservations: the proportion of militants they show seems rather high.[2]

A count of militants, without any other details, has furthermore no significance, since the term is too loose and too complex. As with supporters, we should undertake counts by categories, taking as an index of militancy some concrete fact easily discovered. Attendance at meetings is quite a good criterion in the case of parties based upon the branch. It is passive in character but the very structure of the party makes it of great importance, and experience shows that those who regularly attend meetings are also generally the active militants in the party. By consulting the minutes of meetings (where they exist), and questioning branch secretaries, it is possible to determine the average percentage of members who attend meetings: but raw figures are insufficient. To say that branch meetings are attended, on the average, by 25% of the members, would throw no light on the situation, for experience

[1] Op.cit., p. 235.

[2] J. Fauvet however estimates at 50% the proportion of militants to members in the Communist party (*Les Forces politiques en France*, Paris, 1951), A. Lecoeur, former party secretary, at only a third (*L'autocritique attendue*, 1955).

shows that there is always a certain turnover, that behind the total figures of average attendance there lies a change from one meeting to another of the actual individuals attending. What is required therefore is a set of figures showing differences in regularity of attendance: the percentage of members attending less than 25% of the meetings, the percentage attending between 25% and 50%, 50% and 100%, and so on. It would then be possible to determine the frequency of attendance by social class, by age-group, and so on. Such counts would be beset with many practical difficulties; they presuppose that the leaders of a number of test-case branches, suitably selected, would make a very careful check of attendances over a period of time, without warning the members. It may be doubted whether the parties would comprehend the scientific value of such research and would comply with its demands. None the less such studies would give us precious information concerning the true nature of the party community.

An inquiry carried out amongst Parisian branches of the Socialist party seems to reveal a fairly close correspondence between the quality of militants and the social environment of the branch; it may be expressed in the following formula: the nature of the militants tends to coincide with the dominant social category. In a branch with a working-class majority, the militants are chiefly workmen, the proportion of workmen amongst them being higher than their proportion amongst the members. On the other hand, in a branch situated in a middle-class quarter, of which the majority of members are civil servants, tradesmen, lawyers, teachers, and so on, the proportion of militants of middle-class origin exceeds their proportion of the membership: there are workmen in the member class but not in the militant class, as a general rule. The inquiry is too incomplete and superficial for results and figures to be published as yet. The previously quoted tendency seems none the less to be present in marked degree. The explanation seems to be fairly clear; in a branch that is predominantly middle class, the workmen feel isolated amongst people who share their political opinions but not their mentality, their daily preoccupations or their instinctive reactions; the same is true for the middle-class members of a predominantly working-class branch. Social differences among members seems therefore to provide an obstacle to the development of militancy. One is tempted to say that the more homogeneous the milieu, the higher the index of militancy. Herein lies the superiority of techniques of organization by separate and homogeneous milieux, such as are to be found in Communist cells, in organizations on a co-operative basis (e.g. the *standen* of the Belgian Catholic Bloc) or in the 'specialized' movements of Catholic Action: Young Catholic Workers, Young Catholic Students, Young Catholic Sportsmen. More numerous, more detailed, and more profound investigations alone will allow us to draw definite conclusions.

In some parties, the measurement of militancy might be attempted on different lines. Besides the criterion of attendance at meetings we might set as criterion the payment of subscriptions. When these are collected monthly by the stamp or book system, it is of interest to discover the average number of monthly stamps taken each year by members. In theory each member should buy twelve stamps; in practice, this ideal is never attained. There are ten-stamp members, eight-stamp members, six-stamp members, and so on. Classification by degrees of financial membership is thus conceivable, and it should further differentiate by age-groups and social classes:[1] such detail would only be obtainable after special investigations, since the financial statistics of the parties do not give enough accurate detail on the point. However, some parties calculate each year the average number of monthly stamps taken by members (by dividing the total number of stamps by the number of members which is obtained from the total of cards or annual books sold). This average might be fixed upon as an index of financial militancy. No doubt the bases of the calculation are not very satisfactory (stamps sold by the centre are not all bought by members, as we have seen): but they give us a satisfactory order of magnitude. Moreover, regularity in the payment of subscriptions is not an element in the definition of the militant: subscribing is purely a function of membership. However, experience proves that the militant is generally more reliable than others in the performance of this financial duty: the criterion may therefore be retained. In the case of a general average of stamps sold, however, we do not know the proportion of militants in the party: the figure obtained is rather an indication of the degree of overall fidelity of the members. This represents a departure from the individual notion of the militant in favour of a purely statistical definition.

[1] In parties with differential rates of contribution, the distribution of membership amongst the various rates might be a valuable index of militancy (although other factors are operative in this field, notably the social position of party members): the greater financial effort of the Berlin subscribers of the German Social Democratic party is worthy of note in this connection. (Cf. Fig. 7.)

In spite of everything the analysis of this average is not devoid of interest, especially if it be compared with the changes in the number of members and electors. The study of variations in the average inside the French Socialist party from 1906 to 1936 reveals some general tendencies (Fig. 17). The average appears to fall when the number of members rises, the newcomers being less loyal than the old members. This movement is however not general, and it can often be explained by purely mechanical reasons: the new members, joining during the course of the year, subscribe for a limited number of months and so depress the general average. Conversely, at periods of crisis in the party, a drop in the number of members often coincides with a rise in the average of subscriptions, as if membership gained in depth what it lost in breadth. But this phenomenon is no more constant than the preceding one. A more exact coincidence can be seen between General Elections and the rhythm of the collection of subscriptions. In the year prior to the election the average falls: this phenomenon was repeated in six cases out of seven between 1910 and 1936 (the exceptional year being 1924). In the year after the election, the average rises: this phenomenon was repeated in five cases out of seven between 1910 and 1936 (the exceptions being 1924 and 1915, when the war may explain the change in rhythm). It will be remembered that the number of members tends, on the contrary, to rise not only in the year following but also in the year prior to General Elections. We must discover the factors capable of determining these coincidences or these distortions, but first we must find out whether the latter occur in other parties of the same type, for no conclusion can be drawn from a few incomplete observations, bearing upon a single party over a fairly short period of time.

Compared with the members, the militants are somewhat restricted in number. In no party do they seem to exceed a half of the membership: when they reach a third or a quarter, the party may be considered to be active. Thus a spontaneous oligarchy is formed amongst the members: they allow themselves to be led passively in the mass by a small nucleus of militants who attend meetings and congresses, who take part in the election of leaders, whose ranks furnish the leaders. It would be scarcely an exaggeration to describe the party according to the following pattern: the militants lead the members, the members lead the supporters, the supporters lead the electors. The members of a party do not constitute an egalitarian and uniform society but a complex and

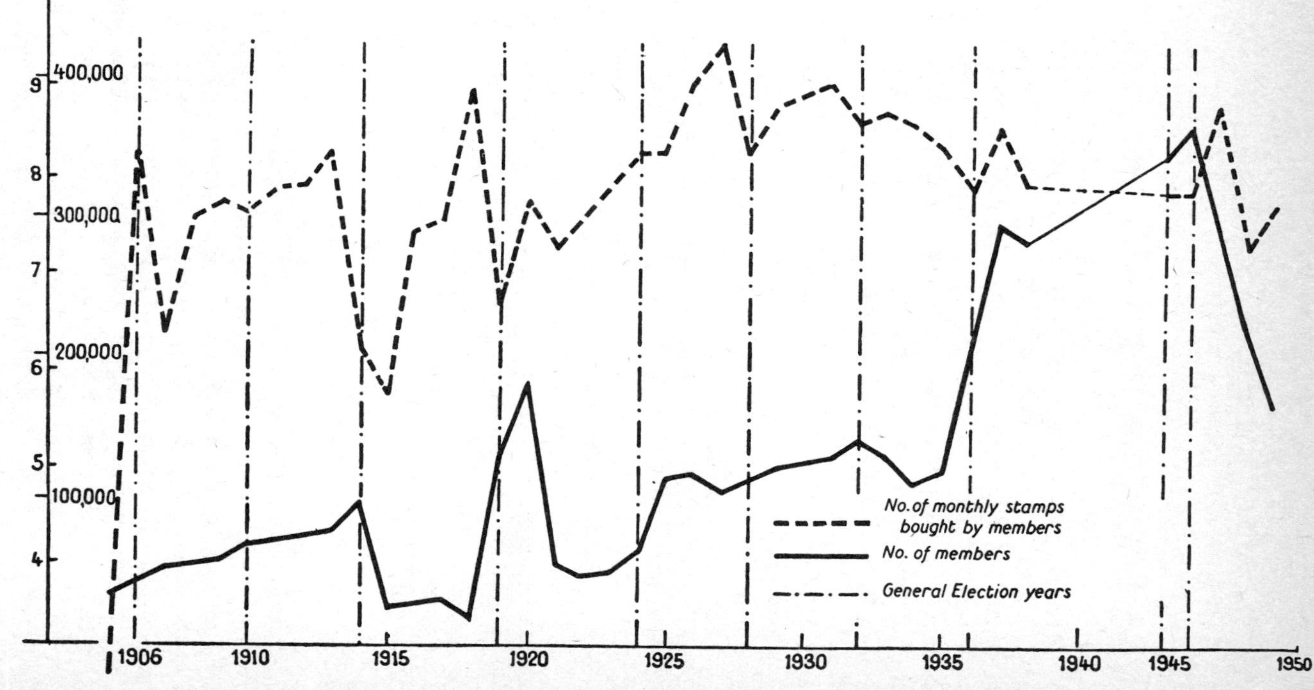

Fig. 17. Subscriptions in French Socialist Party.

hierarchical society; a differentiated society too, for all do not participate in the same way in its activities.

III. NATURE OF PARTICIPATION

We have just drawn distinctions between degrees of participation: but are they really degrees or are they not differences in kind? Electors, supporters, members, and militants differ less in the intensity of their links with the party than in the quality of these links. A militant is not twice or three times more attached to the party than a member: he is attached to it in a different way. Each category of party members corresponds to a type of participation, characterized by its quality rather than by its intensity. But this quality of participation varies even within each category: the links of solidarity are not identical for all members, for all militants, nor for all supporters. When we try to investigate further we come up against this fundamental problem: the nature of participation.

Besides general difficulties of analysis, common to all questions relating to membership, this problem presents special difficulties due to the imprecision of sociological terminology. In the present state of sociology there is no general classification of communal relationships which all admit and which might serve as a system of reference for a distinction between kinds of participation. One is therefore obliged either to fix on a classification suitable for this subject or to adopt one, drawn up by a particular sociologist, which others may not consider authoritative. Both methods will be followed in turn—first of all, the ideas of the totalitarian party and the restricted party will be contrasted, and then Tönnies' distinction between 'Community' and 'Association' will be applied to parties and will be revised and completed.

Totalitarian and Restricted Parties. Let us compare a Radical militant and a Communist party member. Party does not play a very large part in the life of the former: from time to time he attends the meetings of his caucus: sometimes he tries to obtain a favour through the intermediary of his parliamentary representative; he follows national political alliances and even more so local ones; he considers the possible candidatures and alliances for future elections. He reads a Radical paper if there is one; he is sometimes a member of the League for the Rights of Man, which is not very active, or of a masonic lodge, or some other similar group. In short only a few hours of his time are devoted to the party, only a few thoughts among his everyday preoccupations. Neither his intellectual nor professional life, nor his leisure, even less his family and emotional life are influenced by Radicalism. Participation is of a purely political character and does not extend beyond this very restricted field: the Radical party is a restricted party.

The situation of the Communist party member is quite different. The party exacts a much more intense political life from him. Every day, in his factory or workshop, he must militate within his cell, that is to say spread the party's orders among his workmates, discuss with them the most important matters dealt with in *L'Humanité*, or the local Communist daily paper, and feed the enthusiasm with which they claim their rights. He is a member of the C.G.T. union, which is affiliated to the party, and in which his cell activity is prolonged and completed. All his working life is thus brought within the party framework, dominated by the party and devoted to the service of the party. It is the same with his leisure time: a great deal of it is taken up by meetings of the party, of the union, or of the ancillary organizations: Peace Campaign, Franco-Russian Friendship Association, etc.; the party sees to organizing what remains: Communist Sports Associations; Communist Youth Hostels; Communist fêtes, fairs, and picnics; Communist cinema shows; Communist Literary or Art Clubs; Communist exhibitions and lectures form the 'diversions' of the party members. The party also penetrates into his family life: normally his wife is a member of the Union of French Women and of various Housewives' Committees; his children are enrolled in the Republican Union of French Youth and its affiliated clubs. There is no longer any distinction between public and private life: there is only party life. This is a totalitarian party.

Two elements are to be distinguished, one material, one spiritual. The first consists in the effort made by the party to organize all the activities of the individual (work, sport, amusements, leisure, culture, and family life) and to extend beyond the purely political domain. This effort takes the form of the development of ancillary organizations intended no longer for supporters but for members. There is no longer any question here of forming a secondary zone of partisans round one central kernel formed by the members of the party, but of multiplying the organizations to which one individual may belong—the party, the Union, the Sports Club, the Art Society, the Camping Club, the Franco-Russian Friendship Association, the Tenants' Union, the Family Association, etc.—so as to leave no activity outside the control of the party. Under single-party regimes, everything is arranged so that the citizen never disposes of a minute of real leisure in which he may remain alone with his thoughts: all official leisure time (that is to say time not taken up by work, sleep, or eating) is thus devoted to the service of the party and the ancillary organizations. Nevertheless certain parties which are not really totalitarian parties also try to multiply their ancillary organizations. The development of these is a good way of attracting members or of keeping them: a man who is bored at the branch meetings of the party will enjoy its Sports Club; a man who will not attend meetings will be quite willing to listen to the few words spoken by the leaders at a fair or a rural fête. The ancillary activities of the party can be a means of retaining lukewarm members, as well as a means of strengthening the loyalty of the faithful. The technique of ancillary organizations is rather like that of the band and processions used by the Salvation Army, which is not a proof of its power over souls. This material organization of the whole of a man's activities has not a really totalitarian significance unless it is accompanied by a spiritual organization of the whole of his thought. A party which endeavours to develop ancillary organizations in order to make membership more attractive is not really totalitarian if its doctrine implies only a political attitude and leaves a freedom of choice in other spheres. Real totalitarianism is spiritual.

Let us return to our militant Communist. The party not only provides him with organizations for all his material activities, more important still it gives him a general organization of ideas, a systematic explanation of the universe. Marxism is not only a political doctrine but a complete philosophy, a way of thinking, a spiritual cosmogony. All isolated facts in all spheres find their place in it and the reason for their existence. It explains equally well the structure and evolution of the state, the changes in living creatures, the appearance of man on the earth, religious feelings, sexual behaviour, and the development of the arts and sciences. And the explanation can be brought within the reach of the masses as well as being understood by the learned and by educated people. This philosophy can easily be made into a catechism without too serious a deformation. In this way the human spirit's need for fundamental unity can be satisfied. In the light of this totalitarian nature of Marxism the ancillary organizations of the party take on fresh significance. It is important to organize non-political activities not only in order to strengthen discipline or the loyalty of members, but to ensure that Marxist doctrine shall permeate all these activities. A Communist Sports Club is not set up in order to keep members within the party by offering them facilities for taking part in their favourite game but in order to bring about the application of Marxism to the realm of sport: for sport can be Marxist just as can genetics, painting and medicine. The material organization of all human activities takes on its true significance when they are united around a fundamental doctrine. At the same time it acquires a really totalitarian character; for the political label of a sports or literary club is of no importance as long as its members remain as free in it as members in non-party clubs: everything is different on the other hand if the club propounds a definite doctrine and insists on loyalty to it. We must then distinguish between a pseudo-totalitarianism, which is achieved by the multiplication of ancillary organizations aimed at encompassing the whole life of the party member, and an authentic totalitarianism, the characteristic of which is that party doctrine is not limited to politics and economics alone, but constitutes a systematic explanation of the universe, exclusive of any other. Material totalitarianism then becomes the reflection and result of spiritual totalitarianism.

The totalitarian character of the party can be more or less emphasized according to the members. Certain militant members of restricted parties take their task so much to heart and show such a liking for politics that these gradually absorb their whole life; for these enthusiasts the restricted party becomes totalitarian in character. This psychological state is common among elected representatives or leaders—conversely, certain moderate members of totalitarian parties will not allow themselves to be enslaved by their doctrine and retain an independent private life from which the party is excluded: for them the totalitarian party becomes restricted in character. The nature of participation is never uniform, and considerable individual differences can always be found amongst the members of one party. Nevertheless the general characteristics remain quite clear. Communist and Fascist parties are clearly totalitarian; Conservative and Liberal parties clearly restricted. Socialist parties tended towards totalitarianism at the outset, but in practice discussion and dissidence, as well as their gradual ageing, made them restricted in character. In so far as Christian parties declare that their political and social position is the inevitable outcome of religious principles they are totalitarian; in so far as they recognize the liberty of the Christian in this respect they are restricted.

The nature of participation is obviously very different in totalitarian parties from what it is in restricted parties. In the latter the amount of the individual's life that is caught up in the bonds of the community remains small; in the former it is the whole life of a man that is caught in the nets of the group. Amongst all the communities to which individuals belong restricted parties occupy only a secondary place; on the other hand totalitarian parties take first place: party solidarity takes precedence over all other bonds instead of being subordinate to many others. For a Communist, country, family, wife, friends are all subordinated to the interests of the party; for a Liberal or a Conservative the party ranks far below them. Hence the general characteristics of the totalitarian party: homogeneous, exclusive, and sacrosanct. Restricted parties are heterogeneous: that is to say that they are composed of members whose ideas and points of view are not absolutely identical in all their details. A wide diversity in personal points of view is tolerated; in Liberal and Conservative parties, for example, this diversity is very marked: each party member retains a great deal of freedom of thought. Elsewhere heterogeneity takes a more collective form: instead of individual differences we have communal differences: within the party ranks there are factions and wings more or less organized. They still retain something of the character of coteries grouped around influential personalities, but they also take on a fairly distinct doctrinal tone, as with the wings that formed within the Socialist parties. In the French Socialist party for example, between 1920 and 1940, some factions were very highly organized: members belonged to a faction, they bought the paper of the faction (*La Bataille Socialiste*—daily paper of the P. Faure-Zyromski faction until 1933; *La Vie Socialiste*, weekly paper of the Marquet–Déat–Renaudel faction; *Le Pays Socialiste*, daily paper of the Pacifist faction after 1936; *Les Cahiers Rouges*, occasional journal of the 'revolutionary Left', etc.); sometimes they took a *carte d'ami* (friend's card), obtained from the local representative of the faction, and this implied a supporter's subscription larger than the ordinary subscription and therefore a kind of contribution for the benefit of the faction. In American parties factions sometimes take the form of groups in revolt against the *bosses* and the 'machine' which ensures their domination: within the Democratic party, for example;

there have been factions against Long in Louisiana, against Kelly in Illinois, against Talmadge in Georgia, against Prendergast in Missouri, and so on. There is also the fundamental opposition between the Democrats of the North and of the South (the *Dixiecrats*) within the Congressional parliamentary groups.

In totalitarian parties such practices are unthinkable: internal divisions, sects, factions, dissidence, wings, 'sectionalism' are not tolerated. Homogeneity is strict. There is neither majority nor minority: whoever does not approve of the party doctrine in its entirety must leave the party. Those who oppose it have the choice only between submission and expulsion. This insistence on orthodoxy is natural. In restricted parties doctrine is not of fundamental importance: it takes up only a small share of the thoughts and minds of party members. Their ideological or tactical differences are of secondary importance, provided they agree on the general strategy of the party, on its electoral and governmental methods. Moreover this doctrine is not rigid by nature: often it is more a state of mind, a general tendency, rather than a real doctrine. It is natural that differences of interpretation should be allowed. It is equally natural that they should be prohibited in a totalitarian party: here doctrine becomes of fundamental importance and at the same time rigid. It is the intellectual and moral thread of the whole life of party members, their way of thinking, their philosophy, their faith. It is presented as a complete and coherent system explaining the universe, and all its parts are interdependent. Doctrinal differences here imply a difference in the orientation of one's whole life: they cannot be tolerated without destroying the unity of the party.

The closed nature of totalitarian parties is a natural result of their homogeneous character. Membership is strictly regulated. When the party is functioning under a democratic regime in which the competition from its rivals obliges it to seek to increase its membership the regulations are not very strict, but they are still much more so than in restricted parties. When the totalitarian party has become the only party, on the other hand, its closed character becomes marked. It is only possible to enter after a waiting period of varying length—like a catechumen—after obtaining sound references from reliable sponsors and even appearing before examining and screening committees and giving proof of the sincerity and strength of one's allegiance. Once you have entered, it is difficult to leave. 'The only way out of the party is feet first', says one of Jean-Paul Sartre's characters in *Les Mains Sales*. He exaggerates somewhat, although totalitarian parties usually take advantage of times of crisis to 'liquidate' their deserters. But the very nature of the membership makes a break difficult. The totalitarian party forms the mainspring of the life of its members, the fundamental belief which directs all their activities, the moral basis of their existence: to leave it is to abandon one's reasons for living, to break with the whole of oneself, to make a void and a desert within one, for the party fills all. Think of the wretchedness of the medieval Christian when he was excommunicated: the Communist or Fascist party member is in like state when he is condemned to be 'purged'.

This comparison leads to the third fundamental characteristic of totalitarian parties, their sacredness. The vital distinction made by Durkheim between the 'sacred' and the 'profane' is well known. A social fact or an object is sacred when it is surrounded by special respect and reverence, when it is considered as superior and transcendent, when it is not criticized or discussed, not joked about or made fun of. Restricted parties are not like this; they are entirely profane. But totalitarian parties are in the 'sacred' category. They are the object of a real cult; the Party is personified (with a capital letter: a typical characteristic of 'sacralization'), the all-powerful, infallible, protective, transcendent Party; the Party raised to the dignity of an end in itself, instead of remaining in the domain of ways and means. Thus participation becomes really religious in nature. It has been suggested that Communism should be called 'a secular religion': the term applies equally well to Fascism and to all totalitarian parties. And the religious character does not come only from their structure—very like that of a church—or from their totalitarianism (by nature a religion is totalitarian, for it forms an all-embracing system explaining the universe), it depends even more on the truly sacred nature of the bonds of solidarity.

The appearance of totalitarian parties coincides moreover with the decline of organized religion in the West. Certainly during the last twenty years there has been a revival of religious thought in Europe, in Protestant communities as well as within the Catholic Church; a parallel revival of religious feeling is quite clearly perceptible among the 'enlightened' classes. But during the last century the spread of irreligion among the masses has not ceased; among the working class especially, truly religious preoccupations have little place today—it is precisely among the masses of the people and within the working class that totalitarian parties have developed the most. It is in Russia and in Germany, countries with a profoundly religious mentality, that they have reached their peak of perfection. It all looks as if the masses could not exist without religious beliefs, so that the decline of traditional religions must necessarily be accompanied by the birth of new religions. It is striking to find that this idea was familiar to the great Positivists of the last century, to Auguste Comte and to the followers of Saint-Simon; that they were all convinced of the unconquerable nature of the people's need of the irrational, their need of the absolute, their need for spiritual unity, and that consequently they tried to create religions. Their error lay in not understanding that the new religions would not be metaphysical but political. Auguste Comte alone seems to have had a glimmering of this evolution. The decline of organized religion among the masses of the people at a time when the latter were invading political life may be considered as one of the factors in the rise of totalitarian parties.

The second factor seems to be the transformation of political doctrines into beliefs truly religious in character. Two changes have taken place in this connection: we have passed from the purely political doctrine to an all-embracing philosophy; we have passed from the rational idea to the myth; on the day when political theories were no longer restricted to the explanation of power, its nature, its characteristics, its forms, and its evolution, but claimed to explain all social phenomena, and through them all human phenomena, politics became a general system of explanation, philosophic in character. In the Middle Ages politics were deduced from philosophy (itself a daughter of religion); today philosophy is deduced from politics; social relationships are no longer explained by the nature of the human mind, but the nature of the human mind by social relationships. It only required the passage from idea to myth, from scientific demonstration to irrational belief, in accordance with the process described by Sorel and many others after him, for politics, already transformed into philosophy, to become a real religion. Such was the development of Marxism, the basis of totalitarian Communist parties and of Nationalism (or Racialism), the basis of Fascist totalitarian parties. The first, however, is much more elaborate and more complete than the second. It is extremely difficult to explain all the phenomena of nature, of society, and of the human mind by differences in race or nation; the Marxists, none the less, succeed quite well in connecting them with the class struggle and with dialectical materialism, without any more mystery or strangeness than is found in any other religion.

Finally the evolution of party structures favours the development of totalitarian parties and secular religions, although it is no doubt itself an effect rather than a cause. At all events a regular correlation is to be observed between the totalitarianism of parties and the structure based upon cells and militia with vertical links and strongly centralized articulation: the Communist and Fascist parties provide a striking example of this concomitance. On the other hand parties based upon caucuses, weak in articulation and decentralized, are always restricted, as witness the Conservative and Liberal parties. As for parties of the Socialist type, built up on the branch and on a stronger and more centralized system of articulation, they generally remain restricted, although participation tends in them to be more extensive than in the others, and we have noticed from time to time some tendencies towards totalitarianism.

Community—Association—Order. In 1887 Tönnies distinguished between two categories of social groups, the *Gemeinschaft* (Community) and the *Gesellschaft* (Association). He was thinking more of normative concepts, of ideal types, than of a concrete objective classification. The distinction entailed a certain judgement of value, as the *Gemeinschaft* seemed to Tönnies a method of grouping superior to the *Gesellschaft*: this conception seems to have influenced the National Socialist ideology. Leaving aside this metaphysical romanticism and transposing Tönnies' conception into the realm of purely scientific fact we may use these ideas to make an interesting classification of social groups which remains very general but seems capable of throwing light on the problem of the nature of the links of solidarity within parties, especially if it be completed by a third category of group, as when H. Schmalenbach, in 1922, gave the name of *Bund* to this additional type: it will be translated by the word 'Order' (in the sense in which this term is used in 'religious order', 'Order of Malta', and so on).

The Community (*Gemeinschaft*) has two essential characteristics. First of all it is a social group founded on proximity, neighbourhood (Durkheim would say: on solidarity through similarities). It can be a geographical proximity: this is the case for the village, the commune, the parish, the nation. It can be a physiological proximity, a blood relationship (Tönnies insisted a great deal on the community of blood): here the family is the best example. Finally it can be a spiritual proximity, a kind of consanguinity of minds, which discover a certain nearness and resemblance between themselves. According to Tönnies friendship comes into this category, but it is not a community in so far as it involves an 'elective affinity' based on freedom of choice, for the Community constitutes a spontaneous natural social group, older than the individual. That is the second characteristic of the Community. A Community is not created, it is discovered. One does not really become a member of a Community: one belongs to it automatically, willingly or unwillingly. One is born into a Community and does not escape from it. Being part of one's family, one's village, one's country, and one's race is natural and involuntary.

The Association (*Gesellschaft*) shows diametrically opposed characteristics. It is a voluntary social group, based on the contract and the adhesion of the members. One joins it deliberately: one could stay out. It is created in its entirety: it does not exist naturally. It is created because it is in someone's interest to create it: instead of being based on neighbourhood, geographical proximity, or blood relationship, the Association is based on interest. Membership of the group is founded here on the advantages obtained from it. But this notion of interest must be understood in a very wide and extensive sense. Obviously it includes material interests, which serve as a basis for trade associations. Trade Unions, Friendly Societies, and associations for fellowship, as well as intellectual interests, which are the origin of learned societies, of literary or philosophical clubs, of Academies and art groups; or moral interests which animate charitable organizations, temperance groups, and associations for mutal aid. It extends also to what might be called 'leisure interests', which give rise to various groups which help individuals to divert themselves (in Pascal's meaning of the word), these diversions being rarely solitary ones; sports clubs, bridge circles, bowls or anglers' clubs, camping associations, amateur theatricals, billiards clubs, and Scouts groups. Finally we must include interests that might be called affective if the two terms did not conflict: people are bored on their own, they feel the need to meet others, they find a certain pleasure in being in company and at the same time their pride is satisfied (association allows one to make an appearance, to shine, to dazzle), and they derive a certain satisfaction from activity (if it is true that action is a source of pleasure, as Plato affirmed). Many women's associations have no other real foundation, notably those catering for middle-aged ladies which are so widespread in Nordic and Anglo-Saxon countries, especially in America. It should be added that these various forms of interest are generally mixed, that some often serve as pretexts for others (many charitable associations really depend on the pride taken in making an appearance or on the pleasure of meeting others). The varieties of *Gesellschaft* are therefore very numerous; but the idea of *Gesellschaft* itself remains quite precise.

The *Bund* (Order) described by Schmalenbach holds an intermediary position between Community and Association. Like the latter the *Bund* is founded on voluntary membership: it is not the product of a natural spontaneous evolution but of deliberate human creation. Nevertheless entry into an Order does not mean the same as membership of an Association. Here we must distinguish between membership and dedication, the former indicating a much weaker form of allegiance than the second. Dedication is complete membership, the direction given to the whole of one's life; membership is only a restricted dedication, affecting only part of the member's activity and not committing his inner self. In other words membership is restricted, dedication is totalitarian. One should add that dedication is not felt as being entirely voluntary; he who dedicates himself always has to a greater or less degree the feeling of an inner compulsion, of a profound obligation, of a duty. We must recall here the ideas of 'vocation' or 'conversion', which are essentially connected with entry into an Order or with changing from one Order to another. It will be understood then that the Order, unlike the Association but like the Community, is not founded on interest. To dedicate oneself to an Order, on the other hand, often entails an element of sacrifice, of renunciation, of passing through the 'strait gate' of which the Gospel speaks. The Order is based on a profound need for communion, for passing beyond one's own personality, for the fusion of individuals within a group that transcends them. Certainly one could find traces here, both of that spiritual consanguinity which according to Tönnies is one of the elements of the *Gemeinschaft*, and of that affective interest which constitutes one of the bases of the *Gesellschaft*, but the *Bund* differs from them both by the intensity, depth, and extent of the communion and the feeling of its transcendence experienced by its members. One should add that the *Bund* is characterized by a certain internal tension, by a certain enthusiasm, and a certain effervescence: by contrast with a 'cold' Association, one might speak of the warmth of the order. A young religion, a monastic order, a love marriage; these are the examples of *Bund* given by Schmalenbach and his disciples.

One may question whether the Order really founds a third category of social groups, contrasting with the 'Association' and the 'Community', or if it does not define a certain particular intensity that sometimes enters into one or other of these. François Mauriac has described tragic, passionate families where the community is very like the Order; similarly patriotic enthusiasm can confer this characteristic of the Order on nations or at a less advanced stage of evolution on tribes or villages. On the other hand monastic orders and totalitarian parties would furnish examples of Orders resembling Associations. This point of view would be strengthened by Schmalenbach's statement about the ephemeral character of the Order, and the law of internal decline to which it is subject: progressively the tension of the Order lessens and enthusiasm diminishes. The Order cools, so to speak, until one day it becomes a Community or an Association: religions finish as churches, love marriages as communities of habit. This question cannot be discussed in this book: it is enough to establish that, from any point of view, the Order corresponds to a reality and that this conception makes it possible to define the nature of membership. It throws light, however, upon the intersection of the two classifications, already established, that of totalitarian and restricted parties and that opposing the Community, the Association, and the Order. As far as parties are concerned it may be considered that the ideas of Order and totalitarianism correspond almost exactly: all totalitarian parties are like a *Bund* in character and all parties resembling a *Bund* are totalitarian. The concept of Order is only useful in that it throws light on the structure of totalitarian parties. The distinction between Community and Association is only to be seen as a rule in restricted parties, whose nature it makes clearer. Nevertheless traces could be found in totalitarian parties: for a young Russian brought up since childhood in the Communist ideology the party is a Community: for the convert from Western countries it is more an Association. Here we again encounter the idea that the conception of *Bund* designates perhaps a particular form taken sometimes by the Community or the Association rather than a separate category.

If, with the reserves already mentioned, we apply the Tönnies–Schmalenbach classification to parties, we note the complexity of the links of participation. In each party the three types of social links coexist. For some members, governed by tradition, class necessity, family, local or professional habits, the party is a Community. For others, who are attracted by possible material advantages, by the desire for political action, by a moral or idealistic impulse, the party is an Association. For still others, who are driven by enthusiasm, passion, or the desire for communion the party is an Order: this is often the case for the young or the intellectual. But the different methods of participation may interweave and become superimposed on each other within the same individual conscience. Coincidence between tradition and interest is frequent and then we have the amalgam between the Community and the Association: similarly, in Communist parties, natural membership, based on the social class, can be found added to totalitarian passion, and then we have an amalgam between the Order and the Community. But with this totalitarian passion, which is characteristic of the *Bund*, there is sometimes mingled, consciously or not, pride and the need to assert oneself, as well as the desire for action, that is to say an affective interest and a leisure interest, foundations of the 'Association'. For the purposes of classifying a party in one of the three categories (Community, Association, Order), the only possible basis is the greater importance among the members of one social link by comparison with the others. A party will be considered as a *Gesellschaft* when Association links predominate, as an Order when *Bund* links predominate, and so on. Within these limits, the concepts of Community, Association, and Order make it possible to establish a classification of political parties and at the same time to perceive among them traces of an evolution.

There are Association parties in which interest and desire predominate and in which the passion of the Order and the tradition ot the Community have scarcely any place. The middle-class parties of the nineteenth century are a good example of this, even though for many of their members they corresponded to a Liberal or Conservative tradition which gave them a Community character. Certain Centre parties at the present time are similar. The main reason for membership is the advantage that their intermediate position gives them in political struggles and the quest for favours. American parties partially belong to this category, although a great many of their members support them because of a family or local tradition: for the mass of real militants, nevertheless, interest is the real reason for participation. This example shows that the nature of participation can be very different according to the categories of members: especially does it seem probable that electors and members are not joined to the party by links of the same nature and that it is the Community type that is predominant among electors, even in parties where members and militants belong rather to the Association type. A careful distinction must also be made between ordinary members and real militants. Any all-embracing classification would easily fall to the ground here.

Other parties correspond more clearly to the Community type, for example the Socialist parties. They call themselves—at least they did so at the beginning of the century—class parties: belonging to a social class is a *Gemeinschaft* link. In so far as membership of the party is determined by class the party becomes a Community. By replacing the Liberal idea of party as founded on ideology or interests by the conception of the party as the political expression of a social class, Marxism has substituted a Community theory of party for the earlier Association theory. This Community theory has flourished most in certain People's democracies where each party corresponds officially to a definite class; in the U.S.S.R., on the other hand, the suppression of differences of class leads to their being only one party, according to the official argument. Nevertheless the concept of a Community party is a far wider one than that of the class party. In American parties, for example, where the variety in social class is striking, people often belong because of custom, habit, or family or local traditions. Many are Republicans because their parents were so, because their grandparents were, and because Republicanism is one of the fundamental rules of good behaviour in the family. In the South, people are Democrats because they are white, because they are descended from the rebels of the Civil War, and because it would be contrary to etiquette and shocking to announce that one was a Republican. The vulgar but forceful French expressions 'sucer le lait républicain à la mamelle' (to suck in Republicanism with one's mother's milk), and 'avoir la tripe républicaine' (to have Republican guts) are well known. They describe the same Community support for a traditional party.

Finally Communist and Fascist parties correspond to the idea of *Bund*, as it has been described by Schmalenbach. The National Socialists expressly affirmed it in their Germany in which the concept of the Order seems to have corresponded to a certain profound aspiration; most Fascist parties have followed this example. The mystique of the Order is an important element in Fascist ideology. On the other hand, at first sight it does not seem to have any place in Communist ideology; party terminology bars the term Order. Nevertheless the ideas of Lenin and Stalin on the fundamental role of the party, which groups the most conscious, the most loyal and the most courageous elements of the working class, lead to the same conception. This complete dedication which the party asks of its members, this spirit of communion and self-denial which it develops in them (this 'virile fraternity', as Malraux called it, when he belonged to the party), this detachment from material goods and the rough austere life it demands of them, all these characteristics are typical of the Order. The same may be said of the absolute discipline it demands of its members, this obedience *perinde ac cadaver* which is like that of the greatest and most celebrated religious orders. Similarly the conception of the party as the 'elite of the revolution', 'the leaven which causes the masses to rise', 'the spearhead of the working class' is related to the same idea of Order. One has only to compare the characteristics of the Communist party with the description of the *Bund* to establish their complete resemblance.

The distinction between Community, Association, and Order does more than make possible this classification of political parties according to the nature of the links of solidarity which prevail in them. Thanks to it an interesting evolution may be noticed. In a first stage parties seem to pass from the Association type to the Community type. When parties were formed in the nineteenth century they necessarily took the *Gesellschaft* form: by their very definition they did not constitute natural, spontaneous, inescapable groups, since human initiative—impelled by events—had just created them, and since their first members had to make a deliberate act of will in order to join them. In the middle-class democracies, based on a property franchise, in which they functioned first of all, they were clearly based on material interests and ideologies, the latter quite often serving to conceal the former. Loyalty to the party had scarcely any meaning: one changed one's party if one's interests changed, unless the party itself changed its ideology and tactics. In European Conservative and Liberal parties successive changes in the attitude towards Free Trade, Agrarian policy, social legislation, and so on can be clearly seen. So also can the migration of politicians from one party to another, and this seems quite natural. Two things seem to have transformed this system of Association parties into a system of Community parties. Firstly the ageing of the middle-class parties which created traditions. For its founders the party was a *Gesellschaft*; for the founders' sons, for whom membership was part of the family inheritance, it took on the characteristics of a *Gemeinschaft*. These characteristics grew stronger from generation to generation, in the same way as usurpations become legitimate monarchies: it is a natural law of general application that progressively changes Associations into Communities. Today's innovation is tomorrow's custom: the Association of today engenders the Community of the future. In the domain of parties the change was accelerated by the entrance of the proletariat into political life in the shape of class parties: from the very beginning Socialist parties did indeed take the form of Community parties, depending on a social class, and they proclaimed this loudly and affirmed its general application. The old parties reacted by becoming conscious of their own class character, which naturally brought about a speedier transformation into Community parties. In this way the appearance of Marxism and of Socialist parties and the ageing of the middle-class parties together brought about the transformation of Association parties into Community parties.

Furthermore the decline of organized religions and the elevation of political doctrines to the religious plane that has already been described have tended to drive parties towards the Order structure. On this point we shall do no more than simply refer to the analysis of the factors that produced the totalitarian parties, for a perfect coincidence has already been indicated in this field between the nature of the *Bund* and totalitarianism. In this way, the second phase in the evolution of parties would consist in their development from Communities into Orders. However, this phase remains much less clear and much less widespread than the preceding one: the totalitarian parties, that are by nature Order-like, still remain exceptions amongst the great mass of political parties. Within the Order-parties, moreover, a change seems perceptible. In the first place we might point to a certain transformation of the Association-Order into the Community-Order, noticeable in the totalitarian parties in power (here we are considering Order as an exceptional pattern that Associations and Communities can assume and not as a distinct sociological category contrasting with them, cf. *supra*, p. 127). Before the seizure of power the National Socialist party was an Association-Order; for the Young Nazi trained from infancy and segregated in the Hitler Youth it constituted much more of a Community-Order. It will be observed that totalitarian parties when in power tend to restrict direct recruitment and to reserve admission to those who have passed through the party youth-movements, a fact which tends to make them Communities of a special type.

Perhaps the Order parties however have also a tendency to evolve into a Community type pure and simple, to divest themselves gradually of their totalitarian nature, of their enthusiasm, of their effervescence, and of their internal tension. At the beginning of the century the first Socialist parties had a hold upon their members very like that exercised by the Order: they experienced this type of decline, which Schmalenbach considered in fact a natural law of the *Bund*. There seems to be no doubt that the Communist and Fascist parties would tread the same path *if they were allowed to do so*. But their very structure, as well as the efforts of their leaders, tend in fact to guard them against this weakening. The machinery of purges and cleansings, of excommunications and deviations, as well as the regular recruitment into the leading strata, the increasingly strict training of new leaders, the hold maintained over members (thanks to the cell and the militia), have as their essential aim the prevention of the loss by the party of its structure as an Order. There is a systematic campaign waged against the decline in energy which tends to show itself in any social group. It is not possible to pronounce any definite judgement upon the results achieved. We are still too near. Nevertheless the evolution of the Communist parties during the last twenty years shows no lessening of their totalitarianism, no weakening of their Order; both seem on the contrary to be reinforced, just as much within parties in power, in the position of single party (in U.S.S.R.) as within those parties which still fight in the multi-party democratic system. It does not seem as if within the historically foreseeable future their transformation from an Order to a Community could be the result of a mere internal evolution.

CHAPTER III

PARTY LEADERSHIP

IN every human community the organization of power is the result of two opposed forces: beliefs on the one hand, practical necessities on the other. In consequence the leadership of political parties—like that of most present-day social groups: Trade Unions, associations, business firms, and so on—presents dual characteristics: it is democratic in appearance and oligarchic in reality. Only a few Fascist parties provide exceptions to this rule: they are bold enough to confess in public what others practise in secret; they are not to be congratulated on this score, however, if it is true that hypocrisy is the homage vice pays to virtue.

This almost universal reverence paid to democracy is explained by the fact that it appears legitimate in the eyes of contemporaries. In every age men formulate their own ideal of the organization and devolution of power within social groups: it is natural for them to offer obedience to the leaders who conform to this common ideal and to refuse obedience to others. The dominant belief determines the legitimacy of a leader, in the sociological sense of the term legitimate. Those who adhere to the belief hold that it is an absolute; the investigator notes that it is relative. Every civilization has built up its own doctrines of legitimacy, usually very different from any other. In the Western world the French Revolution replaced the legitimacy of monarchy by the legitimacy of democracy. For centuries it seemed right that power should be transmitted on the principle of heredity, just as today it seems right for it to be done on the principle of election. Democratic legitimacy is beginning to find itself opposed by a class legitimacy, quite clearly admitted by the Communist parties, but already breaking through in others: membership of the working-class being a precondition for the exercise of authority. The Fascists set up in opposition an aristocratic legitimacy: power should reside in the members of the 'political elite', that is to say, in those alone who are capable of shouldering it, as a result of their natural gifts. But both these remain as yet of secondary importance: democracy remains the dominant doctrine of the contemporary age, that which determines the legitimacy of power.

The parties are the more compelled to take this into account in that their activity lies directly in the political field, in which there is constant reference to democratic doctrines. Beliefs concerning legitimacy are general in character and valid for all social groups; but they are more immediately applicable to the state, its organs, and its machinery. If a commercial organization or an anglers' club were to adopt an oligarchic structure, entrusting authority to a few individuals not chosen by election by the body of members, this would shock the general belief in democracy, but much less profoundly than if the same structure were adopted by a political party, which worked within the framework of a democratic state and sought to gain the support of the masses who consider that the only legitimate form of power is the democratic. Parties must in consequence take the greatest care to provide themselves with leadership that is democratic in appearance.

Practical efficiency, however, drives them hard in the opposite direction. Democratic principles demand that leadership at all levels be elective, that it be frequently renewed, collective in character, weak in authority. Organized in this fashion, a party is not well armed for the struggles of politics. If all adopt the same structure, no great harm is done since the conditions of battle are the same for all. But, should one of them organize itself along authoritarian and autocratic lines, the others would be placed in a position of inferiority. It has often been observed that a democratic state at war with a dictatorial state must progressively adopt the methods of its rival, if it is to defeat it. The same phenomenon occurs on the party level in political warfare: in order to safeguard their existence the parties of democratic structure must follow the pattern of the others. They do it the more easily because their leaders tend naturally to retain power and to increase it, because their members scarcely hinder this tendency and on the contrary even strengthen it by hero-worshipping the leaders: on all these points the analysis made by Roberto Michels continues to hold true. The parties are none the less anxious to maintain the appearance of democracy: authoritarian and oligarchic methods generally develop without constitutional warrant by a series of devious but effective contrivances. This technique of camouflage may be compared with that employed by some contemporary states to achieve the same ends: the setting up of autocratic power behind the formulae and façades of democracy.

This is a general tendency, but it is more or less developed according to the party. How far it extends depends upon many factors: the social composition of the party, the strength of democratic sentiment among the members, the party doctrine (which is obviously reflected in its structure), and also the age of the party. Like all human groups parties are conservative: they do not easily change their structure, even if the general trend urges change upon them. The more democratic character of some parties often arises from the fact that they were created before more authoritarian methods of organization were perfected.

I. THE SELECTION OF LEADERS

Officially the party leaders are almost always elected by the members and given a fairly short period of office, in accordance with democratic rules. The Fascist parties alone openly repudiate this procedure and replace it by appointment from above: the subordinate leaders are chosen by the supreme chief of the party; the latter—being self-appointed—remains in office all his life: co-option is used to appoint his successor. In practice the democratic system of election is replaced by autocratic methods of recruitment: co-option, appointment by the central body, nomination, and so on. The situation is aggravated by the fact that the real leaders of the party are often distinct from the apparent leaders.

Tendency to Autocracy. We must first make a distinction between open autocracy, which is the exception, and disguised autocracy, which is the rule. The former is to be met with in Fascist or pseudo-Fascist parties in which the *führer prinzip* replaces election as the ground of legitimacy. Supreme control is therefore in the hands of a leader who has taken it unto himself, by reason of his own nature or of circumstances. Two kinds of Fascist doctrine on leadership may be discerned: the German theory which considered the *Führer* to be the man of Providence whose very nature it is to incarnate the German People and for that reason to exercise sovereign power; and a less mystical doctrine which sees the hand of Providence only in the circumstances which placed the leader at the head of the party. In the first case, the leader is a true superman: this is a modernized application of the ancient beliefs concerning the divine nature of rulers, the theory of the Divine King. In the second case, the leader is simply the man whom destiny (an all-seeing Providence, say the devout; blind chance, say the rest) has placed in such a position that he alone can assume the supreme leadership of the party. The Latin forms of Fascism, less mystical and more sceptical than the German model, generally prefer the second theory, and this entails a less intense atmosphere of veneration surrounding the party leader and wider scope for criticism. Both forms are identical in the methods for selection of subordinate leaders: all are appointed by the party chief, by virtue of his own sovereign power.

Sometimes, however, parties of this type are led to compromise with the democratic principle and to give it some place, at least in appearance, so strong are the general beliefs in the legitimacy of election. In general the concessions made are greater at the local levels than at the higher level—the centralization of the party in practice thus robbing them of much of their effectiveness. As an example we can quote the organization of the French People's Rally (R.P.F.), created in 1947 by General de Gaulle. At the Commune level, the officers are officially elected: all the leaders are thus democratically chosen, in appearance at least. At the Department level, there exist side by side elected officers forming a committee and a delegate appointed by the central authority; in theory the initiative lies with the committee, while the delegate has a power of veto; in fact the prerogatives of the nominee of the centre appear more important, as we have already pointed out. At the level of the Region, there is nothing but an appointed delegate. Finally, at the central level, all the leaders alike are appointed by the leader of the party, with the exception of the delegates to Congress and to the National Council. The former, however, meets only once a year; its debates are conducted behind closed doors in specialized working parties; the plenary sessions are given over to the hearing of speeches by the leaders of the party and to the ratification of the working parties' recommendations; in the same way the National Council has no more than a consultative role. The effective power, outside the leader of the party, belongs to the Council of Administration and to the secretariat, the members being directly appointed by General de Gaulle (the secretariat is even made up of his personal assistants). The central authority is entirely autocratic.

From the example of the French People's Rally we may turn to other parties in which autocracy is only partially admitted: alongside the elected leaders we find appointed or co-opted leaders who are able to counterbalance the influence of the first. In the famous Birmingham caucus, which exercised considerable influence at the end of the nineteenth century on the organization of British parties, there was to be found this kind of ingenious mixture of election and co-option. At the basis there were the district caucuses composed of delegates elected by the party members and of as many co-opted members as the elected members wanted to nominate; at the apex was the Executive Committee composed of 110 members of whom 48 were directly elected by the members in each district, 32 elected by the district caucuses constituted as above, and 30 members co-opted by the 80 already mentioned. Between the two there was a General Committee, a kind of deliberative assembly, comprising the 110 members of the Executive Committee and 480 delegates elected by the district members: in appearance the system seemed broadly democratic. With it can be compared the present-day organization of some Christian Democratic parties. For example in the French Popular Republican Movement (M.R.P.) the National Committee includes 10 co-opted members and the Administrative Committee 5. In the Belgian Christian Social party, the committees at commune and arrondissement level have the right to co-opt members to a number equal to that of the elected members; at the central level the General Council includes 12 co-opted members out of more than 100 and the National Committee 4 co-opted members out of 21. At the local level the number of co-opted members is sufficient to give the system a semi-automatic character; at the central level their number is too few: the aim of co-option is to bring into the directing councils of the party various people (intellectuals, political experts, etc.) who take no part in the political life of the federations, but who can be useful because of their experience. The co-option of leaders in the M.R.P. is of the same kind.

In the French Communist party the appointment of leaders by the superior bodies or by co-option (with ratification by the central body) is expressly provided for in Article 7 of the constitution 'in special circumstances of which the Central Committee is qualified to judge, in the event of any hindrance to the free development and activity of the party'. The second formula is meant implicitly to meet the situation in which the party has to go underground; the first is vaguer and broader: in practice it permits the Central Committee to make use of co-option or nomination whenever it considers it of value. Any opposition can thus be stifled without difficulty.

As we shall see later the freedom left to the section committee to determine the method of representation of the cells at the section conference makes it possible to suppress any democratic element in the selection of leaders, if need be.

Partial recourse to open autocracy does not moreover prevent the employment of methods of disguised autocracy: they are employed by *all* parties which are officially democratic in structure. The extent of autocracy is greater or less but there is always some element that is autocratic. Two techniques may be thus made use of to camouflage autocracy: the manipulation of elections and the distinction between real leaders and apparent leaders. The former is frequently used by governments: from the 'official candidates' of the Second Empire to the 'controlled' ballots in Latin-American or Balkan countries, through 'gerrymandering', governmental pressure, forged voters' cards, and so on, there is a whole range of widely differing processes which make it possible to fake political representation. Within parties, where elections take place in a narrower circle and where publicity is less considerable, these tricks are even more numerous and effective. In democratic countries the manipulation of elections is not widespread and does not noticeably falsify the results of the ballot; within political parties, on the other hand, manipulation is systematically resorted to and makes the recruitment of leaders markedly autocratic in character.

The first point to notice is the widespread use of indirect representation: except at the local level (branch or cell) the leaders of the party are not elected by the members directly, but by delegates who are themselves elected. Often delegation occurs in several stages: the Communist party in particular has greatly developed this system of pyramidal election (Fig. 18). The whole edifice is based upon the section conference made up of 'representatives of the cells' (Article 17 of the constitution), chosen by 'a method of representation decided upon by the section committee' (Article 15). The conference can therefore be made up of the secretaries and officers of the cells, or of members nominated by these officers: in the former case it is based upon first-remove representation from the members at the base, in the second case upon second-remove representation. But the text of Article 15 is so vague that there is, if need be, nothing to prevent the section committee from itself nominating the representatives of the cell to the section conference, in which case the system is no longer in any way democratic, since the first election, *the only one carried out* by *the members of the party*,

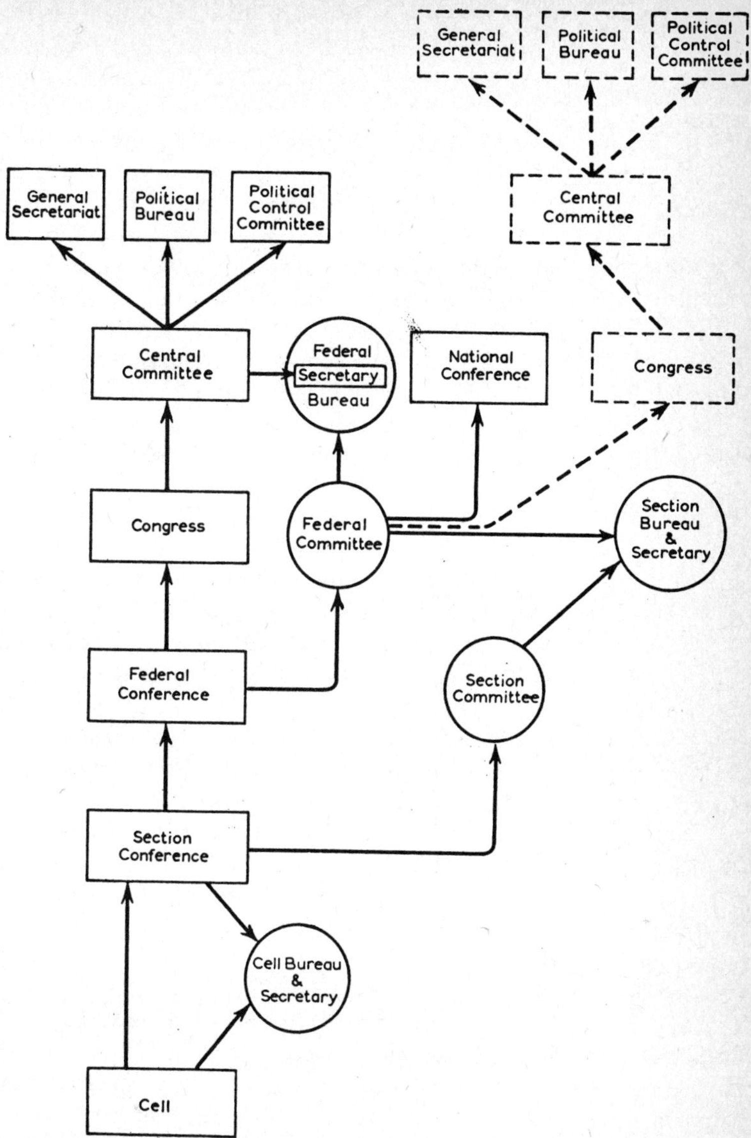

Fig. 18. Indirect election in the French Communist Party.
Dotted lines show the exceptional organization provided for in Art. 26 of the constitution.

is cancelled out: the whole pyramid rests upon a vacuum. In any case, the section conference elects a committee which itself appoints a bureau. At federal level the federal conference made up of the delegates from the sections (second or third remove from the members) elects in the same way a committee (third or fourth remove) which likewise appoints a bureau (fourth or fifth remove); at central level the National Congress, made up of the delegates appointed at the federal conferences (third or fourth remove from the members), elects a Central Committee (fourth or fifth remove) which itself nominates the Political Bureau, the Secretariat, and the Political Control Committee (fifth or sixth remove). Between conferences the National Conference is in session, and its members are appointed by the federal committees (fourth or fifth remove). Article 26 of the constitution even lays it down that 'in the event of circumstances being such that the free operation and activity of the party is hindered the federal committee may exceptionally, with the agreement of the Central Committee, nominate the delegates [to Congress]', in which case Congress would be the fifth or sixth remove of representation from the base, and the Political Bureau, the Secretariat, and the Control Committee, the sixth or seventh remove.

All parties do not apply indirect representation with the same rigour, but all make use of it. Now indirect representation is an admirable means of banishing democracy while pretending to apply it. Rousseau was aware that sovereignty cannot be delegated: all the legal artifices concerning the representation of the mandator by the mandatary cannot conceal this fundamental truth: that the mentality of the delegates is never the same as that of those who delegate them, with the result that every additional stage of delegation increases a little more the gap between the will of the base and the decision of the apex. The election of the leaders of a party by a small group of delegates is not the same in character as their direct election by the mass of the members. Nor does this take into account the fact that the use of other means of manipulating the elections is made much easier in such cases by reason of the restricted number of voters. Furthermore such manipulations are superimposed one upon another, in the course of the various successive ballots, with the result that the election is progressively falsified as the pyramid of ballots is scaled. In particular, an effort is sometimes made to have the party officials appointed as delegates to the conferences and congresses at which leaders are elected (this is all the simpler because the officials, e.g. the secretaries of

Departmental federations, are well placed to influence the members at the base): in such circumstances the party congresses are just like a meeting of employees facing their employers: obviously the former will tend to keep in office the latter, whose creatures they are.

Alongside indirect representation a place of honour in the list of election tricks is reserved for the nomination of candidates. Some parties in their constitution officially limit the party electors' freedom of choice by laying down a procedure for nomination. Frequently, moreover, this system is linked not only with the desire to introduce an element of autocracy into the party, but also with an attempt to increase centralization or decentralization. The election of local leaders is sometimes subject to nomination by the central body, which obviously increases centralization: thus the constitution of the French Communist party lays it down that 'the federal committee must discuss with *the Central Committee* the candidatures for the post of federal secretary'. In the Austrian Socialist party the leaders of local organizations are chosen exclusively from the list of 'party co-operators' (*Parteimitarbeiter*), drawn up by the district organization at the higher level: co-operators are members who are considered to be particularly loyal and capable, and who have attended courses of instruction organized in the central schools of the Social Democratic party: at the present moment, there is approximately one co-operator per twelve members. In the Belgian Christian Social party candidates for the presidency of local committees are nominated for election at a general meeting of members by the local committee itself, with the prior approval of the arrondissement committee; the presidents of arrondissement committees are similarly nominated by the arrondissement committee with the prior approval of the Central Committee. Conversely, the nomination of central leaders may be left to the initiative of local bodies, which has the effect of increasing decentralization, but this tendency is much less noticeable than the contrary. In the Belgian Socialist party, candidatures for the party Bureau emanate from the arrondissement federations, which have to nominate a list of names equal in number to the places to be filled: in fact, this increases the influence of the leaders at the federal level. In the Belgian Catholic party, candidates for the National Committee are nominated by the National Committee itself or by province or arrondissement committees. In the Austrian Socialist party, the election for the National Council is prepared by an electoral committee which must include representatives of the provincial bodies, 'all due regard' being paid to their numerical importance; this committee submits a report to the Assembly of provincial delegates and the final proposal is then submitted to Congress.

However, semi-official nomination of candidates is much more widespread than official nomination. In many parties a single candidate (or a single list) is referred to the suffrage of members. Such for example is the normal practice of the Communist party: there is no true election of the Central Committee at the meetings of the National Congress but merely a simple ratification; election in this case is but a formality, a rite deprived of all efficacy. It would seem that similar methods are in use at the lower levels. But parties which lay claim to orthodox democratic principles make use of analogous techniques: the elections of the officers of the French Radical Socialist party often takes the form of the ratification of a single list of candidates. The same is true for right-wing and conservative parties in a great many countries. There is less democracy, moreover, the nearer one approaches the base of the party, contrary to general belief. From time to time some opposition to the semi-official candidates is manifest in National Congresses; it is much less frequent inside the branch, the caucus, or the cell. It is quite exceptional for the members of these basic groups not to appoint as leaders the candidates that are put forward to them: the difficulty of concerting action to ensure the success of the contingent opposition, the dearth of personalities capable of forming the opposition, the failure of the majority of members to attend meetings, suffice to explain such docility in the face of autocratic methods. Sometimes a branch rebels, a cell revolts against the party's proposals, but such acts of local indiscipline are too infrequent, too dispersed, and too isolated to imperil the system. This passive attitude adopted by the base is serious: since the elections are of the indirect kind, the whole organization in fact depends on this initial appointment of delegates. The absence of real democracy, which is a feature of it, has repercussions at every point of the party structure. In the last resort the occasional opposition that occurs at the higher levels, particularly in National Congresses, looks more like a struggle for power between several leaders, all owing their places to autocracy, than the democratic resistance of the rank and file.

The material organization of the voting complements the effects of nomination. Two different series of manipulation can be simultaneously employed in this field: the packing of the electoral body on the one hand, the faking of votes on the other. The first system is in great use at the Radical Socialist Congress meetings where the machinery of representation is such that skilful leaders can profoundly affect its composition. Since every fully paid-up member of the party is able to buy a Congress ticket (granted the money), the very decision as to where the Congress shall meet assumes fundamental importance: for the members of nearby caucuses will easily be able to attend it, whereas the members of distant caucuses will only very exceptionally be able to take part. By arranging for the Congress to meet within a Department favourable to its members the outgoing Administrative Committee can exert a strong influence in favour of its own re-election. However, the purchase in bulk of Congress tickets that are then distributed amongst temporary members of the party makes it possible to achieve similar results. Even in parties where the system of representation is laid down most strictly the use of such devices is merely restricted, not suppressed. When in 1872 Karl Marx and the supporters of the authoritarian wing summoned the General Council of the International to meet at the Hague they were surely aware that they had chosen a town 'difficult of access for certain opponents, completely inaccessible for others'.[1]

In present-day Socialist parties, in which the rules of democracy are more respected than anywhere else, the methods of calculating the number of representatives allow of some 'sleight of hand'. In the French Socialist party, for example, each federation has a right to one Congress representative for every twenty-five subscribers with twelve monthly stamps; that is to say the total number of stamps bought by the federation's treasurer is divided by twelve in order to compute the representation to be accorded to the federation. There is, therefore, nothing to prevent a rich federation from buying many more stamps than it can sell to its members. A deputy or an influential militant who can find financial assistance is therefore able, indirectly, to buy mandates for the Congress.

On the other hand, representation is often calculated in a way that is disproportionate to the power of the federations. In the Radical party up to 1945 the number of delegates to the Executive Committee was determined, as to half by the effective membership of the federation, as to the other half by the population of the Department: a skeleton federation in a highly populated Depart-

[1] Roberto Michels, *Political Parties*, London, 1915, p. 204.

ment might have a greater number of representatives than a large federation operating in a small Department. The system reveals the secondary importance in the party of the member. In the Popular Republican Movement the representation of the federations is calculated on a decreasing scale: one representative per 50 members for the first 200, one per 100 members from 200 to 5,000, one per 200 members thereafter. The system is obviously intended to

Democratic Party Convention		*Republican Party Convention*	
State	*No. of Democratic Voters per Delegate*	*State*	*No. of Republican Voters per Delegate*
New York	28,960	New York	29,290
Pennsylvania	26,955	Pennsylvania	19,021
S. Carolina	1,721	S. Carolina	894
Louisiana	5,680	Louisiana	5,589
Maine	11,191	Ohio	27,277
Vermont	7,443	Kansas	24,884
Connecticut	21,164	Georgia	5,478
Illinois	33,245	Alabama	2,923
Wyoming	8,725	Mississippi	630
Nevada	3,129		
Texas	15,014		

Fig. 19. Unequal representation in the National Conventions of the American Parties.[1]

favour new groups and at the same time to limit the influence of the strongest federations at the Congress: it thus leads by indirect means to increased power for the central authority, as experience shows that opposition to the centre almost always comes from the big federations. In the American parties the National Conventions are based upon a system of representation which gives the advantage to the thinly populated rural States over the urban and densely populated States. This falsifies the whole orientation of the country by displacing the centre of political gravity from North to South and from East to West (Fig. 19).

At the local level, similar packing of the electoral body is also very common. In the regional Congresses representation is less well

[1] Figures for 1948, according to the report of the Committee on Political Parties of the American Association of Political Science. (Supplement to *The American Political Science Review*, September 1950, No. 3, part ii.)

organized than in national Congresses, with the result that the influence of the leaders is all the greater. Within the framework of the branch the problem is no longer one of manipulating the system of representation, since voting is direct, but of keeping out members who do not support the semi-official candidates and would have the right to vote, or else of introducing in support pseudo-members who in fact should have no vote. The methods employed at one time or another by some parties include the following: calling of meetings without adequate notice so as to prevent the hostile members from being notified in time; fixing meetings at awkward times so as to keep them away; using teams of strong-arm men to come and spread through the hall and to take part in the vote. The American 'bosses' know every trick in the art of faking an election. The creators of the Birmingham caucus had perfected their methods; they made use of 'travelling companies' going from district to district to attend electoral meetings in order to ensure by the decisive addition of their votes the appointment of those delegates who enjoyed the benefit of semi-official support. Moreover it must never be forgotten that attendance at branch meetings is always poor and that those who take part in the vote are only a small proportion of the members of the party. In any event, therefore, the appointment of its leaders is not fully democratic.

Finally the manipulation of elections can affect the ballot itself. Democratic principles would demand a ballot with sealed voting papers: this condition is not always realized. At the lower levels the vote often takes place by show of hands, those present being invited to show their acceptance or rejection of the candidates put forward; this completely alters the nature of the ballot: what we have here is not an election but plebiscitary approval. This same procedure is sometimes employed at higher levels in regional or national Congresses: at the Radical party Congress it is not unusual for the bureau or the President to be elected by acclamation; in the Communist party Congress this procedure is the rule, and a unanimous vote is always secured. Sometimes voting by secret ballot is organized, but the only voting slips distributed bear the names of the semi-official candidates, with the result that votes in opposition are more difficult and run the risk of being dispersed among various candidates. More current and more subtle, but no less effective than such manipulations of the machinery of the ballot, is psychological manipulation of the voters. At the lower levels, some important person (member of parliament, journalist, member of the

Executive) will take the trouble to go and speak in support of the semi-official candidates: his prestige with the members will have a considerable influence on their vote, the more so that they will feel flattered by the self-importance which the special visit of the great man will confer on them. In national Congresses such personal influence upon the voter becomes more complicated and more complete. There is an art in 'working the conference', in lobbying, in undermining support for the opposition, in plotting in the wings: in this respect a full account of a French Radical party Congress or of the Presidential Convention of an American party would read like a scenario, but in all parties similar practices are current.

Titular Leaders and Real Leaders. The total effect of these electoral tricks is to hide a greater or less degree of autocracy in appointments under a more or less democratic mask. There is another method capable of achieving the same result that can be used concurrently with the manipulation we have described. It consists in setting up two categories of leader within the party: titular leaders and real leaders—the former elected, the latter autocratically appointed. The former enjoy power in theory, the latter exercise it in reality or else share it with them. Here we touch upon the general question of the real repositories of power. The Marxists complain that classical democracy is purely formal: deputies, parliaments, and ministers being invested only with the form of power, the essential substance remaining in the hands of capitalist organizations: banks, heavy industry, trusts, and so on. Historians attempt to discover behind the sceptre and the throne of absolute monarchs the men or institutions who were really in control: Palace Chamberlain, the Pretorian Guard, Prime Minister, favourite mistress or protégé. In considering all social groups, and not only states, it is proper to make such attempts to discover the Grey Eminence behind the Imperial Purple, the wire-pullers manipulating the puppets who dance on the stage. This is a particularly important question in the case of political parties, for in many the real authority is very different from the titular authority. But it is necessary to proceed cautiously in this matter: by definition Grey Eminences remain hidden or half-concealed, and precise information about them is always difficult to obtain; moreover, the popular imagination being particularly fond of stories of secret influences and mysterious leaders, popular opinions on the subject must be treated with the greatest caution.

Many parties have only an indirect acquaintance with this duality of power, real and apparent; their official leaders are also their real leaders. What happens is simply that small circles sometimes form around certain men, thus increasing their authority and giving them a preponderance of power in fact that is not provided for by the constitution. Or, alternatively, the exceptional personality of a leader sets him, in similar fashion, above the official rules: take, for example, the parts played by Jaurès or Léon Blum in the French Socialist party, or by Branting amongst the Swedish Social Democrats, or by Stauning in Danish Socialism. In other cases the duality may go very deep: the official hierarchy is paralleled by a semi-official or secret hierarchy; the two share effective power, with the second tending to take the lion's share. Such a distinction is made for American parties between the official organization controlled by the *leaders*, and the *machine*, an unofficial organization in the hands of the *bosses* and their followers, although the terminology is not always very clearly defined and the two hierarchies sometimes fuse. Now this 'second power' is not democratically organized: those who wield it do not derive it from election but from co-option or appointment from above, from conquest or from inheritance.

How is this 'second power' created? It seems possible to formulate no general conclusion on the matter: we must restrict ourselves to quoting a few examples, suitably chosen as representative. American *bossism* seems to be based upon profit. In France an election makes possible only indirect and limited action on behalf of the friends and supporters of the successful candidate: he can indeed secure them some advantages, a few jobs, a few honours, but not easily. Posts in the Government service are filled by competition and enjoy the protection of law which guarantees them a certain security independent of normal political changes; the administration enjoys considerable independence. In the United States an election brings into power not only a Senator, a Representative, a Town Council, or a State Legislature, but the judges, sheriffs, policemen, tax-collectors, fire-chiefs, school inspectors, and almost all the heads of the public services. Moreover the officials in these services are appointed by the party in power; its defeat means their loss of office, by virtue of the principle: 'To the victor the spoils.' In consequence an electoral victory is highly profitable. It is so even when the winning party remains honest and uses the mandate and the duties entrusted to it in the general interest. It is even more so when the winning party traffics in the vast powers that have fallen into its hands: misappropriation, abuse of power, and corruption allow enormous profits to be made. Such are the economic foundations of bossism: a *machine*, that is an unofficial organization which is in effective control of a party, is fundamentally an organization aiming at securing positions of power and the legal and illegal advantages that they afford; the boss is the leader and creator of the organization. The picture drawn is scarcely exaggerated, though it must be acknowledged that it applies only to certain types of machine (albeit the most widespread, of which Tammany Hall is the best-known example); in the South bosses and machines have not quite the same significance.

In Europe unofficial bodies of this kind are little known. Civil Service regulations make it impossible for such bodies to have a financial basis, preventing corruption from becoming systematized and permanent, and thus making it a much less important influence in the leadership of parties. We could draw comparisons touching the influence of financial backers, but it seems slighter than popular opinion believes. There is no direct proportion between the size of the donations made to the party and the authority of the donor in its councils. Most men and institutions which subsidize parties are notoriously incompetent in politics; it is no more difficult to handle them than to handle the delegates to Congress. They exercise very considerable pressure on restricted issues which concern their immediate personal interests: a campaign against a certain tax which inconveniences them, a vote for a certain Bill which suits them. Their interference in some points of the party's policy is obvious but this does not imply any true share in its permanent leadership. The financial backers themselves have no real status as concealed leaders of the party; they simply take action on certain occasions in their own interests to ensure that the party will take a particular line. There are, of course, exceptions to this rule; there is a certain kind of megalomaniac capitalist, bitten by the political bug, who wants to exercise effective leadership of the party that he is financing; but the major parties do not take kindly to this sort of domination, with the result that such men often end up at the head of short-lived organizations set up by adventurers or cranks.

With the behaviour of financial backers may be compared that of groups and coalitions set up to defend private interests by means of political action: Workers' and Employers' Federations, Ex-Servicemen's Associations, Women's and Family Leagues, Regional Associations, Temperance and Ethical Societies, and so on. The

Americans have given them the very expressive title of *pressure groups*. Like the financial backers the pressure group operates in a clearly defined and limited field. It is even less interested than the backer in linking itself with any particular party; it prefers to exert an influence upon all parties in order to guide them in the direction favourable to its interests. In the nature of things, however, the general coincidence between the aims of a pressure group and the political line of a particular party may lead the group to take special interest in the party and to exercise a permanent influence upon its leadership. The influence of the Congress of Industrial Organizations on the American Democratic party provides a good example of this. It is simultaneously exerted at the apex, upon the leaders of the party at the various levels, and at the base, where within the framework of the primary elections the Trade Unions try to get their candidates elected. As a result it sometimes happens that they work in opposition to the bosses and their machines and that they are in direct competition with the party leaders. Similar action by independent Unions upon the leadership of parties is moreover fairly widespread: the influence of Trade Union leaders on Socialist or Christian Democratic parties is very considerable.

Pressure groups must not be confused with associations of intellectuals—Philosophical Societies, as they were called in the eighteenth century—which have at certain periods exercised an important influence on the leadership of political parties. Perhaps the clearest example of this is to be found in the influence exerted by Freemasonry, about 1900–10, upon the leadership of the French Radical party. It is undeniable that at that time Masons formed the leading strata of the party, that Freemasonry provided the party with its framework, its unity, and its general lines of policy; that its influence was dominant in the party Congresses, in its Executive Committees, and over its leaders; and that, thanks to Freemasonry, the party acquired an effectiveness and a power such as it has never since recovered. At the same period the influence of Freemasonry was evident in various parties of the same political complexion as the French Radical Socialist party, like the Belgian Liberal party for example. Other instances could be found of the part played by Philosophical Societies in the councils of parties: a noteworthy example is the influence of the Fabian Society upon the British Labour party, though this is much more a case of spiritual influence than of leadership proper.

Another kind of 'second power' is furnished by the teams which collect around a newspaper whose circulation reinforces their influence on the leadership of the party. Often the dominating personality of one man will make them more or less noticeably a clique. In France, for example, *La Dépêche de Toulouse* and Maurice Sarraut for long exercised a veritable moral sway over the Radical party without having any official position corresponding to the role. The influence of *Le Quotidien* in 1924 might be compared with it, though this paper was more concerned with uniting like parties than with urging any particular course upon one of them. Many similar examples could be adduced. The influence of Lenin within the Russian Social Democratic party before 1917 was founded on *Iskra*: the bitter campaign he waged to keep the control of the paper out of the hands of the Central Committee aimed at maintaining the foundation of this 'second power'. In almost all Socialist parties provision is made in the constitution to ensure the strict subordination of the party's newspaper to the party's directing bodies; none the less an editorial team still retains a certain amount of independence which allows it to influence in greater or less degree the members, the officers, and the directing bodies.

Finally the subjection of a party to an international authority constitutes a last type of 'second power': it may be democratic in appearance, if the authority in question is made up of delegates freely elected by the national parties in numbers proportional to their membership. However, since each national party enjoys no more than minority representation inside the international body the latter still retains the characteristics of autocracy in relation to it; furthermore the appointment of members of each party to the International constitutes yet one more remove in indirect representation, which increases the gulf between elector and elected. In fact experience proves that the Internationals were made up autocratically or else were without any effective power. The First International (of Karl Marx) provides an example of the first method, the Second International of the second. With the Third International a return was made to autocracy, heightened by the preponderance of the Russian Communist party, which disposed of five votes in the Executive compared with the one vote accorded to each of the largest Communist parties. In practice its authority was further increased by reason of its power and its prestige. The dissolution of the Comintern did not diminish this autocracy; it has tended rather to increase it in so far as the relationship between Moscow and the individual Communist parties has taken on the pattern of a dialogue between unequal partners; at a meeting within the framework of the Comintern the preponderance of the Russians was less considerable. However, the degree of autocracy diminishes if the members of the individual national Communist party recognize the authority of the Russians and acknowledge the Russian leader, Lenin or Stalin or Malenkov, as their leader: such appear to be the facts.

II. OLIGARCHY IN LEADERSHIP

The leadership of parties tends naturally to assume oligarchic form. A veritable 'ruling class' comes into being that is more or less closed; it is an 'inner circle' into which it is difficult to penetrate. The phenomenon is just as true of titular leaders as of the real leaders, of autocratic as of democratic rulers. In theory, the principle of election should prevent the formation of an oligarchy; in fact, it seems rather to favour it. The masses are naturally conservative; they become attached to their old leaders, they are suspicious of new faces. Socialist parties, in which the recruitment of leaders is more democratic than in others, find correspondingly greater difficulty in finding new leaders.

The Formation of the 'Inner Circle'. The electoral system of the State seems to exercise a certain influence upon the oligarchic nature of party leadership and the formation of 'inner circles'. In so far as no candidate has a chance of being elected without the approbation of the committees of the party, its leaders play an essential part in the selection of future parliamentary representatives: they are nominated by the inner circle. On the other hand, if free candidature is possible, or if the personality of the candidate plays an important part in the election, with the result that the party committees depend more upon the candidate than he upon them, then the recruitment of parliamentary representatives occurs outside the inner circle, and outside the party oligarchy. Since, under such circumstances, the parliamentary representatives too play a very important part in the leadership of the party, the inner circle opens and the elites become more mobile. In consequence, voting by lists, which is by its nature collective and dependent on the party, strengthens oligarchy, whereas single-member voting weakens it. The internal oligarchy reigns supreme in the P.R. system with fixed lists and the ranking of candidates in a strict order which determines their election, for here the parliamentary representatives are chosen by the inner circle; the party in this case is a closed circuit. The same effects are also observable in the two-party system because the quasi-monopoly of the two parties gives them preponderant power in the selection of candidates in spite of the single-member voting system.

From the point of view of their formation the classes of leaders and inner circles can be divided into several kinds. No doubt the simplest is to be seen in the *camarilla*, a small group which makes use of close personal solidarity as a means of establishing and retaining its influence. Sometimes it takes the form of a clique grouped around an influential leader: this leader's retinue has a monopoly of the positions of leadership and takes on the characteristics of an oligarchy. Some examples of cliques in Socialist parties have already been cited. They flourish best in conservative and moderate parties in which the rivalry between cliques takes the place assumed elsewhere by the struggles between 'wings' or 'tendencies'; control of the party is almost always in the hands of the dominant cliques. The structure of the party favours the development of cliques; we need only recall the composition of the central bodies of the Radical party to see that everything is so arranged as to allow of the interplay between personalities with their retinues. In American parties the way the machines are organized around the bosses shows similar characteristics.

There is a distinction to be made between such clans and 'teams of leaders' which are not united by any personal attachment to a dominant chief: the distinctive feature of the team is the comparative equality that rules among its members, the fact that its bonds develop horizontally and not vertically. Such teams are formed in very different ways. Sometimes it happens that they are the result of a deliberate compact entered into by a few men, generally belonging to a new generation, who unite in order 'to shake the fruit tree', to win the positions of control from those in possession, and to monopolize them for their own advantage: this is the phenomenon that in literary and artistic matters produces schools and coteries, but it is to be seen occurring quite frequently in politics. Sometimes they are mythomaniacs pursuing their dream of 'synarchy', that is the formation of a secret team uniting influential leaders from several different parties, in which case they are not to be taken seriously. There are however serious teams set up within individual parties: round about 1933–4 a team of this kind could be seen forming around the French Radical Socialist party (around Pierre Cot, Jean Mistler, Pierre Mendès-France, etc.), but the events of 6 February 1934 broke it up: its members were not averse to being called 'Young Turks', with the 1908 Revolution in mind. More frequently such teams are the result of a spontaneous fellowship arising out of shared origins or training: there is the local group (e.g. 1792 Girondins), the old boys' group (e.g. the former students of the École Polytechnique in Paris), the group that arises from collaboration in one organization (e.g. the Treasury), the group knit by war (e.g. Old Soldier of the —— Regiment).

The first of these is the most important: in districts in which parties have long held sway there naturally grow up local teams which often play an important part in the life of the party. Albert Thibaudet was ironical at the expense of Old Sarrien and the Radical teams in the Department of Saône-et-Loire; Daniel Halévy observed that the evolution of the Radical party at the beginning of the century was synonymous with the decline of the Parisian teams and the rise of those from the Centre and the South. In the history of the French Socialist party during the last half-century the passage of the various teams, from the North, from Languedoc and Provence, from the Centre, and from Toulouse and so on, has left fairly clear traces. Similar phenomena can be observed in all parties. Some, the Communist parties in particular, attempt to prevent them by such measures as 'rotation' and 'uprooting', which we shall study later. The other types of team are much less common within parties. It is comparatively rare to find in them traces of influence similar to that exercised by Treasury officials or by Old Polytechnicians upon certain French ministries: one example that might be quoted is the part played within the M.R.P. by teams that arose out of the Catholic Association of French Youth. In many present-day European parties there are to be found teams of leaders that grew out of common action in the Resistance Movement during the Occupation: on occasion there has moreover been some rivalry between the London team and the team from the internal Resistance. A similar state of affairs was to be seen in the Russian Communist party after its seizure of power. The recent purges in Western European Communist parties generally aimed at eliminating the London teams to the advantage of the internal Resistance (or the Moscow) team; it is also worth noting that some purges were directed against the teams brought together in the struggle against Franco during the Spanish War.

Teams and cliques are personal oligarchies. On the other hand bureaucracy provides us with a type of institutionalized oligarchy. Unimaginable in the old parties based upon caucuses linked by a weak system of articulation, it came to birth with the branch system and complex structure and has developed more especially in the parties that are linked with Trade Unions, Co-operative and Friendly Societies. Thus, the German Social Democratic party had 3,000 permanent officials in 1910 (that is approximately one official per 250 members).[1] These permanent officials tended to play a dominant role: since their duties put them in daily contact with the base, they easily secured appointment as delegates to Congress and were thus able to exercise a decisive influence upon the composition of the governing bodies. Moreover their position within the party gave them immediate authority over the members: the permanent secretary of a Departmental federation obviously became the king-pin of the federal committee in which the other members, taken up with their private work, could not play so active a part. As a result of this twin mechanism the growth of a bureaucracy, in the proper sense of the term, could be observed. Some parties sought to react against the tendency by limiting the number of permanent officials who could be sent as delegates to Congress. Thus the constitution of the Belgian Socialist party laid it down (Article 23) that federal delegates to the National Congress must be drawn as to at least one-half from outside the ranks of the party's parliamentary representatives and permanent officials. But the rule was relaxed for the General Council, which is in fact the most important organ of control: federations which send more than three delegates to it need to choose only a minimum of one-quarter of the delegates from outside the ranks of the parliamentary representatives and permanent officials (Article 31); other federations may make up the whole of their delegation with representatives and officials: the restriction is slight.

Other parties on the contrary seek to develop into a system the use of permanent officials. In their view, the party resembles a professional army, at least so far as its leading strata are concerned. On this question Lenin wrote a few pages that are crucial for this question, particularly in *What is to be done?* He was impressed by the terrible restrictions imposed on revolutionary action by daily work in the factory, the shop, and the workshop. He thought total

[1] According to a report on the 1910 Congress, *Revue politique et parlementaire*, 1910, p. 509.

and permanent devotion to the party, with no interruption or hindrance due to external cares, was essential for the formation of the real agitators in the new party. Hence the idea which he expounded on many occasions of the creation of a veritable class of professional revolutionaries who would act as the central nucleus of the party and would provide its basic militant members. 'No working-class agitator', he said, 'who has talent and shows promise should work eleven hours a day in a factory. We must arrange that he be maintained by the party.[1] He makes it clear that the party should 'reply upon people who devote to the revolution not their free evenings but their whole life',[2] 'people whose profession is that of a revolutionary'.[3]

The ideas of Lenin seem to concern not only the leaders but also the militants. In practice, in so far as the latter are maintained by the party, they are naturally given positions of control because they alone dispose of sufficient leisure to fill these positions effectively. To create a 'class of professional revolutionaries' is equivalent to creating a class of 'professional leaders of revolutionary parties', an inner circle which stirs up the masses and which is founded upon the official duties performed within the party; it is equivalent to creating a bureaucracy, that is to say an oligarchy. If the posts for the party's permanent officials were strictly elective bureaucracy could coincide with democracy. But this is not so and cannot be so: the militants who are capable of filling a permanent position and willing to do so are not very numerous; the leaders of the party are anxious to keep close control of them so as to be certain of their technical ability and of their political trustworthiness; the leadership, as we have seen, is largely made up of permanent officials already in office. Thus there is born an authentic oligarchy which exercises power, retains it, and transmits it by means of co-option.

Sometimes the bureaucratic oligarchy assumes the form of a technocratic oligarchy. 'Courses for leaders' are set up inside the party which one must attend before being given a post of leadership. The system was first used by the Socialist parties in an attempt to form a political elite within the working class. In 1906 the German Social Democratic party founded in Berlin the *Parteischule* which aimed at completing the training of the permanent officials already in office in the party and at training candidates for employment in the party or in Trade Unions.[4] In 1910–11 141 students

[1] *Op. cit.* Cf. *Selected works*, London, 1947, Vol. I, p. 240. [2] *Iskra*, No. 1.
[3] *What is to be done? Op. cit.*, p. 225. [4] Roberto Michels, op. cit., p. 34.

attended its courses: 52 party officials and 89 candidates, of whom 49 found positions on finishing the course. The Communist parties developed such training courses systematically. In the French Communist party at the present moment there are three kinds of course: the central, federal, and elementary. The first is further subdivided into 'four-month courses' intended for the higher leaders (parliamentary representatives, members of the Central Committee, federal delegates; 96 militants attended them in 1947–8) and into 'four-week courses', more particularly intended for leaders in agricultural areas and in ancillary organizations (in 1947–8 at least, when 292 militants attended them). The second category, federal courses, which last a fortnight, are provided for members of the federal and section committees (2,071 in 1947–8).[1] Furthermore there are courses in Moscow for the training of the highest and most trusted leading strata: those who have attended them form the supreme aristocracy of the party.

The Fascist parties and the National Socialist party in particular adopted similar methods. After seizing power the latter created veritable 'leadership schools' for its higher and middle-ranking leaders. The machinery for selecting and training future leaders was very highly organized. A thousand individuals a year were chosen from the total membership of the Hitler Youth Movement. After a period of initial training in the 'Adolf Hitler Schools' a further drastic selection took place. A small number of future leaders was then admitted to a special course of training for three years. After a period of foreign travel intended to broaden the mind the first year of study was designed to test their resistance and their character, the second to form them spiritually, the third to provide them with technical knowledge. There was provision for a period of practical work with a party leader. Obviously a system so highly organized is possible only under a single-party regime when the selection of leaders for the party is tantamount to choosing the leading political strata of the state.

The present-day Austrian Socialist party has organized a very interesting system for the privileged category of militants that are called in its constitution the 'party co-operators' (*Parteimitarbeiter*). They must attend the central training courses organized by the party (Article 1 of the constitution). If they wish to 'rise to the

[1] Information taken from report of M. Casanova to Central Committee on 28th February 1949 and from article by A. Parinaud, *Cahiers du Communisme*, October 1949, p. 1241.

highest posts in the party' (ibid.), they must attend the more advanced training courses. The list of 'co-operators' is drawn up by the district committees, which are themselves elected by the delegates of the local branches. But the latter can elect as members of their committee only 'co-operators'. Since the leaders of the branch are generally chosen by it as its delegates to the district conferences at which the district committees are elected the result is that everything takes place in a closed circuit: the 'co-operators' play the fundamental part in the appointment of the district committee which itself nominates the 'co-operators'. This is an oligarchy into which entrance is gained by co-option combined with attendance at leaders' training courses. This system reproduces, officially and with refinements, practices that other parties follow without acknowledgement. It corresponds moreover to an attempt to make the party democratic. There is a list of co-operators from which branches may choose their responsible officers; each branch has the right of proposing to the district committee names for the list; the co-operators are numerous (50,000 out of 614,000 party members in 1950). A remarkable effort is made to give the base an opportunity of choosing the oligarchs.

Composition and Renewal of the Inner Circle. When the leadership of the party assumes the characteristics of an oligarchy, of whatever form, two important problems arise: first, the composition of the inner circle, and second, its renewal. The first consists in the measurement of the disparity that exists between the social make-up of the members in the mass and that of the members of the inner circle. In brief we have to apply to those in control of parties the methods used by J. F. S. Ross in the case of British parliamentary representatives.[1] This has never been done in any systematic way; the many investigators have done no more than formulate empirical observations, often of great interest none the less. For example attention has often been drawn to the very high proportion of lawyers, doctors, and members of the liberal professions amongst the leaders of the middle-class parties and the relatively small number of merchants, industrialists, artisans, or farmers, that is to say of those who form the mass of the middle class. In the same way, the 'intelligentsia' (teachers, writers, journalists) occupy at the head of the working-class parties a very large place out of all proportion to their numerical importance. But such

[1] J. F. S. Ross, *Parliamentary Representation*, 2nd ed., London, 1949.

remarks are far too vague, being based upon no statistical evidence, upon no general calculation. Moreover they refer only to the higher ranks of leadership, taking no account of the subordinate ranks, the non-commissioned officers in the party, who play an important part. Finally, they do not deal with the social origins of the leaders.

It would however be stimulating to make some comparison between the social composition of leaders who have been really elected and that of leaders appointed by autocratic methods. It would no doubt lead us to envisage the problem of democracy from a new angle. It is not at all certain that the social make-up of a group of elected leaders is more akin to that of the mass of the members than is the social make-up of an oligarchy of leaders recruited by autocratic methods: on the contrary, there is every reason to suppose that the opposite is true. Country folk do not choose country folk as their parliamentary representatives, but seem to prefer lawyers, because they consider them to be more capable of defending their interests in parliament. In just the same way the members of any party federation elect their chiefs on the grounds of the ability and the oratorical talents they see in them rather than on grounds of social status. In working-class parties, which are much more class conscious, matters are but little different. It is significant that the proportion of workers is higher amongst the leading strata of the Communist party, who are appointed autocratically, than amongst the leaders of the Socialist party, who are selected by more democratic methods. Basically there is a conflict here between two conceptions of representation, one juridical founded upon election and delegation, the other technical and founded upon a *de facto* similarity between the masses and those who govern them. One's thoughts turn to the possibility of a truly scientific democracy, in which parliament would be made up of a true sample of the citizens reproducing on a reduced scale the exact composition of the nation, made up, that is, according to the very methods that are used as a basis for public opinion surveys like the Gallup polls.

Some parties, which are autocratic and oligarchic in the ordinary sense, would seem to come near to such a scientific democracy, in particular the Communist parties, which make systematic efforts to increase the representation of the working class in their leading strata so as to make of their leadership a true reflection of the base. They experience great difficulty in this respect: a report of M. Léon Mauvais to the Central Committee stated that in 1949 there were no more than 9 representatives of the working class out of the 40 members of the federal committee of the Ain, 15 out of 40 in the Aisne committee, 7 out of 46 in the Côtes-du-Nord committee, 17 out of 52 in the committee of the Haute-Garonne, and 13 out of 43 in that of the Gironde.[1] At the Congress held at Gennervilliers in 1950 M. Auguste Lecœur was at pains to emphasize the dearth of working-class leaders. He pointed out that in the 15th Arrondissement in Paris, in which the Citröen and over a hundred other factories are situated, out of 17 section secretaries only 7 were of the working class 'and that, after the last section conferences which introduced remedial action'; he considered that in the Seinè Federation alone it was necessary 'to find immediately a good thousand secretaries for cells'.[2] It will be observed that the question at issue is not simply to reproduce in the inner circle the same social composition as prevails amongst the members at the base; the efforts are directed solely towards the working class, because of the special qualities attributed to it by Marxist doctrine in the field of revolutionary activity. None the less, the effort involved also brings about better contact between the base and the leaders in accordance with the general trend of the party, which in this respect fulfils the concept of 'scientific democracy'.

The concept is however more theoretical than actual. In the abstract one can conceive of the inner circle representing exactly the social composition of the mass that it controls, just as those questioned for the Gallup poll exactly represent the make-up of the group that is the object of the survey. In actual fact there is a fundamental difference between the two systems: Mr. Gallup's clients remain a part of the masses whose opinion they express, whereas the members of the inner circle are separated from the masses. In the case of the professional leaders the isolation is complete: it would not be accurate to say that they are composed of 50% working class and 50% intelligentsia. What should be said is 50% *former* working class and 50% *former* intelligentsia.

The French expression '*sorti du peuple*', like the English '*sprung from* the working class', does in fact indicate both origins and a breach with them. Roberto Michels has laid considerable emphasis upon the psychological transformation that occurs in political leaders of working-class origin. The same separation, although less clearly marked, is to be found in the non-professional ranks of leaders: the exercise of responsibility produces a change in the

[1] Quoted by H. Chambre, *Vie économique et sociale*, November 1949.
[2] A. Lecœur, *Report to the 1950 Congress*, pp. 24 and 26.

man who assumes it; the mentality of leaders is never identical with that of the masses, even if the leaders are of the same social composition as the masses. In fact, whatever may be their origins, leaders tend to draw closer together and to constitute naturally a leader class. The idea of scientific representation is an illusion: all power is oligarchic.

Further, all oligarchy tends to age. The problem of the renewal of the leading strata in parties, of the rejuvenation of the inner circle, consists in the struggle against this natural tendency. When the party oligarchy is based upon appointment and co-option the tendency towards age is a result of the fact that the duties of leadership take on the nature of a life interest, for leaders but rarely agree voluntarily to abdicate their power and to retire when retirement is not automatic. Events follow much the same course when the leaders of the party are elected by the members. 'Much is said of the fickleness and unpredictability of the favour of the masses,' the German Socialist Bernstein observed, 'but it is a fact that a leader who conscientiously carries out his duties is more secure in the labour movement than is a minister in the Prussian kingdom founded on the grace of God.'[1] In fact the tendency for leaders to be old appears to be stronger in democratic parties than in others. Merriam and Gosnell observed that in 500 elections for party committees in American wards only 13 people were not re-elected: all other changes were the result either of the death or the voluntary retirement of the former leader.[2] A close study of Socialist parties would show the great difficulty experienced by the youthful elements in securing recognition by the militant members. It is much less the opposition of the higher ranks which prevents the rejuvenation of the party than the opposition of the base: the branches do not like new faces; more especially they do not like speedy advancement. To attain to the posts of real command, a slow *cursus honorum* must be completed; you have to be 'apprenticed' to the party.

Other factors in the situation are the fundamental conservatism of the masses and their fondness for the faces they know. But these do not seem to be the only influences: what is perhaps the decisive factor is a certain deep and unacknowledged jealousy. Superiority in age is the only kind that arouses no envy, the only one that does no violence to the feeling that all are equal. There is no confession

[1] Quoted R. Michels, op. cit., p. 106, n.4.

[2] Merriam and Gosnell, *The American Party System*, 4th ed., New York, 1949, p. 179.

of personal inferiority implied in acknowledging the superiority of a veteran, for as one grows older one can become a veteran too. By contrast the superiority of youth assumes the appearance of an aristocracy. Egalitarian envy and rivalry between different generations combine here to hinder the introduction of young blood into the leading strata of democratic parties. It is a striking fact that

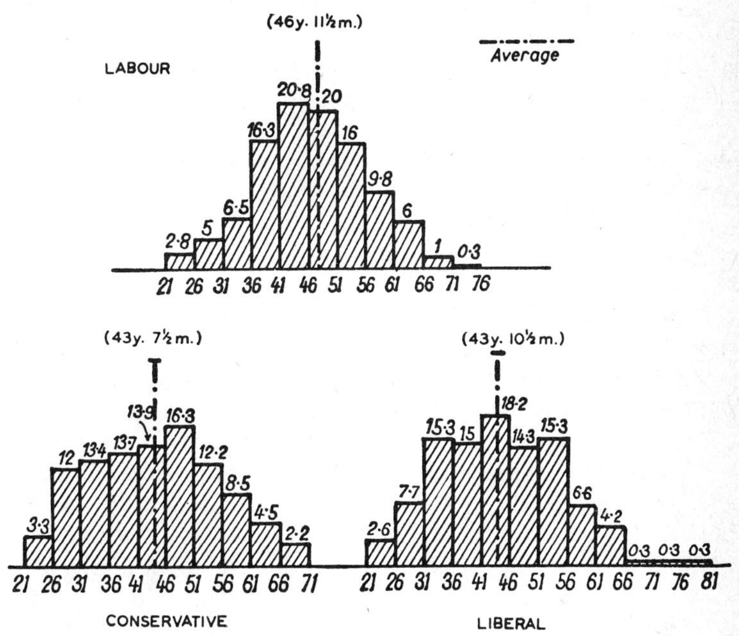

Fig. 20. Age of Members of House of Commons on first election, 1918–35.[1]

Communist leaders, more autocratic in origin, should generally be younger than Socialist leaders who are recruited democratically. The social composition of the parties plays an equally important part: the average age of leaders in working-class parties is higher than that of the leaders in middle-class parties. The average age of members entering the House of Commons for the first time is definitely higher for the Labour party than for the Liberal and Conservative parties: 43 years 7 months for Conservatives, 43 years 10 months for Liberals, nearly 47 years for Labour members. (Figures for the 1918–35 period. Cf. Fig. 20.)

To be born wealthy or noble is equivalent to gaining a few years'

[1] Cf. J. F. S. Ross, *op. cit.*

start over workmen's sons. The middle-class parties can select younger leaders than can working-class parties because in the first place the middle-class leading strata are more easily trained. In spite of the scholarship system the percentage of workmen's sons receiving secondary and higher education is much lower than for the sons of industrialists, merchants, doctors, lawyers, and so on. In England between the wars 50% of the Conservative Members of Parliament were university educated compared with 42·5% of the Liberal and only 22·2% of the Labour Members; 96·5% of the Conservatives had been to secondary or public schools compared with 86·5% of the Liberals and only 28% of the Labour Members. The figures speak for themselves, but they apply only to the parliamentary representatives of the party, that is to the higher levels of leadership. In the lower ranks the proportion of working-class leaders who have had a secondary-school or university education would be much lower. Even if it should be held that secondary or higher education constitutes an inadequate training for politics it is none the less true that such an education provides a background of culture and a skill in the analysis of facts and in their exposition —a rhetoric—which are highly advantageous in the leading strata of a party. Because they have not acquired them in their youth many working-class militants are compelled to learn them later, a fact which delays their admission to positions of responsibility. Even within the proletarian parties middle-class elements have therefore more likelihood of attaining posts of responsibility while still young. Nor must it be forgotten, on the other hand, that by definition the mass of the middle-class parties is middle class in origin, and that a large proportion will have had the advantage of secondary or even of higher education: this causes considerable competition for the posts of leadership. Renewal of their leading strata is consequently far from being ensured in any satisfactory way. The 'greybeards' of the middle-class party correspond to the 'high priests' of the working-class party.

Furthermore the ageing of the leading strata and the possibilities of renewal depend to a large extent on the particular organization of the party. It has been shown that, contrary to general opinion, election does not satisfactorily ensure the infusion of new blood. But parties that are autocratic in structure are no better protected against senility. In fact growing old is equally natural to both, with the sole difference that in autocratic parties energetic action by the centre to ensure the mobility of talent remains possible, whereas the machinery of election makes this difficult in democratic parties. Another factor of some importance is the degree of centralization or decentralization of the party. Experience seems to indicate that the renewal of the leading strata is easier in centralized parties, for opposition to youth is particularly strong amongst the lower ranks of leadership that are often manned by the mediocre. Incapable of rising to higher positions, but very jealous of their authority and thoroughly convinced of their importance, they instinctively raise a barrier against those who seem to them likely to threaten their own position as leaders. In some Socialist parties the action of the local leaders is thus combined with the tendencies to conservatism of the militant members to produce a very serious state of stagnation; the French Socialist party provides a typical example of this. Immediately after the Liberation the young groups formed during the Resistance were ready to take over command and to infuse new blood into an organism which was greatly in need of it. In almost every case the combined opposition of the local leaders and the militant members prevented them from attaining the positions of responsibility they merited. The new constitution of the party made their elimination the easier since it required five consecutive years' membership of the party as a condition of admission to its central bodies or for nomination as its candidate at elections for the legislature (the 1906–11 constitution required only three years' membership: the change is symptomatic). The breach between the Socialist party and the Movement for National Liberation consummated the failure of the young groups. Some joined General de Gaulle in the French People's Rally, most gave up politics. The loss to the Socialist party was very considerable, for the elimination of its reserve teams is one of the prime causes for its decline since 1946.

On the whole it seems to be the centralized parties alone who bother to establish a system for replacing leaders; it is closely linked with their system of training schools. For the granting of responsibility to young men presupposes that they have received the appropriate political and technical training. The Communist parties pay great attention to this question. In his report to the French Communist party in 1950 M. Auguste Lecœur strongly emphasized the necessity 'of not letting the party grow old'. Quoting the sentence of Pascal 'It is a great thing to be a nobleman, you start with twenty years' advantage', he added, 'twenty years that the sons of princes did not lose in waiting upon patrons. . . . Today, the proletariat is no longer obliged to wait upon patrons',[1] and recalled that Maurice Thorez was a member of the Political Bureau at the age of twenty-five, and Benoît Frachon at the age of thirty. The whole proceedings of the 1950 Congress were moreover dominated by the idea of

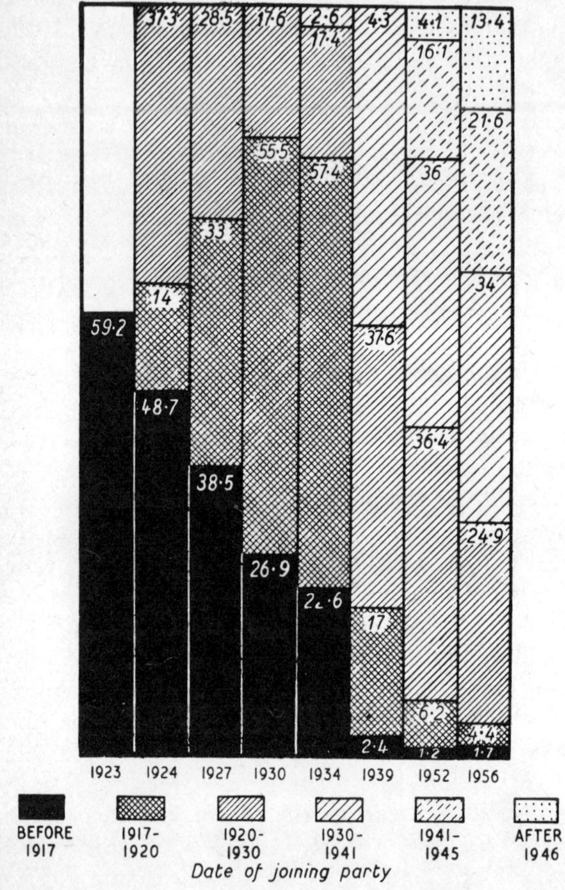

Fig. 21. Renewal of leading strata in Russia Communist Party: distribution by seniority of delegates to the Party Congress.

rejuvenating the leading strata. Similar tendencies seem to be manifest in Communist parties in the other countries in which they are linked with a development in the political line of the party: in Russia great efforts have been made on several occasions to renew

[1] Op. cit., p. 23.

the leading strata, and they have often coincided with changes of policy.

Evidence of this can be found in the statistics relating to the date of admission to the party of delegates to the National Congress (Fig. 21); there is no strict coincidence between the date of admission and the age of the delegates: however, there is probably some approximate correlation between the two phenomena. The greatest effort of rejuvenation took place between 1934 and 1939 (Fig. 21). At the 1934 Congress 22·6% of the delegates were old Bolsheviks who had joined before 1917; 57·4% were Bolsheviks who had joined during the civil war period (1917–20); 17·4% had joined the party between 1920 and 1929, and only 2·6% were Communists joining after 1929. On the other hand, at the 1939 Congress, 43% of the delegates had joined after 1929 and 37·6% between 1920 and 1929; only 17% belonged to the war years, and 2·4% to the old guard, members before the Revolution. Although in Communist parties there is a marked desire to introduce new blood it seems to function intermittently; there are periods of renewal, generally linked with transformations in the party's policy. Outside these periods there is no neglect of the need to renew the leading strata, but there is no systematic or organized effort to that end. Some measure of ageing in the higher ranks can moreover be observed. The National Socialist party on the other hand had attempted after seizing power to set in train a regular procedure to ensure mobility amongst the elite by means of the system of 'leadership schools' that has been described.

In democratic and decentralized parties the renewal of the inner circle is exceptional or indirect in character. In the first case it is a result of special or abnormal circumstances: an example can be found in the case of the French Radical Socialist party after the Liberation. Habit and the Press have led the public to look upon the Radicals as an old party. In fact, the average age of its deputies in parliament is still higher than that in other parties; this is caused by the high proportion of old men to be found in it (29% of its parliamentary representatives are over sixty, compared with 6% in the Socialist party and 3% in the Communist party and the M.R.P.). But there are groups of young men alongside the old and these are more numerous than the young in other parties, with the exception of the Communists and the M.R.P.: 14% of Radical deputies are under thirty-six compared with only 8% of the Socialists; 4·5% are under thirty-one as against 1% of the Socialists (Fig. 22). These groups grew up in the Resistance Movement, as did those of the Socialist party to which we have referred. The difference is that the latter did not succeed in entering the controlling bodies of the party, whereas the Radicals did. The Socialist groups were hindered by the opposition of the lower ranks and of the militants at branch level; the Radicals often found neither militants nor lower ranks barring their way, as a result of the disorganization of the party brought about by the war and the occupation. The weak organization of the Radical party stood up to these events less successfully than the strong organization of the Socialist party; many of its leaders were compromised in the Vichy regime: the result was that the new groups often found the ground free for manœuvre. If this example is compared with the formation of the so-called 'Young Turk' Movement in the party in 1934 and with analogous symptoms in various conservative and moderate parties outside France, it will be appreciated that the absence of strong organization may favour the rejuvenation of parties after exceptional crises: whereas the barrier of 'high priests' and lower ranks which tempers the violence of crises in parties of strong structure also prevents them from profiting by the event to rejuvenate themselves. The situation presents some analogies with the elimination of the less fit by free competition and with the danger of stagnation in semi-planned economies.

As an example of indirect rejuvenation we may quote the influence of research groups. They make it possible for young experts to exercise a controlling influence upon the party, without having to go through the long *cursus honorum* that is exacted by the militant members in the branch. The experts work first behind the scenes but their work is no less effective, since the research groups prepare the draft Bills tabled by the parliamentary representatives of the party and draw up its programme and its electoral 'platform'. The leaders can then 'push' them by first getting them into parliament and then into ministerial committees. In the British Labour party young intellectuals are in this way given the opportunity of advancement; the rise of a man like Mr. Hugh Gaitskell is a good example of this 'lateral' infusion of new blood. Other examples are to be seen in the Belgian Socialist party, in which the Emile Vandervelde Institute plays a similar role, in the Belgian Christian Social party which, on the same pattern, has set up a Research and Information Centre, in the specialized working-parties of the M.R.P., and so on. It would be interesting to make a comparison with the French Socialist party, which has been abandoned by the

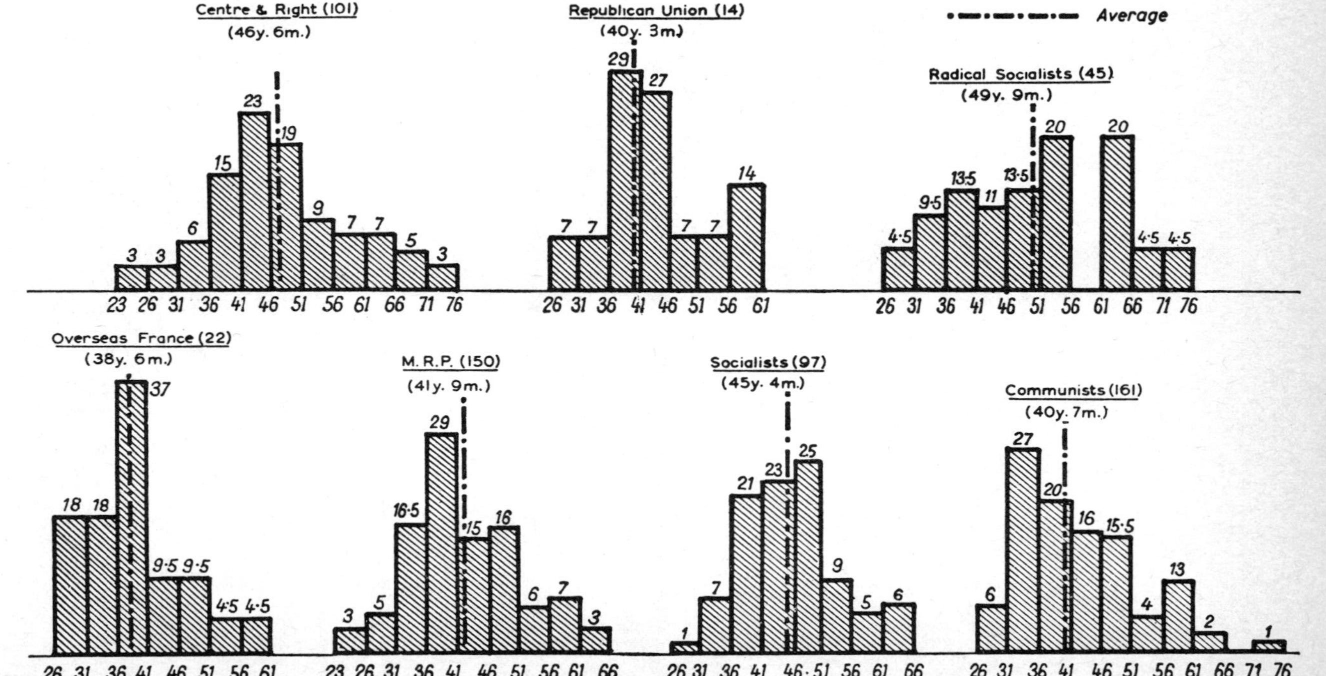

Fig. 22. Distribution by age of Deputies in French National Assembly (1946).

groups of young intellectuals because its structure gave them no opportunity for effective action. It is to be noted that the system requires a high degree of centralization: the research groups are an expression of the strength of the party's central authority, and the latter is obliged to take action to ensure the promotion of their members. This corroborates our earlier observations.

In brief the two fundamental obstacles to the infusion of new blood into the inner circle are the opposition of the lower ranks (that is, of the majority of the members of the inner circle), and the tendency to conservatism of the mass of active members. The result is that promotion of the elite is possible only in parties with a considerable degree of centralization, in which the leaders can 'impose' the young upon the party, or else in very weakly organized parties in which the lower ranks are not numerous and in which free competition makes it possible, in some exceptional circumstances, to 'collect the plums'. The distribution by age of deputies in the French National Assembly supports this conclusion: the highest percentages of young members (under thirty-six years of age) are found in the Communist party (33%) and the M.R.P. (24·5%), which are very centralized; next come the Radical party and the *Union Démocratique* (14%) and the Right (12%) which are weakly organized; at the bottom comes the Socialist party (8%), in which strong organization coincides with a high degree of decentralization and a highly democratic system for the appointment of leaders (Fig. 22).

III. THE AUTHORITY OF THE LEADERS

In this respect two essential facts seem to have dominated the evolution of political parties since the beginning of the century: the increase in the authority of the leaders and the tendency towards personal forms of authority. Increase in power, personalization of power; both phenomena can be seen today in many human groups, and not only in parties. This is not what Durkheim had hoped, for he saw in the weakening of power and in its progressive 'institutionalization' the fundamental characteristics of democratic evolution. In reality this evolution seems, on the contrary, to constitute the principal factor in the growth and personalization of authority; for these correspond to the rise to power of the masses, that is to say to the application of democratic principles.

* * *

The Growth of Power. As early as 1910 Roberto Michels noted an increase in the obedience of party members when he analysed the structure of Socialist parties and especially of German Social Democracy. What would he say if he could see modern-type parties, Communist or Fascist? He would observe not only that the obedience of the masses has become stricter and more precise, but that its nature has changed, that automatic docility has given way to psychological docility and that indoctrination has become one of the fundamental bases of discipline.

On the whole the advent of authoritarian parties coincides with the advent of mass parties. Certainly this coincidence is not absolute. In the period of caucus parties authoritarian phenomena had already made their appearance. The discipline imposed on British Members of Parliament by the Whips is a good example of this, as are the quasi-dictatorial tendencies of certain American bosses. The Birmingham caucus had tried to perfect the system by insisting on strict discipline from both elected and electors.

The celebrated slogan 'Vote as you are told' prefigures our epoch and the fixed lists of P.R. But these cases remained exceptional and this discipline tolerated divergencies. In reality Members did not always vote alike in the British Parliament, despite the Whips. The dictatorship of the bosses was exercised over the narrow circle of caucus members who were trying to obtain advantages and situations and accepted this discipline as a condition of efficiency. At Birmingham the electors did not always vote as they were told, and the elected kicked against the authority of the caucus. Elsewhere parties took the form of groups of personalities very independent of each other. Uniformity of voting played almost no part: local caucuses remained very independent of the centre; caucus members were too few in number and too influential individually for there to be any question of subjecting them to strict discipline. This corresponded not only to the organic structure of the parties but to their social composition: they were made up of members of the aristocracy and the middle class, profoundly individualistic and generally liberal-minded, and these members found all real discipline repugnant. In short, with various degrees and shades of difference according to the party and the country, a pleasant anarchy reigned everywhere.

The creation of Socialist parties profoundly modified this system. First of all for a mechanical reason: from now on large masses of people had to be organized, and discipline alone made that possible.

It might be said that intensity of power is necessarily proportional to the number of those who are subject to it. In a small group of fifteen people anarchy may be pleasant; in an assembly of ten thousand it becomes dangerous disorder. When a party is composed of a few hundred members the problem of power does not arise; when there are a million members this problem becomes vital. But the mechanical factor was reinforced by a social factor: instead of uniting individualistic 'bourgeois', the Socialist parties were formed essentially for the working-class masses, who by their very nature are given to communal institutions and discipline. It has already been pointed out that for the tradesman, the industrialist, the artisan, the lawyer, the doctor, and the civil servant freedom is a personal conquest, an affirmation of individuality. He makes his own place in the sun by seeking his clients in the face of competition; by acquiring his diplomas through personal effort, by struggling against his rivals for success in competitive examinations. For him originality is a strength, the refusal to conform to established ideas an element of success: a great middle-class success awaits those who invent something: a slogan, an idea, a product, a remedy, a method of procedure. The American atmosphere is typical of this mentality: that is why American workers have no class-consciousness and why their way of thinking remains essentially middle-class.

For the European working classes, on the other hand, freedom was a collective conquest. Apart from some individual charity and some kind words—of the type: 'Get rich'—no serious social reform took place until the proletariat discovered the weapon of its liberation: common action. It is always being said that it opposed 'the strength of numbers to the power of money'. That is not exact. By themselves numbers were of no avail: the thousands of people who came to beg the Czar to help them to a better life, on 9 January 1905, and who were shot down by a few hundred Cossacks, were quite powerless. The masses have been liberated not by numbers but by discipline: the success of Lenin and his disciples comes from their having understood this truth and always given priority to party organization. The masses know it: they have seen with their eyes and touched with their hands the successes engendered by their common disciplined action and the failures resulting from their dispersal. When strikes were sporadic and unorganized the strikers did not obtain much; when discipline was introduced into the launching and conduct of strikes the Trade

Unions were often victorious. When working-class votes were divided between Liberal and Radical candidates the proletariat could not influence parliaments: when they were able to form a block in favour of the Socialist parties the masses gained a political influence which brought about the passing of reformist legislation. For the masses the classic contrast between freedom and discipline which appeals to the middle classes has no meaning: they won freedom by discipline, not only technically, because of their size, but sociologically because of the mental attitude of their members; the parties of the masses had a natural tendency to be disciplined parties.

This tendency was strengthened by the leaders, who systematically acted so as to obtain from members obedience as complete as possible. They had two motives for this. First of all the taste of power: he who possesses a little power always tries to increase it. This natural 'authoritarianism' seems moreover to be particularly strong in the case of the working-class leaders. A leader who has risen from the people is generally more authoritarian than one of aristocratic or middle-class origin. The latter thinks himself superior to those he commands by reason either of birth, education, or fortune; the former knows he is their equal: his position of authority is all that distinguishes him from them. For the patrician leader power results from his natural superiority; for the plebeian leader the superiority is the result of his power. The former may retain a certain indifference to discipline: he may accept discussion and opposition without really fearing that he may be reduced to the level of the masses; the latter needs their obedience so that he may feel above them. The authoritarianism of plebeian leaders arises from a kind of inferiority, or rather equality, complex. To this must be added the different mentality of the two classes: Alain makes the subtle observation that the bourgeois lives in the realm of words in which the problem is to convince and to persuade (the tradesman persuades his customer, the lawyer the court, the teacher the class) whereas the workman lives in the realm of things which are resistant to rhetoric, and only yield to force.

A second motive drives the leaders into the path of authoritarianism: efficiency. Discipline is not the principal force of armies alone but of parties as well. At the parliamentary level the homogeneity of groups, which voted as a block according to the directions of the party leaders, was a considerable advantage over the individual dispersion which was the rule for so long. At the level of 'agitation and propaganda', and of that extra-parliamentary action which characterizes the new parties, discipline showed itself to be even more powerful. A party which has an organized mass of members, capable of following blindly the orders of their leaders in the most varied fields, of launching a strike because they say so, of stopping it because that is their order; of organizing on orders from the centre campaigns and demonstrations in support of their claims, and of ending them just as automatically when the orders are countermanded; of starting, if necessary, sabotage, disorders, and riots because its leaders wish it, and of returning to legality at the appointed time—this party constitutes through its power a formidable weapon: even in opposition, even in a minority it can weigh heavily enough on the life of a regime to destroy it or transform it radically. Without discipline what would the Communist party be in France? Without discipline what would the National Socialist party have done in Germany or the Fascists in Italy?

In Socialist parties, nevertheless, a sincere desire to act democratically has to a certain extent offset this increase in the authority of the leaders. In spite of its general decline electoral procedure has retained a greater influence amongst them than anywhere else: nowhere are its rules more detailed and precise, and nowhere do they afford more safeguards: with the result that nowhere do members retain in theory so developed a power of control and repeal. In certain Socialist parties, the proportional representation of 'wings' within the Executive Commitees ensures a constant watch on the group in power by minority elements: in others the right of members to participate directly in the government of the party is recognized in an internal referendum. The system functioned in Italy before 1914 and it made it possible to consult members on points not decided by the Congress: in 1906 the problem of Freemasonry was dealt with in this way. In the Swedish Social Democratic party the present constitution recognizes the right of the referendum to modify or suppress a decision of the Congress, and not only to intervene in a matter on which it has not come to a decision: recourse to the referendum is decided by the party Executive; but the latter is obliged to have recourse to it if 5% of the members ask for it. In the Swiss Socialist party the decisions of the Congress must be subjected to a general vote of the members if two-fifths of the delegates or a quarter of the branches (representing at least a tenth of the members) demand it: in 1919 affiliation to the Third International was rejected in this way. But these limitations on the authority of the leaders remain more formal than real: in practice the referendum is not much used,[1] proportional representation has been slightly extended (in France itself proportional representation on the Executive Committee of the French Socialist party was suppressed in 1945: but in fact it is still partially operative); the election is restricted in the way that has been described. This effort of the leaders to diminish the importance of the procedures which limit their freedom and their prerogatives constitutes in fact the first form of the tendency to strengthen the authority of the leaders. The second consists in the development of the techniques that make it possible to obtain the obedience of the troops: coercion and persuasion.

A disciplinary repression has been progressively established in parties which, in principle if not in content, is analagous with the classic disciplinary repressions. Jurisdictions and courts of appeal have been set up, more or less perfect according to the organization of the party and the importance of obedience to it. As early as the beginning of the century Socialist parties had provided for 'discipline committees' which moreover they distinguished from 'committees for the settlement of disputes': the former judged individual acts of indiscipline on the part of the members; the latter collective differences between two party bodies (between a branch and its federation, between two branches or two federations, between the federation and the centre). Jurists may find here the beginning of an interesting distinction and the indication of a considerable development of the juridical function. In Communist and Fascist parties it is even more perfect. Within the National Socialist party, for example, the juridical spirit of the Germans and their liking for corporative tribunals, where a man is judged by his equals, had given rise to a very developed organization. At the same time a coherent system of sanctions was established, some purely moral (censure), others material: loss of status (for the leaders), suspension, prohibition from holding any office in the party, finally expulsion, the most severe of all. In countries where there is a single party, which is in power, expulsion is moreover a very serious punishment, reaching beyond the party community and entailing consequences affecting the whole social and professional life of the person expelled: he risks losing his job, he becomes a political suspect, he suffers a kind of civic *capitis diminutio*. Even under a

[1] In the Swiss Socialist party it has not been used since 1921, if we are to believe F. Lachenal, *Le parti politique*, Bale, 1944, p. 79, note 140.

multi-party regime Communist or Fascist parties take expulsion very seriously, as has been seen: in addition to the moral suffering caused by rejection from a totalitarian community, the outcast is still pursued by the watchful hatred of his former co-religionists, who bring pressure and social weapons to bear upon him and do not always shrink from 'settling accounts' if the opportunity offers. It is not only the mechanism of jurisdiction, the pronouncement of sanctions and their application, that is worth studying: the number of sanctions pronounced is equally revealing. The disciplinary system has aged in certain parties (for example Socialist parties), in which the number of expulsions pronounced is very small or non-existent. On the other hand in Communist parties it functions with a great deal of efficiency. It tends however to assume a cyclical rhythm: at certain periods the party proceeds to a more or less general control of the discipline of its members and pronounces a rather large number of expulsions. This is the system of 'purges' and 'cleansings' which seems very efficient in remedying the natural loss of energy that is to be observed in all social groups, and in maintaining the cohesion and rigidity of the party.

The development of obedience implies moreover the homogeneity of the party, the absence of 'fractions' and wings. In practice the disciplinary institutions and the system of purges serve to preserve the orthodoxy of the party and to maintain strict unity among its members. Nevertheless the development of fractions is not a sign of the liberty of members and of a weakening in the authority of the leaders: rather does it point to differences of opinion between members of the ruling class. Each fraction is itself authoritarian in structure: it is composed of a few leaders and the party members whom they have gathered around them and whom they generally submit to a discipline similar to that which exists within the party itself. Splitting does not take place at the level of the masses but at the level of the leaders: generally it is the result of an attempt by subordinate leaders to oust leaders of higher rank, or of certain higher-ranking officials to obtain the majority in collective executive bodies. By their very nature these fractions are not opposition coming from the base but opposition coming from the apex. Their existence entails a natural weakening of the authority of the leaders because of the division it introduces among them: in short, their effect can be compared with that of the separation of powers in the State, which sets limits to each one through the others and weakens the power of the whole.

Persuasion, even more than sanctions, has aided the development of obedience. In all parties calls to discipline and unity have multiplied. In some obedience has become the very foundation of the party community, the source of the solidarity which unites its members. Instead of the definition of a party being a 'group of citizens united in acceptance of one doctrine' it becomes 'a group of citizens united in acceptance of one discipline'. The French Communist party expressly declares that it 'opens its ranks to all those who, even if they do not share its philosophical ideas, respect party discipline, and do not develop within the party philosophical ideas other than those of the party'.[1] Consequently, in theory, a non-Marxist may enter the Communist party on condition that he does not criticize Marxism within the party (but he remains free to criticize it outside), provided he accepts the party discipline. In practice members of this kind form only a small minority. None the less the principle reveals the fundamental priority accorded to discipline and its strength within the party: for one must be quite sure of the cohesion of an organization before admitting elements heterogeneous from the doctrinal point of view. Here again parties can be seen to approximate to the sociological type of the army, in which the power of the organization and the strength of the discipline are capable of establishing cohesion between elements very different from each other, and of imposing unity on this basic diversity.

This priority given to obedience naturally entails an ideological decline: it is not immediately noticeable in Communist parties compared with the others because they have a very developed doctrinal and philosophical foundation. Nevertheless if the present state of Communist parties is compared with their position between 1925 and 1930 the doctrinal impoverishment is striking. Marxism has been reduced to a few rigid elementary principles, to a simplified catechism, to a collection of practical policies whose essential objective is to motivate obedience to the organization. It is true that such a simplification is necessary in order to penetrate the masses: the strength of Marxism lies precisely in the fact that it can be brought 'within the reach of every intelligence', like the catechism of our childhood. But the doctrinal impoverishment has reached the summit: the intellectual life of the leaders is remarkably restricted, no real theoretical and doctrinal activity can be observed

[1] Quoted by F. Goguel, *Encyclopédie politique de la France et du monde,* 2nd ed., Paris, 1950, p. vol. 286.

among them. It is a striking fact that of all the political reviews published or inspired by the Communist party in France, the *Cahiers du Communisme*, devoted to organization and discipline, is the only interesting one.

This intellectual poverty is even more marked in Fascist parties, which explicitly profess to despise doctrines or to give them second place. 'Fascism is first of all action', said Mussolini. It is essentially organized, that is to say disciplined, action. The appeal to members of every philosophical complexion is stronger in Fascist parties than in Communist parties; the necessity of not developing within the party philosophical ideas other than those of the party has no longer the same strength, since the party usually affirms that it has no philosophical ideas. Discipline is really the essential foundation of the community. However, it becomes a doctrine itself, or rather a myth: the basis of Fascism is a desire for order, conceived in the direct visible form of military order. The finest passage in the Nazi propaganda film *Hitlerjugend* showed a German boy who was taking part in a picturesque, anarchical, and disorderly outing for young Communists being attracted by the neighbouring group of Hitler youth, encamped a few hundred yards away in the forest, in admirably straight ranks, singing hymns in an impeccable chorus: here discipline springs from the depths of one's being: it becomes an aesthetic system and a religion: it is a myth and a faith.

But this desired obedience, willingly accepted, is still felt to be obedience. Ultimate perfection is achieved and the authority of the leaders finds its most certain foundation when obedience becomes automatic: this anaesthesia of discipline supposes a very developed technique of contact with the masses. By a series of perpetual actions and reactions, closely intermingled, the centre knows in detail the positions and influences at the base and at the same time modifies its tactics accordingly. One cannot really say either that the centre follows the base or that the base follows the centre. Party leadership listens to the masses and speaks to them at the same time, its speech being modelled perpetually on what it hears. Thus it proceeds by light touches, by infinitely supple pressure: but the less its influence gives offence to those who are subjected to it, and the better it corresponds to their thought, the more profound and lasting it is. Without being aware of it the mass is thus slowly orientated, directed, and transformed. Its attitude derives less and less from itself, from its own spontaneity, but from the initiative of the leaders: it still thinks it has freedom of choice, whereas it is more and more obedient. It can no longer distinguish between what is its own and what is whispered to it. Progressively there is more and more whispering but the mass is less and less conscious of it.

Admittedly it is a theoretical pattern that is being described: in practice things are less perfect: the leaders have not always the extreme wisdom and skill necessary. Such is nevertheless the general import of the system: 'listening-in to the masses', this formula is a good description of the general line of Communist parties, if one adds that the masses repeat more and more what is said to them, so that the leaders progressively tend to hear no longer anything but the echo of their own voices. It is made possible by the admirable articulation of the party and the nature of its doctrine, which is remarkably well adapted to the times and to its massive structure: but the influence of doctrine is undoubtedly less important than the influence of articulation. It is less the content of the doctrine than the technique of indoctrination which brings about this veritable image of a 'freely accepted discipline'.

Personalization of Power. The form of authority becomes modified within parties: a double evolution can be seen. The first phase is one of a slow change from personal government to institutional government. In the second phase a certain reversal of the process can be seen. Authority has taken on a personal character again, while retaining the framework of the institutions. This evolution is moreover not confined to political parties: it is met with in other communities and first of all in the State.

The development of Socialist parties at the end of the nineteenth century and later imitation of their methods by others, notably the Christian Democratic parties, had as a consequence the perfecting of the governing institutions. Formerly they were often very sketchy. Locally authority belonged to the party representative in parliament, to a boss or to some influential notability who either occupied the official function of a President or who remained in obscurity. Nationally there were indeed official committees and offices, but effective government was ensured by recognized leaders. It was men who were obeyed: Disraeli, Gladstone, Gambetta. Official institutions remained either factitious or supple; factitious when they remained ornamental in character, their members exercising no effective authority; supple when they allowed free play to personal influences. On the contrary Socialist parties made a great effort to establish an organized, institutionalized leadership in which the office was more important than the person who held it. Two principles seem to have guided them here. On the one hand they gave authority a pyramidal character, so as to avoid concentrating the power in a few hands. Hence the usual differentiation between three superimposed organizations (with various names according to the country): the Central Office, a permanent organization consisting of very few members; the Committee, larger and semi-permanent, in which a few representatives from the federations are added to the Central Office ('General Council', 'National Council', etc.); finally the annual Congress, formed by delegates from the whole party. In principle the Congress has the power of decision; the National Committee may act in the interval between Congresses, within the limits set by them; the Central Office is only an executive body. In practice the Central Office plays a fundamental role. On the other hand, Socialist parties have established a kind of horizontal separation of powers, placing beside the administrative Committee and the Central Office, which are entrusted with political management and administration, a 'Control Committee', invested with a power of financial supervision: the creation of this body is a sign both of the desire to remove all temptation from the leaders and of the distrust the militant party members have of them. The establishment of party tribunals, of discipline committees, and disputes committees completes this separation of powers at the jurisdictional level.

There seemed therefore to be a very high degree of institutionalization, but in reality it was otherwise. To begin with this perfected organization was not set up without some difficulty. Some of the creators of Socialism were very authoritarian, very imbued with their personal power, and not much inclined to dilute it in institutional forms. The influence of Karl Marx was in actual fact preponderant in the First International. The creator of the first German Socialist party, Lassalle, had given it a definitely dictatorial structure in which his authority was predominant. Once the institutional organizations were set up the personal influence of one leader or another was always great: Stauning, Branting, Jules Guesde, Jaurès, Vandervelde, Léon Blum—the roles that these men played in their respective Socialist parties clearly exceeded their official functions. In fact, behind the institutional façade power tended to become just as personal in character in Socialist parties as in the earlier middle-class parties. The explanation lies in the massive structure of these parties: it is true, as M. Maurice Thorez has said, that 'the working class is not prone to the affliction that is particularly rife among the lower middle class: lack of recognition of the role of individuals'.[1] Their natural realism perceives the man behind the function, obeys the individual and not his title, and trusts in personal qualities rather than in ranks and uniforms. Belief in institutions is dependent on a certain abstract juridical culture and a respect for form and titles which belong to the middle class.

But it was precisely against this tendency towards the personalization of power that Socialist parties tried to struggle. In their structure they sought to limit it as far as possible. Here the collective character of all the executive bodies reinforced the division of responsibilities already described: in principle there were no 'leaders' or 'presidents', but only committees, officers, and secretaries entrusted with the responsibility of putting their decisions into practice. The first Communist parties acted in the same way. At that time the cult of the leader did not exist in Russia. The prestige of Lenin was immense, but Lenin himself tried to hold it within bounds and avoid the development of personal power. Proceedings in the Russian Communist party did actually remain collective; discussion in committees was real, decisions were indeed taken in common. It must not be forgotten that the sense of equality was so profoundly developed in the early days of Bolshevism that in the first place it was decided that all officials should receive the same salary, the People's Commissars being on the same footing as the others. Foreign Communist parties showed the same characteristics; there, too, an attempt was made to check the inclination of the masses towards personal power. The desire of the Comintern to banish the great figures of Socialism and to place reliable men in the posts of command was very effective in this respect: the parties found no leaders of first rank, no brilliant personalities like those who had worked in the early Socialist parties.

The tendency was reversed by the Fascist parties: they were the first to develop the cult of the leader, considered as a person and not as the holder of an office. They were the first to utilize the natural aspiration of the masses towards personal power, instead of keeping it in check, in order to strengthen the cohesion of the party and establish its framework. For them all authority comes from the leader and not from election; and the authority of the

[1] Quoted by *Le Monde*, 23 December 1949.

leader comes from his person, from his individual qualities, from his own infallibility, from his being a man of destiny. 'Mussolini is always right', the Fascists used to say. The Germans went further and invented a completely new juridical theory, that of the *Führung*, to explain and justify the sovereignty of Adolf Hitler. In the end Communist parties followed this example, and, for various reasons, reversed their previous policy. The transformation of the Russian Communist party and the evolution of power in the U.S.S.R. no doubt played an important part here, as each national party modelled its organization quite closely on that of the big brother. The growth of the cult of Stalin in Russia is a partial explanation of the development of tendencies towards the personalization of power in France, in Germany, in Italy, and in all the Communist parties in the world: it was on the occasion of Marshal Stalin's seventy-first birthday that M. Maurice Thorez sketched the analysis of the role of leaders in Marxism and in working-class mentality which was alluded to above.

The influence of the Resistance and of party martyrs should also be pointed out. After the Liberation the party based its propaganda to a large degree on the memory of those who had been lost by developing a real hagiography around them. The cult of dead heroes leads quite naturally to the cult of living heroes. Finally reasons of efficiency no doubt played a great part in this evolution, the successes of Fascist propaganda having made the Communists realize what sympathetic vibrations are aroused in the masses by the leader mystique: with its habitual realism the party deduced the lesson from the facts. At all events, since the Liberation the Communists have been systematically developing the personal loyalty of members to leaders. This they do not do in the same way as Fascist parties, at least for national leaders (apart from Stalin). They do not consider them as supermen: on the contrary they try to relate them carefully to their background, to give them an important place in daily life, by presenting them as nothing but models of all the virtues (the general tone of the biographies of Communist leaders recalls that of the edifying stories of the 'good little boy' at whom Mark Twain poked fun). This personalization of power can go very far. On the occasion of the fiftieth birthday of M. Maurice Thorez the party circulated special membership forms drawn up in the form of a letter: 'Dear Maurice Thorez, I wish you long life and good health, and on the occasion of your fiftieth birthday I am joining the French Communist party, etc.'

At the top the form bore the words: 'I hereby join the party of Maurice Thorez'—and not 'to the Communist party' (Fig. 23).

J'adhère au Parti de Maurice THOREZ

- LE PARTI des Travailleurs, de la Classe ouvrière, de la Nation Française.
- LE PARTI qui n'a jamais eu un de ses élus souillé par la moindre éclaboussure.
- LE PARTI de tous les honnêtes gens qui se refusent à faire la guerre aux héros de Stalingrad et qui exigent la fin immédiate de la guerre colonialiste du Viet-Nam.
- LE PARTI qui donnera à la France, dans la Paix, le Pain, le Bonheur et la Liberté.

Cher Maurice Thorez,

Je vous souhaite longue vie et bonne santé, et, à l'occasion de votre cinquantième anniversaire, j'adhère au Parti Communiste Français dans la promotion de la Paix.

Je m'appelle ....

J'ai .... *ans et exerce la profession de* ....

à l'entreprise ....

J'habite ....

à ....

Adresser ce bulletin au siège du Comité Central à Maurice THOREZ, 44, rue Le Peletier, Paris (9e).

I hereby join the Party of Maurice THOREZ

- THE PARTY of the Toilers, of the Working Class, of the French Nation.
- THE PARTY which has never had a single leader besmirched by scandal.
- THE PARTY of all decent folk who refuse to fight the heroes of Stalingrad and demand an immediate end to the Imperialist war in Viet-Nam.
- THE PARTY which will give France, Food, Happiness and Liberty, in Peace.

Dear Maurice Thorez,

I wish you long life and good health, and on your fiftieth birthday I am joining the ranks of the French Communist party and of Peace.

My name is ....

I am .... *old and I work as* ....

in ....

I live at ....

Send this form to Maurice Thorez at the office of the Central Committee, 44, rue le Peletier, Paris (9e).

Fig. 23. French Communist Party Membership Form.

The personalization of power is sometimes accompanied by a real deification of power. This is a revival of a very ancient form of authority, that of the Divine King. This is the case in Fascist parties and in Communist parties as far as Stalin is concerned.[1] The leader is omniscient, omnipotent, infallible, and infinitely good and wise: every word that falls from his mouth is true; every wish emanating from him is party law. Modern techniques of propaganda make it possible to invest him with extraordinary ubiquity: his voice pentrates everywhere, thanks to the radio; his picture is in every public building, on every wall, and in the house of every active member. Sometimes this real presence is accompanied by invisibility of the person: everywhere in Russia the effigy of Stalin was to be seen, but Stalin rarely appeared in public. The extreme case would be the dictator, child of a novelist's imagination, the 'Big Brother' of George Orwell, whose voice and haunting image accompany each man at each instant of his life: but Big Brother is nothing but an image and a voice; Big Brother does not exist. In the end deified personal power becomes depersonalized: the leader becomes no more than an effigy, a name, a myth, behind which others give the orders. In a way the leader becomes in his turn an institution.

IV. PARTY LEADERS AND PARLIAMENTARY REPRESENTATIVES

The distinction between parliamentary representatives and party leaders corresponds to that between electors and members of the party: the members of parliament (and, to generalize, the 'elected representatives', national and local) represent the electorate, the leaders are the heads of the party community. The problem of their reciprocal relations is of great importance: democracy requires that parliamentary representatives should take precedence over party leaders and the members of the electorate over the members of the party, since the electors constitute a larger group than party members, who are moreover included in it. In practice the opposite often takes place: in many parties there can be seen a tendency of party leaders to give orders to the parliamentary representatives in the name of the militant members. This domination of the party over its elected representatives constitutes a form of oligarchy that might

[1] Since the death of Stalin, there has been in the U.S.S.R. a marked reaction against the personalization of power and a return to the principle of 'collective leadership' laid down by Lenin. Certain Communist parties, however, notably the French, are resisting this tendency.

be termed 'external' by comparison with the oligarchic nature of leaders within the community of party members.

This tendency is neither general nor absolute: moreover there is frequent interpenetration between party leaders and parliamentary representatives. In practice the principal leaders hold both elective mandates from the country and leading positions in the party. The separation of the two functions has only taken place slowly and the domination of the party has been established only by successive stages. Thus three phases in the evolution of parties may be distinguished: the domination of parliamentary representatives over the party; a state of relative equilibrium between parliamentary representatives and party leaders, finally the domination of the party over parliamentary representatives. They each correspond to a certain type of party.

Nevertheless general factors seem capable of strengthening or weakening the tendency implied by the internal structure of the party. Thus proportional representation with fixed lists and the ranking of candidates in strict order naturally makes parliamentary representatives dependent on the leaders within the party who prepare the lists and determine the order of the names. Yet the system of cross-voting attenuates this tendency, as does the simple-majority system. By contrast, the system of voting for a single candidate makes the elected representatives very independent, except under a two-party regime where the obligation to stand for election under the colours of one or other of the rivals, which is almost like a system of monopoly, brings the candidate once more under the domination of the party electoral committees.

Domination of Parliamentary Represenatives over the Party. The French Radical Socialist party provides a good example of the methods employed to ensure the preponderance of parliamentary representatives in the party. Before the 1955 reform the Executive Committee included, as *ex officio* members, all senators, deputies, departmental and town councillors of towns of more than 50,000: relative to them it may be estimated that the elected delegates from the federation, together with their presidents and general secretaries, totalled about one third of their number. The national and local elected representatives belonging to the party had therefore absolute preponderance in the committee; among them the members of parliament retained a dominant influence: morally, first of all, by the prestige which surrounded them, but numerically too, because of the rules for a quorum, since the presence of only 150 members of the committee was required for its deliberations to be valid (in 1936 there were 1,800 members); among those present the proportion of parliamentary representatives was naturally very large. Moreover delegates from the provinces were not summoned to all meetings. It should be added that the parliamentary group was very independent of the Executive Committee. No precise ruling existed with regard to general policy, nor even with regard to participation in a government. When particular congresses brought about the resignation of Radical ministers (in 1928, when they participated in the Poincaré government and in 1934, when they participated in the Doumergue government) it was not done because of pressure from militant members at the base, who had risen against the parliamentary representatives, but under the influence of one parliamentary coterie arrayed against another, and with the approval of most of the Radical ministers, for whom the decision of Congress served as a pretext and an excuse. After the First World War an attempt was made to give to active party members a certain power over the behaviour of the party at times of ministerial crisis: on the proposal of the president of the Radical caucus of Cadillac in the Gironde it was decided that the problem of the participation of the Radical members of parliament in the new cabinet would be examined by a committee (called the 'Cadillac committee'), composed both of the parliamentary groups and of those members of the Executive committee who happened to be in Paris. But members of parliament were almost always in a majority on this committee, in which their word was law.

This domination of parliamentary representatives over the party gives it a very decentralized structure. Each deputy being very independent of his colleagues controls the local caucuses as he pleases. The central leadership is rather like a feudal king without either power over his vassals or prestige in their eyes. It is only through his personality that the party leader can command a certain authority, and this remains precarious. The parliamentary group has no will of its own, no common action, no discipline in its voting. When it comes to an important ballot it is exceptional to see the Radical deputies adopt the same attitude: generally the group divides into three, some voting 'for', others 'against', and the rest abstaining. Sometimes the very idea of a 'parliamentary group' is unknown. In many countries on the continent of Europe the idea of a group dates from the introduction of proportional representation: formerly deputies were classified in a purely unofficial way according to their leanings. Within the French Radical party, up to 1911, the situation was even more curious: the deputies met in the Chamber in *two* groups, often rivals: the 'Radical Left' and the 'Radical Socialist Left'. A certain number of them had moreover joined the Democratic Alliance (a Centre party), at the same time as they joined the Radical party. As from 1st January 1911, the Executive Committee decided to form a single group in the Chamber, with the name 'Radical Republican and Radical Socialist party group'. But the Radicals in the Senate continued to give their group the name of 'Radical Left', and their policy was often different from that of the Radicals in the Chamber. Thus parliamentary domination coincided with a weak structure and a large measure of decentralization.

This coincidence may be considered to be a general rule. Parliamentary domination is characteristic of a certain phase of party evolution and a certain social structure. It applies especially to parties of the old type, founded on caucuses, which are at the same time parties of the 'middle-class' type, that is to say conservative and centre parties. Participation in elections and in the working of parliament constitutes the very aim of their existence, their sole justification, their only form of activity. All their effort is concentrated on ensuring the election of as many deputies as possible and on participating in the government or in the opposition through the intermediary of these deputies. It is therefore natural that the deputies should occupy positions of power in the party. Besides, there is nobody to challenge them, except defeated candidates or rivals for the candidature, that is to say possible parliamentary representatives. No party hierarchy can be established outside the electoral and parliamentary domain; for it would have no foundation. Militant members are too few in these cadre parties to serve as a base; they are too dependent on the elected representatives who dispense favours and advantages; they are too filled with respect for parliamentary and ministerial offices. Moreover party administration is too weak and too elementary to give rise to a class of bureaucrats. Finally, in these middle-class parties, going into parliament does not involve for the elected representative that change of class in relation to the militants that takes place in Socialist parties where it tends to create hostility between the 'proletarian' base and the deputies 'turned bourgeois'. The power of money alone can counterbalance the power of the parliamentary representative.

But, as we have seen, financial backers rarely exercise any permanent action upon the party's leaders. Describing the English Conservative party at the end of the nineteenth century, Ostrogorski made the very just observation that they left this task to the 'small men'. They generally intervene on particular occasions with specific aims in view. They can thus secure that the leaders of the party turn its energies in some particular direction: but they do not replace them by any true rival hierarchy; they do not themselves lead the party. They cannot be considered as true rivals to the parliamentary representatives.

Certainly these general rules admit of exceptions. We sometimes encounter very definite tendencies towards parliamentary domination in parties based on the branch, well-organized and highly centralized: the M.R.P. provides a good example. Its militants are sufficiently numerous to allow of the establishment, distinct from the parliamentary representatives, of an internal hierarchy which might equally be based upon other forces such as the Christian Trade Unions, or upon the 'specialized teams' of the party: in fact such a hierarchy exists. But the M.R.P. has taken great pains in its constitution to prevent this hierarchy from playing the fundamental part in the control of the party: every precaution is taken to guarantee the preponderance of the elected representatives. In the National Committee the delegates of the parliamentary groups officially occupy one-third of the seats (Article 32 of the constitution) but their real weight is much greater. In fact, we find alongside the official representatives of the groups from the National Assembly and the Council of the Republic: (1) the President and the General Secretary of the M.R.P. (who may be senators and deputies, and in fact generally are); (2) the Presidents of the two Chambers of Parliament, when these are members of the M.R.P.; (3) the ministers in office and those who were ministers at the date of the last Congress; (4) two ordinary members of parliament; (5) co-opted militant members (who may be senators or deputies); (6) members elected by the group in the Assembly of the French Union 'in such numbers relative to its strength, as to give this group representation proportional to that of the two others'. Being nominated to the Assembly by parliament or by local bodies the latter have the mentality of parliamentarians: grouped with them, the parliamentary representatives enjoy a majority in the Committee; the representatives of the local federations are in a minority. Furthermore, though deputies and senators may not be selected as titular delegates by the federations, they may be chosen to deputize for delegates: their presence in Paris makes this arrangement very advantageous.

In the Executive Committee, a permanent body entrusted with the management of the party, the preponderance of deputies and senators is even more marked: compared with eighteen delegates from the federations there are twelve from parliament, plus the ministers in power or five former ministers, plus the chairman and the general secretary of the party (who are, in fact, often members of parliament), plus five co-opted members (who may be members of parliament), plus two members of the group of the Assembly of the French Union. The presence of the ministers in power in the two bodies is moreover a source of additional strength to the members of parliament, because of their obvious prestige with the militants. These constitutional arrangements may be compared with the absolutely opposite ones adopted by the Belgian Christian Social party, where the position of minister is incompatible with membership of the National Committee (analogous arrangements exist in the Italian Christian Democratic party). This parliamentary and ministerial predominance causes a great loss of force in the M.R.P. and reduces it to a kind of Christian Radical Socialism. It is probably to be explained by the very great discrepancy between the advanced social doctrines professed by the militants of the party and the general conservatism of its electors. In order to retain the latter something had to be done to prevent the former from taking over the leadership of the party and swinging it very definitely towards the Left. Certainly, this contrast between the militants and the electors, between the moderation of the latter and the intransigence of the former, is met with in all parties. Nowhere else, however, does it seem to have become so marked: and nowhere is the disproportion between the two communities so great. These points may explain the exceptional influence of parliamentary representatives in the management of a party of this type.

American political parties would provide examples of a different kind of exception: viz. a decentralized party with a weak structure, based on caucuses, in which parliamentary representatives do not always play a leading role. Here, however, certain vital distinctions must be made. The organization of American parties is very difficult to study because of regional differences which are very great, and differences in time, which are also great. Parties are not organized in the same way in New York State as in the Rocky Mountains, in the North as in the South. Within the same state the organization changes within a few years, because of a change in the leading personalities. When the Congressman (senator or representative—but more especially senator) is the head of the local party machine and acts as the boss he is in effect the leader of the party, and it is right to call this Congressional domination. On the other hand if the machine is in the hands of a boss who is not a Congressman the senators and representatives are very dependent on him: the party then dominates its Congressmen. The two-party system or even the one-party system (the Democratic party in the Southern States) strengthens this domination: the nomination of the candidate by the party becomes more important than the election. The party makes and unmakes deputies, as happens with proportional representation. The system of primaries was established precisely to check this power of the caucuses over the candidates and the representatives, and to restore a certain independence to the latter. It does not seem to have achieved this everywhere, especially in the large towns and in the South. Several examples might be given of outgoing Congressmen being rejected in the primaries through the influence of the leaders of the party machine, in spite of the electors' trust in them.

The evolution of British parties in the second half of the nineteenth century makes it possible to complete these few remarks on parliamentary domination: here, contrary to the general rule, it coincides with quite definite centralization. The internal organization of the parliamentary groups no doubt provides an explanation of this fact. The Members of Parliament led the party: but the Members themselves were led by their leaders and their Whips: the discipline of Members constituted the centralization of the party. Certainly this discipline was not yet very strict; nevertheless it was far superior to that of most other parliamentary groups at the same period. Nevertheless, about 1880, the authority of Members of Parliament over the party was attacked, in the case of the Whigs as well as of the Tories, by the increasing development of organizations at the base and of internal hierarchies. The crisis declared itself first of all in the Liberal party, following the transformations in its structure brought about by the Birmingham caucus. In 1878, at Bradford, there was a violent dispute between the out-going Member of Parliament, W. F. Forster, a former Minister, who had represented the town in Parliament for eighteen years, and the local party caucus, concerning paragraph 15 of the constitution of the local caucus, which said that candidates must give the caucus an assurance that they would submit to its decisions. Forster refused. Throughout the country there arose a lively controversy over the problem of the relations between Members of Parliament and caucuses. Finally there was a compromise, quite favourable to the party. If Forster had not died during the following legislature he would not have been renominated by the party caucus at the elections.

At Newcastle, a few years later, the well-known Radical leader Cowen was beaten by the caucus. Moreover, after the Liberal victory of 1880 the Party Central Office invited local organizations to call to order recalcitrant Members of Parliament: but the Central Office itself was in effect controlled by parliamentary leaders. Finally the reorganization of the Liberal party strengthened centralization rather than diminished the influence of Members of Parliament: at the local level the authority of each Member over the caucus in his constituency was diminished; at the national level the authority of the leaders over the whole of the party was, on the contrary, strengthened. But their authority over the Members of Parliament was increased even more: the discipline of the group became stricter and more severe. On the occasion of the vote on the Marriott amendment (Marriott was a recalcitrant Liberal) the government threatened to dissolve Parliament if it were defeated and warned the Liberals who were ready to follow Marriott that their caucuses would not renominate them if they did not conform to party discipline. In the end most capitulated: only five followed Marriott (1882). After the Home Rule crisis Liberal organizations came entirely under the authority of parliamentary leaders.

The Conservative party had passed through a similar crisis after the reforms brought about by Randolph Churchill: in 1883 the Council of Union, formed by the leaders of party organizations, asked for the dissolution of the Central Committee, composed of the Whips and a few Members of Parliament, which was responsible for party funds, dealt with election nominations, and in fact controlled the party. In the end after vain negotiations the parliamentary leader, Lord Salisbury, turned the Council of Union out of the premises it occupied at the General Headquarters of the party. Finally there was a compromise: two internal leaders came into the committee alongside the Members of Parliament; they were to deal especially with general policy, candidatures, and finances. After the retirement of Randolph Churchill the parliamentary leaders once more took over the effective leadership of the party. By the end of the century parliamentary domination was re-established. But at the same period the development of Socialist parties was about to raise the question again in every country.

Rivalry between Parliamentary Representatives and Leaders. The history of British parties at the end of the nineteenth century shows that the development of party structures naturally gives rise to rivalry between the internal leaders and the parliamentary representatives. The larger the organization the stronger the rivalry and the more does the authority of parliamentary representatives decrease to the advantage of the authority of internal leaders. In the end we have Communist or Fascist parties in which parliamentary representatives have become nothing but executives, without any power over the management of the party. Socialist parties form the intermediate type (moreover many Christian Democratic parties have an approximately similar structure): officially parliamentary representatives are subordinate to the leaders; in practice they retain quite considerable prerogatives. There exists a state of tension, if not of equilibrium, between the internal leaders and the parliamentary representatives. It would not be correct to speak either of domination of the party over parliamentary representatives or of the parliamentary representatives over the party; rather is there a separation of powers between the internal leadership and the parliamentary leadership, and a permanent rivalry between them.

The reasons for this rivalry are clear enough. The nature of the party's organization plays a preponderant role here. From now on we have mass parties, constituted on the basis of branches, with a strong structure and a considerable administration. These different characteristics create the conditions for an internal hierarchy, which, with the backing of a large body of militants, a powerful bureaucracy and a fixed constitution, disputes with the parliamentary representatives the effective leadership of the party. This is made all the more possible by the fact that a natural opposition nearly always shows itself between the militants and the parliamentary representatives, for reasons both social and political, which are not always avowed, not always even clearly felt, but always deep and strong. Socially the parliamentary representatives become, from the working-class militants' point of view, members of the middle class. A working-class deputy is always more of a deputy than a member of the working class—and as time passes he becomes less and less working-class and more and more of a deputy. In a comedy by Robert de Flers one of his characters, a Socialist deputy, dictating to his secretary biographical notes for *Le petit Larousse* says, 'Put down "sprung from the people"', 'And quite determined not to return to them', adds the secretary in an aside. This is amusing, but also true to life. The great mass of militants is very conscious of the deputies' standard of living: Communist parties are well aware of this and rise in true demagogic fashion against any increase in the parliamentary allowance. But even more than the income figure it is the general mode of existence which separates the member of parliament and the militants. Through his surroundings, his connections, and his contacts the deputy leads a typically middle-class existence. The general atmosphere of parliament is a middle-class atmosphere. To go more deeply into the matter, the manner of parliamentary activity is truly middle-class in its nature, if we accept the statement of Alain, who sees in influence over men by persuasion something peculiar to the middle class.

It must be added that the militants are very much on their guard against the possible corruption of the elected representatives. The members of the Constituent Assembly of 1791 (and the English in the seventeenth century) feared that the King might make use of ministerial posts to win over the people's representatives through favours: consequently they forbade him to choose his ministers from the Assembly. Party members today fear lest the members of parliament should be bribed by the financial powers whom they imagine to be concealed and formidable. Hence their desire for supervision and control. Hence, also, their veiled opposition to participation in a ministry: we pass from the social and financial field to the political field, as there is a close connection between the two. The militants are afraid both of the political corruption of ministers and their financial corruption, the first fear being admitted to more than the other and being deeper at the time when Socialist parties were revolutionary. The problem of 'Socialist participation in a middle-class ministry' dominated the debates of the National Congresses and of the International before the 1914 War. It was bound up with the more general question of 'reformism' or revolutionary tactics. In 1904 the Amsterdam Congress had condemned reformism, which implied a condemnation of participation: but the latter was not explicit. In France participation was refused by the French Socialists until 1936 except for the war period and the period of 'Sacred Union'. This refusal to participate represented the feeling of the militants: the members of parliament were generally 'participationists'. Personal interest and desire for power are not the only reasons here: the deputies accepted the idea of participation because they were attracted to reformism. Placed at the very hub of the state they visualized the laws that might better the lot of the working class, and the means of drawing them up: their very duties as legislators inclined them to reformism, rather than to revolution: this is a combination of the tendency to become middle-class and the tendency towards professional deformation.

The tendency to become middle-class combines also with consciousness of the profound desires of the elector. For the conflict between militants and members of parliament conceals a wider and more serious conflict, that between militants and electors. The militants are more revolutionary than the electors, who are scarcely revolutionary at all. And the deputies are naturally more prone to follow the electors than the militants. This divorce between militants and electors was particularly marked in the French Socialist party between 1919 and 1936, when the obvious moderate reformism of the electors made a violent contrast with the purely verbal 'revolutionariness' of the militants. The tactics of 'support without participation', which consisted in making the Socialist deputies vote for middle-class governments without allowing them to form part of them, was a result of the parliamentary representatives being divided between their electors and their party. It does not seem to have really protected the party against reformism, nor to have preserved its revolutionary purity: but many other factors entered into this.

What means did the party employ in its attempt to keep its deputies dependent and to replace parliamentary domination by party domination? First of all it restricted the number of deputies in the controlling bodies. In the early days of parties these bodies were composed entirely of members of parliament. Later, when the organization had become more developed and an internal hierarchy had arisen, the members of parliament took every precaution to retain the majority over the militants' delegates. The Socialist parties tried to reverse the proportion and give the majority to the delegates. In France, according to the first constitution of the Socialist party, the parliamentary representatives were represented as a body on the National Council without being allowed to number more than a twentieth of its members; no deputy could be delegated as an individual to the National Council: none of them could be members of the permanent adminstrative committee. In 1913 it was made possible for parliamentary representatives to enter this committee provided they did not exceed in numbers a third of its total membership. Today there is no longer any *numerus clausus* for deputies in the National Council, on which they may serve as delegates of the federations; but they are still limited to a third of the controlling committee which has replaced the former administrative committee. In the Italian Unitary Socialist party the role of member of parliament is incompatible with that of member of the party management: the exception is the president of the parliamentary group, who is present in a consultative capacity. In both, however, the deputies exert a great influence: it seems that the constitutional precautions taken against members of parliament are more precise and strict in proportion as the danger of seeing them play a leading part is greater. It also seems as if these precautions were not very effective. In other parties the constitution simply forbids ministers in power to lead the party. Thus in the Belgian Socialist party the Bureau can hear the ministers only in a consultative capacity: the member of the Bureau who becomes a minister loses his right to a vote: he must be replaced during the whole time of his presence in the government. Similar arrangements exist in the Austrian Socialist party for the members of the National Council, the administrative committee, and the control committee. Their existence in certain Christian Democratic parties has already been noted.

Moreover the Socialist parties tried to subordinate the parliamentary representatives to the controlling bodies of the party either individually or collectively. The principle is that each deputy is subject to the authority of his federation: in practice this subjection often remains illusory. Here the electoral regime plays a very important part. In a single-member constituency system in which the elections have an individual character and the constituencies look rather like strongholds devoted to the man rather than to the party label, the local position of the elected representatives is very strong and the party caucuses cannot do much against them: they must continue to provide the support of the party lest they lose the seat. Individual subordination is very slight. On the other hand when there is list-voting, in which the party becomes essential, in which the support of its caucus can determine success or defeat, this subordination is much greater. When there is proportional representation with fixed lists and the presentation of candidates in a strict order the power of the caucuses reaches its zenith. A comparison of the beginnings of the Third and Fourth Republics is very instructive in this respect. But the electoral regime is far from being the only factor involved. Certain Socialist parties have sometimes used a technique later widely used by the Communists: the parliamentary representatives have been obliged to pay over the whole of their allowance to the party, which in exchange grants them a more or less modest salary. Thus deputies become salaried employees of the party, which places them in a position of dependence. In 1890 the Revolutionary Socialist working-class party, created in France under the leadership of Allemane, had adopted a system of this kind. This financial control was not to the liking of its deputies; in 1896 all the party representatives broke away from him and founded the 'Communist Alliance', in order to preserve their liberty and their allowance.

The clearest sign of the subordination of the deputy to the party remains the voting discipline: it is the rule in all important divisions. A member of parliament who does not conform to it risks expulsion. Fairly numerous examples of expulsions of this kind could be quoted, notably in the British Labour party and the French Socialist party. Voting discipline is more a consequence of the subordination of parliamentary representatives than a means of ensuring it: the deputies follow the instructions of their group because they are dependent on the party for other reasons (electoral, financial, etc.). Moreover it has a collective character. Each deputy must vote according to the decision taken by the group after discussion: but the group itself is not always free to make its own decision; it must conform to the general policy of the party as defined by its congresses and controlling bodies. Thus the parliamentary group as a body is subordinate to the party. In 1929 the French Socialist group accepted the participation in the government offered to it by President Daladier; but a National Council, specially called by the permanent administrative committee, revoked this decision, and the group had to give way. Nevertheless this subordination of the group is essentially dependent on the preciseness of the directives adopted by the National Congresses and committees. The tactics of parliamentary representatives consist in bringing pressure to bear on the National Congresses and committees so as to obtain the passing of general motions which leave the group the greatest possible margin of autonomy.

The militants often react by obliging the parliamentary representatives to confer with 'internal leaders' when there are grave decisions to be made: participation in a government, votes of confidence, attitude to be adopted towards an important reform, etc. This meeting may take place within the National or General Council when the parliamentary representatives have seats there, either as a block in a consultative capacity (General Council of the Belgian Socialist party) or through delegates with the right to vote (National Council of the French Socialist party). It may equally well take place through the presence of one or several delegates of the party Office at the meetings of the parliamentary group (Italian and Belgian Socialist parties, etc.) or even take the form of a special contact committee (National Labour Council and Liaison Committee of the Labour party, Contact Committee of the Belgian Christian Social party). The role of the Research Bureaux must also be mentioned. They are entrusted with the duty of preparing the plans for reform and drafting the bills proposed by the party deputies. If these bureaux are more dependent on party leadership than on the parliamentary group, and if the group is obliged to have recourse to them in order to draw up its texts, they exercise over it a very important influence, though one very infrequently pointed out. The system is also very much employed in parties in which the deputies are reduced to a completely subordinate position.

Theoretically all this procedure ought to ensure a very definite preponderance of internal leaders over the parliamentary representatives. In practice the parliamentary representatives employ various devices by which they make certain of a great deal of actual power, so that the result is a two-headed leadership. The first means is the prestige which the deputies enjoy as a result of their office. The militants are suspicious of the elected representatives, but they envy them: they criticize the ministers but they are pleased to rub shoulders with them at the party meetings. The reputation of parliamentary representatives is a variable factor, but it is almost always greater than that of the internal leaders among party members. Moreover the parliamentary representatives are usually more able than the internal leaders: apart from a few intellectuals and enthusiasts, the internal leaders are often rather mediocre. Being used to lobby intrigues, the deputies often manage to outmanœuvre those adversaries, who are not as well armed. But the internal leaders can take refuge in principles, intransigence, and purity—a demagogy which pleases the militants and discomfits the deputies: so that the struggle becomes equal once again. But the parliamentary representatives have the advantage locally: by a mixture of prestige and services rendered they exercise a dominant influence over the party caucuses: with their backing they can stand up to the central body. In short, everything depends on the degree of authority of the central body and on the degree of domination by the parliamentary representatives of the local organization; here the electoral regime plays an important part, as has been seen.

But the distinction between parliamentary representatives and party leaders is not so definite, and the confusion benefits the former. In the first place, parties suffer very often from a dearth of internal leaders: they can manage to find subordinate leaders but not leaders at the higher levels. Those who have the qualities required become parliamentary representatives: 'absorption' represents one of the most effective devices for avoiding subordination. Many leaders who are potential parliamentary representatives hope for it, being naturally inclined to respect the body to which they dream of belonging. It is a necessary consequence of this dearth that parliamentary representatives are entrusted with responsibilities for the leadership of the party: hence the development on a considerable scale of 'dual status', another form of absorption, more widespread than the first. Sometimes the constitution seeks to set limits to it, but they are generally wide: necessity knows no law. Thus, deputies often get themselves nominated as delegates to Congress, representatives of federations in National Committees, members of the Executive, and so on, not in their capacity as deputies but in their personal capacity. Now, in parties of this type, when one man combines in himself dual functions, experience proves that of the two roles the parliamentary takes precedence over the party leader. In this case, the duality of status is a sign of the predominance of the parliamentary representatives.

As a result of this system of checks and balances there is created permanent rivalry between the deputies and the party leaders representing the militants. The respective positions of the two groups vary with the party and the period. In general it may be said that parties allied with Trade Unions offer more successful resistance than others to the influence of the parliamentarian, no doubt because the organization of the Trade Unions makes it possible to bring into being a powerful internal hierarchy capable of rivalling the deputies and of refusing both absorption and dual status. The Australian Labour party has given us the first example of a party in which parliamentary representatives are subject to the authority of the internal leaders; in the British Labour party the subordination of Members of Parliament to the party and the Trade Unions is fairly marked, in spite of the relaxation of the formal regulations on party discipline in 1945. On the other hand Socialist parties in the Latin countries present a picture of very profound influence by the parliamentary representatives. However, the German Social Democratic party was very subject to the influence of its deputies, although it was based upon a powerful Trade Union movement; the same is true of the Belgian Socialist party. In both cases, it is true, the Trade Unionism in question was quite markedly subordinate to the party.

Furthermore the ageing of parties seems to increase the influence of the parliamentary representatives. Such an evolution can be fairly clearly seen in the history of the French Socialist party: the power of the deputy was not considerable at the outset owing to the very great distrust of the deputy by the militant. On the eve of the 1914 War, this power had already considerably increased, as is shown by the amendment of the constitution in 1913 which opened to the deputy the doors of the permanent administrative committee. It grew slowly between 1919 and 1936, in spite of the opposition of militant members to this participation. The party's accession to power increased it even more. Finally, immediately after the 1939 War, the part played by parliamentary representatives seemed more important than ever. No doubt this is partly attributable to the fact that the party has gradually become more bourgeois since the development of Communism has diminished its working-class membership. But the exercise of governmental responsibilities seems to have played the decisive role: the influence of ministers is very much greater than that of ordinary deputies. This example seems to point to a general conclusion: the very measures taken by some parties to restrict the part played by ministers in their controlling bodies bears witness to the importance of this factor.

Domination of Parliamentary Representatives by the Party. With the Communist and Fascist parties we reach the last stage of the development: the parliamentary representatives here do not control the party, the party controls the representatives. The second Congress of the Communist International reminded every party deputy in precise terms that he was not 'a legislator seeking a basis of understanding with other legislators, but a party agitator sent among the enemy to apply the party's decisions'. And facts in this case coincide with theory.

Two kinds of factor seem to explain such domination: the first relate to the structure of the party, the second are external to the party. The extra-party factors play only a secondary role. Here let us recall the effect of the electoral system: voting by list and proportional representation favour the domination of the party and, further, fit in with the collective organization of Communist and Fascist parties. We must also note the constitutional provisions which, in some countries, compel a parliamentary representative expelled from his party to present himself again to the electorate, or which, in others, give parliamentary groups, collectively, an important part to play in the functioning of parliament. The factors internal to the party are much the more important. First of all there is a whole series of technical devices which make it possible to increase the subservience of the parliamentary representatives. The old idea of making over the parliamentary salary to the party has acquired a new force in this connection. The Socialist parties had made use of it primarily for financial reasons: the representative contributed a share of his salary to the party funds as a special subscription. On the contrary in the Communist parties the procedure assumes political significance: in the first place, the intention is to make the deputy into a salaried worker of the party, as had been attempted by the Allemanists in France. But the device is more subtle still: the party pays the deputy only a modest wage but provides him with 'benefits in kind' which make it possible to exercise control over him. Communist deputies have no private secretarial help; they use the services of the party's secretariat, which is thus able to exercise strict and close supervision of their parliamentary activity down to the smallest detail. The system is most effective.

In spite of its spectacular nature the device of the blank resignation is much less important. Candidates in some parties are compelled to sign, before their election, an undated letter of resignation; the party will fill in the blanks and forward the resignation should the representative once elected ever prove insubordinate. In other cases candidates have only to give their word of honour that they will resign if they break with the party (e.g. Article 16 of the French Socialist party constitution): the use of a term like 'word of honour' clearly reveals the purely moral nature of the system. The blank resignation is no more effective. In practice it is easy for the recalcitrant deputy to denounce the system and to claim that the resignation is null and void because consent was extracted under duress: the opponents of the party, only too happy to cause it embarrassment, would no doubt refuse to recognize an extorted act of resignation. The written undertaking can only turn away independent candidates and constitute a ceremony likely to strengthen the obedience of the others. However, for achieving the same results Communist and Fascist parties have other methods that are much more trustworthy.

A more important device is the systematic uprooting of parliamentary representatives. The aim is to prevent them from turning their constituencies into personal strongholds and strengthening local ties which might make it possible for them to take an independent line towards the party. With this aim in view care is taken to choose candidates from outside the district that they will be called upon to represent: the back is unflinchingly turned upon 'localism', which is so widespread in other parties because it pays electoral dividends. The party is prepared to lose votes in order to guarantee the loyalty of its deputies: it will put up a Breton in Périgord, although it is well aware that a man from Périgord would have more chance. The system of voting by fixed lists makes it possible however to minimize the difficulty: the 'foreign' candidates are named at the head of the list and to them are added the names of authentic 'locals', as well known as possible, so that the local ties of the latter will help the former to be elected. This first step in uprooting is, however, not enough: the transplanted deputies soon begin to grow new roots in their new soil. It is therefore expedient to give them a frequent change of constituency, to organize a kind of 'general post' to avoid any acclimatization that might imperil obedience to the party. Systematic uprooting of this kind is not practised generally. The Communist parties in particular have at their disposition many other methods to prevent the elected member from becoming independent. Since they are well aware of the very considerable importance of local ties, not only from the point of view of electoral dividends but also for the general influence of the party, they do not always disdain 'localism'. Before the war it was thus possible for some Communist deputies in France, like Renaud-Jean for example, to be considered as feudal lords.

With systematic uprooting may be compared the system of the elimination of celebrities. The party generally chooses its candidates from the 'unknown, the unhonoured', the men who have no individual fame. We can leave out of account the case of its own leaders, although it substantiates the point of view, since they owe their fame to the party and not to themselves. In several countries the Communist party numbers amongst its members well-known writers, artists and scholars; it scarcely ever gives them a seat in parliament, except in the case of very long-standing members of the party whose loyalty has long since been tried. No doubt the proletarian nature of the party and its aim to give the working class as large a place as possible in its representation in parliament could be advanced as explanations for this. But the Communist party is no longer solely proletarian and the hyperbole of praise that it generally lavishes on its intelligentsia would justify finding them a place in parliament. Moreover it does on occasion give parliamentary seats to writers, but only to the most mediocre and most obscure: for the others could find support in their fame for the adoption of a relatively independent attitude and the party would be very embarrassed, no matter whether it expelled them or kept them. Celebrities are in consequence promoted to the headlines, their function is strictly confined to the realm of publicity; no post of responsibility in the party, no parliamentary seat is entrusted to them.

The technique of the study or research bureau is similarly much used by Fascist and Communist parties. No bill tabled by a deputy ever emanates directly from him; it is prepared by the party specialists and the deputy is simply given the task of defending it. In this way one whole section of parliamentary activity is directly undertaken by the party. Furthermore the party takes good care to give its deputies a very intensive training in its doctrines. Within some parties there are to be found veritable 'deputies' schools', which the deputies attend to deepen their knowledge of the party's principles and at the same time to receive instructions pertaining to their parliamentary status. We have already noted that certain stages in the national courses of the French Communist party are specially reserved for parliamentary representatives. The procedure offers the dual advantages of preparing deputies for their task and of making them clearly aware at the same time of their situation as dependants of the party.

Finally, dual status provides the last device used to guarantee discipline amongst parliamentary representatives. The weapon is two-edged; an instrument of domination by parliamentarians in middle-class and Socialist parties, dual status here becomes the instrument of domination by the party. Instead of parliamentary representatives taking up positions of leadership in the party it is the leaders of the party who take seats in parliament. This means that party solidarity is stronger than parliamentary solidarity. Then the inner circle leader can utilize the prestige conferred by the status of deputy or minister to bolster his own authority in the party: the very foundations of parliamentary power are shattered. This reversal is made possible by the general atmosphere in the party; this it is, in the last resort, which explains the obedience of deputies much more profoundly than the various technical devices, for they exert only a secondary influence. First we must emphasize the fact of party discipline and the respect for the party leaders that it systematically encourages. Inside Communist parties the Political Bureau and the Central Committee enjoy considerable prestige. Every effort is made to foster obedience to them by emphasizing their ability, their value, and their importance. On the other hand middle-class parliamentary institutions are an object of scorn and derision, with the result that the status of deputy confers no prestige. To a Communist it is quite obvious that a member of the Central Committee is much more important than a member of the parliamentary group. When a leader unites both functions in his own person it is obviously the former that he prizes, being himself trained in the party attitude and himself convinced that the Party (with a capital letter) is far superior to bourgeois Parliaments, that Party office is far more meritorious than Parliamentary office.

The general line of the party reinforces this attitude. As we have seen, electoral and parliamentary activity plays only a minor role in it. The party's parliamentary representatives are troops engaged upon the less important fronts (except during some periods when legal political action is provisionally put in the forefront on strategic grounds; but no one in the leading strata of the party has any illusions about the provisional character of such an attitude). In general parliaments are used by the party as platforms for agitation and propaganda; deputies are therefore strictly confined within the role of agitators, as the resolution of the International already quoted makes quite clear. To it we may add this directive issued in 1924 by the Political Bureau of the French Communist party: 'The elected representatives are to introduce Bills of purely publicity value, conceived not with a view to their being adopted but for purposes of propaganda and agitation.' In parliaments therefore Communist representatives are clearly distinct from the rest: they remain aloof from the general spirit of comradeship of parliamentary solidarity: they somewhat resemble foreigners encamped in a hostile country. To quote Robert de Jouvenel, 'Two deputies of different parties have more in common than a deputy and a militant member of the same party.' This is not applicable to Communist deputies: they are close to the militants, they are far removed from the other deputies. When they become ministers, there is no change in essentials: the party explains to the members that the ministers are primarily representatives of the party, who are carrying out the party's policy at the ministry, and that they must not be confused with bourgeois or Socialist ministers. This robs the post of minister of the essence of its prestige. It seems that the ordeal of ministerial responsibility in 1945–6 did not noticeably diminish the proletarianism of the leaders of the party in France: they did not 'go bourgeois'. Nor do ministers or former ministers seem to enjoy any special prestige in the party.

Domination over the parliamentary representatives by the party is the result of the general structure of the party and of its general orientation much more than of particular technical devices. In consequence Communist and Fascist parties can deliberately neglect certain of these devices. For example in the French Communist party no limit is set upon the admission of parliamentary representatives to the controlling bodies; no *numerus clausus* is established in contrast with the practice of Socialist parties. Parliamentary representatives may hold a majority in bureaux and committees: this is of no importance because they are not parliamentary representatives in the true sense, because their status as members of the party's 'inner circle' takes precedence over their status as members of parliament, because the Communist party constitutes a community powerful enough and homogeneous enough to unify all the elements of which it is composed. The struggle against parliamentary representatives seems indeed to exist only in parties that are vulnerable to action by them. The others have no need to fight an opponent who does not exist.

BOOK II

PARTY SYSTEMS

With the exception of the single-party states, several parties coexist in each country: the forms and modes of their coexistence define the 'party system' of the particular country being considered. Two series of elements enter into this definition. In the first place there are the similarities and disparities that can be discovered in the internal structures of the individual parties that make up the system: a distinction will be made between systems with centralized parties and those with decentralized parties, between systems with totalitarian parties and those with restricted parties, between the flexible party and the rigid party systems, and so on. In the second place a comparison between the various parties makes it possible to distinguish new elements in the analysis that do not exist for each party community considered in isolation: numbers, respective sizes, alliances, geographical localization, political distribution, and so on. A party system is defined by a particular relationship amongst all these characteristics. Just as different types of structure have been defined, so we must seek to define certain types of party system. The distinction drawn between the single-party, the Anglo-Saxon two-party, and the multi-party system is classic; many other distinctions are superimposed upon it and combine with it: systems with independent parties or with parties in alliance; systems with parties in balance or with a dominant party; systems with major or with minor parties; with stable or unstable parties; systems in which power moves leftwards (Leftism) or immobile systems, and so on.

Party systems are the product of many complex factors, some peculiar to individual countries, others general. Amongst the first may be cited tradition and history, social and economic structure, religious beliefs, racial composition, national rivalries, and so on. The opposition between Republicans and Democrats in the U.S.A. stems from the rivalry between Jefferson and Hamilton in the early years of the Union; the breaking-up of the Right wing in France and the existence of the Radical party are a result of the political situation between 1875 and 1900; the persistence of

Agrarian parties in Scandinavia can be traced back to the middle of the nineteenth century when the Democratic country areas were struggling against the Conservative nobility of the towns. The controversy over secular and confessional schools gave rise directly to the nineteenth-century Belgian party system, to the rivalry between Left and Right in France which still shows through more recent divisions, to the division of the Dutch Right wing into Catholic party, Anti-Revolutionary party, and Christian Historical party. In pre-1914 Austro-Hungary and in pre-1938 Czechoslovakia the party system reflected racial differences and hatreds; the same is true of the three-party system in Great Britain at the end of the nineteenth century when the Irish disturbed the traditional two-party system; so too with the contemporary divisions amongst South African parties. In Sweden and Norway the rivalry between parties was long dominated by the problem of union or separation of the two countries; in Ireland the attitude towards Great Britain played a considerable part in the first party divisions.

There are three chief factors common to all countries, socio-economic, ideological and technical. The first are mainly concerned with the influence of class structure on political parties, and there is no doubt that this influence is very great. The division of European parties in the nineteenth century into Conservative and Liberal can be described as the opposition between the landed aristocracy and the commercial, industrial and intellectual middle class; the appearance of Socialist parties at the beginning of the twentieth century coincides with the entry of the working class into political life, and so on. Nevertheless, there are exceptions: American parties do not correspond to definite classes and there is no party completely homogeneous in social composition. To a certain extent political ideologies themselves correspond to class attitudes, but the correspondence is neither general nor absolute. Ideologies are never simple epiphenomena in relation to the socio-economic structure, and some are related to class in ways that are indirect and of minor importance.

The most important technical factor is the electoral regime, to which particular attention will be paid in this book. Its influence upon certain aspects of party structure has already been studied: even in that field it constitutes an element in the party system, since the method of ballot moulds the structure of every party in the country in the same way. Its effect upon number, size, alliances and representation is important. Conversely, the party system exercises a vital influence upon the electoral regime: the two-party system favours the adoption of the simple-majority single-ballot form, the existence of parties with a Bund-like structure works against it, the natural tendency towards alliances is hostile to proportional representation, and so on. In brief, the party system and the electoral system are two realities that are indissolubly linked and even difficult sometimes to separate by analysis: the degree of accuracy in political representation, for example, depends upon the electoral system and the party system, considered as features of the same complex, rarely distinguishable from one another. The general influence of the system of balloting may be set down in the following three formulae: (1) proportional representation encourages a system of parties that are multiple, rigid, independent, and stable (except in the case of waves of popular emotion); (2) the majority system with two ballots encourages a system of parties that are multiple, flexible, dependent, and relatively stable (in all cases); (3) the simple-majority single-ballot system encourages a two-party system with alternation of power between major independent parties. But these very general propositions define only fundamental tendencies; they are far from including all the influences of the electoral system on party systems. We shall make use of them solely as a first working hypothesis. The decision to analyse in particular detail this influence of electoral regimes was due to the fact that until the first appearance of this book in 1951 it was a subject to which very little attention had been devoted. There was a great gap to be filled. This does not mean, however, that we have ever considered it to be more important than the rest. The influence of ballot systems could be compared with that of a brake or an accelerator. The multiplication of parties, which arises as a result of other factors, is facilitated by one type of electoral system and hindered by another. Ballot procedure, however, has no real driving power. The most decisive influences in this respect are aspects of the life of the nation such as ideologies and particularly the socio-economic structure.

CHAPTER I

THE NUMBER OF PARTIES

THE contrast between the multi-party and the single-party systems has become a commonplace in discussion; there is even a tendency to see in it the political criterion distinguishing the two worlds, East and West. This is an error, for the single party flourishes in Spain, in many Latin-American states, and in some parts of the territory of the U.S.A., whereas multipartism continues to exist officially in Eastern Germany and in some People's Democracies. In the salient features, however, there is in fact a real correspondence between totalitarian regime and single-party system, between democracy and multi-party system. In comparison with this antithesis the contrast between the two-party and the multi-party systems is of much less importance; it is understandable that it should long have been neglected and that it should be even less well known. However, it is undeniably a fundamental distinction.

Let us compare the system in England with that in France under the Fourth Republic. For some observers the capital difference between them lies in the form of the Executive and in the prestige accorded to the British monarch compared with the unobtrusiveness of the French President; they forget that the Head of the State never plays anything but a very minor role in a parliamentary system: the President 'presides but does not govern' just as the King 'reigns but does not govern'. Other observers are impressed by the difference in parliamentary structure, and grant the British two-chamber system all the virtues they find lacking in the French single-chamber system: they allow themselves to be deluded by appearances, not noticing that since 1911 the House of Lords has had few powers, that its influence is almost entirely moral, and that it is tending to join the ill-fated French Council of the Republic in limbo. The experts emphasize the fact that the British Cabinet enjoys at all times the right to dissolve Parliament, whereas the French government is less well-armed against the National Assembly: for them the threat of dissolution appears to be the essential means of avoiding ministerial crises. This explanation is advanced even by some Englishmen who reproach the French with having adopted the parliamentary 'motor' and having forgotten to include a 'brake'. This explanation, although closer to the truth than the other, is still very inadequate: in practice the British Cabinet never uses the power of dissolution to bring pressure to bear on Parliament in order to avoid a vote of censure or to escape its consequences, for the very good reason that such a vote is almost always impossible, since an absolute majority is in the hands of a single party. And here the fundamental difference separating the two systems clearly shows itself: the number of parties. In one case for practical purposes only two parties share the parliamentary seats: the one assumes the entire responsibility for government, the other limits itself to the free expression of criticism in opposition; a homogeneous and powerful Cabinet has at its disposition a stable and coherent majority. In the other case a coalition between several parties, differing in their programmes and their supporters, is required to set up a ministry, which remains paralysed by its internal divisions as well as by the necessity of maintaining amidst considerable difficulties the precarious alliance on which its parliamentary majority is based.

I. THE TWO-PARTY SYSTEM

It is not always easy to make the distinction between two-party and multi-party systems because there exist alongside the major parties a number of small groups. In the United States, for example, in the shadow of the two Democratic and Republican giants there are to be found a few pygmies: the Labor, Socialist, Farmer, Prohibitionist, and Progressive parties. In some state legislatures or municipal councils, one or another of these will on occasion exert a considerable influence: in Minnesota, for example, the Agrarian party, Farmer-Labor, has reduced the Democrats to the position of a third and comparatively weak party; in Wisconsin La Follette's Progressive party has often taken first or second place; in New York the Labor party got five members elected to the City Council and five to the State Legislature in 1937. Frequently they even capture a few seats in Congress, particularly in the House of Representatives and even in the Senate (cf. Fig. 32). However, the obvious disproportion between them and the major traditional parties, as well as their local and ephemeral character, makes it possible for us to consider the United States system as typically two-party.

In Great Britain the question is more complicated. Indeed a French Ministry of Information pamphlet published in 1945 declared that Great Britain (like France at that date) enjoyed a three-party system. It is a fact that the Liberal party is based upon an ancient and sound tradition; it still corresponds to the opinion of an important section of the British people. In 1950 more than 2,600,000 voters put their trust in it, but many others, far greater in numbers, whose views are closely akin, were driven away from the Liberal party by the electoral system. Between 1918 and 1935 it was not possible to speak of the British two-party system, for the British people were really divided amongst three major parties. It may seem arbitrary to talk of the British two-party system today, especially if the Belgian system be considered multi-party, since the influence of the Liberal party is scarcely any greater in Belgium than in Great Britain; the electoral system alone ensures the party a markedly higher degree of representation. Yet the dual nature of the British system is undeniable. For we must rise above the restricted and fragmentary view to examine the general tendencies of the system. We then note that England has had two parties throughout her whole history up to 1906, when the Labour movement began to show signs of development, that since 1918 and especially since 1924 there has been a gradual process of elimination of the Liberal party tending to the re-establishment of a new two-party system, and that at the present moment this process seems to be near its end, the Liberals being reduced to ·96% of the parliamentary seats (Fig. 24). A comparison of this development with those in other countries of the Commonwealth reveals a striking general resemblance. By contrast the difference with Belgium is definite since the Liberal party there, though weak, has occupied the same relatively stable position since 1918.

Types of Two-party System. It is generally thought that the two-party system is a specifically Anglo-Saxon phenomenon. Such a view is only approximately true, for some Anglo-Saxon countries have a multi-party system, while the two-party system is also met with in Turkey and in some Latin-American countries; evolution towards it is even to be seen in some States in continental Europe. Within the framework of the Anglo-Saxon two-party system a clear distinction must be made between the U.S.A. and the British

Commonwealth. In the United States dualism has never been seriously threatened; the parties have changed profoundly since the rivalry between Jefferson and Hamilton which epitomized the opposition of Republicans to Federalists, the former defending State rights, the latter urging an increase in the powers of the Union. After the break-up of the Federalist party and a period of

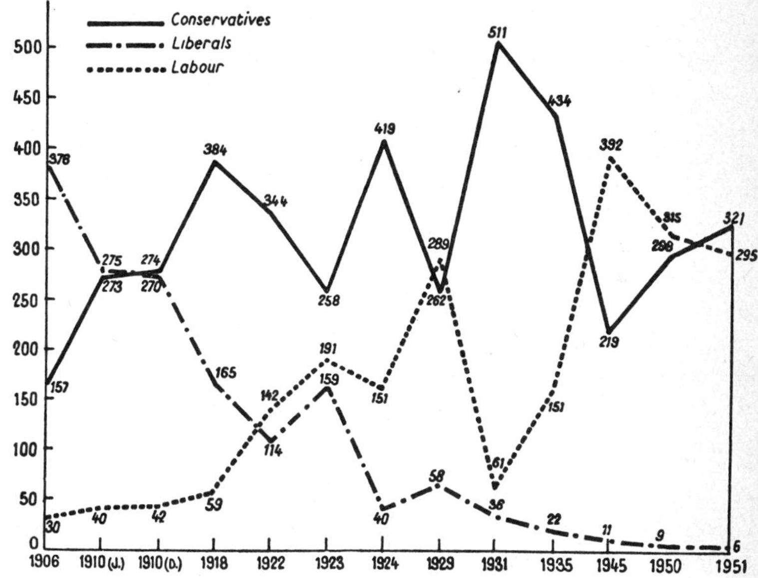

Fig. 24. Return to the Two-party system in Great Britain. (The Irish-Nationalists have been omitted between 1906 and 1918).

confusion the two-party system reappeared during the 1828 presidential elections with the opposition between the Democrats grouped around Jackson and the 'National-Republicans', led by Clay and Adams, who were also called 'Whigs': these different names masked the old Jeffersonian party. The Civil War naturally introduced considerable confusion into the position of the parties and their organization: none the less it did not appreciably modify the two-party system, which reappeared after the war in the antithesis between Republicans and Democrats. In the course of the history of the United States frequent attempts have been made to create a 'third party': all have failed or have given birth only to minor parties, ephemeral and localized.[1] By contrast, in the

[1] Cf. especially W. B. Hesseltine, *The Rise and Fall of Third Parties*, Washington, 1948.

countries of the British Commonwealth the traditional opposition of Tories and Whigs, of Conservatives and Liberals, underwent a profound crisis at the beginning of the twentieth century, when the birth of Socialist parties gave rise to a three-party system. The question could then be asked whether this system was not going to become permanent. However, the two-party system triumphed in the end, as a result either of the elimination of the Liberal party or of its fusion with the Conservatives. By contrast with the United States, a 'third party' did therefore succeed, but its success in fact consisted in its becoming the 'second party' by the elimination of one of the parties already installed. In Australia and Canada, however, the two-party system has not been re-established: there are three major parties in the first country, four in the second.

The British and American two-party systems differ also in the structure of their parties. In Great Britain organization is based upon a high degree of centralization, less considerable in the case of the Conservative than of the Labour party, but infinitely greater than on the other side of the Atlantic. In the United States the caucuses are very largely independent one of another: the precinct captains and their committees are linked with the county committees; the latter are subject to the authority of the State leaders and committees; but beyond the State there is in practice almost no organization, the powers of national leaders and committees being extremely restricted. This presents a striking contrast with Great Britain, where the centre retains strict control of party finances and reserves the right to ratify the candidates proposed by the local associations; in the Dominions the degree of centralization varies without ever descending to the United States' level. Finally we must recall that American parties are founded on no ideological or social bases, that they include elements and doctrines that are completely heterogeneous, that fundamentally they are simply organizations for the conquest of administrative and political offices and for the nomination of candidates in 'primaries', which are often more important than the real election; British parties on the other hand are much nearer to the classic notion of the political party.

In Latin America, a general tendency towards the two-party system is perceptible, though it is generally thwarted and deformed by the revolutions, *coups d'état*, gerrymandering, and factional strife that are characteristic of the political life of that sub-continent. In Uruguay, however, the two-party system has endured almost intact; the two parties date from the 1835 civil war; they have retained their old names (*Colorado* party and *Blanco* party) based upon the colours of the emblems adopted at that time; they are internally divided into factions, but these rarely lead to schism. Moreover an ingenious electoral system makes it possible for each faction (*sublema*) to put up its candidate for the presidency and for the elective high offices of state, the sum of the votes obtained by all the factions in the same party (*lema*) being credited to the candidate of the strongest faction: in 1950, for example, the *Colorados* put up three candidates; the most favoured, M. Martinez Trueba, was elected, the total of the votes obtained by him and his two *Colorado* competitors being higher than that credited to the *Blanco* candidate. A faction of the *Blanco* party seceded however in 1941 under the title of 'Independent White party'; at present it has very few representatives in parliament (less than 10%). In Turkey the single-party system came to an end in 1945 on the creation of the Democratic party by M. Celal Bayar: at the 1946 elections there were two parties; however, governmental pressure considerably reduced the representation of the Democrats. In 1948 a schism occurred in this party, giving birth to the Nationalist party organized round the person of the veteran Marshal Tchakmak. At the free elections of 1950 the Democratic party won a resounding victory, gaining 55% of the total poll and 408 seats compared with 39 (but nearly 40% of the votes) for the People's Republican party; the Nationalist party secured only one seat. At present there is a two-party system in Turkey.

Such is the geographical distribution of the two-party system. It will be observed that it does not exist in continental Europe. At the present moment, however, two countries display a fairly marked tendency towards it: Germany and Italy. Under the outward appearance of a multi-party system the political struggle is restricted to two major formations that are quite disproportionate compared with the others: Socialist and Christian Democratic parties in Germany, Communist and Christian Democratic parties in Italy. The weakness of the Communists in Germany, Socialist divisions and the 'colonization' of the Nenni group by the Communists in Italy, together with the impotence of the Right in both countries, have produced this situation, which is quite exceptional for countries which had until recently known a multi-party system before they succumbed to a single-party dictatorship. It is rather interesting to compare this example with the situation in Turkey: of course the nature of the dictatorship was very different in the different cases as were the circumstances of its fall and the previous political situation. It remains a fact that in all these countries the suppression of the single party produced dualist tendencies. The question may well be asked how far this fact results from the natural characteristics of the two-party system; they will be defined below.

A study of the distribution of the two-party system in time, following the description of its distribution in space, leads to the conclusion that since the nineteenth century three types have succeeded one another. The property franchise first gave rise to a 'bourgeois' two-party system, with the characteristic opposition between Conservatives and Liberals, whose social and ideological sub-structure varied somewhat from country to country. In general the Conservatives found their support chiefly amongst the aristocracy and the peasantry; the Liberals theirs amongst the trading, industrial, and intellectual middle classes in the towns. However, this summary distinction is no more than approximate: the line of demarcation in practice is much more complicated and subtle. In some countries, in Scandinavia for example, the Conservative aristocracy was grouped in the towns; in consequence the tendencies towards Liberalism first made their appearance in the countryside: it would be more accurate to say that an Agrarian Liberalism grew up in opposition to the more intellectual and industrial Liberalism of the towns, which turned the fundamental two-party tendency into a three-party system. From the point of view of doctrines the Conservatives preached the virtues of authority, tradition, and submission to the established order; the Liberals, being individualist and rationalist, claimed descent from the American and French revolutionaries and the ideas of liberty and equality that they had trumpeted to the world; yet many of them showed some timidity on the question of universal suffrage, and especially over the social changes demanded by the working classes. In Protestant countries the two-party system was not on the whole complicated by religious antagonisms; in Catholic countries the *de facto* linking of the clergy with the *ancien régime* gave the Conservatives the air of a party supported by the Church and threw Liberals into the anti-clerical camp: the political struggle became in some cases a religious struggle, particularly acute over the schools question (e.g. in France and Belgium).

In the second half of the nineteenth century the development of Radicalism seemed to threaten the reign of the two-party system; but in fact this proved to be rather an internal division amongst the Liberals, whose moderate elements witnessed the growth of a left-wing tendency opposing them. In most cases this left-wing tendency remained within the party or joined it again or else disappeared; however, a viable Radical party seceded from the Liberals in the Netherlands in 1891, and in Denmark in 1906; the creation of the French Radical party in 1901 corresponds to a different situation. The development of Socialism, on the contrary, provoked the general modification of this first two-party system. In some countries Socialism was long held back by the restriction of the franchise, with the result that dualism still held the field in parliament, whereas in the nation there were three parties in the field: the franchise often being wider at the commune and local level, Socialist representatives gained a foothold in town and village councils without being able to enter parliament (except in very small numbers). A coincidence is therefore frequently to be observed between the establishment of universal suffrage (or the extension of a limited suffrage) and the appearance of Socialist parties at the parliamentary level. In Belgium the electoral reform of 1894 allowed twenty-eight Socialists to enter the Chamber, thus replacing the traditional two-party by a three-party system and reducing the Liberals to third place; in the Netherlands the first Socialist deputies appeared when the Van Houten law was brought into force (increasing the electorate from 295,000 to 577,000); in Sweden the electoral law of 1909 doubled the number of Social Democratic representatives in the Riksdag. Elsewhere (Germany, Great Britain, France, Norway, and so on) since universal suffrage existed prior to the burgeoning of Socialism, the latter was therefore able to develop without hindrance.

The birth of Socialist parties was an almost universal phenomenon in Europe and the British Dominions at the turn of the century. However, the two-party system was not everywhere destroyed. As a matter of fact only one of the countries in which a two-party system flourished previously was unable to re-establish it: Belgium, because of the electoral reform of 1899. Everywhere else the two-party system suffered a period of eclipse of varying duration, to be reborn later in a new guise approximately in conformity with the class-struggle pattern of Marxist doctrine: opposition between a Bourgeois and a Socialist party. The former is sometimes the product of a fusion between two older parties, Conservative and Liberal, as is the case in Australia and New Zealand. In other countries the Conservative party has remained alone in opposition to the Socialists, the Liberals having been eliminated (e.g. Great Britain); but the converse has not occurred (Conservatives eliminated to the advantage of Liberals). This last feature can be explained on natural grounds: the Liberals at that time had realized the essentials of their programme and so found themselves constrained to adopt a conservative attitude: the appearance of a Socialist party naturally took from them a section of their left-wing support, whilst fear of the 'Reds' threw another section into the arms of the Conservatives; finally, the operation of the simple-majority ballot (which in fact was in force in the countries being considered) is unfavourable to Centre parties.

What we are considering is much more a 'Conservative-Labour' than a 'Conservative-Socialist' dualism. The new two-party system was established only in countries with Socialist parties based on Trade Unions, indirect in structure, with little doctrinal dogmatism, and of reformist and non-revolutionary tendencies. The last feature is fundamental: a two-party system cannot be maintained if one of the parties seeks to destroy the established order. At least it cannot endure unless that party remains always in opposition. Today the question no longer arises in the case of Socialist parties, which have all become reformist parties, direct and indirect alike. There would, for example, be no danger if Western Germany attained the two-party system (Christian Democrats—Social Democrats) towards which its present development is visibly leading it. But the question assumes a new urgency with the appearance of a third type of two-party system which as a matter of fact has nowhere so far come into existence, but which is already obviously developing in some countries, as for example in Italy: the opposition of the Communist party and a 'Western' party. The adoption of the simple-majority single-ballot system would undoubtedly bring it into being, but this event would be catastrophic. The first task of a Communist party in power would obviously be the suppression of its rival; in consequence the first duty of its rival once in power would be to take the initiative to prevent the establishment of a dictatorship of the Soviet type. This would be equivalent to setting up a dictatorship of a different type. It is therefore necessary to distinguish between two kinds of dualism: technical dualism, where the difference between the two rivals concerns only secondary aims and means, whilst a general political philosophy and the fundamental bases of the system are accepted by both sides, and metaphysical dualism, where the rivalry between parties concerns the very nature of the regime and the fundamental concepts of life and so assumes the aspect of a veritable war of religions. Only the first type is viable. This is equivalent to saying that the two-party system is inconceivable if one of the two parties is totalitarian in structure.

None the less the two-party system seems to correspond to the nature of things, that is to say that political choice usually takes the form of a choice between two alternatives. A duality of parties does not always exist, but almost always there is a duality of tendencies. Every policy implies a choice between two kinds of solution: the so-called compromise solutions lean one way or the other. This is equivalent to saying that the centre does not exist in politics: there may well be a Centre party but there is no centre tendency, no centre doctrine. The term 'centre' is applied to the geometrical spot at which the moderates of opposed tendencies meet: moderates of the Right and moderates of the Left. Every Centre is divided against itself and remains separated into two halves, Left-Centre and Right-Centre. For the Centre is nothing more than the artificial grouping of the right wing of the Left and the left wing of the Right. The fate of the Centre is to be torn asunder, buffeted and annihilated: torn asunder when one of its halves votes Right and the other Left, buffeted when it votes as a group first Right then Left, annihilated when it abstains from voting. The dream of the Centre is to achieve a synthesis of contradictory aspirations; but synthesis is a power only of the mind. Action involves choice and politics involve action. The history of Centre parties would provide examples in support of this abstract argument: take, for example, the fortunes of the Radical party under the Third French Republic, the fortunes of the Socialists or the M.R.P. under the Fourth. There are no true Centres, only superimposed dualisms, as we shall see: the M.R.P. is politically Right, socially Left; the Radicals are Right in economics, Left in mystique.

The idea of a natural political dualism is to be encountered moreover in widely differing sociological conceptions. Some writers contrast the radical temperament (in the nineteenth-century sense; today we should call it the revolutionary temperament) with the conservative temperament.[1] It is a summary and approximate view but not altogether inaccurate. It is true that some find themselves completely at home amongst commonplace ideas, accepted traditions, and conventional habits, whereas others experience the

[1] Cf. especially Macaulay, *History of England*, London, 1849, I, pp. 82–3.

compelling need to change everything, to modify everything, and to innovate in all domains. The expression 'Better the folly of our ancestors than the wisdom of our children' epitomizes the conservative temperament. It has been suggested that the two tendencies could be identified with different ages, youth being 'radical' and maturity 'conservative': legislators have long been familiar with this fact; they raise the qualifying age for voters to favour the Right and lower it to favour the Left. Marxism re-establishes this deep-seated Manicheism in a modern and different form, that of the opposition between the bourgeoisie and the proletariat, which is given approximate expression in the present-day two-party system of the Anglo-Saxon countries. Contemporary studies in political science reveal a duality of tendencies in countries that are to all appearances most divided politically: underlying the multiple and diverse parties of the French Third Republic François Goguel has succeeded in demonstrating the permanence of the conflict between 'order' and 'movement'. In small French villages public opinion spontaneously distinguishes between 'Whites' and 'Reds', 'clerical' and 'anti-clerical'; without bothering with the more varied official labels, it seizes on the essential. Throughout history all the great factional conflicts have been dualist: Armagnacs and Burgundians, Guelphs and Ghibellines, Catholics and Protestants, Girondins and Jacobins, Conservatives and Liberals, Bourgeois and Socialists, 'Western' and Communist: these antitheses are simplified, but only by neglecting secondary differences. Whenever public opinion is squarely faced with great fundamental problems it tends to crystallize round two opposed poles. The natural movement of societies tends towards the two-party system; obviously it may be countered by tendencies in the opposite direction; these we shall attempt to define below.

The Two-party System and the Electoral Regime. If we accept the idea that the two-party system is natural we still have to explain why nature should have flourished so freely in the Anglo-Saxon countries and their few imitators and why nature should have been thwarted in the countries on the continent of Europe. As a matter of form we may mention the explanations based upon the 'genius of the Anglo-Saxon peoples' (frequent with American authors), and upon the 'temperament of the Latin races' (though the multi-party system exists in Scandinavia, in the Netherlands, and in Germany); not that they are entirely false but they belong to a realm of generalizations too vague and too approximate to allow of the formulation of valid conclusions; it is pointless to repeat the work of Gustave Le Bon. In passing we may glance as well at the explanation furnished by Salvador de Madariaga, who connects the two-party system with the sporting instincts of the British people, which lead them to view political campaigns as a match between rival teams: the sporting instincts must have disappeared between 1910 and 1945, when the three-party system was in operation. Nor can we take more seriously the picturesque comments of André Maurois, who contrasted the rectangular arrangement of the House of Commons and its two rows of facing benches leading naturally to the two-party system with the French semi-circle in which the absence of any clear line of demarcation encouraged the multiplication of groups. It is an amusing comment but it works both ways: is the seating arrangement in parliament the cause or the consequence of the number of parties? Which came first, the semi-circle or the multiplicity of parties, the rectangle or the two-party system? The reply is disillusioning: in England the shape of the chamber is anterior to the two-party system but in France the topography of parliament is posterior to the tendency towards the multi-party system; moreover the Americans have adopted the semi-circular chamber and their two parties are none the worse.

The historical explanation is more worthy of consideration. The age-long habit of dualism in England and America is obviously a factor in its present strength. It remains to be discovered why this habit has taken such firm root: otherwise the problem is simply referred back in time. Only individual investigation of the circumstances in each country can determine the real origins of the two-party system. The influence of such national factors is certainly very considerable; but we must not in their favour underestimate the importance of one general factor of a technical kind, the electoral system. Its effect can be expressed in the following formula: *the simple-majority single-ballot system favours the two-party system.* Of all the hypotheses that have been defined in this book, this approaches the most nearly perhaps to a true sociological law. An almost complete correlation is observable between the simple-majority single-ballot system and the two-party system: dualist countries use the simple-majority vote and simple-majority vote countries are dualist. The exceptions are very rare and can generally be explained as the result of special conditions.

I

We must give a few details about this coexistence of the simple-majority and the two-party systems. First let us cite the example of Great Britain and the Dominions: the simple-majority system with a single ballot is in operation in all; the two-party system operates in all, with a Conservative-Labour antagonism tending to replace the Conservative-Liberal antagonism. It will be seen later that Canada, which appears to present an exception, in fact conforms to the general rule.[1] Although it is more recent and more restricted in time the case of Turkey is perhaps more impressive. In this country, which had been subjected for twenty years to the rule of a single party, divergent tendencies were manifest as early as 1946; the secession of the Nationalist party, which broke away from the opposition Democratic party in 1948, might have been expected to give rise to a multi-party system. On the contrary, at the 1950 elections the simple-majority single-ballot system, based on the British pattern (and intensified by list-voting), gave birth to a two-party system: of 487 deputies in the Great National Assembly only ten (i.e. 2·07%) did not belong to one or other of the two major parties, Democrats and Popular Republicans. Nine were Independents and one belonged to the Nationalist party. In the United States the traditional two-party system also coexists with the simple-majority single-ballot system. The American electoral system is, of course, very special, and the present-day development of primaries introduces into it a kind of double poll, but the attempt sometimes made to identify this technique with the 'second ballot' is quite mistaken. The nomination of candidates by an internal vote inside each party is quite a different thing from the real election. The fact that the nomination is open makes no difference: the primaries are a feature of party organization and not of the electoral system.

The American procedure corresponds to the usual machinery of the simple-majority single-ballot system. The absence of a second ballot and of further polls, particularly in the presidential election, constitutes in fact one of the historical reasons for the emergence and the maintenance of the two-party system. In the few local elections in which proportional representation has from time to

[1] Australia too offers an exception since the development of the *Country party*. But the system of preferential voting in operation there profoundly modifies the machinery of the simple-majority poll and makes it more like a two-ballot system by allowing a regrouping of the scattered votes. It is moreover a striking fact that the appearance of the Country party coincided with the introduction of the preferential vote.

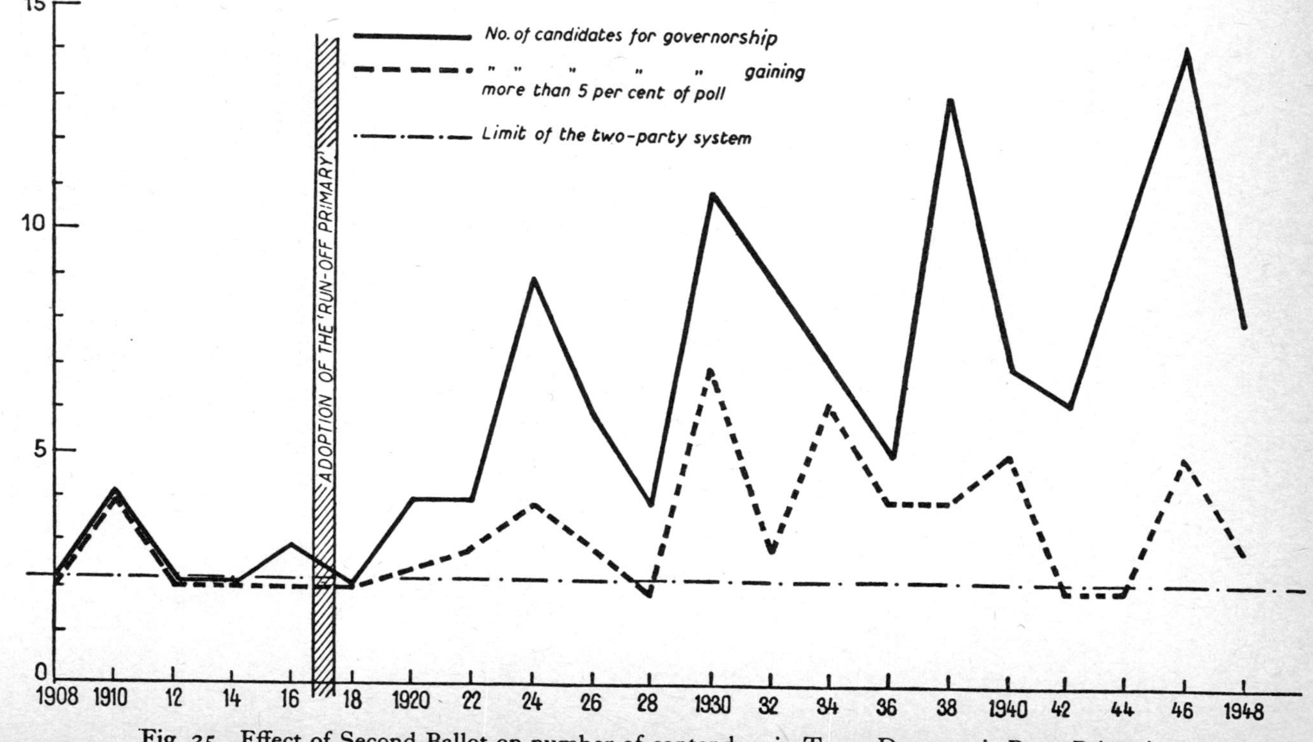

Fig. 25. Effect of Second Ballot on number of contenders in Texas Democratic Party Primaries.

time been tried it shattered the two-party system: for example in New York between 1936 and 1947, where there were represented on the City Council 5 parties in 1937 (13 Democrats, 3 Republicans, 5 American Labor, 3 City Fusionists, 2 dissident Democrats), 6 parties in 1941 (by the addition of 1 Communist), and 7 parties in 1947 (as a result of an internal split in the American Labor party supported by the Garment Trade Unions). The same influence of the simple-majority single-ballot system is also to be noted in the sphere of the primary; Key has observed that in primaries in the South where the nomination is conducted at a single ballot the Democratic party generally divides into two factions; on the other hand, in the system with two successive primaries which correspond to the second-ballot system—the second or run-off primary operating in the event of no candidate securing an absolute majority at the first primary—the factions tend to increase in number; statistics comparing the number of candidates for nomination before and after the adoption of the run-off primary seem to confirm its multiplying effect (Fig. 25).

Not counting Latin-America, which may be neglected because the frequent and effective interference of the government in both polls and parties denatures the whole system, four countries provide exceptions to the rule: on the one hand pre-1894 Belgium, where the two-party system coexisted with the second ballot, on the other, pre-1911 Sweden, pre-1920 Denmark, and present-day Canada, in which the simple-majority single-ballot system is to be found alongside the multi-party system.

In the first case the exception is more apparent than real: the second ballot was provided for in the Belgian electoral law, but in practice it scarcely ever operated before the introduction of universal suffrage. In 1892, for example, in 41 constituencies there were no more than four *second* ballots, of which three (at Nivelles, Charleroi, and Tournai) were the result of cross-voting and incomplete voting, only two lists being presented at the first ballot; in fact, only in a single arrondissement, at Mons, did the second ballot truly operate as a result of votes being shared amongst three rival lists. After the introduction of universal suffrage the appearance of the Socialist party brought the full legal machinery into play: the three-cornered fight caused twelve *second* ballots in 1894 and fifteen in 1896–8. But during the period of dualism the elections took place in practice after the pattern of the single-ballot system. It remains to be determined why practice was not in conformity with the letter of the law, why the possibility of a second ballot did not produce three-cornered fights, party splits, and the break-up of the two-party system: we shall attempt an answer below (cf. p. 243).

The case of Sweden before 1909, when proportional representation was introduced, is scarcely less exceptional. In reality, under the complicated system of limited suffrage then in operation (direct election in the towns and indirect in the countryside, voting for single candidates or several candidates according to the constituency) the lines of demarcation between the parties long remained fluid and vague. There were scarcely any true organized parties in the country; there were not even any clearly delimited parliamentary groups; it is impossible to arrive at any precise electoral statistics giving the political complexion of candidates for the pre-1911 period. The system can be called neither two-party nor multiparty. Rather was there an absence of parties. Furthermore certain special political or social problems (secession from Norway, opposition between town and country, growth of a rural left-wing movement) here modified the natural duality of opinion. However, within each constituency the struggle was often limited to two candidates, which restored the two-party system at the local level. On the national level we can also discern below the surface variations among the short-lived and fluid groups a fairly marked tendency towards two parties. From 1867 to 1888 there were two oposing parties: the Conservatives, drawing their support from the towns, and the *Lantmannapartiet*, whose strength lay in the rural areas. As from 1888 the Lantmanna split into two groups, the 'Old Lantmanna' standing for Free Trade, and the 'New Lantmanna' which was protectionist: but the two groups reunited in 1895. In 1906 a new split divided the National Progressives from the Lantmanna but the two factions worked in close agreement: they were much more like two tendencies within the same party than two different parties. The coagulating effect of the simple-majority ballot is noticeable. Meanwhile the old Right was gradually disappearing and a Liberal party based upon the urban middle class was taking shape; at the end of the nineteenth century, therefore, there was to be found in Sweden the classic two-party system: Conservatives (Lantmanna) *v.* Liberals, modified however in 1896 by the appearance of the Socialist party. In fact, at the beginning of the twentieth century, the political divisions in the Riksdag, in so far as lines of demarcation between the parties can be drawn, resembled those in the British Parliament, the presence of Socialists making a breach in the Conservative *v.* Liberal dualism.

Denmark is a much clearer exception to the general tendency. In spite of the simple-majority single-ballot system there were four major parties just before the reform of the electoral system: Right, Liberals (*Venstre*), Radicals, Socialists. But in fact this four-party division at the national level often masked a two-party division at the local level; in very many constituencies only two candidates fought the campaign; thus, in 1910, out of 114 constituencies, 89 were in this position, compared with 24 constituencies having 3 candidates only and 1 with 4; the reduction in the number of candidates was moreover very marked in comparison with previous years (254 candidates in 1910, 296 in 1909, 309 in 1906). In 1913 there was a sudden rise to 314 candidates with only 41 constituencies in which there was a straight fight, 55 with 3 rival candidates, 15 with 4 and 1 with 5. This increase can however be largely explained by the desperate effort made by the Right to avert the decline with which it was seriously threatened: compared with 47 candidates in 1910 it managed to put up 88 in 1913; however, in spite of this considerable effort, its seats fell in number from 13 to 7 (although the total vote it polled increased from 64,900 to 81,400, and the 17,000 extra votes, chiefly won over from the Liberals, cost the latter party 13 seats). In 1910, furthermore, there was a close electoral understanding between the Radicals and the Socialists, since in no case did these two parties put up candidates against one another; this agreement would appear to have broken down in 1913, however, when we find that 17 Socialists were put up against Radicals, and also 7 Radicals against Socialists. Finally, if a comparison be made of the situation of the parties in 1913 with their earlier position, a definite concentration is apparent. Indeed, in 1906 there were five parties (as a result of the creation of the Radical party); in 1909 the fusion of the Agrarian party (moderate) with the Liberals reduced this number to four; lastly, we must take into account the fact that from the beginning of the century onwards there was a growing process of elimination of the Right which seems to have been accelerating, for the disparity between the percentage of the poll and the percentage of parliamentary seats continually increased. In 1913 the Conservative Right, with its seven deputies, had only 6·14% of all the seats in parliament. In reality the situation was undoubtedly tending towards a tripartism analogous to that in England at the same period where the Socialist party was for the first time taking up a position alongside the two 'bourgeois' parties. The majority ballot was in fact exercising its normal reducing effect, and the agreement between Radicals and Socialists made it possible even to anticipate the coming of a new form of bipartism, resultant upon a fusion of the two left-wing groups. It was proportional representation that put a stop to this development.

Of the four political parties in Canada only two have national status, the Liberals on the one hand and the Conservatives on the other. It is only in certain provinces that the other parties (Labour and Social-Credit) have any real power, so that they may be said to be local parties. This example, in common with the examples provided by Sweden and Denmark, makes it possible to define the limits of the influence of the simple-majority single-ballot system: it tends to the creation of a two-party system inside the individual constituency;[1] but the parties opposed may be different in different areas of the country. The simple-majority system therefore makes possible the creation of local parties or the retreat of national parties to local positions. Even in Great Britain there existed from 1874 to 1918 an Irish party that was remarkably stable. The British Liberal party too shows a distinct tendency to become a Welsh party. None the less, the increased centralization of organization within the parties and the consequent tendency to see political problems from the wider, national standpoint tend of themselves to project on to the entire country the localized two-party system brought about by the ballot procedure: however, the true effect of the simple-majority system is limited to local bipartism.

The effect is produced in a very simple way. Take for example a British constituency in which the Conservatives have 35,000 votes, Labour 40,000, and Liberal 15,000: it is obvious that the success of Labour is entirely dependent on the presence of the Liberal party; if the Liberal party should withdraw its candidate it can be assumed that a majority of the voters supporting him will transfer to the Conservative, the minority being divided between Labour and abstention. Two alternatives are therefore possible: either the

[1] Note that in Canada this tendency to have only two parties within each constituency is by no means absolute, especially since the 1957 elections, which put an end to Liberal supremacy. In several constituencies there are, in fact, three or four parties, and this is an obstacle to true representation. The situation is rather like that in Great Britain between 1920 and 1935, when there was temporarily a three-party system. The situation in Canada today seems to have the same transitory character.

Liberal party may reach agreement with the Conservatives to withdraw its candidate (in exchange for some form of compensation in other constituencies), in which case the two-party system is restored as a result of fusion or of an alliance very like fusion; or else the Liberal party may persist in its independent line, the electors will gradually desert it, and the two-party system will be restored by elimination.

The first alternative has already taken place in its weaker form (alliance akin to fusion) in Great Britain with the Conservatives and National Liberals as well as in Germany with the Christian Democrats (C.D.U.) and the Liberals (F.D.P.) in the simple-majority district elections in some *Länder*, e.g. Westphalia, N. Rhineland, Schleswig-Holstein. Frequently it is but the prelude to the extreme form, total fusion, which is the normal term of the development and is often attended by schism, some members of the former Centre party preferring to join the opposition party. In Australia Liberals and Conservatives coalesced as early as 1909 in face of the growth of Labour. In New Zealand they waited until 1935 to do so: from 1913 to 1928 the Liberal party had pursued a progressively declining path which threatened its natural extinction; in 1928 a sudden renaissance put it on equal terms with the Conservatives; but as from 1931 it began to decline again and once again became the third party; faced with the Labour threat, increased by the economic crisis, it resolved on fusion after the 1935 elections. In South Africa the secession of the Nationalists in 1913, coupled with the growth of the Labour party, had produced by 1918 four parties of almost equal strength; in face of the danger of such a situation in a simple-majority single-ballot system the old Unionist party fused with General Smuts' South African party, while General Hertzog's Nationalist party signed an electoral pact with Labour which proved fatal to the latter: the two-party system was restored by both fusion and elimination.

Elimination in this sense (the second way in which bipartism is restored) is itself the result of two factors working together: a mechanical and a psychological factor. The mechanical factor consists in the 'under-representation' of the third, i.e. the weakest party, its percentage of seats being inferior to its percentage of the poll. Of course in a simple-majority system with two parties the vanquished is always under-represented by comparison with the victor, as we shall see below, but in cases where there is a third

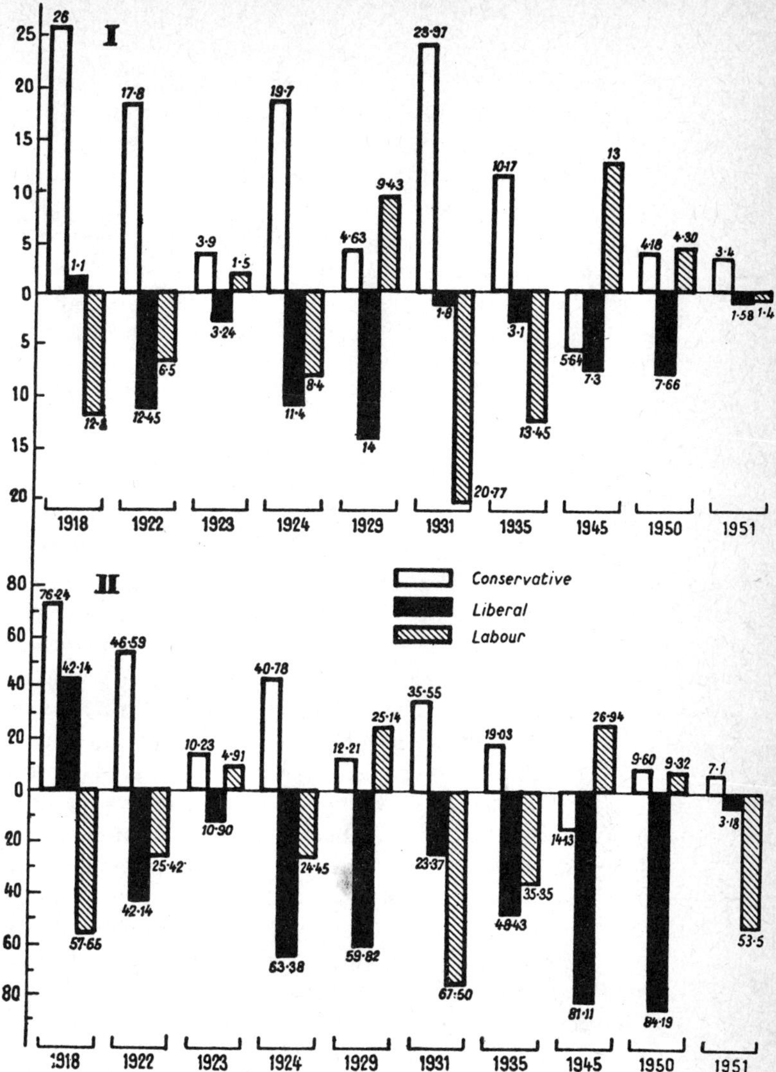

Fig. 26. Disparity between percentage of votes and percentage of seats in Great Britain.

I. Gross disparity. *II. Net disparity* (related to percentage of votes).

party it is under-represented to an even greater extent than the less favoured of the other two. The example of Britain is very striking: before 1922, the Labour party was under-represented by comparison with the Liberal party; thereafter the converse regularly occurred (with the one exception of 1931, which can be explained by the serious internal crisis in the Labour party and the crushing victory of the Conservatives); in this way the third party finds the electoral system mechanically unfair to it (Fig. 26). So long as a new party which aims at competing with the two old parties still remains weak the system works against it, raising a barrier against its progress. If, however, it succeeds in outstripping one of its forerunners, then the latter takes its place as third party and the process of elimination is transferred.

The psychological factor is ambiguous in the same way. In cases where there are three parties operating under the simple-majority single-ballot system the electors soon realize that their votes are wasted if they continue to give them to the third party: whence their natural tendency to transfer their vote to the less evil of its two adversaries in order to prevent the success of the greater evil. This 'polarization' effect works to the detriment of a new party so long as it is the weakest party but is turned against the less favoured of its older rivals as soon as the new party outstrips it. It operates in fact in the same way as 'under-representation'. The reversal of the two effects does not always occur at the same moment, under-representation generally being the earlier, for a certain lapse of time is required before the electors become aware of the decline of a party and transfer their votes to another. The natural consequence is a fairly long period of confusion during which the hesitation of the electors combines with the transposition of the 'under-representation' effect to give an entirely false picture of the balance of power amongst the parties: England experienced such drawbacks between 1923 and 1935. The impulse of the electoral system towards the creation of bipartism is therefore only a long-term effect.

The simple-majority single-ballot system appears then to be capable of maintaining an established dualism in spite of schisms in old parties and the birth of new parties. For a new party to succeed in establishing itself firmly it must have at its disposal strong backing locally or great and powerful organization nationally. In the first case, moreover, it will remain circumscribed within the geographical area of its origin and will only emerge from it slowly and painfully, as the example of Canada demonstrates. Only in the second case can it hope for a speedy development which will raise it to the position of second party, in which it will be favoured by the polarization and under-representation effects. Here perhaps we touch upon one of the deep-seated reasons which have led all Anglo-Saxon Socialist parties to organize themselves on a Trade Union basis; it alone could put at their disposal sufficient strength for the 'take-off', small parties being eliminated or driven back into the field of local campaigns. The simple-majority system

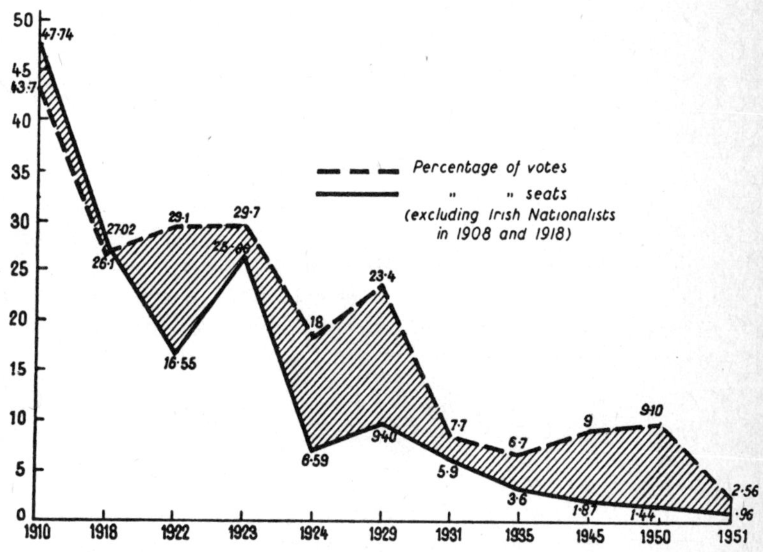

Fig. 27. Elimination of Liberal Party in Great Britain

seems equally capable of re-establishing dualism when it has been destroyed by the appearance of a third party. The comparison between Great Britain and Belgium offers a striking contrast: in both countries a traditional two-party system was broken up at the beginning of the century by the emergence of Socialism. Fifty years later the majority system restored bipartism in Great Britain by the elimination of the Liberals (Fig. 27), whereas in Belgium proportional representation saved the Liberal party and later made possible the birth of the Communist party, without counting a few other parties between the wars.

Can we go further and say that the simple-majority system is capable of producing bipartism in countries where it has never existed? If they already show a fairly clear tendency towards two parties, the answer would unquestionably be in the affirmative. The establishment of the simple-majority single-ballot system in Western Germany would undoubtedly have the effect of gradually destroying the small and medium-sized parties, leaving the Socialists and Christian Democrats face to face; there is undoubtedly no country in which the technical conditions more nearly approach those required for the establishment of a parliamentary system after the British pattern. In Italy an electoral reform of the same kind would have the same results—with the sole difference that the Communists would be one of the two parties, which would greatly imperil the future of the democratic system. However, the brutal application of the single-ballot system in a country in which multi-partism has taken deep root, as in France, would not produce the same results, except after a very long delay. The electoral system works in the direction of bipartism; it does not necessarily and absolutely lead to it in spite of all obstacles. The basic tendency combines with many others which attenuate it, check it, or arrest it. With these reserves we can nevertheless consider that dualism of parties is the 'brazen law' (as Marx would have said) of the simple-majority single-ballot electoral system.

II. MULTI-PARTISM

Multi-partism is often confused with absence of parties. A country in which opinion is divided amongst several groups that are unstable, fluid, and short-lived does not provide an example of multi-partism in the proper sense of the term: it is still in the prehistoric era of parties; it is to be situated in that phase of general development at which the distinction between bipartism and multi-partism is not yet applicable because there are as yet no true parties. In this category we can place many Central European countries between 1919 and 1939, most of the young nations in Africa, the East, and the Middle East, many Latin-American states, and the great Western states of the nineteenth century. However, some of these countries might be better classified in an intermediate category: in them there are to be found authentic parties possessing a minimum of organization and stability in juxtaposition to inorganic and unstable groups. In this case the line of demarcation between multi-partism and absence of parties is blurred, all the more so because vestiges of inorganic groups subsist inside many countries that have organized parties: in France, for example, that whole sector of opinion to the right of the Radicals is almost entirely without true parties and consists rather of the fluid groups which are characteristic of an earlier phase of development.

In this sense multi-partism is fairly characteristic of Western Europe, Great Britain excepted but Ireland included. It is of course true that some of these states have had experience of the two-party system at some periods in their history: Belgium was dualist until 1894; contemporary Germany is very near to being dualist. Other states have had experience of single-party systems: Italy from 1924 to 1945, Germany from 1933 to 1945, Spain and Portugal at the present day. It may also be thought that the European multi-party system is to-day in peril and that its future is uncertain. None the less in 1956 the multi-party system continues to hold sway throughout continental Western Europe; it seems too to correspond to the most general of her political traditions.

Formation of Multi-partism. The typology of the multi-party system is difficult to establish: innumerable varieties can be imagined ranging from three parties to infinity, and within each variety innumerable patterns and shades of difference are possible. Post-Liberation tri-partism in France has nothing in common with Belgian traditional tri-partism; Scandinavian quadri-partism is fundamentally different from Swiss quadri-partism; the dispersal of the French Right means something quite different from the splitting of parties in pre-war Czechoslovakia or Republican Spain: each national organization seems to retain its own extraordinary and unique characteristics which prevent it from being classified in any general scheme. However, we can discover some traits that they have in common if we consider the ways in which multi-party systems come into being. In this connection we can construct a theoretical pattern which fits most of the facts if we take as our point of departure the idea that the two-party system is natural, and then consider this fundamental tendency to be subject to modification as a result of two different phenomena: internal divisions of opinion and their overlapping.

Take for example a two-party system like that in Britain in 1950. In the Labour party there was a fairly clear distinction between the moderates who supported the Attlee Government and a more radical, more extremist group which was sometimes at odds with Ministers and which followed its own line on some important questions, notably foreign affairs. Inside the Conservative party the divisions were less clear because the party was restricted to the role of opposition: when it came to power the differences became more obvious, as in pre-war days. We may proceed to generalize from this particular example: inside all parties there are moderates and extremists, the conciliatory and the intransigent, the diplomatic and the doctrinaire; the pacific and the fire-eaters. The cleavage between reformers and revolutionaries in European Socialist parties at the beginning of this century was simply one particular instance of a very general tendency. In fact the sociological distinction between 'radical' and 'conservative' temperaments should be complemented by a second distinction contrasting the 'extremist' temperament with the 'moderate'; each is complementary to the other, for there are extremist conservatives and moderate conservatives, extremist radicals and moderate radicals (e.g. Jacobins and Girondins). So long as this second distinction is limited in its effects to the creation of factions and rivalries inside parties produced by the first distinction, the natural two-party system remains unchanged. If, however, the factions become exasperated and can no longer meet on common ground the basic tendency to dualism is thwarted and gives way to multi-partism. It was in this way that the split in Switzerland between Radicals and Liberals breached the original 1848 two-party system (Conservatives *v.* Liberals) and created a three-party system that the Socialists later transformed into a four-party system. The same is true of France: the gradual formation of the Radical party split the Republicans, with the result that by the end of the nineteenth century there were three basic tendencies visible: Conservatives, Moderate Republicans (Opportunists), and Radicals. In Denmark and Holland the birth of the Radical party was the product of an identical tendency: a split over the opinions common to moderates and extremists. About 1920 there were many cases in Europe of an increase in the number of parties due to splits between Communists (revolutionaries) and Socialists (reformers).

Such splits give rise to Centre parties. It has already been shown that there exists no Centre opinion, no Centre tendency, no Centre doctrine separate in kind from the doctrines of the Right or of the Left—but only a dilution of their doctrines, an attenuation, a moderate doctrine. If an old Liberal party (on the Left in a two-party system) splits into Liberals and Radicals, then the former become a Centre party. The same happens when a Conservative party divides into Moderates and Extremists. Such is the first method by which Centre parties are created (the second is a consequence of 'Leftism' and will be considered later). In theory an authentic Centre party would presuppose that right-wing Moderates and left-wing Moderates, breaking away from their initial tendencies, had united to form a single party; in practice, however, the origin of the central party is of little account; its very position and the contradictory attractions that are exerted on its members produce inside it a fundamental cleavage: every Centre party is by its very nature divided. An exception occurs when two Centre parties coexist in a country: this was approximately the case in Denmark before proportional representation was set up—the Liberals represented the Right-Centre and the Radicals the Left-Centre; the attraction of the two extremes still proved stronger than the solidarity of the Moderates, for the Radicals co-operated with the Socialists and not with the Liberals, illustrating thereby a tendency which is very common in Scandinavia. In France the Radical-Socialists (Left-Centre) alternated throughout the Third Republic between Central solidarity (which produced the 'concentration') and Left-wing solidarity (which produced the Left-wing Cartel, the Popular Front, and so on): these different patterns in the political ballet will be met again when we come to define party alliances.

'Overlapping' is a phenomenon however that seems to be more widespread than the 'split'. It consists in the non-coincidence of a number of different dualisms of opinion with the result that their combinations produce a multi-partite division. In France, for example, the old division of opinion 'Clerical' *v.* 'Anti-clerical' does not correspond with the division between 'West' and 'East' or with that between 'Freedom' and 'Planning' (Fig. 28). By superimposing these bipartite divisions we can draw a diagram showing the main spiritual families in France: Communists (East, Planning, Anti-clerical); Christian Progressives (East, Planning, Clerical); Socialists (West, Planning, Anti-clerical); M.R.P. (West, Planning, Clerical); Radicals (West, Freedom, Anti-clerical); Right (West, Freedom, Clerical). Of course this classification is somewhat arbitrary and much oversimplified; none the less it corresponds on the whole to the main lines of cleavage in opinion as well as to the real division of parties (it gives too much importance to the Christian Progressives who are weak). The multi-party system in France is a result of the non-coincidence of the main cleavages in opinion.

Here we see the limits of the field within which the two-party system is natural. All antitheses are by nature dualist where they involve rivalry between two points of view that are diametrically opposed (always remembering however that either can be defended with moderation or with zeal); if, however, there are various sets of

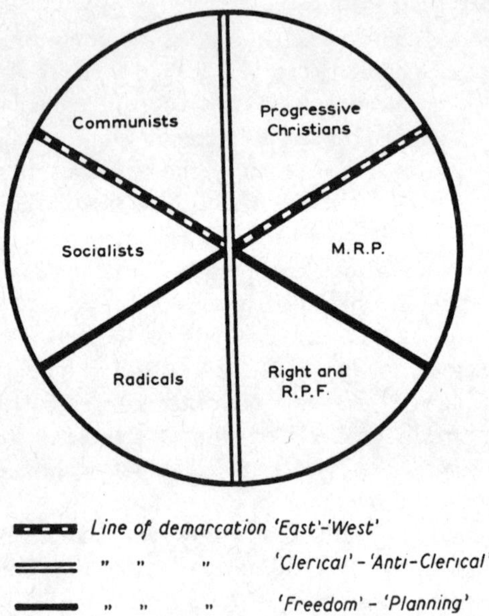

Fig. 28. Overlapping of Cleavages in France.[1]

antitheses and these are largely independent of one another, then one can adopt a viewpoint in one field and still be relatively free to choose one's point of view in other fields. Multi-partism arises from the mutual independence of sets of antitheses. It necessarily presupposes that the different sectors of political activity are relatively isolated and sealed off one from the other: the distinguishing characteristic of every 'totalitarian' concept lies precisely in its

[1] The diagram takes no account of the strengths of the respective 'spiritual families': the Progressive Christians, in particular, are not numerous, though their intellectual influence is considerable. Moreover, as the M.R.P. has moved further to the Right since 1951 many of its members are fairly Liberal from the economic point of view. On the other hand, the Radical followers of Mendès-France are more in favour of planning, and in this respect are more to the Left.

establishment of a rigorous interdependence of all questions, with the result that an attitude to one necessarily involves a corresponding attitude to all others. Totalitarian ideologies may coexist, however, and produce a multi-party system on condition that they are not agreed upon the one supreme issue which determines for each of them the attitudes to be assumed on all other issues. If all Frenchmen were in agreement in holding that the antagonism East *v.* West took precedence over all others, then there would be only two parties: Communists and Anti-Communists. If they all accepted as fundamental the rivalry between freedom and planning, there would be only two parties: Conservatives and Socialists. If on the other hand they thought that the Clerical *v.* Anti-clerical issue was basic, as is still held in some corners of France, then there would be only two parties: Catholics and Free-thinkers (there was a trend towards this at the beginning of the century). It is on the contrary the very fact that some emphasize the Freedom *v.* Planning issue, others the Clerical *v.* Anti-clerical, and yet others the East *v.* West that maintains multi-partism.

Very many antitheses can overlap in this way. First there are political antitheses proper, concerning the form or organization of the government, e.g. the Republican-Monarchist opposition, sometimes made more complex by subtle differences similar to those between Bonapartists and Royalists, or between Orleanists and Legitimists. Then there are social antagonisms: Aristotle noted, for example, in his Athenian Constitution, that there existed three parties, that of the port fishermen and sailors, that of the lowland agriculturists, that of the town workpeople; Marxism affirms in fact that social antitheses are fundamental and primordial in character. Next there are economic antagonisms illustrated by the controversy between planning and freedom, but this masks a more deep-seated social antithesis: tradespeople, industrialists, producers, and distributors defending freedom which favours them, the salaried classes, workers, clerks, and office workers supporting planning which protects them. There are religious antagonisms: the struggle between clerical and anti-clerical elements in Catholic countries (France, Belgium, Spain, Italy, etc.) where the ecclesiastical authorities have often preserved some political influence; the struggle between Protestants and Catholics in countries divided on religious questions—in Holland, for example, parties are primarily organized on this basis, the Anti-Revolutionaries (Conservative and Protestant) opposing the Catholic Conservatives, while the Christian Historical party was formed at the end of the last century in protest against the co-operation of the first two. There are national and racial antagonisms in states which comprise different racial and political communities: Czechs *v.* Slovaks in the Masaryk and Beneš Republic; Serbs *v.* Croats in the former Yugoslav kingdom; Germans, Hungarians, and Slavs at odds in the Habsburg Empire; Catalan and Basque independence movements in Spain; Irish movement in Great Britain before the independence of Eire; Sudeten movement in Czechoslovakia, and Alsatian independence movement in the German Empire and in the French Republic; antagonism between Flemings and Walloons in contemporary Belgium, and so on. There are diplomatic antitheses that are the reflections within states of international rivalries: Armagnacs and Burgundians, Guelphs and Ghibellines, Axis supporters and supporters of democracy, Easterners and Westerners. And finally there are the antitheses of history: like so many sedimentary deposits, new antitheses overlay old antitheses without destroying them, with the result that divisions of varying ages may coexist in the mind of the nation at the same point of time. In France, for example, the dispute between Monarchists and Republicans which was fundamental in 1875 no longer subsists today except amongst a very small minority of the population; on the other hand the division between 'clericals' and 'anti-clericals' which was dominant around 1905 still retains a large measure of influence in the provinces (and in the subconscious of Frenchmen) although for the most part events have made it obsolete; the Socialist-Liberal antithesis only really began to be important after 1940 and is only primordial so long as the economic situation is difficult (it has diminished somewhat since 1950–51); lastly, the East *v.* West antagonism (Communists *v.* Non-Communists), not born until 1947, is not always very clear: many workers, farm-labourers, and lower-middle-class people, who have no desire for a Soviet regime, vote Communist to show their discontent; moreover, the 'neutralists' are in an intermediate position.

Types of Multi-party System. If we consider established multi-partism and not the methods of its establishment we can distinguish several varieties according to the number of rival parties, e.g. tri-partism, quadri-partism, polypartism, but this classification is even more precarious than the preceding one. We shall therefore describe a few concrete examples instead of seeking out general explanations which would remain too theoretical. There are two chief cases of tri-partism which will repay analysis: 1900 tri-partism and contemporary Australian tri-partism. As we have seen, the fundamental dualism of opinion was transformed into tri-partism in England, Belgium, Sweden, Australia, New Zealand, etc., as a result of the development of Socialist parties at the end of the nineteenth and the beginning of the twentieth centuries. We might consider basing a system on this example and try to discover whether the tendency of the country to swing to the Left has not the effect of modifying in the direction of tri-partism the natural dualism of opinion. It is a fairly common occurrence that reformist or revolutionary parties become conservative once the reforms or revolutions they have fought for are accomplished: they move from the Left to the Right, leaving a gap which is filled by the appearance of a new left-wing party that in its turn evolves in the same way. Thus after an interval of twenty or thirty years the Left of one period becomes the Right of the next. The term 'Leftism' can be applied to this constant drive. In theory the movement of the old Left party towards the Right should entail the disappearance of the old conservative party, with the result that the initial two-party system would be perpetually reborn (as in Anglo-Saxon countries). In practice parties are very long a-dying, their social structures tending to persist long after they have lost their usefulness. The swing to the Left would therefore combine with the fundamental tendency to dualism to produce a tri-partism. Thus the tri-partite system 'Conservatives–Liberals–Radicals' would be followed by a new tri-partism, 'Conservatives or Liberals–Radicals–Socialists', and that by the tri-partism 'Liberals–Socialists–Communists'. Traces of such a tendency could be discovered in several countries, but it is combined with too many special phenomena for us to accord it any great weight. Since the old organizations often persist for a very long time, the swing to the Left increases the total number of parties instead of destroying one of them. The factors which led to the birth of the 1900 tri-partite system do not seem to offer the materials for any valid conclusion.

The contemporary three-party system in Australia has a social basis. The 'Conservative–Labour' dualism which corresponds to the 'middle-class–working-class' pattern is here modified by the separate political representation of the farming community by the Country party. The latter is the result of a marked effort to give the agriculturist a means of expression like that provided by

Labour for the working class: the very fact that it has deliberately moulded its organization on that of the Labour party proves this. It is interesting to compare this example with the attempts made in certain People's Democracies to set up a multi-party system based on social considerations; in every case it ended in the same trinity, Workers', Peasants', and Liberal-Bourgeois parties. The increasing dominion of the Workers' party (Communist in practice) prevented the experiment, which might have been of interest, from bearing fruit. But the major difficulty of every Agrarian party comes from the perpetual conflict within it between Right and Left, springing from the variety of social strata amongst agriculturists: there exists no agricultural class, only a division between the agricultural proletariat and the agricultural proprietors, and a deeper division still between the smallholder and the large-scale farmer. Whence a natural difficulty in creating Agrarian parties, the inevitable limits to their expansion and their fairly general tendency towards the Right and conservatism: the smallholder and the agricultural worker prefer to join Socialist or Communist parties.

Agrarian parties are in consequence comparatively rare; in any case they have not become so widespread as Socialist parties. In some countries, however, their development has given rise to a quadri-partism which deserves mention, for the phenomenon involved is somewhat uncommon. The four-party system in question results from the addition of an Agrarian party to the Conservative–Liberal–Socialist tri-partism general in Europe about 1900. Such is approximately the present situation in the Scandinavian countries with which can be compared Switzerland and Canada. Why has the peasantry in these countries succeeded in creating and maintaining an independent political party whereas it has not succeeded elsewhere? The Scandinavian example can be associated with historical traditions. In the nineteenth century the antagonism 'Conservative *v.* Liberal' assumed in Scandinavia the form 'town *v.* country', the latter being more Left than the former, contrary to what happened elsewhere: it was a sign of a still elementary social structure resting upon a very limited industrial development (the first revolutions were Jacqueries). Thus a fairly powerful Agrarian party opposed the aristocrats and middle classes of the towns. However, the development of an urban Liberal party, then of a Socialist party, gradually drove the Agrarian party back towards conservatism, where it joined its former adversaries: at the end of the nineteenth century, the old Agrarian parties were tending to become Conservative parties pure and simple, either through the elimination of the old Right wing or by fusion with it. But a certain tradition of independent Agrarian policy remained and no doubt played some part in the reappearance of Agrarian parties when proportional representation encouraged multi-partism. In Denmark the decline of the Conservatives was arrested and the Left (*Venstre*, very moderate) was able to remain truly agricultural in character. A new Agrarian party, much more moderate than its nineteenth-century predecessors, was formed in Sweden in 1911 and in Norway in 1918. In fact the rural parties in these three countries today represent one fraction of right-wing opinion, in spite of the fact that their social basis is the lower and middle agricultural classes; it seems that agrarian civilization and the peasant's mode of living encourage political conservatism. The same might be said of the Swiss Peasant and Bourgeois party (which is not moreover entirely agrarian). In Canada, however, the Social Credit party is more progressive in outlook; in the United States the farmers established parties, quite strong locally (especially before the measures taken in their favour by Roosevelt in 1933) and markedly reformist. Some Agrarian parties operating in Central Europe between 1919 and 1939 displayed similar characteristics; they were based on Co-operatives and Trade Unions after the fashion of Labour parties; in Bulgaria in particular their organization was quite remarkable. From time to time a four-party system seemed to be emerging in these states, notwithstanding electoral manipulations and *de facto* dictatorships.

Over and above four parties classification is no longer possible. Separate consideration must be given however to *polypartism*, or the tendency to extreme multiplication of parties, which can be explained by general causes that are rather variable. There are several types of polypartism. One might distinguish a nationalist or ethnic polypartism, peculiar to countries divided into several traditional or racial groups: here racial antagonisms overlay the social and political, producing extreme complexity; 'Twenty-five parties!' sadly noted Andrassy, Minister of Foreign Affairs in Austro-Hungary on the eve of the 1914 War, as he looked at the Viennese Parliament in which the rivalries between Conservatives, Liberals, Radicals, and Socialists were complicated by rivalries between Austrians, Poles, Czechs, Serbs, Croats, and so on. In the same way in Czechoslovakia there were in 1938 as many as fourteen parties, including one Hungarian, one Slovak, and four

German parties; amongst those which seemed to be active throughout the whole Republic some were in fact especially concerned with Bohemia or Slovakia. In the 1871–1914 German Reichstag places were occupied by a Polish, a Danish, and an Alsatian party. The Irish party played an important part in England towards the end of the nineteenth and the beginning of the twentieth centuries.

Furthermore it will be observed that there exists in many countries a right-wing tendency towards polypartism. In France, for example, since the beginning of the century, the Left has coalesced into two or three clearly defined parties whereas the Right is scattered into a swarm of small groups. In Holland religious divisions have the same effect in fundamentally dividing the Right and the Centre, while the Left remains united in support of the Socialist party. Sometimes this right-wing polypartism is due to 'Leftism': several of the present-day right-wing groups are nothing but old left-wing parties that have been driven to the Right by the pressure of new parties and that have not succeeded in completely absorbing the old right-wing parties. It also occurs as a result of the tendency of Conservative parties to split internally and to become dispersed into rival fractions. This is no doubt connected with the deeply individualist streak in the bourgeoisie, already frequently mentioned, and probably also with the fact that the most developed social class is naturally the most differentiated, which leads it to adopt a variety of political attitudes. The coincidence between party and class that is affirmed by the Marxists is valid only for primitive social classes that are undeveloped and undifferentiated; all progress in a class introduces into it diversities which tend to be reflected on the political plane and in the division of parties.

Finally there is a fairly clear tendency towards tri-partism amongst the Latin peoples as a result of the profound individualism of their citizens, their taste for personal originality, and a somewhat anarchic side to their character. In this connection it is worth while pondering the example of the Italian Socialists with their classic propensity for splitting into rival groups. More definite still is the example of the Spanish Republic (Spain being much more anarchist-minded than the other Latin peoples): there were 17 parties in the constituent Cortes, 20 in the Chamber elected in 1933, 22 in that elected in 1936; the number of parties under the Dual-Monarchy was almost attained. None the less it appears difficult to arrive at a generalization: in Imperial and Weimarian Germany the parties were also very numerous (the antagonism between states no doubt aggravated this dispersion, but polypartism there was not primarily based on national and ethnical considerations; anarchic tendencies were clearly manifest on the Right and they are to be seen reappearing today); in Holland polypartism is also evident; in Italy, on the other hand, in spite of some indications of scattering, opinion today is grouped around two main tendencies. Considerations drawn from national psychology and from 'national temperament' do not seem to lead to any very clear conclusions.

Multi-partism and the Second-ballot System. Underlying all the special factors in multi-partism there is one general factor present which combines with them, viz. the electoral system. It has been seen that the simple-majority single ballot encourages the two-party system; on the contrary both *the simple-majority system with second ballot and proportional representation favour multi-partism.* These influences are not entirely identical, that of the second-ballot system being more difficult to define. It is in fact an old method which is little used nowadays. France alone remained faithful to it until 1945 (the last General Election having taken place in 1936); most other countries abandoned it towards the beginning of the twentieth century: Belgium in 1899, Holland in 1917, Switzerland, Germany and Italy in 1919, Norway in 1921. In consequence there is available only a limited number of elections in which the effects of the second ballot can be studied; furthermore many of them occurred under a limited franchise (until 1874 in Switzerland, 1894 in Belgium, 1898 in Norway, 1913 in Italy, 1917 in Holland). Moreover at that period detailed electoral statistics were not very often compiled (no reliable statistics in Switzerland, Sweden, or Italy before the establishment of P.R., nor in Norway before 1906, nor in Holland before 1898). Further, there were variations of procedure in the simple-majority second-ballot system: voting by list in Switzerland, Belgium, and partially in Holland (until 1888), and in Norway until 1906; voting for single candidates in Germany, in Italy (except from 1882 to 1891), in France most of the time, in Norway from 1906 and in Holland from 1888; a second ballot limited to the two most successful candidates in Germany, Belgium, Holland, and Italy; free second ballot in France, Norway, and Switzerland (after 1833); a third ballot (an absolute majority being also required at the second) in Switzerland before 1883. The general influence of the system cannot therefore be identical in all cases.

With these reserves the tendency of the second ballot to give rise to multi-partism appears to admit of no doubt. It operates quite simply: the variety of parties having much in common does not adversely affect the total number of seats they gain since in this system they can always regroup for the second ballot. The phenomena of polarization and under-representation are not operative here, or operate only at the second ballot, each party retaining unimpaired its chances at the first. In fact, observation confirms the conclusions emerging from the argument: almost all countries with a second ballot are also countries with a multi-party system. In Imperial Germany there were 12 parties in 1914, which corresponds to the general average (11 parties from 1871 to 1887; 12–13 from 1890 to 1893; 13–14 from 1898 to 1907); if, from this total, we deduct the three national groups—Alsatian, Polish, Danish—the formation of which cannot be attributed to the electoral system, there remain 9 parties of which 2 are major (Catholic Centre and Social Democrats, each with about 100 seats), 3 medium (Conservatives, Liberal Nationals, Progressives, each with about 45 seats), and 2 minor (with 10 to 20 seats); this is then a true multi-party system. In France, under the Third Republic, the number of parties has always been very high; in the 1936 Chamber there were twelve parliamentary groups, and this figure has on occasion been exceeded. Some very small groups of course did not really correspond to any real party organization, none the less there were rarely fewer than six parties. In Holland throughout the twenty years up to 1918 there were seven parties. In Switzerland four principal parties were represented in the Federal Parliament. Lastly in Italy there was a swarm of unstable and short-lived minor groups that did not succeed in combining to form real parties.

The tendency towards multi-partism is obvious. It seems to assume two somewhat different patterns. In Switzerland and in Holland the multi-party system is limited and orderly; in Italy it is anarchic and disorderly; in Germany and France the situation is intermediate between the two. It might be thought that the variations could be explained by differences in the ballot procedure, but attempts to do this have proved disappointing. The list-vote seems to encourage orderly and limited multi-partism in Switzerland and Belgium, but it did not modify the anarchy of the Italian system during the years 1881–92, when it was applied there; it is true that the period of application was too brief for the reform to have shown all its potentialities. However, voting for single candidates was in operation in Holland, where the system was even more orderly than in Switzerland (the parties being more numerous but better organized). Neither freedom nor restriction of the second ballot seems to have any greater effect; if freedom appears to have accentuated the tendency towards multi-partism in France, it does not seem to have done so in Norway, where only three parties existed (plus a fourth towards the end of the period); moreover the second ballot was restricted in Italy and in Germany. The degree of limitation of the suffrage possibly played a more definite part in this matter: in Holland the Van Houten Law of 1896, which doubled the number of electors, also increased the number of parties from four to seven; however, the suffrage was very limited in Italy, where the greatest degree of anarchy was attained. We ought perhaps to leave Italy entirely out of the comparison for, before 1914, she had not so much a multi-party system as a complete absence of parties, which is not at all the same thing. In the last resort the differences in the number and stability of parties under the simple-majority second-ballot system seem to arise more from individual national factors than from the technical details of the electoral system; they do not disprove its general tendency towards multi-partism.

In order to determine the nature and the strength of this tendency, we should have to compare within the same country the state of the parties under the second-ballot system with their state under some different electoral system, e.g. single-ballot or proportional representation. The comparison with the single ballot would be particularly interesting, since it should be possible to see the operation of the multiplying effect of the twin ballot contrasted with the dualist effect of the single ballot. Unfortunately no country has had consecutive experience of the second-ballot and single-ballot systems. The only example that can be referred to on this score is that of some American primaries. We have seen that in Texas the establishment of the second ballot had led to an increase in the number of candidates and of internal factions in the Democratic party (cf. Fig. 25, p. 219). Out of 5 primaries on the single-ballot system between 1908 and 1916 there were 4 cases of the nomination of 2 candidates and only 1 of 3 candidates; out of 15 primaries under the second-ballot system between 1918 and 1948 there were only 4 cases of the nomination of 2 candidates as against 4 cases of 3 candidates, 3 with 4 candidates, 2 with 5, 1 with 6, and 1 with 7 (nor has any account been taken of 'freak' candidates who did not obtain at least 5% of the poll). The same phenomena is to be observed in Florida. On the other hand in Georgia and Alabama there is scarcely any difference between the number of factions before and after the establishment of the run-off primary, that is of the second ballot: this exception to the general tendency of the second ballot towards multiplication seems explicable by the fact that in these two states there existed throughout the period under consideration a very influential faction which threatened to obtain a majority in the first ballot, thus driving its opponents to combine.[1]

Although comparisons with the single-ballot system are rarely possible, this is not true of porportional representation; almost everywhere indeed the second-ballot system has been replaced by P.R. However, both systems tend to produce multi-partism, and the comparison is of much less interest. It only makes possible the measurement of the degree of influence exerted by each system. In Germany under the Weimar Republic, between 1920 and 1932, the average number of parties represented in the Reichstag was a little over twelve, which resembles the figure for Imperial Germany, but the three nationalist parties had disappeared after 1919: there is therefore an increase to be noted of 33%. In Switzerland proportional representation led to the appearance of the Peasant and Bourgeois party. In Norway the Agrarian party (born at the last election held under the majority system) found its importance suddenly increased. In Holland there are seven parties under P.R., as under the two-ballot system, but one of the seven is the Communist party, the Liberal Conservatives and Liberal Union having fused in 1922, with the result that what has happened is rather a decrease in the number of former groups. In France P.R. seemed to have reduced the number of parties in 1945, but in 1946 there were already fifteen groups in the National Assembly (compared with twelve in the 1936 Chamber of Deputies); it is true that the overseas deputies, who did not exist in 1936, figure in the 1946 total. Really the system has been in operation for too short a period for its effects to have had time to make themselves felt. The 1919 Reichstag included only five parties, which also might have led to a belief in the reducing effect of P.R.; there were, however, ten in 1920, twelve in 1924, and fourteen in 1928. In sum, the effects of

[1] V. O. Key, *Southern Politics*, New York, 1950, p. 422.

the second ballot and of P.R. upon the number of parties seem not to differ appreciably, it is rather the internal organization which is changed; the personal and flexible structure yields to a rigid one, as was seen in France between 1936 and 1945, in Italy from 1913 to 1920. It is possible that the two-ballot system has a less marked scattering effect than P.R., for the application of the latter seems to have resulted in a slight increase in the number of parties. The former works in the direction of greater individualism, with the result that parties are more deeply divided within themselves.

The only real exception to the multiplying effect of the second ballot is provided by Belgium. Until 1894, as we know, a strict two-party system was in operation there, and at that date the appearance of Socialism immediately set in motion a process of elimination of the Liberal party that was checked by P.R., yet the second ballot existed in Belgium. It is true that voting was by list and that the second ballot was restricted differing from the system in France: the only candidates allowed to continue to compete were those at the head of the poll, two going forward to the second ballot for every seat to be filled. This feature seems however to exert no influence on the point at issue: in Germany, Holland, and Italy the second ballot was also limited without any tendency towards a two-party system being detectable; in Switzerland the list-vote had given rise to five parties without any marked dualist symptom. What is more to the point is the distinction between the letter and the practice: although the second ballot was provided for by the electoral law of Belgium, it was scarcely operative in practice, since only two parties were in competition. We must here emphasize the interdependence of political phenomena: although the electoral system influences the organization of parties, this in its turn influences the system. Thus the two-party system in Belgium was hostile to the application of the second ballot. However, the question is only transferred: the real problem is to discover why the possibility of a second ballot did not bring about the disintegration of the major traditional parties. Here two factors seem to have exercised a decisive influence: on the one hand the internal structure of the parties, on the other, the nature of the political struggle in Belgium. All observers have been impressed by the originality displayed by Belgian parties in the second half of the nineteenth century: all have referred to their cohesion and their discipline, and the complex and hierarchically organized network of committees that they maintained throughout the country. No other

European country at that time possessed so developed a party system, not even Great Britain or Germany. Their strong internal structure made it possible for the parties in Belgium to resist successfully the disintegrating effect of the second ballot, by preventing the schisms that it would have perpetuated. The high degree of organization of the electorate was an obstacle to the appearance of new parties, which found it difficult to set up rival machinery, all the more so because voting by lists prevented in practice the intervention of independent personalities. In this way the powerful organization of parties tended by combining with their dualism to checkmate the legal provision for a second ballot. The dualism was a consequence of the nature of the political struggle in Belgium at that period. The antagonism between the Catholic party and the Liberal party was entirely based upon the religious problem and the confessional school problem, under a system of limited suffrage which prevented the development of Socialism. The influence of the Church, which had created the Catholic party, was a powerful factor in maintaining its unity and safeguarding it againstany schism: faced with this powerful bloc the Liberals would have been reduced to impotence by any internal division. Catholic unity was cemented by religious and educational pressure and by the centralizing influence of the clergy; but the bloc thus formed enjoyed in the country a position such that it was capable of securing an absolute majority in parliament; indeed it held a majority from 1870 to 1878 and from 1884 to 1914. It was therefore extremely dangerous for the Liberals to disagree. As a result of committing this error in 1870 after thirteen years in power, and dividing into Old Liberals (doctrinaires), Young Liberals (progressives), and Radicals, they lost office. In consequence they made a determined effort to reorganize and to re-establish unity, which restored them to power in 1878 after the creation in 1875 of the Liberal Federation. However, once again divided over the question of the franchise, they lost power in 1884 and did not succeed in regaining it until the establishment of universal suffrage. As a matter of fact the Belgian Liberal party was never anything but a coalition of varying tendencies, only united on the electoral plane because of the strength of the opponent, but soon disunited when in power. Thus the different fractions of the Liberal party never went as far as real schism because the power of the Catholic party prevented this: the factors involved are almost identical with those which, in spite of the development of the run-off primary, prevented the multiplica tion of factions amongst Democrats in Georgia and Alabama because of the dominant power exercised by the Eugene Talmadge and Bibb Graves groups. The evolution of political parties in Belgium in the nineteenth century provides a vivid example, showing how the solidifying effect on the Liberal party of the danger from the Catholics checked the effect of the simple-majority second-ballot system towards the multiplication of parties.

The Multi-party System and Proportional Representation. The multiplicative tendency of proportional representation has been the object of numerous controversies. It is generally accepted nowadays, but has been criticized with great penetration by some observers, for example Tingsten.[1] In actual fact, if French parties before 1939 (simple-majority second-ballot system) and after 1945 (proportional representation) are compared, no increase in their number is to be observed. There was even a certain decrease in their numbers in 1945–6; but, since then, the Right has split again, the Radical party has recovered its importance, the Rally of the French People has come into being, and this puts matters back where they were before. No doubt Belgium furnishes a much more striking example: proportional representation has been functioning there for fifty years, and we still find in Belgium the same three-party system as at the beginning, only slightly modified by the presence of a Communist party, which is moreover weak.

The controversy seems to have its origin in a confusion between the technical idea of the multi-party system as it has been defined in this book (a system in which there are more than two parties) and the current idea of multiplication, implying an increase in the number of parties existing at the time of the change to proportional representation. It is possible that such an increase does not take place: which makes Tingsten right. But it is certain that proportional representation always coincides with a multi-party system: in no country in the world has proportional representation given rise to a two-party system or kept one in existence. Certainly at present in Germany and in Italy polarization around two parties can be discerned. The Christian Democrats and the Socialists and Communists (who may be considered as a single bloc, the first blindly following the second) occupy 488 seats out of 574 in the Italian Chamber; the Social Democrats and the C.D.U. 270 seats

[1] H. Tingsten, *Majoritetsval och proportionalism* (*Riksdagens protokoll bihange*) Stockholm, 1932.

out of 371 in the Bundestag. Nevertheless there are six parties in Germany and eight in Italy, and their number tends to increase rather than to decrease. In fact there is apparent in German opinion a two-party tendency which began during the last years of the Empire (with the growth of Social Democracy), which asserted itself during the early years of the Weimar Republic, and which is at present developing again in the Bonn Republic: but proportional representation has mercilessly opposed its transfer to the party level by preventing polarization around the Christian Democrats and the Socialists. In any case Germany and Italy have multi-party systems, like all other countries with proportional representation. There are four or five parties in Ireland, Sweden and Norway; between six and ten in Holland, Denmark, Switzerland and France, as well as in West Germany and Italy; there were more than ten in the Germany of the Weimar Republic, in Czechoslovakia before Munich and in Republican Spain. Even then no account is being taken of very small parties, which obtain only one or two seats at isolated elections. Belgium is the exception. At present there are four parties and with the weakening of the Communist party the tendency is to revert to three: but this is still a multi-party system.

Moreover this last example warrants closer examination, since here one can see proportional representation in action opposing any change towards a two-party system that might have been observable when it was established. Here we must resume the comparison between Belgium and England, both subject to a dualism destroyed by the appearance of the Socialist party at the beginning of the twentieth century. Fifty years later England, which has retained its simple-majority system, has returned to dualism, whereas the three-party system of 1900 has been maintained in Belgium through the adoption of proportional representation. Belgian elections between 1890 and 1914 are very interesting to study in this respect (Fig. 29). In 1890 restricted suffrage had not yet allowed the Socialists to be represented in parliament. The two-party system was still functioning. In 1894 the adoption of universal suffrage gave 28 seats to the Socialists while the Liberal party fell from 60 to 21 (although it had twice as many electors as the Socialists: under-representation worked to its detriment). In 1898 there was a further decline of the Liberal party, which dropped to 13 seats; this time polarization had combined with under-representation, a great number of former Liberal electors having voted Catholic. The process of elimination of the Liberal party was by now well advanced: one might legitimately have considered that two or three more elections would finish it. But proportional representation was adopted in 1900 precisely because the Catholics wished to put an end to this annihilation of the Liberal party in order to avoid being left to face the Socialists: immediately the number of Liberal seats rose to 33. It was to rise to 42 after the elections of 1902–4 (probably through a depolarization:

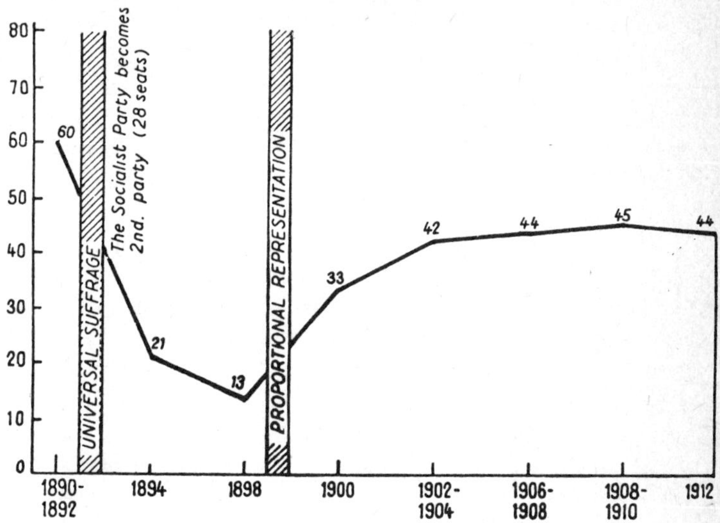

Fig. 29. 'Rescue' of Belgian Liberal Party by P.R. (No. of seats in Chamber of Deputies.)

the former Liberal electors, who had left the party after 1894 to join up with the Catholic party, returned to their first love, once they had understood the workings of proportional representation), and finally to settle between 44 and 45. This rescue of the Belgian Liberal party by proportional representation may be compared with that of the Danish Right. The process of elimination had overtaken it in the last simple-majority elections (13 seats in 1910, 7 in 1913 in spite of a desperate effort to increase the number of candidates). In 1918 the adoption of a mixed system (correcting the results of the simple-majority vote by additional seats allocated by proportional representation) increased this number to 16; in 1920 real proportional representation gave 28 seats to the Right and kept the party representation stable round about this figure until 1947.

It is to be noted that the Belgian Liberal party was rescued in two stages. At the first election with proportional representation the increase resulted chiefly from mechanical factors: the absence of under-representation and the increase in the number of candidates; at the second election and thereafter there was in addition a psychological factor: depolarization. These are the opposite phenomena to those which give rise to the two-party system when there is a simple-majority vote. As long as the latter applies the party placed third or fourth is under-represented compared with the others: its percentage of seats is lower than its percentage of votes, and the disparity remains constantly greater than for its rivals. By its very definition proportional representation eliminates this disparity for all parties: the party that was at the greatest disadvantage before is the one to benefit most from the reform. Moreover the party that was gradually being eliminated through the simple-majority system was forced to fall back on certain constituencies and to withold candidates from those in which there was no longer any hope of victory: when proportional representation restores its chances everywhere (in so far as it is complete) it benefits from votes which were not given to it before because of its absence. These two results are purely mechanical: the first is in complete operation at the very first election; the second does not always operate fully immediately, especially if the party 'resuscitated' by proportional representation was really moribund, for it is not always possible to have candidates ready to stand as soon as the opportunity offers. But at the second election it regains lost ground, and as it progresses it recovers electors who had left it under a simple-majority single-ballot system because they did not wish to waste their votes and play into the enemy's hands. The polarization of the single-ballot system is pointless under proportional representation where no vote is lost (at least in theory); hence we have the opposite process of 'depolarization'.

The first effect of proportional representation is therefore to put an end to any tendency towards a two-party system: in this respect it may be considered as a powerful brake. There is no encouragement to parties with similar tendencies to fuse, as their division does them little or no harm. There is nothing to prevent splits within parties, for the total representation of the two separate factions will not be mechanically reduced by the effect of the vote; it may be psychologically, by the confusion it sows among the electors, but the ballot plays no part in this. The only attenuation of the fundamental tendency to preserve an established multi-partism comes from the collective nature of proportional representation: the party must have organization, discipline, structure. It is therefore opposed to the individualistic anarchical tendencies which sometimes develop under the two-ballot system, and therefore causes a certain coagulation of the small unstable groups which result from it. In Italy, for example, proportional representation seems to have reduced the number of parties in 1919 by strengthening the Socialists and especially by creating the Christian Democratic party of Dom Sturzo. The phenomenon of reduction is to be seen most on the Right and in the Centre, where anarchy is most developed. Proportional representation played a certain part in the uniting of the upper and lower middle classes around Catholic parties, in France in 1945, and in Italy in 1920 and in 1945, as well as in their unification round the Fascist parties in Italy and especially in Germany. To this extent proportional representation sometimes modifies the multi-party system without ever killing it and bringing about a two-party system.

The problem of the increase in the number of existing parties caused by proportional representation is quite a different one. Does P.R. confine itself to maintaining an established multi-partism within the limits that have just been defined, or does it bring about a multiplication of parties? The answer is not easy: though it cannot be denied that proportional representation has a multiplicative effect, it does not seem to be as great as is sometimes suggested, and above all it takes place in certain well-defined directions. Most interesting information concerning the very existence of this multiplicative effect may be obtained from present-day Germany in which several *Länder* have an electoral system combining the simple-majority single-ballot with proportional representation. Some of the deputies (three-quarters in Westphalia–North Rhineland, two-thirds in Schleswig-Holstein and in Hamburg, three-fifths in Hesse, half in Bavaria, etc.) are elected by a simple-majority single ballot: the others are elected according to proportional representation, either on supplementary lists or by means of a rather complicated double vote. The system is moreover modelled on the elections to the Bundestag of the Federal Republic in which 242 deputies are elected by a simple-majority single ballot, and 160 are nominated from lists established by the parties, in such a way as to correct in a proportional sense the results of the direct vote. In so far as electoral statistics make it possible to distinguish between the results of the simple-majority ballot and those of the later proportional distribution we can measure the multiplicative influence of the latter. Nevertheless it must not be forgotten that the whole election takes place in a proportional setting that has an influence on the psychology of the electors: the most important thing is that they know that the votes they give to candidates who seem likely to be placed third or fourth will not be lost, as in a simple-majority single-ballot system, since the supplementary distribution aims in fact at rescuing them. Consequently polarization takes place little if at all. The result is that the coagulating effect of the simple-majority single-ballot system is attenuated and also the multiplicative effect of proportional representation in relation to it. The latter is, however, still perceptible.

In the Federal Diet the members returned by the constituencies represent only five parties: when the proportional distribution has taken place there are four more parties in the Bundestag: Communists, *Zentrum*, D.R.P. (extreme Right), and W.A.V. (Lorentz' party). In the 1950 election for the Schleswig Diet the electoral bloc formed by the C.D.U. (Christian Democrats), the F.D.P. (Liberal party), and the D.P. (German Conservative party) obtained 31 seats at the simple-majority single ballot, as compared with 8 for the Social Democrats, 5 for the Expropriated and Despoiled bloc, and 2 for the South Schleswig party (pro-Danish): after the proportional distribution the government bloc retained its 31 seats without any change, but the Social Democrats advanced to 19, the Expropriated to 15, and the pro-Danish to 4. Although the actual number of parties has not increased, the growth of small groups has much the same effect. The results are similar in Hesse, the Social Democrats having obtained 36 seats at the simple-majority single ballot, the Liberals 8, and the Christian Democrats 4, these figures rising respectively to 47, 21, and 12 after being corrected by the proportional distribution. In Bavaria the multiplicative effect is clearer: on the result of the simple-majority single ballot 46 seats were allotted to the Bavarian Christian party (C.S.U.), 38 to the Social Democrats, 16 to the Bavarian party, and 1 to the Liberal party; in practice therefore three parties alone were represented. When the proportional distribution had taken place, however, the C.S.U. had 64 seats, the Socialists 63, the Bavarian party 34, the Liberal party 12, and the bloc formed by the Expropriated and

Despoiled and the 'German Community' 26, so that finally five parties had seats in the Diet. This result may be compared with that of the elections to the Hamburg Parliament on 10 October 1949: the 72 representatives elected on the plural vote belonged to two parties only, the Social Democrats (50 representatives) and a coalition of Liberals and Social Democrats which presented single candidates (22 representatives); after the proportional distribution there were three more parties in the Assembly: the German Conservative party (9 representatives), the Communist party (5), and a Radical party (1).

The multiplicative effect of proportional representation seems therefore undeniable. But it is generally limited: it must also be ascertained whether proportional representation applies after a two-ballot poll which itself encourages multi-partism, or after a single ballot which favours bipartism, the multiplicative effect being naturally less marked in the first hypothesis than in the second. It has already been seen that the increase in the number of parties is not very obvious when the second-ballot system is replaced by proportional representation: no increase of note in Holland or in France; a slight increase in Switzerland and Norway and a more considerable one in Germany. This slight increase after years of proportional representation may be explained by different factors: the rise of Communist parties in 1920 is not the result of the electoral system, although the latter may have favoured it. If the change to proportional representation is from the single ballot the multiplicative effect is clearer, though difficult to determine because information is very limited here, only two countries, Sweden and Denmark, having replaced a plural vote system by proportional representation. Sweden had three parties in 1908 and now has five; in Denmark the number has risen from four in 1918 to seven: the increase seems fairly limited. Nevertheless the 1939 War restricted the number of parties in most countries, so that the comparison is not quite accurate: if the comparison had been with a period before the war the increase would have been more noticeable. Moreover the preceding figures do not take into account the very small, ephemeral, and shifting parties which are precisely the kind that tend to abound under proportional representation, as will be shown.

In order to define the mechanism of the multiplicative effect of proportional representation one must distinguish between the division of old parties and the appearance of new parties. The first is not peculiar to proportional representation: schisms and divisions are not infrequent under a simple-majority single-ballot system. The British Liberal party has known many of them, before and after the appearance of the Labour party. But they remain provisional and limited in character: either the two fractions reunite after a certain time or one of them joins the rival party (for example the National Liberals, who have to all intents and purposes become part of the Conservative party). On the other hand under proportional representation the splits tend to endure because the ballot prevents the divergent fractions from being crushed by the opposing parties. The establishment of proportional representation has therefore often coincided with splits within old parties, either open (an old party breaks into two new halves, which continue to pay it allegiance) or disguised (a party calling itself new is set up with some of the leaders and organizers of an old party which continues to exist). For example in Switzerland proportional representation gave rise in 1919 to the 'Peasant and Bourgeois party' which actually was the result of a split in the Radical party. In Sweden a few years passed (1911–20) before an Agrarian party, resulting in fact from a split in the Conservative party, was created, while in 1924 the Liberal party divided into two branches (which reunited in 1936 as a result rather of the disappearance of one of them than of a real fusion). In Norway proportional representation provoked both a split amongst the Socialists, divided into Socialists of the Right and Socialists of the Left (they were not to join up again until 1927), and at the same time two splits at the expense of the Liberal Left, through the creation of 'Radical Democrats', who were to obtain two seats, and the sudden growth of the small Agrarian party created at the last election and so far very weak, which advanced from 36,493 votes to 118,657 votes and from 3 seats to 17.

Nevertheless this effect of proportional representation is very limited; on the whole P.R. maintains almost intact the structure of parties existing at the time of its appearance. It never has the disintegrating effect that some people claim for it: in most cases schisms take place through the division of one large party into two others, which then retain their positions throughout the following elections. The multiplying tendency is shown less through the division of old parties than through the creation of new parties: it should be quite clear that these are essentially small parties. Failure to realize this has caused some people to deny, with every appearance of truth, that proportional representation has a multiplying effect. Most of the countries where proportional representation has been effectively used took precautions to avoid this rise of small parties which is the natural result of the system: for example the Hondt method or the method of the highest average, which function in most states with proportional representation, definitely discourage small parties and tend to offset in this way the consequences of proportional representation. The same may be said of the Dutch system, in which no list is eligible for the distribution of the remaining seats unless it has obtained at least the electoral quotient. Fundamentally, 'full' proportional representation exists nowhere, not so much because of the technical difficulties of its application (which are relatively easy to overcome) as because of its political consequences, and particularly its tendency to multiply the more or less minute and shifting groups.

Nevertheless, this deep-seated tendency always triumphs over the barriers set up against it. Let us confine ourselves here to a few typical examples. In Norway, at the first elections with proportional representation held in 1921, two new small parties appeared, the Radical Democrats with twoseats and the Socialists of the Right with eight seats; in 1924 they were joined by a third party, the Communist party, with six seats; in 1927, a fourth, the Liberals, with one seat; in 1933, a fifth, the Social party, with one seat, and a sixth, the Christian Democrats, also with one seat: a similar development has taken place in the other Scandinavian countries. The phenomenon is still more obvious in Holland: in the first elections with proportional representation in 1918 ten new parties obtained one seat (Economic League, Independent Socialist party, Communist party, Neutral party, Social Christians, Christian Democrats, Christian Socialists, League of National Defence, Rural party, Middle-class party). The result of this disturbing abundance was that a clause was introduced into the electoral law eliminating from the distribution of remainders any list that did not obtain 75% of the quotient. Nevertheless four small parties were still in the running after the 1922 elections: three old and one new (Reformed Calvinists); two more arose in 1925 (Reformed Political party and Dissident Catholics); one more in 1929 (Independents); two more in 1933 (Social Revolutionaries and Fascists), and one of the 1918 parties, which had disappeared after the 75% bar, was reborn (Christian Democrats). It became necessary to make further modifications to the electoral law in order to set up fresh obstacles to the tendency of proportional representation to multiply minor parties; so, in 1935, the proportion of the quotient that had to be obtained in order to participate in the distribution of remainders was raised from 75% to 100% and a deposit was introduced. But there were still four

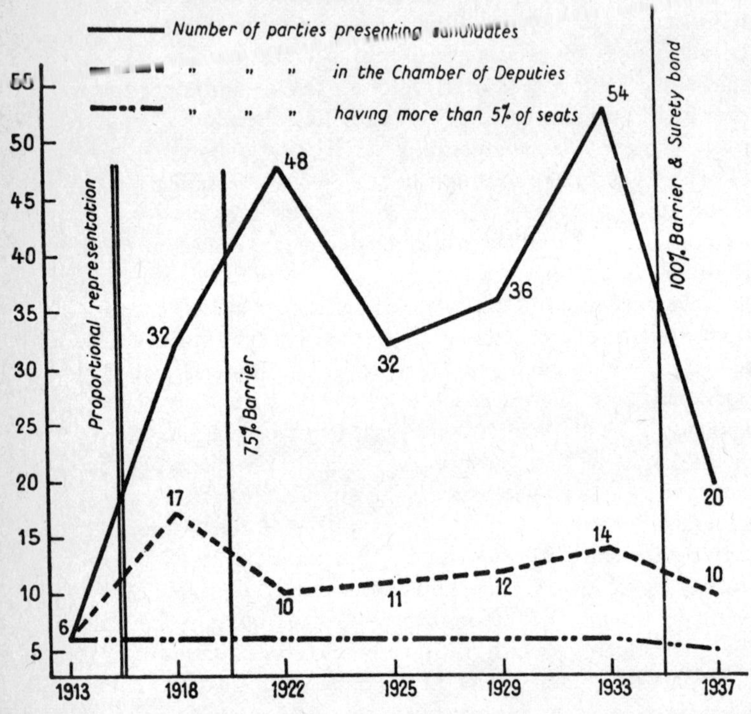

Fig. 30. Multiplication of parties by P.R. (Holland, 1918–39)

small parties represented in the 1937 Parliament, of which one, the National Socialist party, was new. This brought to seventeen the total of small groups which had developed through proportional representation between 1918 and 1939 (Fig. 30). Moreover it should be noted that these are not truly local parties, explained by the personality of such and such a candidate: as Frederick S. A. Huart has shown in his article in *The Encyclopaedia of Social Sciences*, the system of proportional representation applied in the Netherlands, which in practice turns the whole country into a single electoral district, has given rise to minor parties that are national and no longer local in character. On the eve of proportional representation the Parliament at The Hague contained seven parties: between 1918 and 1939 it never counted less than ten, and this figure rose to seventeen. It was the 1939 War that brought it back to its 1913 figure: but between 1946 and 1948 it had already risen from seven to eight. Moreover these figures do not give a clear idea of the reality: they should be completed by a list of the number of parties presenting candidates at the elections. In the Netherlands, for example, it rose from 36 to 54 between one election and the next (1929–33). In Switzerland 67 parties have presented lists in various cantons between 1919 and 1939, out of which 26 obtained representatives on the National Council at one time or another.

But the tendency of proportional representation to give rise to new parties is not always confined to minor parties. Because it is very sensitive to waves of popular emotion, to those great enthusiasms that sometimes rouse a people like a tide, it favours their coagulation into parties which can then prolong the original passion and prevent the ebb of opinion. The phenomenon is the more marked since it is accompanied by an agglomeration around these new movements of small Right and Centre groups of a personal character. In this way proportional representation seems to have favoured the development of Fascism. Hermens has perhaps exaggerated its role in relation to National Socialism; in this sphere the electoral system cannot be considered as a preponderant factor. Neither can its influence be denied: it is curious to note that the only countries in which the Fascist tendency has succeeded in finding corporate expression in parties represented in parliament are countries with proportional representation. This problem will be met with again in connection with the strength of parties, their variations in size, and the representation of new movements of opinion.

III. THE SINGLE PARTY

Usually the single party is considered as the great political innovation of the twentieth century. Actually, although dictatorship is as old as the hills, dictatorship based on a party, as was the case in Germany and Italy, and as it is today in Soviet Russia and the People's Democracies, is a new kind of political system. But there is hardly less difference between the nineteenth-century democracies, based on personal representation and the independence of deputies, and the present form of democracy which is based on an advanced degree of organization of electors and elected. The real novelty lies in the existence of organized parties: the single-party system is only the adaptation to the needs of a dictatorship of a general technique that had its origins within a democratic framework. The great political innovation of the twentieth century is not the single party but the party.

There is no fundamental difference in structure between single parties and the parties of democratic regimes: the French Communist party resembles the Russian Communist party more than the Radical party. In the United States there is not a very marked difference between the Democrats of the South, a single party, and the Democrats of the North, a pluralist party: the first have much more in common with the second than they have with the German National Socialist party or the Italian Fascist party. The common tendency to equate single party and totalitarian party and single party and Bund is contradicted by the facts: there are single parties that are not totalitarian: there are totalitarian parties in multi-party systems. To say that these have copied the structure of single parties precisely because they desire to imitate them and to suppress their rivals, and that consequently they are really virtual single parties, is not consistent with the facts. Historically most large single parties were first of all opposition parties functioning in a multi-party system; some, for instance the Italian and Russian, were not definitely aiming at becoming one day the only party; their structure did not suffer any essential modification after the seizure of power and the acquisition of the monopoly; their totalitarian nature, their Bund character, their autocratic and centralized structure originated within a democratic system. To start with, single parties imitated or retained structures that had their origin in a multi-party system: the opposite course was only followed afterwards. It is true that the totalitarian nature of a party drives it to suppress all other parties if it can: but the tendency to unity is a consequence of its totalitarian nature more than a cause. A party tends to become the only one because its structure is totalitarian; it does not adopt a totalitarian structure because of a desire to become the only party: this seems at least to be the point from which development originates. There is no clear line of demarcation separating the internal organizations of pluralist parties and single parties: one derives from the other and often remains quite close to it.

As a 'party system' the single party is obviously different from the multi-party system or 'pluralism', and it is indispensable to analyse it separately. Nor has this system the homogeneity that is usually attributed to it. There are *several* single-party systems, not one. This diversity will be emphasized in the following pages, because it seems capable of throwing light on the true nature of the single party and its autocratic character.

General Characteristics of the Single Party. Practice preceded theory in the case of the single party. It has even happened that the theory has never followed: certain states, for example Turkey and Portugal, have put the single-party system into practice without integrating it in their doctrine of power. Even in Soviet Russia it was not until the 1936 Constitution that the Communist party monopoly received legal consecration in Article 126: 'The most active and politically conscious citizens from the ranks of the working class and other strata of the toilers unite in the All-Union Communist party of Bolsheviks which is the advance detachment of the toilers in their struggle for the strengthening and development of the Socialist order, and the directing nucleus of all the workers' organizations, both social and state.' The justification of the single party on the grounds that class differences have been abolished was only put forward later. Finally the theory of the single party was worked out in Italy and in Germany. Moreover each of these countries produced a theory that fitted its own single party: the Fascist party theory in Italy and the National Socialist party theory in Germany, differing considerably from one another. The first analysis of the single party as a general institution dates from 1936.[1] The supporters and the opponents of the single party do not see it in quite the same way. The latter are willing to accept the general plan suggested by the former, but on many points they do not agree with their interpretation. The apologists of the system claim that it serves a double purpose: the single party is both an elite and a bond. The era of the masses has entailed the decline of the traditional social elites: the aim of the single party is to form new elites, to create a new ruling class, to unite and to shape the political leaders capable of organizing the country, for the masses cannot themselves govern. Through its youth organizations, their hierarchy, and the channels which take their members into the party itself, or by its organization of controlled methods of entry

[1] Mihaïl Manoïlesco, *Le Parti Unique*, Paris, 1936.

into the party after a waiting period, sponsorship and tests, the party forms a sieve which retains the elites in its meshes. It instructs them at the same time; it makes them capable of fulfilling their tasks: it also organizes them in a permanent fashion; it gives them a structure and a hierarchy. For this new ruling class is organized, and in this differs from the old ruling class where individualism reigned; it forms a community of its own within the community of the people, to whom it serves as an example and a guide. The elite thus chosen and prepared by the party can, thanks to it, fulfil its role of leadership. The principal political, administrative, and economic leaders are taken from the party, but the party itself, as a body, unceasingly supervises all state organizations. Its function is not so much to administer as to ensure the vitality of the administration and to ensure its fidelity. The representatives of the party, therefore, have seats everywhere, from the Councils of Ministers to the smallest local or special committees; from the Civil Service to the Trade Unions, Co-operatives, Cultural Associations, etc.; unless the party assumes directly certain functions, for itself or for its ancillary organizations.

Moreover the party establishes direct and permanent contact between the government and the country. The chief difficulty with authoritarian regimes always lies in the fact that their leaders are isolated from the masses: in a democracy elections make it possible for the leaders to become acquainted with the opinion of the masses and to make sure from time to time of their position with regard to them; dictatorship is deprived of this political compass. Its leaders run the risk of becoming more and more isolated from the people, of completely losing contact with them, the more so as they are surrounded by subordinates who flatter and deceive them so as to be in favour. Police reports are insufficient to break through this iron curtain which separates the government from the governed. On the contrary the single party breaks the isolation by its thousands of cells and sections scattered throughout the country, through all the strata of the population and all social groups. The government is constantly 'listening to the masses'; it can know what the people think about it, and the variations in and development of this opinion, and can then model its conduct upon it. It can also shape the opinion itself. For contact is established not only upwards, in the direction 'people-leaders', but also downwards, in the direction 'leaders-people'. Like wireless stations serving both for the reception and the transmission of messages the single party enables the leaders to hear the voice of the country and the country to hear the voice of the leaders. The same pyramidal structure which makes it possible for the summit to know the reactions of the base in all their diversity makes it possible for the base to receive directives from the summit with a commentary adapted to each group. The party gives the government the opinion of the people; it enables the people to understand the decisions of the government. The stalwarts of whom it is composed revive the lukewarm who remain outside its community. Their action is all the more effective in that as individuals they remain part of the people. Civil servants or official propagandists would not achieve the same result because of their own separation from the 'governed'. The efficiency of the party is derived from its twofold nature: it is both a state body capable of understanding state decisions from the inside and of adhering totally to them and a group of citizens who feel the reactions of the people in themselves and in their neighbours and who are able to express these to the leaders.

The opponents of the single party make amendments to this idealized description. For them the party is a new variety of a very old sociological type: the Praetorian guard which strengthens the tyrant's dictatorship. It is less a question of the selection of an elite than of the creation of a privileged class, bound to the regime by the particular favours it enjoys: material advantages, monopoly of administrative posts, more freedom and power than other citizens, etc. In practice loyalty to the dictator much more than personal merit or aptitude for command is the criterion of whether or not one is allowed to join or to remain in the party. The single party tends to become the 'retinue' of the dictator, attached to him by the favours which its members receive: the innovation resides only in the technical organization of this 'retinue', not in its existence, which is common to all tyrannical systems. As for the 'contact' between the people and the government, the opponents of the single party do not deny it, but they think it is very limited in the upward direction. Party discipline, leader-worship, and the mutual admiration which takes place in it very quickly isolate its members from the masses and hide from them the true reactions of the latter. Moreover the necessity of 'paying court' at all levels of the hierarchy makes it inevitable that truth should be deformed in the course of its transmission, that is supposing that it could ever be ascertained at the base. The militant member can still manage to become aware of it if he makes an effort to free himself from the party slogans, but elementary prudence will cause him to distort the truth when he passes it on to his local leader; there will be a fresh distortion for the same reasons when the latter makes his report to the district leader; a fresh distortion when the district leader co-ordinates the reports before presenting them to the centre: a fresh distortion when the centre explains the position to the party leader, who is also the Head of the State. Certainly the latter is hardly less isolated from the people than Louis XIV at Versailles.

Real contact is established in the downward direction. The fundamental business of the party is to spread the dictator's orders among the public, to ensure government propaganda. There lies its most authentic originality. This Praetorian guard does not draw its strength from pike and lance, in the tradition of the tyrants of old; it draws it from propaganda. The single party is bound up with the modern techniques of influencing the masses. It is the most perfect propaganda machine of all. It is an admirable tool for shaping opinion, for forming it, organizing, canalizing and directing it. But persuasion and obsession are not always sufficient; they are therefore accompanied by spying and repression. As well as being an organization for propaganda, the party is also a police organization, and its originality is equally great here. Spying and informing are two essential duties of a good militant. The very organization of the party makes it possible for it to keep a watch on everything. Each tenement cell is made responsible for the loyalty of the inhabitants, and for spotting suspects and denouncing them. The party is an instrument of terrorism. Further, a distinction might be made between external and internal terrorism. The first consists of the supervision of the whole body of citizens by the party members, which guarantees the loyalty of the whole nation. The second is the mutual supervision of party members by each other, which ensures the loyalty of the political 'elite'. Internal terrorism sometimes seems more severe than external terrorism: being a member of the party does not always ensure peace of mind, far from it. Nevertheless this description must not be exaggerated. In most contemporary totalitarian states the functions of the police are assumed by bodies distinct from the party (O.V.R.A., Gestapo, M.V.D., etc.): although collaborating with them in general supervision and in tracking down the unorthodox, the party is not absorbed in them. The same specialization is also observed for propaganda, at least in Germany (where the Ministry of Propaganda was separate from the party); in Soviet Russia on the other hand, agitation and propaganda (Agit-prop) remain fundamental activities of the party. Even if the originality of the single party is often exaggerated by its supporters it should nevertheless not be underestimated by its opponents.

The latter point out that the functions officially attributed to the single party by its defenders do not differ in nature from the functions that all parties assume in a pluralist democracy. Such parties also aim at picking out a political elite and at making possible contact between the people and the powers that be; but in practice the existence of only one party completely transforms these functions. This monopoly itself is justified in various ways; all the single-party regimes do not adopt the same doctrine here. Some see in the single party the reflection of national unity; others the reflection of social unity. The first explanation goes with Fascist or Conservative theories. According to them, democratic pluralism leads to a distortion of the general interest through a struggle between private interests, through sacrificing the interests of the whole people to disputes concerning the special objectives of individual fractions. 'In the cracked mirror of parties the country no longer recognizes its own image' one might say, paraphrasing a well-known metaphor. There are two underlying reasons for this general attitude, one theoretical, the other practical. The first is derived largely from Rousseau and his conception of the general will, which would be falsified by being split up into collective particular wills: the men of 1789 distrusted 'intermediary bodies'; there is no doubt that they would not have accepted the pluralism of parties. The second reason is based on considerations of fact; this pluralism is considered to be contrary to the pursuit of public good by those in power, yet this should be their supreme aim. 'When there are parties in a country, sooner or later a state of affairs exists in which it is impossible to intervene effectively in public affairs without joining a party and playing the party game. Anyone interested in public affairs wishes his interest to have effective results. Thus those who are interested in public welfare either give up the idea and turn to something else, or pass through the party mill. In this case too they have preoccupations which exclude that of the public welfare.'[1]

Really these are arguments rather for the suppression of all

[1] Simone Weil, quoted by Louis Vallon, *Le Dilemme français*, French People's Rally publication, 1951.

parties than for the setting-up of a single party. The same might be said of the Communist doctrine, despite its totally different basis. Here the single party is the natural consequence of Marxist doctrine and the structure of the Soviet Union. It has already been stated that Marxist doctrine considers parties as the political expression of various social classes and not as ideological groups. To be more precise, the ideological character is secondary to the social character, for the ideology is determined by economic relations and the situations brought about by them. Moreover Russian leaders consider that class differences have been suppressed in Russia, where the Marxist pattern of a classless society or a single-class society has been achieved. Diversity of party therefore serves no useful purpose. The Communist doctrine of the single party may be expressed in a syllogism: '(*a*) each party is the political expression of a social class; (*b*) now the Soviet Union is a one-class society; (*c*) therefore the Soviet Union can exist only under a single-party system'. To be quite accurate this rigid formula makes some slight change in the Communist conception of party: it plays upon words by assimilating 'classless society' and 'one-class society'. The idea of social class assumes some differentiation: the term 'classless society' is the only one that is correct and in conformity with Marxism. But the premiss and the conclusion of the syllogism should then be different. If we say '(*b*) now the Soviet Union is a classless society' we must conclude '(*c*) therefore the Soviet Union must have *no* political party'. According to the teaching of Marx and Lenin the party is an organization for the war of one class against another: if there are no more classes there is no more fighting, and no further need for the organization. The Russian conception of the single party, however, is based on a state of affairs less static and final: it considers that classes no longer exist in the Soviet Union since the suppression of the 'bourgeoisie' and 'the exploiting class', but that these have not been completely destroyed, that they could revive, and that strong precautions must be taken against them. Hence the retention of the Communist party, the fighting organization of the working class in its effort to destroy its rivals, as well as the organization for seeing that they do not build up their strength again.

Another justification for the single party has been found by Manoïlesco in the abandonment by contemporary authoritarian states of the principle of political neutrality. For the neutral state has been substituted the state as a 'bearer of ideals', the state as an incarnation of a faith, a moral or an ethical system. When there is neutrality the pluralism of parties is natural: the state respects all moral systems and all ideals, and therefore all the parties which defend them. Its role consists solely in deciding the conditions of their rivalry and in preventing one from absorbing the others. Obviously the situation is different if the state itself adheres to a definite ethical system: it can then accept only the party which defends it: for then the others no longer struggle *in* the State but *against* the State, against the values it embodies. This *a priori* reasoning seems to conform to certain actual facts. It is true that pluralism exists only in democratic regimes which affirm their neutrality. It is true that the single party usually functions in states which have repudiated this neutrality and proclaimed their adhesion to a dogma. The development of the single party coincides with the rebirth of state religions in the new form they have assumed in the contemporary world; we have a Religious State rather than a State Religion. The state does not adhere to an external transcendent faith which places its object and end outside it: it is itself this object and this end. Nevertheless certain single parties have arisen in neutral states which did not claim to be 'bearers of ideals': for example in Turkey. Moreover the neutrality of democratic regimes is often exaggerated, democracy does not lack an ethical system; it defends the Liberal ethic, which is as good as the others. It is true that parties in a multiple system have only functioned correctly in so far as their combat was confined to the technical field; when they have become religious or moral in nature their struggle has assumed an implacable character and pluralism has been threatened. But there would be nothing to prevent pluralism in states that are 'bearers of ideals': in the Soviet Union the rivalry between heavy and light industry might very well have become a party struggle, if the powers that be had desired it. Manoïlesco starts with far too narrow and rigid a conception of political parties, which is not in conformity with experience. He is too attached to the Liberal conception of the party as an ideology and does not take into account the Marxist conception of the party as a class.

Fascist and Communist Single Parties. Any general description of the single party is necessarily vague. As soon as we wish to be more precise we are faced with the fundamental difference between the single party of the Fascist type and the single party of the Communist type. There is first of all the contrast in the doctrinal field, which is beyond the scope of this book. We have already pointed out the difference between Communist optimism and Fascist pessimism: Communist philosophy is the direct heir of the age of enlightenment and belief in progress. The Marxist tendency is to prove that the Golden Age lies before us, the age of the classless society, of the end of the exploitation of man by man, the age of prosperity and of happiness. 'The song of tomorrow', this phrase of Gabriel Péri's is typically Communist. For a Fascist it was yesterday that sang, yesterday, the good old days: we must rediscover a lost tradition and return to our dried-up springs: the Golden Age lies behind us. Or else there is no Golden Age; if it does not adopt a Conservative and regressive philosophy Fascism adheres to a cyclical philosophy: tomorrow will not be better than yesterday; man is ever the same; the wheel turns—the solar wheel represented by the swastika of the National Socialists.

The Communists take up the old doctrine of Rousseau and rejuvenate it a little: man is born good, it is capitalism that corrupts him. The Fascists think that man is naturally corrupt, that he is born corrupt, and that it is society alone that civilizes him. Naturally, the genius, the hero, the saint, and the elite—those 'who have received the mysterious power of giving more to their fellow men'—are excluded. Fascism despises the individual and exalts him at the same time: it despises the ordinary man and exalts the superman. Communism believes in ordinary men—in its pristine purity it did not believe in supermen: Marxism tends to minimize the influence of individuals on the course of history. But there has been a great change in this respect: the cult of Lenin and Stalin has made Communism more like Fascism. Nevertheless it has not nearly such a liking for 'elites', 'leading strata', and 'leaders'; even when forming a new leading class, by means of a party, it considers it only as the most awakened, devoted and enlightened part of the whole proletariat. It remains a fundamentally egalitarian doctrine, in contrast with Fascism which is aristocratic.

It should be added that Communism alone constitutes a complete coherent philosophy. It alone offers an overall co-ordinated explanation of the universe. Fascism aims at the same totality but does not achieve it. To be more precise, it does achieve it vaguely and obscurely. Fascism has lacked the equivalent of Karl Marx and the philosophical movement that grew around his teaching. Marxism, at one and the same time philosophy and logic, framework for thought and system of thought, has an intellectual wealth that Fascism lacks. Rosenberg's stories of race and blood are confused, obscure and vague; the theories of Mussolini concerning the state, corporations and authority are brief and disconnected. There is no Fascist philosophy nor Fascist doctrine: there are myths, tendencies, and aspirations with not much connection between them, and not much coherence. It is true that Fascism does in fact affirm the prime importance of the irrational and of instinct, whereas Communism proclaims the sovereignty of reason and science and often, moreover, assumes the guise of a scientific view of the world together with all the narrowness that such an attitude implies; but this is a distortion by unintelligent disciples; the basic doctrine is much richer and stronger.

From the social point of view the definition of Communist parties as 'the tools of the proletariat to overthrow the authority of the middle classes' and of Fascist parties as 'the tools of the middle classes to retain their power and prevent its falling into the hands of the proletariat' is rather inadequate. Nevertheless on the whole it corresponds to reality. In the Soviet Union the Communist party has not overthrown the power of the middle class but rather the power of the aristocracy; it derived its strength not only from the proletariat but from the peasants. Nevertheless it broke the attempt at a revolution on the 1789 pattern launched by the constitutional Democrats and Kerensky; it liquidated the 'Kulaks' and the land-owning middle class, and for a long time it gave the working class of the towns preponderance over a peasant class that was actually more numerous. In Italy and in Germany the principal objective of Fascism was to keep the middle class in power: in both countries it was subsidized by the important capitalists; in both countries it mobilized the middle classes that were its principal strength. One ought perhaps to distinguish between the seizure of power and the exercise of power. In the first phase the definitions given above are more or less exact: Communism enlists the working class in order to overthrow the middle-class state; Fascism brings together the upper and lower middle classes in order to oppose this overthrow. The presence of an important Communist party is thus one of the factors essential to the birth and development of Fascism.

In the second phase it has been claimed that Fascism and Communism tend to become like each other, the first tending to rely more and more on the working class and to limit the power of the middle class; the second to create a new privileged class, a kind of neo-bourgeoisie: without being absolutely false, this opinion does not seem to coincide with the facts. No doubt party members are clearly distinguished in the Soviet Union from the mass of citizens both by their special duties and their special rights. But one cannot call this the reconstitution of a middle class, for there are neither hereditary advantages nor prerogatives derived from private property and money. The party does perhaps constitute an elite, but not a middle-class elite in the sociological sense of the term; it is true that it is wider open to membership from outside the working class than it was in the first years of its monopoly: the 1939 constitution unified in this respect the rules of sponsorship and the length of the waiting periods and put an end to the privileges of the proletariat, but that is not a direct proof of becoming middle class. On the other hand the proportion of the working class in Fascist parties does not seem to have increased very noticeably during the period of their stay in power. Direct recruitment having been suppressed the only new members came from youth organizations: it does not seem as if their admission has modified the distribution of social classes within the party. Nevertheless the absence of evidence does not allow of a very definite conclusion on this last point.

These doctrinal and social differences are too well known for there to be any need to insist on them. On the other hand less is known about differences in party structure, which are nevertheless very important. Certainly the general framework is the same, with strict centralization and vertical links. Nevertheless it should be noted that the Communist party officially adopts election as the means of appointing its leaders, whereas the Fascist parties rely entirely on a system of nomination. In practice, however, the difference is not so great as in theory. The same may be said of the basic elements. The Communist party is based on cells, the Fascist parties on militias; but after the seizure of power the latter are bound to become less important. Unless they are limited to the thankless role of a supplementary police force the tendency is to disarm them fear lest they should form a state within the state, capable of overthrowing the government they have themselves put in power, lies at the root of this. In Germany there was a general disarming o the Storm Troops after 1934: training exercises were spaced out and members had the right to wear uniform only for drills, ceremonies, and processions. The militia became an army for show only the party sections and cells worked effectively, as in th Communist party.

The most noteworthy difference in structure (but not that of which most notice has been taken) concerns admission into the party. As has already been said, entrance to single parties of the Fascist type is in practice confined to adolescents coming from the youth organizations. In the Italian Fascist party entrance was practically unrestricted until 1922, strictly controlled from 1922 to 1925, and then completely closed, except in year X of the regime, when with the severest of screening it was provisionally restored. In the National Socialist party direct recruitment came to a full-stop on the 1st Mary 1933. In Italy one had first of all, at a very tender age, to join the *ballilas* (aged eight to fourteen), to pass into the *Advance Guard* (fourteen to eighteen), then into the *Young Fascists* (eighteen to twenty-one); only then did one receive the party card after taking an oath during the solemn ceremony of the 'Fascist levy': like conscripts, all the young men born in the same year joined the ranks of the party on the same day. In Germany members of the Hitler Youth who had turned eighteen in the case of boys, and twenty-one in the case of girls, could be admitted into the party on condition they had belonged to the organization for at least four years without interruption and that 'by the zealous accomplishment of their service obligations and by irreproachable conduct within the service and outside they have shown themselves proved National Socialists in feelings and in character and offer the assurance of becoming valuable members when they join the party'. It can be seen that admission was not automatic and that the system was fundamentally different from the Italian technique. Nevertheless there was the same solemn ceremony with an oath-taking on the 9th November, the anniversary of the Munich *putsch*.

In Soviet Russia admission to the Communist party is subject to entirely different rules. Recruitment has always been open and separate from membership of the Communist Youth Organization. Anyone who wishes to join the party must obtain the sponsorship of three persons who have been party members for at least three years and who have known him and worked with him for at least one year. The decision to admit is taken at the local level and approved at the town or district level: the attendance of the sponsors at the discussions is obligatory. If the decision is favourable the candidate must pass through a preliminary stage, lasting a year, which aims at 'making him familiar with the programme, rules, and tactics of the party and at allowing the party organizers to weigh his personal qualities'.[1] During this stage he attends all party meetings but has no vote, and he pays the same dues as members. At the expiration of the period the same process of sponsorship and investigation by the basic organization is repeated: if the decision is favourable the 'candidate-member' becomes a real member of the party. Before 1939 the conditions for admission were stricter and more discriminating. Four categories of people were established; first, industrial workers (of at least five years' standing); second, agricultural workers, industrial workers (of less than five years' standing), engineers or technicians, soldiers who had been workmen or workers on collective farms; third, members of collective farms or co-operative organizations and teachers; fourth, other employed persons. Candidates in the first category were obliged to provide testimonials from three party members of at least five years' standing; those in the fourth category, testimonials from five party members of at least ten years' standing; the length of the preliminary stage was one year for the first category, two years for the others. Members of the Communist Youth Organization enjoyed no special facilities for entering the party: the only difference was that a testimonial from the district committee of the Youth Organization was equivalent to a testimonial from a member of the party. In fact a considerable number of new members came from the Communist Youth Organization but not the majority. Between 1930 and 1934, for example, of one million new members joining the party, only 375,000 came from the Youth Organization.[2] Moreover, at that period, recruitment was somewhat restricted; it has been considerably extended since the war.

These differences in methods of recruitment are fundamental: since the single party seeks to create an elite, the ways in which it selects that elite are of primary importance. Fascist parties are closed: those who did not belong before victory have no longer any chance of joining. Only the new generations can join after a long period of preliminary training. In consequence they tend to become isolated from the nation, to become a rigid caste founded upon a kind of collective heredity. Membership in this case is the result of a system of training exercised upon children or adolescents as yet unaware of the real problems and incapable of pronouncing valid judgements. Isolation became so serious in the Italian Fascist party after seven years with no direct recruitment that this had to

[1] Article 13 of the Party Regulations, 1939.
[2] Cf. *L'Encyclopédie Française*, Vol. X, *L'Etat moderne*, pp. 1082–6.

be restored for some time in 1933; new blood was infused into the party somewhat brutally: it almost doubled its membership. In the Russian Communist party, on the contrary, this caste feature is not to be seen: an ordered mobility of the elite becomes possible; contact with the masses is established. No permanent and rigid barrier separates the 'haves' and the 'have-nots', the 'ins' and the 'outs'. Entry to the party is not easy, but it is always possible. Except during the periods 1921–4 and 1933–8, a policy of widening the political elite has resulted in reasonably easy admission to the party, in contrast with Fascist practice.

Difference in admission policy is complemented by a difference as to expulsion. Fascist parties have never made any regular use of the system of 'purges' which plays so great a part in Communist parties. After the seizure of power they did carry out some considerable 'purging' in order to get rid of doubtful elements and especially of revolutionary elements. Thus in Italy it is reported that 150,000 Fascists were expelled from the party in the first year;[1] in 1925–6 a new wave of excommunications is said to have led to the 'reconstruction of the party from top to bottom'.[2] In Germany, Hitler announced at the Nuremberg Congress in September 1934 a rigorous screening of party members; at the 1935 Congress he confirmed this: 'our membership has been subjected to a drastic purge',[3] a purge consequent on the events of June 1934 and the brutal repression of the Roehm–Strasser opposition. These expulsions remained the exception. On the other hand, in the Russian Communist party 'purging' is regular and systematic in character. Before 1939 it was decided upon at regular intervals by the Central Committee: all members of the party had then to be examined by an investigating committee which subjected them to a close examination of their activities. At the time of the 1933 purge, 17% of the members were expelled and 6·3% were demoted, that is reclassified as probationers. In fact, the great purges almost always coincided with a change in the party line or with modifications of its social structure. The Russian single-party presents therefore the characteristics of a living organism in which the cells are perpetually renewing themselves. Fascist parties on the other hand are more like frozen, unchanging automata. Fear of the 'purge' keeps the militants in suspense, is a perpetual spur to endeavour; the absence of

[1] Statement by Mussolini to Emil Ludwig, quoted by Ludwig, *Entretiens avec Mussolini*, French trans., Paris, 1932.
[2] Mussolini, quoted Kurella, *Mussolini ohne Maske*, 1931.
[3] *Le Temps*, 12 September 1935.

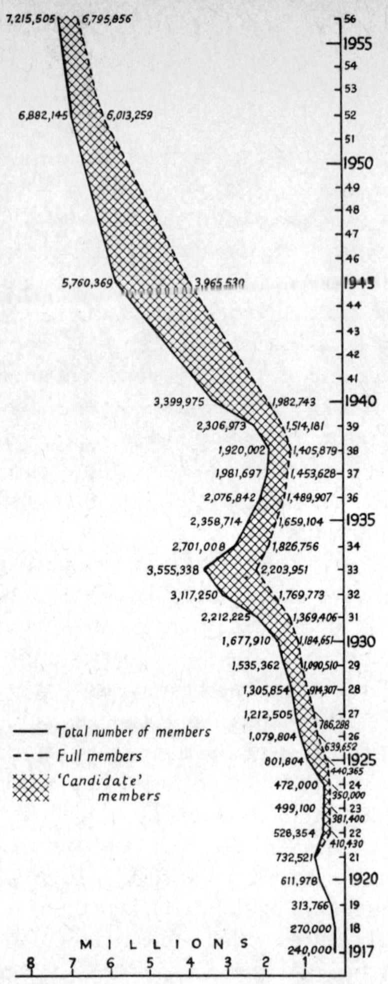

Fig. 31. Development of Russian Communist Party, 1917–56.

SOURCES: For the years 1917–45 (except for 1919 and 1920) *History and Life of the Party*, an article in the review *Partinaïa Jyzn* (Oct. 1947) translated in *Articles et Documents* (Documentation française) 4th Jan. 1948, No. 1168; for 1952 the Malenkov report to the 19th Party Congress (Oct. 1952); for 1919 and 1920 *History of the Russian Communist Party* by Stalin (1938). There are contradictions between the figures given in the *History of the Russian Communist Party* and those in the article in *Partinaïa Jyzn*, and sometimes there is a considerable difference between them. To some extent this may be due to the fact that the *History of the Russian Communist Party* gives the figures on the day of the Congress while the *Partinaïa Jyzn* article gives the 1st January figures for each year.

In the Figure above we have used Congress day figures for 1917–20 and 1952–56 and 1st January figures for 1921–45.

large-scale expulsions lulls them into quiescence. The Fascist single party, closed and stabilized, tends to assume the character of an association of Ex-Revolutionaries; the young join them and mould themselves on the pattern of their elders.

Nevertheless the system of mass purges no longer exists in the Soviet Union. After functioning regularly since the N.E.P. (1921), it was suppressed by the eighteenth Communist Congress (1939), which revised the party constitution accordingly. The resolution adopted by Congress on the 20th March 1939 contains interesting details on the subject. It is stated that collective purges, necessary immediately after the N.E.P., when the capitalist elements had received a new lease of life, no longer serve any useful purpose, since the capitalist elements have been completely eliminated. They are criticized chiefly because they substituted for an individual examination of the members of the party general criteria which did not allow of an appropriate judgement. But the reform of 1939 was not the end of purges: it meant only that they were no longer collective and periodic. Henceforward the party was to drive from its ranks by the ordinary procedure of individual expulsion those who violated its programme or its rules. Combined with the greater facilities for joining the party which were also introduced by the 1939 reform, these measures denote a remarkable increase in the flexibility of the party's structure which makes it even more obviously different from single parties of the Fascist type. Actually the Russian Communist party, which had less than two million members in 1930 and less than two and a half in 1939, has today more than six million. This enormous growth is the direct consequence of the 1939 reforms; it is a sign of a considerable transformation of the regime.

This transformation is all the more important since the place occupied by the party in the state is fundamental in the Soviet Union, which differs from the Fascist regimes in this respect. Theory and practice diverge here. In Germany as in Italy, official speeches and proclamations unceasingly affirmed the prime importance of the party: National Socialist jurists even strained their ingenuity to define a doctrine of the relations between the party and the state, which concluded by subordinating the second to the first. Certainly in neither country could the place occupied by the party be said to be negligible. Its representatives had seats in that capacity on numerous public bodies, at the central as well as at local level. The system of personal union had moreover introduced the party chiefs into the leading positions in the state. But the party does not really seem to have had a preponderant influence on political life. It is certain that precise conclusions are unattainable in this sphere in which analysis is particularly difficult. Nevertheless the role of the Communist party seems much more important in Russia than that of the Fascist party in Italy or the National Socialist party in Germany. In the Soviet Union the place of the party is perhaps less important in doctrines and ceremonies; there is no doubt that it is much more important in the political leadership of the state. If the respective degrees of influence are not easy to determine at any given moment the general direction of their evolution is very clear: in Russia the influence of the party has been continuously on the increase: in Germany and in Italy it has been continuously on the decrease. In 1933 P. Gentizon, the Rome correspondent of *Le Temps*, stated: 'Until the last few months there was an obvious tendency in some circles to consider the party as a negative element, as a dead-weight in the political field', and he described the effort made to 'give the party more influence',[1] which was shown in the temporary opening of recruitment. But in 1937 he stated that this effort had been unavailing and that 'the pre-eminence of the state over the party is now established. The party is absorbed into the state.'[2]

As a matter of fact the decadence of the Fascist party had begun, immediately after the seizure of power, with a series of purges which rid the party of its most dynamic and revolutionary elements, with the progressive replacement of old leaders by new ones coming from the youth organizations and more loyal, and with the disarmament of the militia and the 'assault sections'. In Germany the evolution was identical: as there was a certain amount of disturbance in the party after the seizure of power, the newspapers published on 10th July a government notice announcing 'the conclusion of the German revolution' and more precisely: 'Party organizations and groups must not arrogate to themselves governmental powers. . . . At all costs and in all spheres the authority of the state must be maintained.' In both countries the laws officially sanctioning the monopoly of the party at the same time made it subject to the state. In both countries the party progressively lost its influence to the advantage of the army. In Italy the militia was staffed by army officers after 1924; after 1935 it was entrusted with preparation for the army under the command of army leaders; it progressively lost

[1] *Le Temps*, 22 December 1933. [2] *Le Temps*, 11 January 1937.

its importance as an auxiliary police force and was replaced by the *carabinieri*, who were under the orders of a general of the regular army. The *Giornale d'Italia* itself wrote in 1934: 'As a result of Fascism the army becomes the new national aristocracy.' In Germany the evolution was even more rapid and brutal—the repression of 1934, which broke the autonomy of the S.A., was probably brought about through the influence of the general staff. The denunciation of the military clauses of the Treaty of Versailles increased the power of the army; in 1935 the 'Labour corps' became a preparation for the army, was taken out of the party's control and passed under military authority; the decree of the 17th January 1936 officially entrusted the Reichswehr with the maintenance of order 'in case of political disturbances'; after 1935 the army played a part of first-rate importance in the party Congresses at Nuremberg. The result of the reform in command brought about in 1938 was not to restore pre-eminence to the party but to put an end to the General Staff's dream of being independent of the government.

This difference in evolution is the result of a fundamental difference in the conception of the role of the single party in the state. In the Soviet Union the party is an instrument of transformation. Its essential task consists in enabling the Russian people to understand the necessity of the economic, social and technical upheavals brought about since the Revolution: modification of the system of ownership, the creation of a heavy industry, the mechanization of the countryside, reforms in the methods of agriculture, the moving of the industrial centres to the East, and so on. The party must conquer the natural passivity of the masses, their fundamental conservatism, in order to win them over to the changes that have been undertaken, so that persuasion may make it unnecessary to have recourse to force (as in country districts at the time of the 'liquidation of the Kulaks'). It must overcome the tendency to inertia and conservatism of its own members: for every community naturally tends to become immobile. It must defeat this law of the degeneration of social energy, which has already been mentioned more than once. The party is the instrument of a real 'permanent revolution': it is the expression of an effort to prevent the regime from becoming stable. Its mechanism of selection, its internal structure, its purges, its unceasingly renewed 'self-criticism', aim at preventing it from becoming sclerosed, for it must itself prevent the regime from becoming sclerosed.

Officially, the role of Fascist parties is identical. Practically it is quite the opposite. In the conquering of power phase, Fascism is very free with revolutionary and 'Left' terms; once it is in power, there is a complete change: it has to adopt a fundamentally conservative attitude. No doubt it busies itself with many reforms on matters of detail: but it does not lay hands on the economic and social structure of the system. It is an instrument in the effort of the upper and lower middle classes to avoid being dominated by the working class and it maintains the real foundations of middle-class power. The transformation of the revolutionary into a conservative once he has gained power provides an explanation of the purges which follow victory and the subsequent lulling to sleep of the party. Both in Italy and in Germany, on the morrow of victory, the party troops demanded from the government the reforms for which they had fought. In both countries, party members talked openly of the 'second revolution'. 'We have carried out a revolution; we are ready, if need be, to begin all over again', wrote the *Popolo di Lombardia* on the 13th January 1923. Towards the middle of 1933, at meetings of the Storm Troops in Germany, there was much insistence on the Socialist part of the Nazi programme; Hitler was obliged on the 1st July at a meeting of Troop leaders at Bad-Reuchenhall in Bavaria to declare with some brutality: 'I shall fight to the last breath against any second wave of revolution.' After their victory the Fascist leaders found themselves caught between the revolutionary ardour of their troops, that they had themselves fanned to gain power, and the conservative wishes of the middle class, upper, middle, and lower alike, which provided the real foundation of their power. In consequence they temporized, first breaking down the vitality of the party lest they should be swamped by it, then building it up again to a certain point so as not to be submerged by the most reactionary elements. Thus the Fascist single party essentially acts as a stabilizing force in the system, and this is equivalent to a limitation of the role of the party.

These differences in the conception and in the extent of the role of single parties may explain the different directions in which the energies of Fascist and Communist systems are turned. The structure of totalitarian systems compels them to maintain a certain pitch of internal tension: their citizens must live in an atmosphere of perpetual effervescence which will preserve their faith and justify constraints. In a Communist system the tension tends to be directed inwards; the energy of the party is revolutionary in nature. Its aim is to build Socialism, to increase production, to modernize the countryside, to exceed the forecasts of the Plan. In a Fascist system energy is, on the contrary, turned outwards: it is imperialist and warlike in nature. It is not by chance that the development of Fascism has been accompanied by the increased importance of the army and the exaltation of war, by the demand for 'living-space': this is the very law of the system. In so far as the characteristics of Communism are dominant over nationalism in Russia, such considerations are reassuring for the future of peace. However, they do not take account of two facts: first, Communism proclaims itself as an international doctrine which can succeed ultimately and totally not in a single country but only on a world-wide scale; next, the revolution, however radical and profound it may be, will of necessity come to an end some day, and the internal fires will then die down. None the less, it appears that at the moment, and for some time to come, the internal energy seems capable by itself of maintaining a state of tension adequate for the stability of the regime: imperialism and war are not therefore, for the moment, the natural and necessary consequence of its political structure. A single party of the Communist type is not automatically pacific, but it may be so, at least provisionally. A single party of the Fascist type cannot be.

The Single Party and Democracy. To couple together the terms 'single party' and 'democracy' will seem sacrilegious to many. This does not matter. The only problem is to discover whether such a coupling ever corresponds to any reality. Every science begins with sacrilege.

A good deal of confusion has been introduced into the question by the widespread idea that Communism and Fascism constitute the only two possible types of single party; such an idea does not correspond with reality. In fact, the notion of Fascism, as it has been described, corresponds approximately to the political regimes of Hitler's Germany and Mussolini's Italy and more to the former than to the latter (in spite of terminology); but it does not correspond to the political system in present-day Portugal; still less with the system operative in Turkey from 1923 to 1950; still less with that in existence today in the Southern states of the U.S.A., and so on. To consider, for example, that concentration camps and terrorism are techniques inseparable from the single party is to commit an error of fact; in Italy even there do not seem to have been any concentration camps or real terrorism before the war and the pseudo-Republic of 1943. Within the notion of Fascism distinctions based upon national temperament must be drawn; there were as many points of difference between Italian and German Fascism as between the British and French parliamentary systems. Many of the differences between National Socialism and Communism are furthermore nothing more than differences between the German and Russian temperaments. There is a variety of Fascisms, and there are single parties that are not Fascist. The term 'Fascism' is applicable only to totalitarian single parties (Communism excepted); all single parties are not totalitarian nor are all totalitarian parties single parties.

It has already been noted that totalitarian parties can exist in a pluralist system, e.g. Communist parties in France and Italy at the present time. Obviously their presence modifies the structure of pluralism and constitutes an evident menace to it, since every totalitarian party has a natural urge to become the only party. Conversely some single parties are not really totalitarian either in ideas or in organization. The best example of this is provided by the People's Republican party which operated in Turkey from 1923 to 1946 as a single party. Its first claim to originality lay in its democratic ideology. In no way did it set itself up as an Order or a Church like its Fascist and Communist brethren. It imposed on its members neither faith nor mystique: the revolution of Kemal was essentially pragmatic. Its task was to 'Westernize' Turkey by fighting the prime obstacle to any modernization amongst the peoples of the Middle East, that is Islam. The anti-clericalism and rationalism of the leading strata of the party gave it a definite resemblance to nineteenth-century Liberalism: even their nationalism was not very different from that which convulsed Europe in 1848. The attitude of the People's Republican party has sometimes been compared with that of the French Radical Socialist party in its prime; the comparison is not far-fetched. Its very name 'Republican' links it much more with the French Revolution and the terminology of the nineteenth century than with the authoritarian systems of the twentieth. The resemblance is made clearer in the Turkish Constitution which gives all the power to the Great National Assembly, after the pattern of the Convention, and refuses to create a separate Executive. This Constitution is based in its entirety on the principle of national sovereignty to which it gives forceful expression: 'Sovereignty belongs to the nation without any restriction.' The apologia for authority, which is a daily feature of Fascist regimes, was replaced in Kemalist Turkey by an apologia for democracy: not for a 'new' democracy, variously termed 'popular' or 'social', but for traditional political democracy. The party did not deduce its right to govern from its character as the political elite, or as the spearhead of the working class, or from the providential nature of its leader, but from the majority that it won at elections.

That this majority was rendered certain by the fact that only one candidate stood for election is another side of the question. However this fact was not presented as an ideal but as a regrettable and temporary necessity. The Turkish single-party system was never based upon the doctrine of a single party. It gave no official recognition to the monopoly, made no attempts to justify it by the existence of a classless society or the desire to do away with parliamentary strife and Liberal democracy. It was always embarrassed and almost ashamed of the monopoly. The Turkish single party had a bad conscience—differing in this from its Fascist or Communist brethren, who offer themselves as models to be imitated. For its leaders the ideal remained a plural party-system, monopoly being a result of the special political situation in Turkey. On several occasions Kemal attempted to bring it to an end, and this fact in itself is deeply revealing. Nothing similar was conceivable in Hitler Germany or the Italy of Mussolini. In 1924 the Progressive party of Kazim Karabekir provided a first essay in pluralism; it was ended in 1925 after the Kurdish revolt, by the proclamation of a state of siege and by the expulsion of the Progressive deputies from the Chamber. In 1930, Kemal got his friend Fethi Bey, the Ambassador in Paris, specially recalled for the purpose, to create 'out of the blue' a Liberal party. But this opposition party became the rallying ground for all the opponents of the regime, especially for the clericals and religious fanatics, and so the Liberal party was dissolved. In 1935, with the agreement of the People's Republican party, the election was procured of a number of well-known Independents. These efforts to create an opposition have often been ridiculed. None the less they signified that Kemal's government recognized the greater value of pluralism and that it was operating within the framework of a pluralist view of the state.

Furthermore there was nothing totalitarian about the organization of the single party in Turkey. It was based neither upon cells nor upon militia, nor even upon true branches: it might rather be considered a caucus party, in which the leading strata were more important than the members. It did indeed hold a great many public meetings, people's conferences and congresses, designed for the political education of the masses. But the masses themselves were not directly conscripted into the party, which remained very old-fashioned in its organization, closer in this respect to Radical Socialism than to Fascism. It must be added that membership was unrestricted, that the machinery of expulsions and purges did not exist, and that there were neither uniforms nor processions nor rigid discipline. In fact, there seems to have been a quite well-developed democratic spirit inside the party. Officially, all the leaders at every level were elected; in practice, the elections seem scarcely to have been any more 'manipulated' than inside parties in pluralist systems. It is also worth noting that quite a number of factions were able to develop around influential leaders without any 'liquidation' on the Fascist pattern. For example the rivalry between Ismet Inoneu and Celal Bayar first began inside the People's Republican party while Kemal was still alive. The last point is particularly important. In so far as factions develop freely inside a single party this becomes simply a framework which limits political rivalries without destroying them; prohibited outside the single party, pluralism is reborn inside the party, and there it can play the same part. Thus the internal divisions in the Democratic party in the Southern states of America, where it is for practical purposes in the position of a single party, are such that the party is nearer to classical democracy than to Fascism, thanks to the system of the primaries: as far as they are concerned it is possible to transpose the fundamental distinction between bipartism and multi-partism.

It is therefore conceivable that a single-party system may coincide with some kind of political democrcy. Pre-1946 Turkey had not reached that stage. Although the Kemalist system was not Fascist, no more was it democratic. In practice the elections were plebiscites for a single candidate, and the basic political liberties remained very restricted. The same can be said of the Portuguese system, in which the single party (National Union) presents features somewhat similar to those of the Turkish People's Republican party, although it is less organized and plays a much less prominent part in government. In so far as there is a partial coincidence between the single-party system and democracy it exists less on the static plane than on the dynamic. Just as it is possible to apply the description 'virtual single party' to some totalitarian parties functioning within a pluralist system, so it seems possible to apply the term 'virtual pluralism' to some single parties. They should in consequence be considered to represent a stage on the road to democracy. In this matter a fundamental distinction must be made between the single parties set up in previously democratic systems in which pluralism existed and single parties set up in countries already subject to autocratic rule and without experience of real pluralism. The first type would include Germany and Italy, the second Turkey and the Soviet Union. The significance of the single party is obviously different in the two cases. In the second it represents the modernization of an autocracy of archaic structure; it has almost the same significance as the parties in pluralist systems; like them the single party here seeks to replace a traditional aristocracy by a new elite issuing from the people. The establishment of the single-party system brings in its train a real revolution of the progressive type which sets up a certain social equality or at very least diminishes the previous inequality. In this sense the new system is more democratic than the old. On the other hand when the single party replaces pluralism it suppresses or diminishes democracy.

The dynamic view of the single party must take into consideration not only its past but also its future. A distinction should be made between the provisional and the permanent single-party systems, or more accurately between the single party which claims that it is provisional and the single party which claims to be permanent. The anti-democratic nature of the latter is not open to doubt, that of the former is. At this point we may, in the first place, invoke the Marxist-Leninist doctrines relative to the necessity of a transitional dictatorship of the proletariat in order to allow of the establishment of a completely Communist regime. Undeniably the doctrine is well founded: every real social upheaval requires a period of authoritarian rule during which the resistance of the former ruling classes can be broken down to make possible the rise of a new ruling class. In so far as the monopoly of the Russian Communist party corresponds to the 'dictatorship of the proletariat' stage, it is normal. Yet some disquiet may be felt concerning the tendencies that have been manifest in Soviet Russia during the last few years to consider the single party not as a transitional phenomenon corresponding to the period of construction but as a permanent phenomenon corresponding to the structure of a 'classless society'. That would suppress any chance of democratic development. On the other hand a system that definitely stated that the single party was transitional, that it considered it to be no more than a necessary stage on the road to pluralism, could well be considered to be potentially democratic.

Obviously deeds as well as words are required; the rigid organization and the totalitarian nature of the party must not in fact destroy any chance of seeing the system develop the respect for one's enemy and for the opposition which is characteristic of true democracy. Promises cost governments nothing: to announce that democracy begins tomorrow is meaningless if no attempt, however slight, is made today to bring it into being. The idea of 'potential democracy' may provoke a smile; the idea of a single party evolving towards pluralism may be greeted with scepticism; both ideas however have a basis in fact: the post-1923 evolution of Turkey that ended in the 1950 elections with the peaceful triumph of the opposition. With neither checks nor disturbance, Turkey passed from the single-party system to pluralism. Today, she is the most democratic of the Middle-Eastern states, the only one to possess true parties, not feudal clans, nor phantom groups animated by a handful of intellectuals, nor fanatical religious sects. The example of Turkey does not seem to have been properly appreciated; it is of great importance. In the Middle East, as in the Far East, the failure of the techniques of classical democracy is obvious. Parliaments could not have functioned in twelfth-century Europe: some peoples who are given parliaments today are approximately at the same stage of development. The pluralist system of parties applied to countries of archaic social structure, in which the mass of the people is uneducated, maintains and consolidates the power of the traditional aristocracy, that is to say that it prevents the establishment of true democracy. The example of Turkey, on the contrary, seems to demonstrate that the technique of the single party, applied with discernment, makes it possible gradually to build up a new ruling class and the independent political elite which alone make it possible to establish at some date on authentic democracy. Is it possible to generalize and to hold that the single party might thus serve as a temporary guardian, making it possible for the fragile plant of democracy to grow in soil that is not prepared for its reception? Scientifically speaking, we can draw no conclusions from a single example that is still provisional. The question is however worth asking.

CHAPTER II

STRENGTH AND ALLIANCES

THE measuring of the strength of parties presupposes a standard of measurement. Now three different yardsticks can be employed: members, voters, and parliamentary seats. The first is unusable, for the fundamental requirement in a standard of measurement is that it shall be applicable to all the objects to be measured. Membership does not fulfil this condition: cadre parties have no members and mass parties do not all define membership in the same way; the membership figures can only be of use for considering the development of one party or comparing the strength of similar parties. On the other hand voters and parliamentary seats provide common measures, except that they do not always coincide with one another. In a complete and perfect system of proportional representation the difference between them disappears: but no country has put into operation a system of complete and perfect proportional representation, and many have experience only of the simple-majority system in which the disparity between the number of votes polled and the number of seats won is often very great.

These two criteria each represent a different aspect of party strength: the first measures the strength of the party in public opinion, the second its governmental strength. They should be used together. This method alone would make it possible to study the reaction of parliamentary strength upon public opinion. Those who propose to reduce the parliamentary representation of the Communist party in France by re-introducing the simple-majority ballot, which would decrease the number of its seats in the National Assembly, receive from opponents of the reform the reply 'You do not cool a fever by breaking the thermometer'. This is not so certain. For the relationships between the electoral strength of a party and its parliamentary strength do not seem to present the unilateral features of the relationship between fever and thermometer. Parliamentary strength is one factor in electoral strength. Voters grow tired of seeing their votes lost if they give them to a party which is handicapped by the operation of the ballot procedure: the 'polarization' phenomenon which occurs in the single-ballot system clearly demonstrates this. Furthermore, a party which has fewer deputies has less prestige and less influence: it carries less weight in the deliberations of government, it has less facility in obtaining posts, favours, and information for its voters. The under-representation of the Communist party in the French parliament between 1924 and 1939 undoubtedly hampered its development very considerably; the suppression of the barrier in 1945 gave it on the other hand great encouragement. A systematic comparison of the numerical changes in voting strength with those in parliamentary strength, after an electoral reform which increases the disparity between them, would make possible the determination of the degree of influence exercised by the second upon the first, that is to say it would determine the reaction of the 'fever' to a change of 'thermometer' (cf. *below*, p. 377).

The two yardsticks are complementary. None the less in some cases we have to choose between them, for example if we aim at establishing a classification of parties according to their strength. Not to choose would compel us to draw up simultaneously two classifications which would lead to confusion. The choice will naturally depend on the direction of the research: for an analysis of the development of public opinion towards parties, voters would be taken as the basis; for a study of the part played by parties in the state, the basis would be the parliamentary representatives. In the following pages the second criterion has generally been preferred: whenever party strength is referred to without further definition the size of the parliamentary group is to be understood. This choice is not entirely arbitrary. It is founded upon the primacy of parliamentary activity amongst parties in democracies of the Western type, a primacy that has been much attacked but which none the less still exists. In any case, our choice is not exclusive: we shall compare parliamentary strength with voting strength in order to see how representative parties are.

The idea of strength is inseparable from that of alliance. In every system in which alliances exist the strength of parties depends upon them, materially and politically: materially, electoral coalitions play an essential part in determining the number of seats obtained by the parties; politically, parliamentary and governmental alliances increase or diminish the numerical strength of parties. With 163 deputies in the French National Assembly of 1946–51, the Communist party had less influence than the Radical party with 45, because the former was isolated, whereas the latter made use of its central position to enter into combinations and agreements. The real strength of the Communist party was less than its apparent strength; the real strength of the Radical party, greater

I. TYPES OF PARTY STRENGTH

Classifications based upon size or strength are always arbitrary. When do many ears of corn become a heap of corn? At what age does a child become an adolescent; an adolescent a young man; a young man a man, and so on? This introduction of the concept of quality into quantitative measurement, of differences of kind, into numerical graduation, cannot but be approximate. However it is justifiable if it corresponds to the facts, if differences of size are differences in kind. A man of thirty is not twice the man he was at fifteen, nor is a man of sixty twice the man he was at thirty; he is a man in a different way. A party with two hundred deputies is not twenty times greater than a party which can only muster ten: it belongs to a different sociological category.

Categories of Strength. Three kinds of party can be distinguished on the basis of strength: parties with a majority bent, major parties, and minor parties. The first kind is clearly distinct from the others. We here use the term 'party with a majority bent' for those which command an absolute majority in parliament or are likely to be able to command one at some date in the normal play of institutions. In multi-party systems the existence of parties with a majority bent is quite exceptional: it is encountered only in cases of domination (cf. *below*, p. 307); even then it is often doubtful. On the contrary, their existence is normal under the two-party system: in this case the two parties both have a majority bent, unless their disproportion is so great that one of them is reduced to the situation of being permanently in a minority (this is particularly the case in some states of America). The criterion for this category is therefore relatively precise, and it is fairly easy to discern the parties with a majority bent, in a dualist system at least. In America Democrats and Republicans come under this head at the federal level; the Democrats are alone in the category in many of the legislative assemblies in the Western or Southern states; the Republicans in certain Northern and Eastern states. In England Conservatives and Liberals were so until 1922, when the Labour party replaced the Liberals (who remained a major party for many years) In multi-party systems the ascendancy of one party can confer upon it a kind of majority bent: but here the criteria become much vaguer. It may be considered that the Socialist party assumed that position in Norway as from 1933 when it had 69 seats, the absolute majority being 76 (which it attained in 1945). In Sweden the Social Democratic party seems to have reached the position in 1936, when it obtained 112 seats, the absolute majority being 117 (which it reached in 1940). But any judgement on this question is always delicate in a multi-party system; only a study of the party's position over a long period of time permits a conclusion, and that never exact. The majority bent is therefore never clear except under the two-party system; in others, any distinction between parties with a majority bent and major parties is always delicate and often artificial.

It is based however upon a fundamental fact: the difference in political psychology that exists between parties with a majority bent and the rest. A party with a majority bent knows that it is likely at some date to have to shoulder alone the responsibilities of government, if it is not already shouldering them; other parties, even major parties, know that they will never find themselves in a similar situation, apart from quite exceptional circumstances which would rob the experience of any real meaning. This difference completely changes the sociological nature of the parties. A party with a majority bent is necessarily realistic. Its programme may be put to the test of realization. Any demagogy on its part may one day recoil upon it; by giving it power the electorate can corner it and compel it to keep its promises. In consequence, it must never promise more than what is possible, rhetorical effects and literary exaggeration apart. It will therefore place greater stress on concrete problems than upon theoretical questions, for one cannot govern by theories. Normally it will emphasize precise and limited reforms much more than great revolutionary principles which are difficult of application. In short its effort will be entirely directed towards action, with a very acute realization of the limits that action always sets upon thought. The other parties are not at all subjected to this enslavement to reality. They know that their programme will never have to face facts, because they will never be alone in positions of responsibility: they will always share them with allies, at the very least in the form of parliamentary support. It will always therefore be possible to attribute to their allies the responsibility for failure. The party 'platform' is not a plan for concrete action (even if it sometimes appears in that guise), for the party is well aware that it could never itself put such a plan into execution. An agreement with allied parties alone makes it possible to draw up a common plan for governmental action. All agreements imply mutual concessions: the programme of each of the allies will therefore suffer considerable modifications. Each of them will be naturally led to follow a principle of diplomacy that is as old as the hills: ask for more than you expect to get.

Parties without a majority bent (major and minor parties) are therefore led into demagogy by the very nature of the system. The absence of any practical sanction and of the test of realization makes it possible for them to demand with impunity any reform even if it is unrealizable. The electoral dividends attached to promises of this kind lead to their being formulated. The necessity of a compromise with neighbouring—but not similar—parties encourages intransigence and exaggeration in order to reserve for themselves as wide a field of retreat as is possible. In the end the inventors of fables believe in their own inventions: in the same way parties eventually take their own demagogy seriously, especially when they have made use of it to stir up militant members who then refuse to be cooled down. It would be of some interest to study in detail the operation of this factor in the life of parties on the continent of Europe. The Communists are not alone in 'tabling draft bills of a purely demonstrative value'[1] without worrying about the possibility of their realization: they are alone in confessing it. Nor is demagogy the prerogative of the Left. When in 1949 the Belgian Liberals demanded a 25% reduction in all taxes they knew how absurd such a proposal was; when the French Right campaigned in 1946 for a return to an entirely free economy, they knew how impossible such a programme was, before they were taken in by their own campaign. Between the wars, reference to Marxism in the French Socialist party was purely a matter of words, for the party rejected revolutionary and violent measures for the application of Marxist doctrine, and could not but know that it would never gain sole responsibility for government by parliamentary means, and that no coalition government would ever carry out an upheaval of this kind. The theory of 'going part of the way together', by which all parties justify alliances and the necessary limitations entailed, is a complete illusion. For they will be together until the end of the

[1] Instruction of Political Bureau of French Communist party in 1924.

road, and none of them can advance alone any further than the others.

National temperament may aggravate this basic tendency but it does not create it. The demagogy of French and Italian parties is a result less of any Latin taste for political verbiage and for general ideas than of their lack of majority bent. It may be that the Italian Christian Democratic party will one day acquire a true majority bent that it does not yet possess. Its repugnance for governing alone, its desire to make others share the responsibilities of power, in spite of its absolute majority, clearly demonstrate that it still has the mentality of a party which finds this situation exceptional. In any event, in a multi-party system a true majority bent cannot be acquired by any party unless its ascendancy is assured over a long period of time: otherwise the demagogic campaigns of its rivals (which for their part have no majority bent, no hope of enjoying sole responsibility for government, and therefore no fear of having to put their programme into execution), compel it to be demagogic in self-defence. In a two-party system the absence of demagogy is essentially due to the fact that the opposition party, as well as the government party, cannot afford to bid recklessly, since it too risks incurring the sole responsibility of office. In a multi-party system the opponents of a dominant party, which holds a majority in parliament by itself, remain divided by very definition, and quite incapable of attaining alone a similar majority in the near future: they are therefore free to be demagogic, whereas the governing party is not. Thus the natural trend of circumstances causes it to lose its majority, to lose its ascendancy and its majority bent. Demagogy comes easier, of course, to the opposition than to those in office. But in a two-party system where all parties have a majority bent, the risk of alternation restricts the demogogy of the opposition; in a system in which no party has a majority bent the division of responsibility for government augments the demogogic bent of the parties in power. For they are, it is true to say, both in office and in opposition: each lays upon its allies the responsibility for failure.

The distinction between major and minor parties complements the preceding distinction. It is no less important but is much less definite. Major parties have no hope of ever obtaining an absolute majority save in exceptional circumstances which do not correspond to the nature of the system: if they are alone in office they can only exercise power with the agreement and support of other parties.

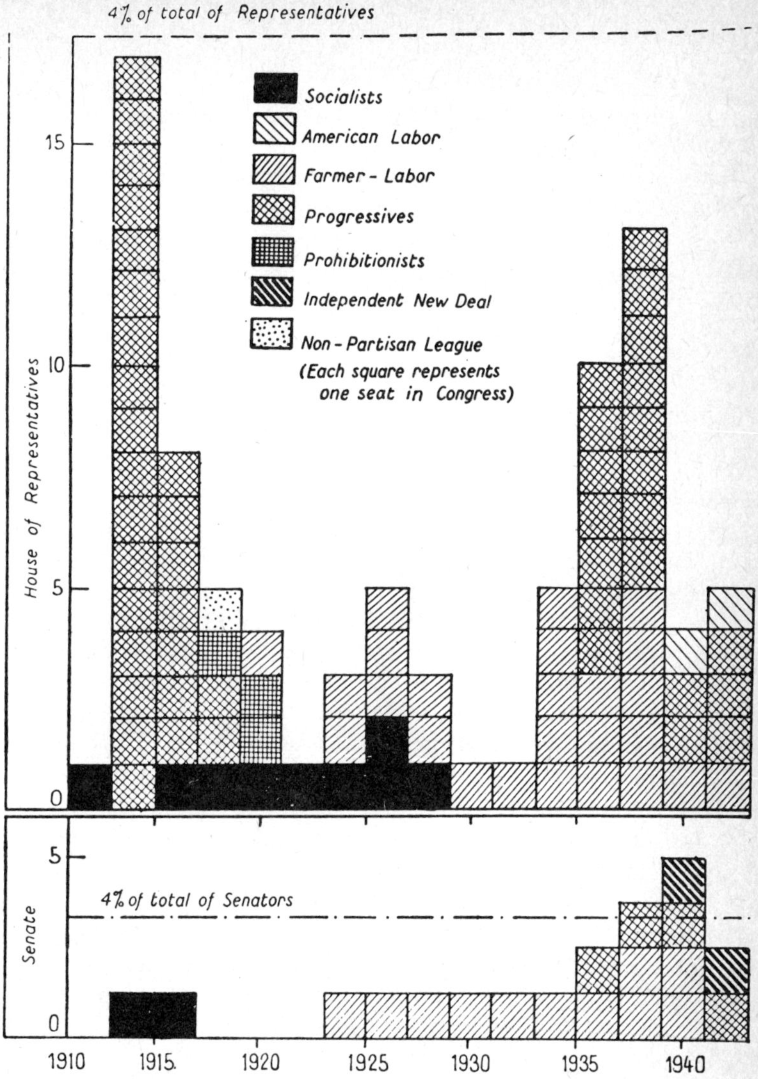

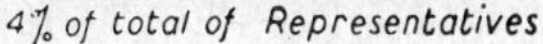

Fig. 32. Minor Parties in Congress.

Normally they govern only in association, inside a coalition cabinet. But their strength allows them to play an important part inside such alliances: they share out amongst themselves the chief ministries and the key-posts. If they remain in opposition, they can exert an effective influence, increased if they form a coalition with their neighbours, but never negligible. On the other hand minor parties are merely makeweights, whether in office or in opposition; they have to be content with a few ministerial back seats or with platonic criticism, unless the gap between the majority and the minority is slight, which may put them in the position of holding the balance, and thus give them a sudden increase in importance. The distinction between major and minor parties evidently corresponds to certain facts, although the lines of demarcation are not clear. It is often difficult to say when a party stops being minor and starts to become major; these intermediate cases however do not abolish the real and profound differences in kind which separate the two categories. It may not be possible to say exactly at what age a child becomes a man, it is none the less true that childhood and maturity each correspond to a particular set of facts.

It is out of the question to establish any general arithmetical standard that would allow us to classify parties as major and minor: it would, for example, be purely arbitrary to fix a limit of 5% of the seats in parliament, even if this figure sometimes corresponds to the facts. Each country must be studied separately over a long and fairly homogeneous period of history. Account must be taken of the number of seats won by a party not only at one election but over a series of elections, and the greatest attention must be paid to fluctuations and their extent. Thus the Communist party figures as a minor party in Scandinavia, Belgium, Holland, and Switzerland during the period from 1920 to 1939: in 1945 a violent surge gave reasons for thinking that it was about to change its nature, but subsequently there was a return to the earlier situation. In the United States all parties save the Democrats and Republicans are minor parties at federal level (Fig. 32). In England the Liberal party has been a minor party since 1935. In all countries with proportional representation there is a swarm of short-lived and changing minor parties (we have already quoted the examples of Holland, Norway, and Switzerland). In France the Communists remained a minor party on the parliamentary plane until 1936 (although they obtained nearly 10% of the total poll in 1924, over 11·3% in 1928, and retained 8·36% in 1932): their rise dates only from the Popular Front which brought them out of their isolation. In the Third Republic the Popular Democrats, Young Republicans, Socialist and Republican Unionists were minor parties. A difficulty arises in dealing with right-wing groups: instead of minor parties, it would be truer to say there were no parties. In fact the French Right was reluctant to accept organization into parties, and the electoral system allowed it to escape (financial needs did not allow this freedom to the Left, which had to use the technique of the mass party in order to collect the funds required to defray campaign expenses). The distinction between major and minor parties can therefore be drawn without any great difficulty. Like the preceding distinction, it is based upon a fundamental difference in the mentality of the parties in each category. Minor parties present individual characteristics which make it necessary to consider them as a special sociological category.

Before going into a detailed description of this last category we may ask whether the notion 'major party' is not too wide compared with the very restricted meaning which has been given to 'minor party'. Observation reveals very important differences amongst the parties that must be called 'major' according to our definition, and suggests the establishment of an intermediate category of 'medium' parties. They are not confined to semi-impotence like minor parties, but their influence is decidedly more limited than that of the true 'major' parties. For example there is no question of their forming a minority government based upon the support of allied parties, except for short and exceptional periods of time: their parliamentary strength is not sufficiently broad-based. In coalition governments their share is small: without being entirely relegated to the second-rank ministries, they can only claim one or two important posts. Outside the government they are incapable of getting an opposition to coalesce around them; they have to follow the lead of a major party or else keep the opposition divided. Quite a number of examples of 'medium' parties could be quoted. In Belgium the Liberal party, which from 1919 to 1936 occupied between 10% and 16·5% of the Chamber, is clearly distinct from the two 'major' parties, Socialist and Catholic, which had something between 31% and 42%. In Holland, over the same period, there is a fairly clear difference between, on the one hand, the Catholics (28%–32%) and Socialists (20%–24%) and on the other the Christian Historical party (10%–7% except in 1937 when they were reduced to 4%), the Liberals (11%–7%), and the Radicals

(7%–5%); the Anti-Revolutionaries (12%–17%) lie somewhere between these two groups, nearer the second than the first. In Switzerland the Peasant and Bourgeois party (between 17% and 10% of seats since 1919) is fairly distinct from the three major parties: Radicals (30%–24%), Socialists (29%–21%), and Catholics (23·5%–21%). In Denmark the Social Democrats and the Left (*Venstre*) constitute major parties, the Conservatives and Radicals medium parties. In France, between 1946 and 1951, it was difficult to put on the same footing the Communists, Socialists, and M.R.P. on the one hand, with their respective 28%, 16%, and 25·5% of seats, and on the other the Radical party, which controlled less than 9%, yet the last-named could not be considered a minor party in the true sense of the term. The distinction between major and medium parties corresponds therefore to certain facts but it is unfortunately too vague to be retained in any general classification: it appears to be applicable only within the framework of each individual country.

Theory of Minor Parties. The concept 'minor party' deserves special consideration. Opinion is much divided over these tiny groups which never have more than a small number of representatives in parliament and do not seem therefore capable of playing an important part either in the government or in the opposition. Some, viewing them as a regrettable source of division and confusion, do their utmost to bring about their disappearance; others grant them the role of useful buffers. These opinions are both right and wrong. For there are two quite distinct types of minor party, and conclusions are very different according to whether they are based upon the one or the other. The two types are personality parties and permanent minority parties.

The former are purely parliamentary groups having no real party organization in the country, no true social substructure. They are made up of deputies who chafe under the discipline imposed by major parties, or who consider that these are not capable of satisfying their ambitions. Many varieties can be distinguished. Some are composed of the retinue of some very influential personage to whom they are attached for reasons of prestige or favour; for example in Great Britain in 1931 there was a Lloyd George fraction of the Liberal party, based upon family ties and grouping around Lloyd George, his son, his daughter, and his son's brother-in-law. Other parties are more egalitarian in character: a general staff having no troops and no chief of staff. From another angle it would be possible to distinguish between independent minor parties, which are not directly linked with any of the major parties, and the satellites, which gravitate round some star of great magnitude: the Union of Progressive Republicans (former Republican and Resistance Union) around the Communist party in France at the present time; Socialist Republicans and Left-wing Independents round the Radical Socialists under the Third Republic; U.D.S.R. around the Socialist party during the first Constituent Assembly; National Liberals round the British Conservative party, and so on. The personality minor parties are in general fairly fluid and shifting. They correspond to caucus parties, with weak organization, a high degree of decentralization, and almost complete absence of discipline (except in the retinue parties and in some satellites). They are not generally based upon any precise doctrine, being founded under the banner of opportunism or of shades of opinion. However, a distinction must be made for those that might be called recalcitrants, for whom the doctrinal basis is, on the contrary, the fundamental ground of their existence: they are composed of the heterodox from the major parties; reproaching them with some ideological deviation or adulteration they seek either to preserve the doctrine in all its purity or else to develop it and bring it up to date. The many 'left-wing' and 'right-wing' Socialist groups furnish examples here. The recalcitrant parties are often composed of pioneers who commit the errors of being right too soon and of believing that a party is built from its apex with no organization at the base.

When such an organization exists we are faced rather with the second category of minor parties, the permanent minority groups. These do not exist solely on the parliamentary level: they dispose of an organization in the country, either national or local. Some are based upon the caucus, others again on the branch or the cell or even the militia. By their structure these are mass parties: they represent the modern type of minor party by comparison with the former which represent an archaic type. They are based upon a social or political sub-structure. They correspond to a section of public opinion, strongly minority-minded but relatively stable. We can thus distinguish parties based upon ethnical or geographical minorities, upon religious minorities and upon political minorities. The first is the most numerous group: Polish, Czech, Slovak, Italian parties in the Austro-Hungarian Empire; Alsatian, Polish,

Danish parties in the German Empire; Sudeten German parties and Slovak parties in pre-1939 Czechoslovakia; Irish party in Great Britain at the end of the nineteenth and the beginning of the twentieth centuries; Basque and Catalan parties under the Spanish Republic; Bavarian Christian party (linked with the C.D.U.) under the Bonn Republic; Algerian and African parties in contemporary France, and so on. They represent either a race or a region which will not accept complete fusion with the national community. Some are separatist, others autonomist, others again federalist, and some simply regionalist: so many descending stages within the same general tendency. Though minor parties in parliament, they are very strong locally, frequently occupying the position of dominant party or even of single party. Parties based on religious minorities are gradually disappearing in Western countries, where religion has ceased to play an important part in the life of the state; on the other hand there are Christian major parties which represent a different type. In Holland, however, the division between the Moderate and Conservative parties has a religious origin, and between 1919 and 1939 there appeared a number of minor parties based upon Protestant sects. In Africa and Asia the religious minority parties are on the contrary well developed: the Lebanon offers a very typical and most complicated example in this connection.

The idea of a political minority is less familiar. We shall apply the term to any fraction of public opinion defined by its ideological standpoint. What we have in mind is a 'spiritual family' quite well marked off, very much in a minority, relatively stable and not reducible to the major tendencies which divide the country. The Communist party in Great Britain, in the Scandinavian countries, in Belgium, Holland and Western Germany could be so defined. Other examples are the American Socialist party and the minor Fascist parties set up in Western Europe before the war of 1939. In France the Progressive Christians approximately fit into this pattern: they are moreover the heirs of an ancient tradition continuing the Young Republic movement, itself the heir to Marc Sangnier's *Sillon*. The origins of these minor parties are varied. Some are the last remnants of major parties that have passed away, historic remains, like fossils, which tell of prehistoric times: the monarchist tendency in France is one such example. Others are geographical remains, so to speak: they bear witness to an attempt to introduce into one country a doctrine that is strong in other countries but which cannot prosper in an unfavourable climate.

The Socialist party in America and the Communist party in Britain and Northern Europe correspond to this type. The minor Fascist parties set up before the war in France, Belgium, Holland and Scandinavia can be included under this head. A sociological analysis of the structure of each country can alone explain the variations in development of some tendencies. Sometimes (but rarely) the cause lies in a difference in maturity, in political age, in which case the minor parties are pioneers. Then they are not fossils but seeds.

The difference in structure is related to a certain difference in function: however, there is no exact correlation. Personality parties tend to be for the government, minority parties to be against the government. The former often function as makeweights to the majority; many of them are nothing more than trade unions of aspirants to office. They sit in the centre of the assembly, which makes it possible for them to act as left-wing backers for a right-wing majority or as right-wing backers for a left-wing majority; in military language, they function as a flank. Their pivotal position on the fringes of the majority and of the opposition confers on them an importance disproportionate to their numerical strength. These nurseries produce not only ministers but also Prime Ministers: their autonomy relative to the major parties predisposes them to act as arbiters between the latter inside coalitions. It is embarrassing for ministers of a major party to serve under the allegiance of a Prime Minister from a rival major party; it is also disagreeable for a major party to accept in the eyes of the public full responsibility for the policy of the government by officially assuming its leadership when others, in collaboration with it, remain free to play the Pontius Pilate. If the Prime Minister comes from a minor party these disadvantages are avoided; if he has some personal authority he can make himself heard by his ministers better than a Prime Minister coming from a major party, who will always encounter resistance from those of his collaborators who come from rival parties. Under the Third Republic the attribution to the minor parties of the post of Prime Minister was much practised: the names of Painlevé, Poincaré, Briand, Tardieu, Laval prove the point to the full. It might be thought that during the early days of the Fourth Republic, owing to the rigidity of parties, complemented by the effects of P.R., the arbitration role of the small groups of personalities would disappear. The case of the U.D.S.R. and M. Pleven shows that this was not so. On the contrary, this rigidity of parties made it more difficult for the ministers of major parties to give obedience to a Prime Minister from another major party, and so increased the minor parties' power as arbiters. From 1948 onwards as party discipline grew weaker this tendency became more pronounced particularly for the small parties of the right and centre.

This relation to the government is not shared by all personality parties: the role of the satellite parties, for example, is rather different. They serve to attenuate the doctrines and standpoints of a major party and attract to it parliamentary representatives who would take fright if they gazed upon the unveiled truth. In brief they play the part in parliamentary assemblies that ancillary organizations play in the country at large. But at the same time they make possible the establishment of transitions and links between two neighbouring major parties: their function resembles therefore that of the minor central parties between the majority and the minority. On the contrary permanent minority parties tend towards opposition. Expressing an opinion which is, they feel, not that of the nation and which has little support, they are led into an attitude of protestation and intransigence by the same psychological mechanism which leads an inferiority complex to show itself in aggressiveness. The absence of responsibilities for government and of a reasonable chance of ever assuming them removes furthermore any check to their opposition tendency. They are demagogic by nature, the most demagogic of all parties. When they are supported by a homogeneous and solid fraction of the population—a geographical or religious minority—the tendency is even more emphasized, for outbidding and violence are ways of retaining their basic supporters, of maintaining their separation from the national community, of keeping their individuality and their heterodoxy unsullied. If a party is clearly in a minority in the country as a whole but in a majority in certain districts its attitude becomes autonomist or even secessionist, which may imperil the unity of the country. Characteristic examples are to be seen in the Alsatian party in Germany and the Sudeten German party in Czechoslovakia.

Minor parties may exceptionally assume the role of arbiters and acquire considerable influence, either on the electoral or on the parliamentary plane. Under the simple-majority single-ballot system they may completely alter the pattern of representation if the numbers of votes polled by the two major parties are so close that it needs only a few votes given to a minor party to turn the scales of victory. This position as arbiter is even more important on the parliamentary plane if the gap between the majority and the minority is so small that the movement of the minor party is enough to alter the balance of power in parliament. In that case the fate of the country comes to depend upon a group that is in a very small minority and is profoundly different from the totality of the national community (in the case of a permanent minority party). It is impossible to govern without its support and its support compromises those who accept it. The Irish enjoyed this position in Great Britain in 1885, in 1892, and in 1910 (Fig. 33).

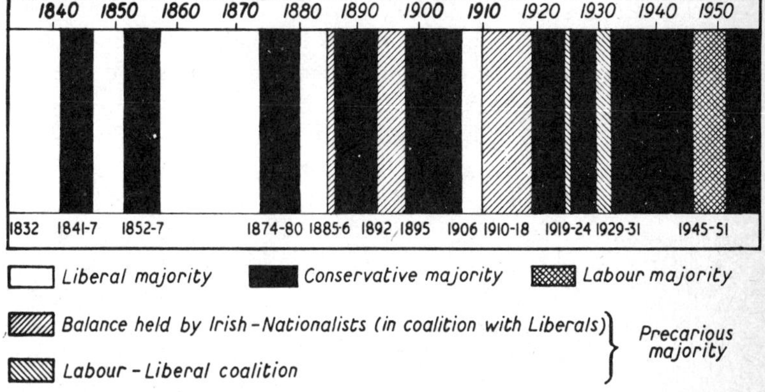

Fig. 33. Majorities in Great Britain, 1832–1957.

In 1885 their alliance with the Liberals, in return for Home Rule provoked the Unionist split in the Liberal party which lost them office; in 1892 a new alliance led to renewed failure and hastened the decline of the Liberal party which was removed from power until 1906. In 1910 the same situation recurred but in graver form: the support of the Irish made it possible to pass the Liberal budget and to effect the reform of the House of Lords; in exchange the Liberals pushed through Home Rule which gave self-government to Ireland. But the resistance of Ulster and of Unionist opinion was serious: political strife assumed a violent character that it had not had in Britain for centuries; in Ireland and Ulster revolutionary armies were formed; protest movements arose amongst officers of the regular army. The gravity of the crisis was of course due much more to the fundamental antagonism which separates Ireland and Great Britain than to the role of arbiter temporarily assumed by the Irish party, but this certainly increased it.

A less marked and less important example of the arbitrament of a racial minority occurred during certain ballots held in the French Constituent Assembly in 1945, when the votes of the Moslem deputies tipped the balance one way or the other. As a result some humorist called the 1946 draft the 'Moslem Constitution of France', which was just as exaggerated a description as that of the 'Irish Constitution of Great Britain' applied to the 1911 Parliament Act. The situation provides however yet another illustration of the danger of permanent minority parties. Some critics go further and talk of the danger of minor parties in general, including the parties made up of personalities and candidates for office in the same condemnation: some distinction should be made. The part played by the last-mentioned both as buffers and as links is undoubtedly very useful: they obviously facilitate the working of the French parliamentary system. Sometimes they are blamed for making it dull, robbing it of all dynamism by setting up a confusion between the parties, diminishing their individuality by suppressing the vigorous items in their programme; this criticism really aims at the multi-party system and the implied necessity for alliances, not at minor parties. They do no more than recognize the consequences of the system and try to make it work; one cannot blame spectacles for the headaches caused by myopia. The personality minor parties have one special disadvantage, however: the opportunity they give to financial interests to interfere in political life. Lobbying is difficult with major parties; they are too vast to be bought *en bloc*, too well disciplined for individual corruption to be effective. It is much easier with a small group that can easily be controlled from without. If this small group is in a position to arbitrate, the danger already mentioned arises: it is then a financial minority which acquires a fundamental influence over the fate of the government. In theory, the danger is very great; in practice it is difficult to assess its extent. It will be noted that the decentralized major parties, with no regimentation of voting, offer almost as great an opportunity for lobbying, and that the corruption of influential members of centralized parties can be very effective. The picture of a financial interest (or a foreign power) controlling the government of a country through the medium of a minor party that holds the balance is obviously very attractive: but real life is rarely to be found following the simplified patterns of the bedtime story.

It remains for us to define the factors producing minor parties. The influence of the electoral system here is incontestable. We have already described the influence of proportional representation and its tendency to increase the number of tiny, unstable groups, so well illustrated by the examples of Holland, Switzerland, Weimar Germany, or pre-Munich Czechoslovakia. The tendency is more or less accentuated according as the system of P.R. is more or less pure. It is attenuated by some systems of distribution at the local level which prevent minor parties from regrouping their votes throughout the country. Often methods are used deliberately to prevent the pullulation of minor groups: compulsory payment of a deposit which is not refunded if the list does not obtain a given percentage of votes, prohibition of any share in the distribution of remainders if the list does not reach the electoral quotient or a proportion of the quotient, and so on. All these devices prove that the influence of P.R. on the development of minor parties is sufficiently great for it to be necessary to restrict it. It must however be made clear that the influence of P.R. is exerted in a fairly well-determined direction and that it favours certain types of minor parties at the expense of others. It appears to discourage personality parties and to encourage permanent minority parties. Since it is a collective ballot the individual candidate disappears behind the party programme, and this militates against the independent character of the men who are the backbone of the personality parties. In the same way, it ill suits the flexibility and lack of dogmatism which are characteristic of them. Personality parties require an individual ballot in which trust is put in a man, personally, without too definite an inquiry concerning his ideas; the tendency of P.R. is the direct opposite. Of course, these are but tendencies affected by other factors: local circumstances, the voters' persistence in using their vote as a vote for a man, and so on. The existence of personality parties under a system of P.R. is not impossible, it is only more difficult. On the other hand, the development of permanent minority parties is made more easy, for exactly opposite reasons. We must, however, treat separately the case of geographical minorities which are in a strong majority in some districts and non-existent elsewhere. P.R. may weaken them by making it possible for their opponents to secure representation even within their sphere of influence, whereas in this respect the simple-majority ballot gives them a monopoly: before 1918 P.R. would have permitted the election of pro-British M.P.s in Ireland, for example; before 1938, it divided German opposition to Czechoslovakia in the Sudetenland. In the same way it would put an end to the monopoly of the Democratic party in the Southern states of America, in conformity with its general tendency towards the 'nationalization' of opinion, which will be described below.

The influence of the simple-majority ballot upon the development of minor parties is much less definite. No general conclusion is possible: the different methods of applying the simple-majority system and the different types of party call for different distinctions. The size of the constituency seems to exert quite a considerable influence. Small constituencies (arrondissements in France) give the election a personal character and bring to the fore the individuality of the candidate; party ties are loosened and the independence of deputies is quite marked: they easily form therefore minor groups which give them greater freedom in parliament and a wider sphere of influence. Large constituencies in which the list vote is in operation restore to the ballot a collective character analogous to that of proportional representation. Personality is at a discount and party discipline is increased; the chances of minor parties are reduced, at least as far as the first type is concerned; if cross-voting is allowed and practised, these consequences are attenuated. The existence or non-existence of a second ballot is extremely important. The single ballot tends to produce two parties and therefore to suppress minor parties in favour of parties with a majority bent. However, this coagulating effect occurs chiefly at the local level: the single ballot tends to produce a duel in each constituency; but the variety of duellists throughout the country makes multi-partism possible nationally. Local minor parties may therefore arise, as is the case in the United States and Canada. None the less their development seems to be more favoured by the second ballot, except in the case of regional minority parties to which the single ballot often gives the opportunity of monopolizing all the seats in their geographical zone (e.g. Irish in Great Britain and Democrats in the Southern states of America). On the whole the simple-majority system, unlike proportional representation, seems rather to favour the personality minor parties—the local minority parties finding it possible to accommodate themselves to it.

The influence of the electoral factor remains however restricted. The rebirth of minor parties under the Fourth Republic shows this clearly; in spite of the difference in ballot procedure they are reviving the tradition of the Third Republic. Electoral reforms might perhaps have affected slightly the number of seats won by the Irish party in Great Britain or by German parties in Czechoslovakia; they would not have suppressed either. The unequal development of minor parties on the Right and the Left of the French Assembly, in spite of the fact that the electoral system is identical for both, offers complementary evidence on the matter. Practically non-existent on the Left (except for the satellites of the Communist party and for the dissident Socialists), they are numerous and influential chiefly in the Centre and on the Right.

II. DEVELOPMENT OF PARTY STRENGTH

In order to define the strength of parties the whole of a period is always studied; this makes it possible to strike an average. So far our argument has been based on such averages. But this static view must necessarily be completed by a dynamic view which will show the variations in stature of the parties within the period under examination. Within each country, this variation makes it possible to follow the development of political forces and public opinion: electoral sociology gives rise in this connection to interesting analyses. But it is also possible to make a comparative study of the evolution of parties throughout the democratic countries in an attempt to define common patterns.

Types of Development. If we examine the party system as a whole we can define certain general types of development. Here we shall limit ourselves to describing the principal types in very schematic form: alternation, stable distribution, domination, and leftism. Alternation exists primarily in dualist countries. It may be defined as a pendulum movement, each party moving from opposition to office and from office to opposition. Great Britain is always quoted as the classic example of this type (Fig. 33). In the nineteenth century the majority in Parliament, which had been in Tory hands for fifty years, passed to the Whigs from 1832 to 1841; in 1847 the Liberals gained a slight majority (2 votes) and in 1852 there was a slight Conservative lead (8 votes); thereafter the majority alternated: Liberal from 1857 to 1874, Conservative in 1874; Liberal from 1880 to 1886 (with Irish support in 1885); Conservative in 1886; Liberal and Irish in 1892; Conservative from 1895 to 1906. In 1906 the majority returned to the Liberals, but they were able to retain it in 1910 only with the support of the Irish; they lost it in 1918 and have never since regained it. The arrival on the scene of the Labour party modified the operation of the pendulum in 1923 and 1929, when no party obtained an absolute majority. None the less the pendulum movement continued to operate: Conservative majority from 1918 to 1923, Liberal-Labour in 1923; Conservative from 1924 to 1929, Liberal-Labour in 1929. Since 1931 alternation has been restored: Conservative majority from 1931 to 1945, Labour 1945 to 1951, Conservative since then. The same swing is to be observed in the United States: after the War of Secession the Republicans held a majority in the House of Representatives until 1875; the Democrats had it from 1875 to 1881;

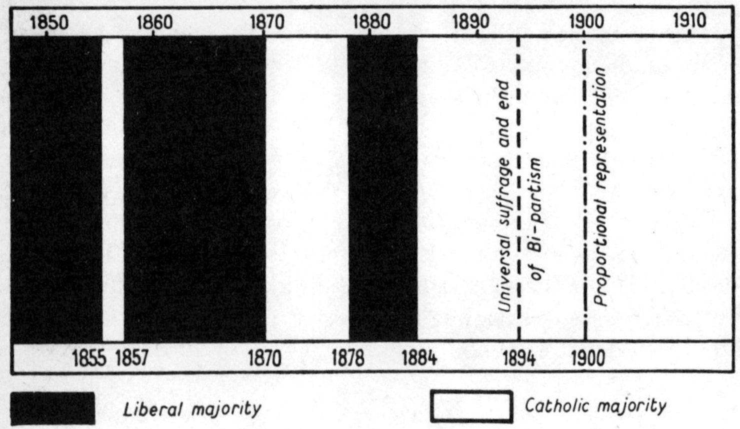

Fig. 34. Alternation of power in Belgium, 1847–1914.

the Republicans regained control in 1881, the Democrats in 1887, the Republicans in 1889, the Democrats from 1891 to 1895; the Republicans had a majority again from 1895 to 1911, the Democrats from 1911 to 1921. Between the wars the majority was Republican from 1921 to 1931 and thereafter Democratic. In 1952 the Republicans returned to power. Before the institution of proportional representation Belgium provided a similar example of alternation of power (Fig. 34).

The pendulum movement has been the subject of many an explanation. In his study of the English political system Hatschek[1] formulated a law governing the disintegration of the majority party, which he based upon two fundamental factors. On the one hand the exercise of power compels a party to attenuate its programme and not to fulfil completely the promises made to its electors: a

[1] Hatschek, *Englische Verfassungsgeschichte*, Berlin, 1913.

certain proportion of them are therefore naturally disappointed and led to transfer their votes to the opposing party; on the other hand the activity of government naturally gives rise to disagreements within the majority party: the antagonism between an intransigent Left wing and a temporizing Right wing. In opposition a party remains united more easily than when in power; whatever their differences, its members all agree to attack the party governing and to take its place; when the place is taken, the disagreements come out into the open. Thus the exercise of power involves a process of disintegration of the party, weakening it to the advantage of its rival. The latter tends therefore naturally to take its place, but once it is installed the disintegration process is turned against it and favours the defeated party. On the whole this description fits the facts. Many examples could be given of erosion and disintegration amongst parties in power. The disagreements amongst English Liberals at the end of the nineteenth century, particularly in 1885 and 1892, directly inspired Hatschek; to this example may be added the crisis in the Labour party in 1931 and the internal rivalries in the Belgian Liberal party in the nineteenth century which brought about its replacement by the Catholics, and so on.

Alternation of power occurs chiefly in two-party systems, whereas the disintegration of parties in office is a general phenomenon: the latter is therefore inadequate as an explanation of the former. The number of parties obviously plays an important part here: alternation presupposes dualism. The electoral system is also an essential factor. It has already been noted that the simple-majority single-ballot system tends to an 'over-representation' of the strongest party (that is to give it a percentage of seats in parliament much higher than its proportion of votes in the country) and to an 'under-representation' of the weakest party. It tends therefore to a resultant exaggeration of changes in the electoral body: this exaggeration however does not produce alternation, it merely makes it more obvious. The true effect of the electoral system remains indirect: the simple-majority single-ballot system tends to produce dualism of parties, and this in turn tends to produce alternation. However, there is no absolute coincidence with the two-party system: alternation may be encountered in a system with electoral coalitions. Before P.R. was introduced in Holland there was an almost perfect alternation of power between Conservative majorities (made up of Catholics and Anti-Revolutionaries) and Liberai majorities (made up of Liberals and Radicals): Conservative majority in 1888, Liberal from 1891 to 1901, Conservative in 1901, Liberal in 1905, Conservative in 1909, Liberal in 1913. The alternation is as regular as in Great Britain.

Stable distribution is in direct contrast with alternation; the latter corresponds to the greatest fluctuations in the strength of parties, the former to their greatest immobility. It is defined by the absence of any serious variation among the parties over a long period. Two elements must be taken into consideration: the slightness of the variations between elections, the rareness of long-term trends. It is obviously difficult to fix precise limits for the definition of the first element. However, observation suggests that we consider as slight variations those which do not exceed 5% of the total number of parliamentary seats and as medium variations those falling between 5% and 10%. For us to be able properly to speak of stable distribution the latter must be the exception and the former the rule. It is equally necessary that the variations, however slight they may be, should not all occur in the same direction, otherwise a profound transformation is taking place, slow but none the less real. Obviously total immobility never occurs, but some countries offer very marked periods of stability. At certain moments technical or political motives cause a 'realignment' of parties: the old distribution of forces is replaced by a new one. But equilibrium tends to be re-established thereafter. Thus the 1939–45 War caused a 'realignment' of parties in stable countries, just as the 1914 War and the electoral reforms at the beginning of the century had done. Between the two wars, on the contrary, stability was clearly evident.

Between 1919 and 1939 three countries presented in this way a picture of great political stability: Holland, Switzerland, and Belgium. In Holland, from one election to the next, the party seats never varied by more than 4% of the whole parliament. Moreover this 4% variation only occurred twice: for the Socialists in 1925 (when they increased from twenty to twenty-four) and for the Christian Historical party in 1922 (when it increased from seven to eleven). Variations of 3% were hardly more common and happened on only five occasions; the most frequent variations were only of 1% or 2%. Moreover no slow long-term trend can be discerned, except for the decline of the Liberal party which went down from ten seats in 1918 to four in 1937: this represents a loss of only 6% of the total number of parliamentary seats through six elections and a period of nineteen years. But the stability of

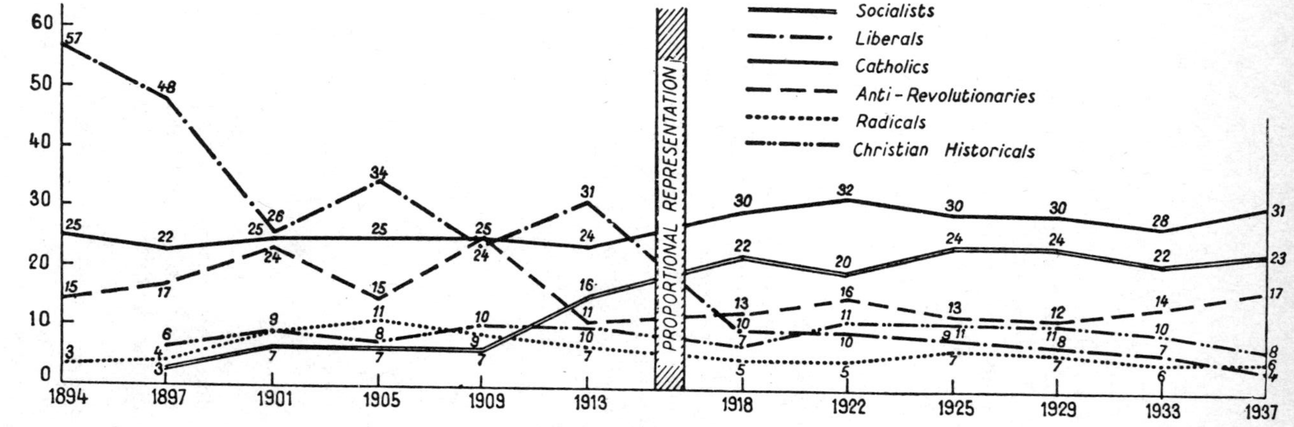

Fig. 35. Stabilization of Parties by P.R. (Holland).

Switzerland was even more marked. There was, it is true, a divergence of 5% (Peasant and Bourgeois party between 1931 and 1935) but it was the only one of its kind. The decline of this party was of exactly the same proportions as that of the Dutch Liberals: loss of 6% of the total number of seats in parliament between 1922 and 1939. There is no variation of 4% and only one of 3% (Socialists, between 1919 and 1922). In Belgium the pro-Flemish and Fascist crisis of 1936 caused a somewhat violent upset, causing the Catholic party a loss of sixteen seats (or more than 8% if the total increase in the number of deputies is counted), giving twenty-one seats to the Rexists who had none, and increasing by eight the Flemish Nationalists (an increase of over 4%). Apart from this crisis the general stability of Belgium remains very high: only two variations of approximately 5% are observable, in the Socialist party between 1921 and 1925 and in the Liberal party between 1936 and 1939. Even during the 1936 crisis moreover the maximum variation attained was only 10% of the seats (21 seats to the Rexists out of 202), which is not considerable.

The influence of the electoral system seems obvious. The stability of Holland, Switzerland, and Belgium is a direct result of proportional representation (Fig. 35). In countries where democracy is of long standing, opinion is naturally stable; the proportions of the votes cast for the parties do not noticeably change from one election to another: by faithfully reproducing in parliament the distribution of votes obtained in the country, P.R. reflects this fundamental stability. 'Floating' votes are too few in number to produce marked changes in the power of parties. When applied to countries that are naturally stable, the proportional system has the effect of petrifying representation, of making it almost completely immobile. The influence of the electoral system is not alone in bringing this about: moreover its effect is shown in action rather than in inaction. That is to say, proportional representation passively registers every variation in opinion, however slight it may be in fact, without amplifying it. National temperament also plays an important part here: it is a striking fact that the three countries under consideration are calm, peaceful and stable by nature. It is even more striking that the distribution of votes amongst the parties should be more stable in Switzerland than in Holland and markedly less stable in Belgium: these differences seem closely related to differences in the degree of national tranquillity. However, even in a new and unstable country like Ireland the variations from one election to another rarely exceeded 10% between 1920 and 1939. None the less the stabilizing tendency of Proportional Representation is not general: some proportionalist countries cannot be classed under the heading 'stable distribution', whereas some non-proportionalist countries do fall within the category. The first case is illustrated by the examples of the Scandinavian countries, Norway in particular, in which proportional representation goes hand in hand with the phenomena of domination. The second case is illustrated in France, where between the wars a simple-majority two-ballot system went hand in hand with fairly marked stability.

The stability of the French system was of course less complete than that of the other countries quoted, but it was very considerable. It is difficult to assess as precisely as the others because the parties were shifting and ill-defined, especially on the Right; only the Radicals, Socialists, and Communists were clearly delimited. None the less it is fairly clear that no variation ever markedly exceeded 10% of the total of parliamentary seats from one election to the next. The maximum divergences were attained by the Communists in 1936 with an increase of 62 seats (out of 608), and by the Radicals with a drop of 42 seats (or 7%). The other variations scarcely touch 5%. But the comparison is limited to the three elections of 1928, 1932, and 1936, the only ones to take place under the simple-majority two-ballot system during the period 1919–39. Obviously the second ballot attenuates the variations of the first. The complicated interplay of withdrawals which sometimes gives one ally the benefit of the progress of the other, and vice versa, leads to a limitation in the extent of the gains and losses of each. If two great rigid coalitions are opposed it is theoretically possible for these individual variations to be the only ones diminished and not the overall variations between the two blocs, although a consideration of the results of the first ballot may lead some moderate voters to change their vote at the second ballot for fear of too violent a swing. But it is rare to find alliances so rigid. In fact the flexibility of the Centre parties decreases the extent of the variations between the major coalitions. In France, for example, the overall variations themselves are quite slight. In so far as the vagueness of majorities permits their measurement it may be taken that the Right was reduced (and the Left increased) by about 6% (still relative to the total number of parliamentary seats) between 1928 and 1932 and that the Left gained (and the Right lost) approximately 10% between 1932 and 1936.[1]

The parties of the French Third Republic provide an example much less of stable distribution than of a slow but regular slide to the Left: they can therefore be equally well considered with the third type of evolution: leftism. We have already studied one of its forms: the birth of new parties on the Left of old parties, which causes the latter to slide to the Right and sometimes brings about disappearances or fusions amongst them. Leftism may assume other very different patterns: the weakening of all right-wing parties to the advantage of left-wing parties without either disappearance or new creation (e.g. France, 1924–39); the preservation of an overall balance between two blocs with internal evolution inside one of them, Liberals increasing at the expense of Conservatives, Socialists at the expense of Radicals, or Communists at the expense of Socialists (Sweden and Denmark approximated to this type between the wars); the replacement of an old Left party by a new, more energetic and intransigent one (cp. England); the rise of the party furthest Left at the expense of all others (cp. Norway between the wars); and so on. Leftism corresponds on the political plane to the social evolution which brought 'new strata' to power during the period in which the modern system of political parties was built up and developed. It seems to be a general phenomenon, with one important exception, the United States. This is no doubt a result of the very slight influence of politics on the development of the country and the life of the community during the nineteenth century and the early years of the twentieth, and especially of the social structure of the American Union which has never really known the stratification into classes common in Europe.

Care must be taken to distinguish true leftism from apparent leftism. To form a just estimate of the movement to the Left in France, for example, it is not enough to count the party votes at different successive periods and to assess the progress of the Left and the losses of the Right. Account must also be taken of the dying down of the initial fervour of the Left parties as they grow bigger and older: this bears them to the Right. An 1875 'Republican' would have voted Radical in 1901, Socialist in 1932, and Com-

[1] Percentage based on an average of 600 deputies. The Left is taken as including Communists, dissident Communists, Socialists, Radical Socialists, dissident Socialists, and 'Republican Socialists'; all other parties are included in the Right. This summary classification, necessary for purposes of calculation, is only very approximate.

munist in 1945. To some extent this development corresponds to a movement of the 1875 Republican towards the Left, but to some extent it also corresponds to a withdrawal by the Left towards 1875 Republicanism. Under the Third Republic the French moved gradually towards the Left, it is quite true; but the Left moved gradually towards the French too: it went halfway to meet them. The passing of the north-bound train on the next track makes the passenger in a stationary train think he is moving south. The remark applies with more point to the political plane than to the social: left-wing ideas lose their savour with age but the rise of the lower classes is an accomplished fact. Conversely, it does happen that true leftism is more marked than apparent leftism. From the outside no movement towards the Left is observable in the United States, the old parties have kept their place; internally the Democratic party is slowly evolving towards a relatively progressive position: this however does not show itself in the strength of parties, the subject under discussion here; it is a question connected with the problem of the relationship of competition between parties to the true divisions of public opinion.

From the situation of French parties under the Third Republic there might equally well be drawn an example of the third type of evolution: the Radical party in fact showed a quite marked tendency towards domination. François Perroux has shown the importance in economics of the phenomena of domination by his description of dominant nations and dominant firms. The history of ideas suggests the concept of a 'dominant doctrine': in every period some doctrine has provided the basic intellectual framework, the general organization of thought, with the result that even its adversaries have been able to criticize it or destroy it only by adopting its methods of reasoning. Christianity in the Middle Ages, Liberalism in the nineteenth century serve as examples. When Marx constructed his theory he made use of arguments taken from Liberalism, he turned its own logic against it: he was the last of the Liberals. Today Marxism tends itself to assume the position of dominant doctrine: it can only be contested within the bounds of its own dialectic. Similar phenomena of domination are sometimes encountered in the evolution of parties; all countries do not possess a 'dominant party', but in some its existence seems certain. We must not confuse dominant party with either majority party or party with a majority bent. A party is a majority party when it possesses by itself more than half of the parliamentary seats. If the political structure is such that a party is likely to find itself in this position as a result of the normal functioning of the institutions a party is said to have a majority bent. The concept of dominant party is not to be identified with these: a party may become dominant although it has never been and, short of a miracle, is never likely to be a majority party. A case in point is the Radical party under the Third Republic. In a two-party system in which all parties have a majority bent and one is, of necessity, in the majority, a dominant party is not always to be encountered.

What then is a dominant party? First of all a party larger than any other, which heads the list and clearly out-distances its rivals over a certain period of time. Naturally this greater strength is to be assessed totally over the whole of the period under consideration. The dominant party may be outstripped at some time or other, exceptionally, without losing its characteristics, in a two-party system at least. Here a party is dominant when it holds the majority over a long period of political development. It is possible for it to lose it exceptionally at one election, because of the way the majority ballot exaggerates the shifts in opinion, whilst still retaining its general pre-eminence. In a multi-party system based upon proportional representation or the double ballot such a reverse generally means the end of dominance. Every party that is larger than all others over a certain period of time is not necessarily dominant in character: sociological factors are at work as well as the material factor. A party is dominant when it is identified with an epoch; when its doctrines, ideas, methods, its style, so to speak, coincide with those of the epoch. France was known as the 'Radical Republic', although many Frenchmen and many Republicans were not Radicals: however, the Radical party did really incarnate the Third Republic at one phase of its history. Did it fashion the epoch after its own image or did the epoch fashion the Radical party? The question admits of no reply, but the similarity between the two is undoubted. In the same way the Scandinavian states are today identified with their Socialist parties, as England was identified with the Liberal party in the latter half of the nineteenth century. Domination is a question of influence rather than of strength: it is also linked with belief. A dominant party is that which public opinion *believes* to be dominant. This belief could be compared with that which determines the legitimacy of those who govern: the two are distinct but closely related. Even the enemies of the dominant party, even citizens who refuse to give it their vote acknowledge its superior status and its influence; they deplore it but admit it.

Fundamentally domination is not a self-contained type of party development but one mode that can be assumed by the other types. Domination may coincide with alternation, with stability, or with leftism by a slight modification of their original pattern. In two-party systems it slows down the swing of the pendulum: instead of

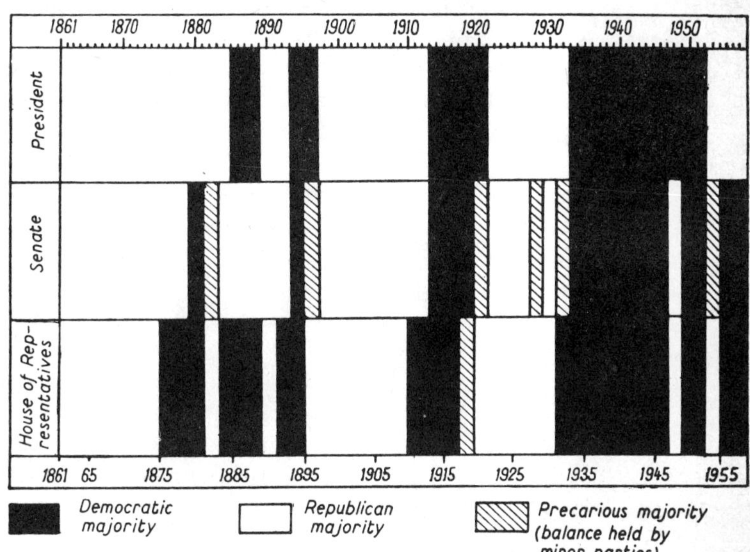

Fig. 36. Alternation of power in U.S.A., 1861–1958.

alternation at each successive election, one finds alternation at long intervals, in between which there reigns relative stability: in fact, slow alternation of this kind seems to occur much more often than changes of majority at each election, in spite of the general belief. In the nineteenth century, for example, Great Britain experienced first the almost uninterrupted domination of the Tories until 1832, then that of the Whigs until 1886, interrupted only three times (or for eighteen years out of fifty-four). In the United States the Republicans can be considered the dominant party from the election of Lincoln until that of Roosevelt: over a period of seventy-two years (1861–1933) the Presidency was in the hands of the Democrats for only sixteen years, a majority in the Senate for only ten years, and a majority in the House of Representatives for twenty-two years. The Democratic party concentrated into its own hands the Presidency and control of both Chambers for only six years (1893–5 and 1913–17), whereas the Republican party had control for thirty-six years. Republican domination was complete from 1861 to 1875, from 1897 to 1911, and from 1921 to 1930; only the period 1875–97 shows signs of a comparative alternation (except for the War of 1914 and the Wilson period). In 1933, on the other hand, America entered a phase of domination by the Democratic party which retained the Presidency, losing the majority in the Senate and the House of Representatives for only a brief interval of two years (1947–9). This trend is not modified by the Eisenhower presidency which is personal rather than party in character (Fig. 36). In Belgium the Liberal party was dominant from 1848 to 1870 except for the years 1855–7; in 1884 a Catholic domination was established which lasted until 1914, in spite of universal suffrage and proportional representation (Fig. 34, p. 300).

In France the domination of the Radical party began about 1905; in practice it continued right up to 1940, the right-wing of the Radicals having always exerted some influence over conservative governments even during the days of the National Bloc. It helped to reinforce the general stability that has already been described. The same can be said of the domination exercised by the Radical party in Switzerland from 1874; it did not lose its majority until 1919. Finally, in the Scandinavian countries, the rise of the Socialist party to a position of dominance brought in its train a general movement to the Left and coincided with leftism. In Norway this dual movement was fairly marked: after 1927 all the other major parties lost seats to the sole advantage of the Socialist party, which thus polarized votes coming from the Centre and from the Right; its rise was uninterrupted after 1930; it gained an absolute majority in 1945 and retained it in 1949. In Sweden and Denmark the evolution is less striking. Leftism there assumed more subtle guises: in Sweden, growth of the Agrarians at the expense of the Conservatives, of the Socialists at the expense of the Radicals, and in general of the second group compared with the first until 1944; in Denmark the Conservatives remained stable but the Agrarian Left and the Radicals decline while the Socialists grew. Here domination is also less marked. In Sweden the Social Democrats obtained a majority on only one occasion, in 1944. In Denmark they never obtained one. In both countries the post-war elections modified the balance of forces (reawakening of the Danish Left and the Swedish Liberals) and weakened the Socialist party (Fig. 37).

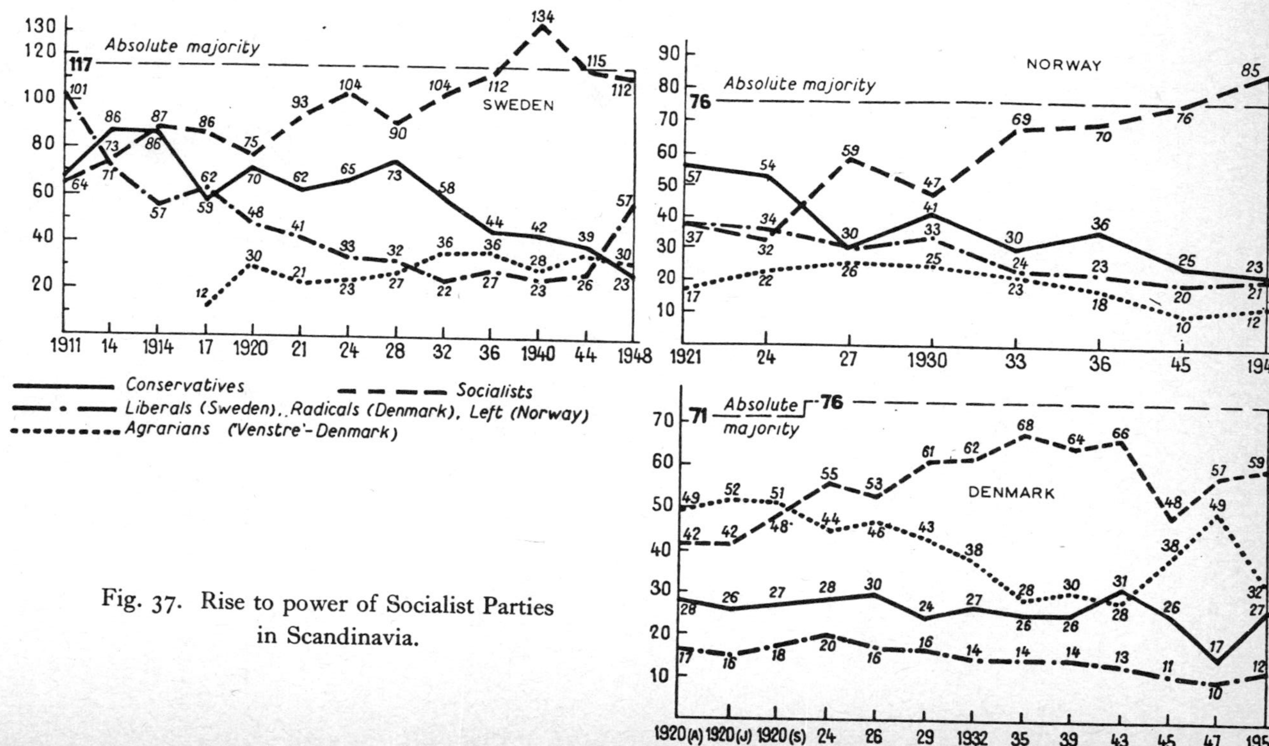

Fig. 37. Rise to power of Socialist Parties in Scandinavia.

Whether it coincides with alternation, stable distribution, or leftism, domination has an obvious stabilizing influence. It slows the rhythmic swing of the pendulum; it diminishes the violence of any trend to the Left. For the dominant party takes up an attitude analogous to that of parties with a majority bent: the continued exercise of responsibility for government diminishes demagogy and the need for innovation. When a left-wing party becomes dominant its appetite for revolution is dulled: apparent leftism is strengthened but real leftism is weakened. Domination takes the zest from political life, simultaneously bringing stability. The dominant party wears itself out in office, it loses its vigour, its arteries harden. It would thus be possible to show, returning to the argument of Hatschek, that every domination bears within itself the seeds of its own destruction. By and large, however, domination produces some fortunate consequences, especially in multi-party systems. It allows of the formation of a relatively solid majority round the dominant party, whether, in exceptional cases, it obtains the majority alone, or forms the centre of a coalition, or constitutes a homogeneous minority government with the support of allies. In this connection, the parts played by the French Radical party under the Third Republic and the present-day Scandinavian Socialist parties are interesting to study although very different, the Radicals being in the Centre and the Socialists on the Left. In particular it appears that a dominant party is alone capable of constituting an enduring minority government that is something more than a caretaker ministry; this practice is fairly common in Scandinavia.

Normal Evolution and Sudden Mutations. The types that have been defined concern the whole of the party system over a period of time. However, history sometimes records sudden changes in equilibrium: the transition from one period to another assumes the character of a breach rather than an evolution. Mutations of this kind are sometimes the result of an internal or external political event: the end of Republican domination and the beginning of Democratic domination in the United States in 1933 were a result of the Great Depression and of an American 'New Economic Policy'; the realignment of parties in Belgium after the 1914 War brought about the end of Catholic domination and the rise of the Socialist party. Generally, complete mutations in a party system are the result of electoral reforms or changes in party tactics. Thus the reversal of alliances in Holland in 1868 caused a breach in the relative stability that had till then prevailed and a trend towards domination by the Liberal party; the 1896 electoral law put an end to this and introduced a new balance of forces that was upset by proportional representation in 1918. In every country in which it has been applied P.R. has profoundly modified the comparative strengths of parties. In Switzerland, Belgium, Scandinavia, and France, the diagrams showing the parliamentary strength of parties at successive elections present entirely different patterns before and after P.R. In this respect the influence of the electoral system is considerable: the respective strengths of parties depend not only upon public opinion but also upon the means for its expression. We shall assess below the fundamental consequences of this fact for the nature of political systems.

Alongside these total changes in party systems, which have often the effect of replacing one type of evolution by another, there exist specific mutations, peculiar to a single party, that do not modify the general type of evolution. It is not a question of a change of period but of the sudden deviation of a party within the same period: e.g. the rapid rise of National Socialism in Germany after 1930, the violent surge of Rexism in Belgium in 1936 followed by just as violent a decline. Here there is no question of any manipulation of the elections to modify the expression of opinion: it is public opinion which is shifting. It seems to display a sudden flash of temper, a gust of passion. Usually such tempers and outbursts are restricted to a very small minority: they are the explanation for certain slight fluctuations in major parties as well as for the ephemeral successes of minor parties. Sometimes they spread suddenly like an epidemic. Such extraordinary mutations in opinion, however, show very different effects upon party strength. Here the operation of the electoral system is a vital factor; it is combined with the influence it exerts for the establishment of one type of evolution or another. One basic fact must be strongly emphasized: the influence of the electoral system is profoundly different according as we are concerned with the normal development of opinion or with its exceptional mutations. If the term sensitivity is used of the capacity of an electoral system to translate the variations of public opinion into variations in the strength of political parties, then we note that its sensitivity to normal variations of opinion and its sensitivity to waves of passion are not identical. A voting system may be insensitive to the former and very sensitive to the latter, in which case it will produce both a tendency towards stable distribution and a tendency to many sudden mutations. On the contrary, a different system may be conducive to alternation and to divergences by exaggerating the normal variations in opinion whilst at the same time strongly attenuating its violent mutations and exercising a stabilizing effect. Systematic investigation of the sensitivity of the different electoral systems to variations in opinion is consequently indispensable for an understanding of the changes in strength of political parties.

It can be summarily expressed in the following three formulae: (1) proportional representation is insensitive to normal variations in opinion and very sensitive to sudden mutations even when they are temporary and slight; (2) the simple-majority single-ballot system is very sensitive to normal developments but insensitive to sudden mutations unless they are deep and lasting; (3) the simple-majority two-ballot system is relatively insensitive both to normal variations in opinion and to sudden mutations. As usual these formulae express only general basic tendencies capable of being modified by the activity of other factors: they admit of many exceptions.

We have already studied the stabilizing effect of P.R. with regard to normal variations in opinion. Of their very nature normal shifts in opinion are very slight, and it is only possible to become fully aware of them with the aid of measuring instruments which amplify their extent, just as the seismograph, in fact, makes us aware of the tremors of the earth's surface that our senses cannot perceive. By faithfully translating the distribution of votes into distribution of seats, without exaggerating the variations, proportional representation ends by crystallizing the position of parties. However, the insensitivity of P.R. to the normal variations in opinion does not always bring about stable distribution and total immobility: P.R. may also coexist with the phenomena of domination. Slight voting shifts at each election, if they always take place in the same direction, end by giving rise to movements that are very marked so long as they are lengthy and regular. The ascending trend of Scandinavian Socialist parties since 1919 is typical: further, it is difficult to say whether the voting system amplified or restricted this development. From one point of view it seems to have checked it, by putting off the moment when the Scandinavian Socialists obtained an absolute majority: they would have reached that position in Sweden and Norway much quicker with a simple-majority single-ballot system; under the same system they would have reached it in Denmark, whereas under proportional representation they have not got that far. From another point of view it may be thought that the voting system reinforced their domination, since it ensured a continuance of the decline of the other parties (a decline which would have been less considerable under a simple-majority system). It is obvious that we must modify the dogmatic tenor of our formulae concerning the stabilizing effect of P.R.; over a long period it may well exaggerate the normal shifts in opinion instead of diminishing them. But it also checks them, both when they are on the increase and when they are declining.

With respect to sudden mutations the sensitivity of P.R. is acute, whether passing emotional disturbances or deep and lasting trends are in question. This forms a curious contrast with its insensitivity to normal variations in opinion. Both phenomena are however explained by the same fact, which arises from the 'passive' nature of P.R. It registers changes in the electoral body without amplifying or diminishing them: whence its insensitivity with respect to habitual variations, slight by nature (the stability of P.R. then reflects the natural stability of public opinion), as well as its great sensitivity to sudden movements which are generally much stronger, being passionate in origin. Belgium, where the number of seats of the traditional major parties varied very little between 1919 and 1939, provides the most striking example of the sensitivity of the proportional system to transitory waves of emotion: the extraordinary success of Rexism in 1936 when it gained twenty-one seats out of 202 (whereas in 1932 it had none) followed by its sharp decline in 1939 (four seats). In France the sudden rise to power of the R.P.F. in 1951 and that of Poujadism in 1956 are just as striking. It is extremely interesting in this connection to observe that the rise of Fascism which occurred throughout Europe in the 'thirties was only visible electorally in the peaceful democracies of the North (Belgium, Holland and Scandinavia) where it seemed to be much less strong than in France. They had a proportionalist system, France a majority system. In the same way the development of Communism immediately after the Liberation produced a considerable increase in the party only in the proportionalist countries of Europe and not in the Anglo-Saxon simple-majority countries. It is true that, with the exception of Sweden only the former had suffered occupation by the Nazis, which encouraged the growth of Communism, thanks to the activity of the *maquis* and the underground campaign. None the less the Communist party would certainly have had more than two members of Parliament in England at the 1945 elections if the proportional system had been in operation there. A study of sudden mutations of a deeper and less transitory nature provides results that are no less

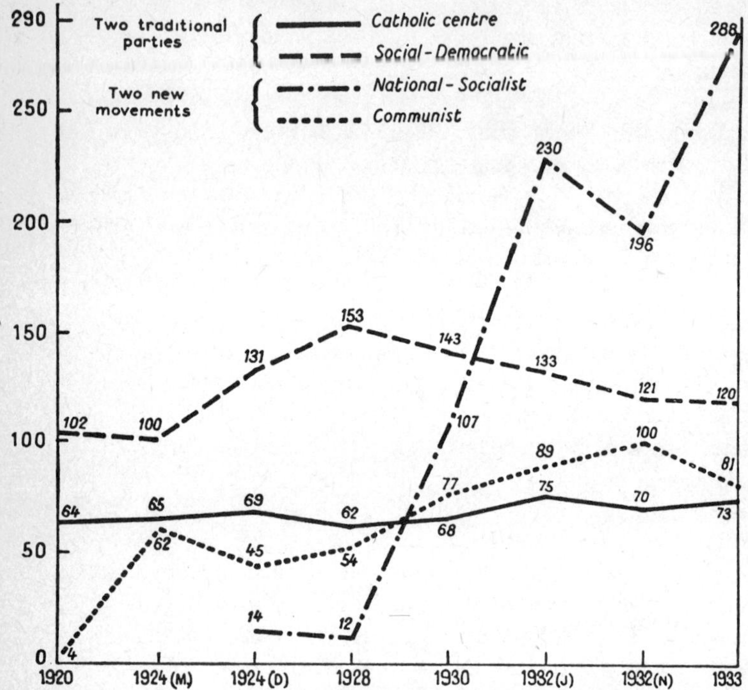

Fig. 38. P.R. and parties in Germany, 1920–33: stability with traditional parties; instability with new movements.

convincing. Between 1919 and 1933 the development of Communism was encouraged in Germany by proportional representation, whereas it was definitely checked in France by the majority system. It is probable that the rise of Nazism would have been much slower and much less powerful if the majority system had continued in operation in Germany; the relative insensitivity of the Empire to sudden mutations forms a marked contrast with the extreme sensitivity of the Weimar Republic (Fig. 38). Similarly the development of the Popular Republican party (M.R.P.) in France in 1945–6 is very symptomatic: under a simple-majority electoral system it would never have attained such proportions.

It is furthermore extremely difficult to distinguish between transitory mutations and deep and lasting mutations, especially as proportional representation tends to transform the transitory into the permanent if they are sufficiently extensive. In this respect the example of the French Communist party between 1945 and 1951 merits special investigation. In the sudden rise which caused it to increase from 15% of the electoral body in 1936 (that election represented a considerable success for it; in 1938 or 1939 it would not have gained such a proportion) to 25% in 1945, and more than 28% in 1946, two kinds of factors can be discerned, some permanent and representative of a real and profound evolution of opinion, the rest purely transitory and resulting from the circumstances of the Liberation. Its Resistance activity, the memory of its martyrs, patriotic propaganda, the backing of General de Gaulle, the capture of seats by violence, government influence: all these factors no doubt played a vital part in the success of the Communists in 1945–6. It has been pointed out that the rural departments in which their influence was most widespread exactly coincide on the map with the *maquis*. On the other hand, it is too often forgotten that the membership of the party at the end of 1944, four months after the Liberation, was very little higher than in pre-war years: the great increase took place in 1945 and a decline had set in by 1947 after their elimination from the government;[1] between 1946 and 1949 the party lost almost 25% of its members. So great a collapse in the electoral influence of the Communists seems scarcely possible. The enormous growth of the party in 1945–6 inevitably drove the Socialists towards the Right, where they endeavoured to replace from the middle classes the working-class voters who had deserted them in favour of Communism: this change in the substructure of the party had an influence on its policy. Furthermore the aloofness of the Communists obliged the Socialist party to support Centre governments, and this accentuated the development. Many voters who had gone over to the Communist party in 1945 owing to special circumstances remained faithful to it in 1951 because they could give their vote to no other party which seemed to them capable of protecting their interests. The sensitivity of proportional representation to important sudden mutations seems therefore to work in only one direction: it encourages the flow but then tends to stabilize it and to check the ebb. It thus crystallizes transitory passions so long as they are sufficiently violent.

[1] Cp. Fig. 11, p. 88.

The simple-majority two-ballot system does not permit such crystallization, since it prevents waves of passion and sudden mutations from showing themselves; moreover, it plays an almost similar role in respect of the normal variations of opinion, without being so insensitive as proportional representation. France provides a fairly clear example of this last point. A study of each election reveals that the second ballot has always toned down the changes of opinion made manifest by the first. On comparing the 1919–24 period with that of 1928–36 one finds that variations in the electoral body were not much more considerable in the former than in the latter, yet they were translated on the parliamentary level into changes of majority that were very marked in the first case because of the single ballot, and much less well defined in the second case because of the second ballot. The process of stabilization is a result both of alliances and of the part played by the Centre party as a buffer: the effectiveness of the process is dependent therefore upon the closeness of the alliances and on the tactics of the Centre party. If very close electoral alliances prevent any see-sawing between Right and Left according to the constituency, such as was practised by the French Radical party, then the situation very nearly approaches that of the two-party system: variations in opinion continue to be toned down within each alliance, but the distribution of votes between the two is exaggerated by the electoral system as in a two-party regime. If, for example, a sum is made of the votes obtained by each electoral coalition of parties in Holland between 1880 and 1913 a saw-tooth graph is obtained which exactly resembles the graph for dualist systems. With respect to sudden mutations the stabilizing effect of the second-ballot system shows the same gradations. If the mutation takes the form of the sudden growth of an existing party, it is very difficult to say whether the system attenuates it or exaggerates it: everything depends on the position the party occupies within the coalitions. If it already occupied first place before the mutation, the operation of the system will tend rather to reduce its progress, especially if this is at the expense of one of its allies, for the total number of votes gained by the coalition will not increase in proportion. Even if it occurs at the expense of the opposition coalition the mutation is toned down: it is spread out amongst all the allied parties. In 1936 the Socialists benefited from part of the mutation in favour of the Communists, who doubled the number of their votes: with 27,000 votes less than in 1932, the Socialists obtained twenty more seats. But if the party benefiting from the mutation were in the second or third place inside an alliance the mutation might have the effect of advancing it to the first place, in which case its candidates would remain in competition at the second ballot, and would profit from the withdrawals of other members of the coalition instead of retiring in their favour. Since the respective positions of the allies vary from district to district, and since sudden mutations are not identical in extent everywhere in the country, no definite conclusion can be drawn.

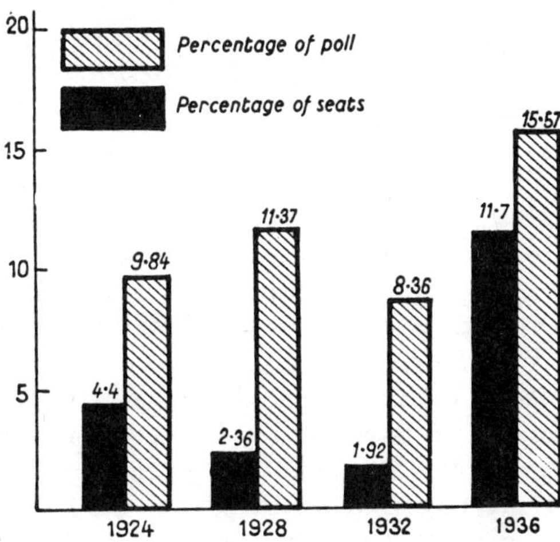

Fig. 39. Parliamentary representation of Communist Party in France before 1939.

If the mutation brings to birth a new party, the stabilizing action of the second ballot seems much more definite. Every party which wishes to face the electorate under this system finds itself in the following dilemma: either to play a lone hand, which means being crushed between the rival coalitions, or else to join one of them, which means sacrificing a great deal of its independence and its originality and not being favoured in the distribution of seats, because a new candidate generally obtains fewer votes than the old and therefore has little chance of being in the running at the second ballot. If the second ballot coexists with single-member voting, that is to say with small constituencies that favour the establishment of personal electoral strongholds, the insensitivity of the system reaches its peak: in order to have any chance of success the new party must accept a battle against candidates who have won their spurs. To escape this dilemma it has to win at the first shot enough votes to put it into the position of securing, in a considerable number of constituencies, the withdrawal from the second ballot of closely related candidates. This rarely occurs; even when it does the composite nature of the votes obtained by the deputies of the new party urges them to moderate their eagerness for innovation and thus diminishes the violence of the mutation. In France, however, the divisions of the Right make such a situation less unlikely, and this gives some opportunity to movements like Bonapartism. Trustworthy observers claim that in this way the French Progressive party (P.S.F.) could have won nearly a hundred seats if elections had been held in 1940; however, there still remains a tendency for originality to be sacrificed to the necessity of seeking allies.

France furnishes a good example of the conservative tendency of the second ballot. Consider, for instance, the development of the Communist party from 1928 to 1939 (Fig. 39). During an initial phase from 1928 to 1936 it went into battle alone, refusing even to withdraw its candidates at the second ballot; it thus preserved both its purity and its individuality but it was crushed (in 1928, with 1,063,943 votes at the first ballot it obtained a total of fourteen seats, whereas the Socialists obtained ninety-nine with 1,698,084 votes); in 1936 it joined the Popular Front coalition, which enabled it to win seventy-two seats, but which corresponds to a marked phase of 'bourgeois contamination' and of resemblance (external at least) to the traditional parties. Further one notes the complete impossibility for movements that are nevertheless dynamic, like the *Action Française*, to obtain any representation in parliament. The fate of the French Socialist party offers similarly a valuable subject for meditation: the permanent necessity of collaborating with 'bourgeois' parties at the electoral level has had a constant tendency to undermine its individuality and to assimilate it to them in spirit and preoccupations; there is no doubt that the electoral system is largely responsible for the fact that French Socialism has lost its savour. To sum up, the second ballot is definitely conservative. It automatically eliminates variations in opinion when they are superficial and transitory; when they are deep and lasting, it puts a check on their representation in parliament as well as eroding their originality and tending to align them with the traditional parties. The progressive decline in energy of parties is, of course, a general phenomenon, but the second-ballot system tends to accelerate it.

The simple-majority single-ballot system has similar results in respect of sudden mutations but not of slow and normal variations in opinion. By contrast with proportional representation, a passive method, it is pre-eminently the active procedure limiting sudden

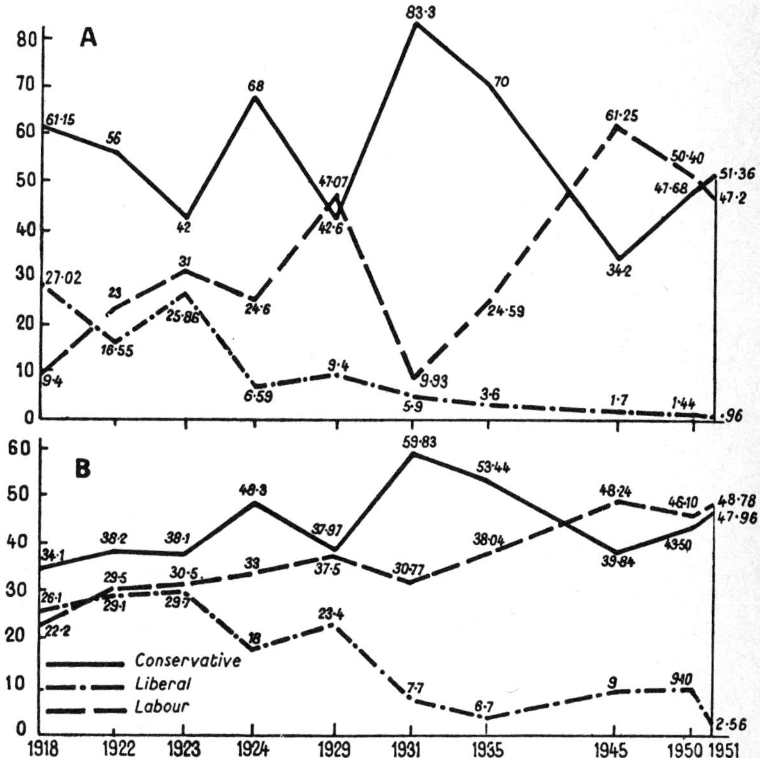

Fig. 40. Exaggeration of normal shifts of opinion by the simple majority, single ballot system: Great Britain.

A. Percentage of seats B. Percentage of votes

mutations and exaggerating normal variations. As we have already seen, under such a system normal variations in opinion tend to take the form of alternation: even in the case of a slow alternation, combined with the domination of one party, the curves for the variations in numbers of parliamentary seats assume a saw-tooth pattern, very characteristic of the system. If with this we compare the curves for the variations in numbers of votes, we note a marked difference in the extent of the variations; in this connection a comparison of the percentage of votes with the percentage of seats in Great Britain between 1918 and 1955 is very instructive, although the presence of the Liberal party profoundly modified the system (Fig. 40). The general way in which this exaggeration is produced is simple: it is a result of the combination of the two tendencies already discussed—the tendency towards 'over-representation' of the majority party and the tendency towards 'under-representation' of the minority party. When the simple-majority single-ballot system functions normally, that is to say when it coexists with dualism of parties in conformity with its natural trend, it forms a political seismograph capable of registering variations in opinion which would go unremarked without it. The system has the merit of preventing the natural immobilizing of public opinion without falsifying the general direction followed by its variations. When the majority system with a single ballot exists in conjunction with multi-partism the results are much less satisfactory: the seismograph is then thrown out of gear and deforms the variations in opinion instead of amplifying them. It must not however be forgotten that the deformation generally occurs in one clearly determined direction (at the expense of the third party) and that it thus tends, of its own motion, to reconstitute the basic dualism of the party system.

In a two-party system the exaggeration of the movements of opinion by the action of the majority ballot seems to be regulated by a definite law which can be formulated as follows: the ratio of the seats won by the parties is the cube of the ratio between the votes cast for them ($A:B=A^3:B^3$). This relation was formulated in 1909 by J. P. Smith in a report to the Royal Commission on electoral systems as a result of his study of nineteenth-century British elections. In fact, the formula is equally applicable to the British elections of 1931, 1935, and 1945 (that is, to those which followed the comparative restoration of the two-party system). After 1948 new constituency boundaries brought about a certain inequality between the two major parties, the Labour party being handicapped: the loss they thus suffered has been valued at one-twenty-fifth of their votes. If a proportionate increase is made in the votes obtained by them in 1950 and 1951 the 'cube-law' continues to operate.[1]

[1] On the 'cube-law' cf. the articles of M. G. Kendall and A. Stuart in the *British Journal of Sociology*, 1950, Vol. I, No. 3, p. 183, and in the *Revue française de Science politique*, 1952, No. 2, p. 270, and D. E. Butler's appendix to H. G. Nicholas, *The British General Election of 1950*, pp. 328 et seq.

In so far as sudden mutations in opinion are concerned the effects of the simple-majority single-ballot system are much more difficult to assess. If the mutation is expressed as a violent increase or decrease in strength of one of the existing parties it is exaggerated by the electoral system according to the operation just described: this is very different from the second-ballot system save in one respect: the originality of the mutation is diminished. In theory new wine can be poured into old bottles, in practice the flavour of the bottle here affects the wine. Numerically the mutation is exaggerated and the extent of the variations increased between elections; politically it is blunted by the leaders and organizers of the old party. This stabilizing effect is even more marked if the sudden mutation finds expression in the appearance of a new party; important distinctions must be made in this case, however. On the one hand, the simple-majority single-ballot system then appears to be conservative in character—even more conservative than the second-ballot system—and to set up an insurmountable barrier to changes, as a consequence of the power of the two major blocs that it has established: here we may quote the example of the U.S.A., where it is generally acknowledged to be impossible to set up a 'third party'. On the other hand, it is to be noted that it clearly favoured the development of Socialist parties at the beginning of the twentieth century, and that the first countries in which they were able to assume office were in fact countries with a simple-majority single-ballot system, Australia and New Zealand. How are we to resolve the contradiction?

To a large extent it is a result of local conditions, unrelated to the electoral system, which defy any attempt at general definition. However, it is explicable also by the nature and strength of new movements of opinion. So long as they remain weak and ill-assured the system pitilessly bans them from parliament: in practice those who might vote for them avoid wasting on them votes which might ensure the triumph of their worst enemies. An absolute barrier is therefore raised against all the sudden and superficial changes of mood which sometimes sweep through a nation. Let us however suppose that a new party—e.g. the Labour party—attains a certain strength in a constituency: at the following election the more moderate of the Liberal voters will throw themselves into the arms of the Conservative candidate for fear of Socialism, whereas the more radical will go over to Labour. This dual polarization starts the process of elimination of the Liberal party, which will only be hastened by the successes of Labour, for it will be paralleled by 'under-representation' as soon as the Liberal candidates take third place. The situation is totally different from that under the second-ballot system: in a French constituency before 1939 the fact that the Socialist party had attained a substantial number of votes did not drive the more moderate voters away from the Radicals; *on the contrary*, for a certain number of right-wing voters began to find the Radicals less dangerous in so far as they offered them protection against the Socialists: polarization worked to the advantage of the Centre and delayed the accession to power of the new party, at the same time as the necessity of allying itself with the old parties diminished its individuality.

Thus the single-ballot system is much less conservative than is often said: it may on the contrary accelerate the development of a new party as soon as it reaches a certain strength, and may rapidly advance it to the position of 'second party'. But from then on the single-ballot system again resembles in its effects the second-ballot system: they both hasten the natural ageing of the new party by tending to draw it closer to its principal rival amongst the old parties. We shall describe below the profound urge which leads the two major parties to grow like one another, as a consequence of the centralizing trend of the electoral struggle.

III. PARTY ALLIANCES

Alliances between parties vary greatly in form and degree. Some are ephemeral and unorganized: simply temporary coalitions which take place in order to benefit the parties concerned in the elections, in order to overthrow a government or to support one from time to time. Others are lasting and are strongly organized, so that sometimes they are like super-parties. The legal distinction between Confederation and Federal State is not always an easy one to make: similarly some very strong alliances are hardly distinguishable from parties fundamentally divided into rival tendencies. Officially the National Liberals in Great Britain form a separate party from the Conservative party: in fact the alliance is so close that they must be considered as completely integrated in the Conservative organization. On the other hand Uruguayan parties, whose different fractions may put up separate candidates at the presidential elections, with a kind of mutual withdrawal of candidature, are more like alliances than unified parties. In Western Germany the Bavarian Social Christians (C.S.U.) may be considered as a fraction of German Christian Democracy (C.D.U.), although in reality they are distinct yet allied parties; the C.D.U. is so decentralized that it might moreover be described as an alliance of local parties.

Factors in Alliances. The number of parties plays a determining role in the formation of alliances. In a two-party regime alliances are quite exceptional: they take the form of National Union when the internal or external situation is serious. There were alliances of this kind in Great Britain in 1914 and in 1939. The United States have also put into practice a bipartisan policy; they have even given us the example of an original kind of alliance, limited to foreign policy. However, South Africa lived between 1933 and 1941 under a coalition of the only two parties then existing in the country. Conversely, multi-party regimes can exceptionally manage without alliances when one of the parties obtains an absolute majority; but in this case the party with a majority most often tries to govern with others (as in Italy since 1948), in order to make them share the responsibilities of power: it remains dominated by the psychology of the regime, which is one of alliances. National traditions also exercise an indisputable influence in this sphere: the tendency of all the 'Republicans' in France to unite, which gave rise to the 1902 Bloc, the 1924 Cartel, the 1936 Popular Front, and even the 1945 three-party alliance; the tradition of the Danish Radicals of collaborating with the Socialists, which dates from the beginning of the century, and of the Agrarian Left (*Venstre*) of uniting with the Conservatives; the customary coalition between Catholics and Protestants in Holland since the 1868 reversal of alliances, etc. In authoritarian regimes governmental interference is also quite marked: in the Balkan democracies between 1920 and 1940 many alliances were concluded as the result of governmental pressure; similarly, in Imperial Germany the famous Cartel of 1887 was brought about by Bismarck. Historical circumstances also play an important part: the financial crisis was instrumental in forming the French National Union of 1926, the events of the Sixth February 1934 in forming the Popular Front, underground warfare in forming the three-party alliance.

But here the influence of the electoral regime seems to predominate. It is moreover sufficiently clear to be expressed in precise formulae. In principle the simple-majority second-ballot system encourages the formation of close alliances; proportional representation, on the other hand, encourages complete independence. As for the simple-majority single-ballot system, its results are very different according to the number of parties functioning under it: in a two-party regime it encourages total independence; in a multi-party regime, on the other hand, it favours very strong alliances. The first tendency is obvious; the very mechanism of the simple-majority second-ballot system does indeed imply that at the second ballot the less favoured parties withdraw to the advantage of the most favoured, within each 'great spiritual family'. We must distinguish between simple withdrawal and 'standing down'. In the case of the latter the candidate abandoning the struggle invites his electors to give their votes to the rival he names. Between the two there are a thousand subtle shades of difference: there are many ways of withdrawing and many degrees of warmth in 'standing down'; but it is natural that candidates of parties which are most like each other should come to an agreement before the ballot in order to make arrangements for their reciprocal 'standing down' or withdrawal at the second ballot. Observation confirms these conclusions based on *a priori* reasoning: in all countries where the second ballot has been working there are more or less clear traces of electoral alliances. The examples of Imperial Germany and the Third French Republic are most typical in this respect.

There were great national alliances in Imperial Germany: the Cartel, grouping Conservatives, National Liberals, and the Imperial party, which won the 1887 elections and lost the 1890 one; the 1906 Bloc, uniting Liberals, National Liberals, and Conservatives against the Socialists; and the coalition of the Left formed by the Socialists in 1912 to oppose the Bloc. The 1906 German Bloc had been formed on the pattern of the French Left Bloc of 1902, which was not the first example of an alliance at the national level in France. The 1877 elections, which took place immediately after the Sixteenth of May, had been fought under the banners of two rival coalitions of Right and of Left. But the 1902 Bloc was something stronger: the functioning of the 'Left Delegation' in Parliament was an important innovation in this respect. The 1936 Popular Front gave itself a similar structure, and the unity of the allies in the electoral campaign was even greater because they had drawn up quite a detailed common programme. Of all coalitions, the Popular Front is probably the one which has had the greatest effect on public opinion. All these great alliances are well known because they have led to national agreements, official and public in character, around which the parties have made a great deal of propaganda: apart from them numerous tacit agreements, often local, have been concluded because they were necessary for election purposes. In the 1907 German elections, the Catholics supported the Socialists in Baden, Bavaria and Austria, either by giving them their votes or by abstaining from voting. In France the two rival blocs took shape again almost everywhere in most of the elections held under the Third Republic. Outside France and Germany, alliances are to be met with in all countries where there is a second ballot. In Sweden the Liberals and Socialists often united against the Conservatives. In Norway, on the other hand, the Right and the Left generally united against the Socialists after 1906: at the 1915 elections their collaboration was so close that it is difficult to separate their votes in the electoral statistics. In Holland alliances were a regular practice until the establishment of proportional representation: between 1848 and 1868 there was a Catholic-Liberal coalition, opposed by a coalition of Conservatives and Calvinists which was not as strong: in 1868 there was a change in alliances (the Catholics collaborated with the Calvinists and the Conservatives tended to disappear); since 1905 there has been an electoral agreement between the Liberals and the Radicals (Fig. 41).

It is difficult to state the exact influence of any particular form of the ballot on the formation of alliances. The limitation of the second ballot to the two most favoured candidates (as in Germany and Holland) does not seem to have played a large part when compared with the integral second ballot (as in the French and Norwegian systems). In theory, on the one hand, it seems to make formal alliances unnecessary by obliging the less favoured candidates to withdraw; but on the other hand it tends to strengthen alliances by obliging the weakest parties to come to an agreement over a candidate at the first ballot, so that they may be able to participate in the second. Only a very detailed study of each particular case could show the respective consequences of these two factors. The different effects of list-voting with a second-ballot system and voting for a single candidate are not clearly perceptible to the observer either. In so far as list-voting strengthens centralization and party discipline it seems to make alliances stronger. The example of France shows that extreme decentralization of parties and the great weakness of their internal organization was one of the principal factors in the rapid breaking-up of electoral alliances.

The action of the simple-majority single-ballot system is totally different according to whether it coincides with a dualist or a multi-party system. In the first case the idea of electoral alliances is logically unthinkable: if the two parties were to unite there would be only one candidate and the election would take on a plebiscitary character which would completely change the nature of the regime. Nevertheless one must be careful about definite conclusions in political science: the example of South Africa between 1933 and 1941 shows that electoral alliances are possible in a simple-majority two-party system without a complete upheaval of the political structure; but this is a very exceptional case. On the other hand if, as a result of particular circumstances, the single-ballot system coincides with multi-partism it will favour the formation of very strong alliances, incomparably closer than those of the second ballot: for it then becomes necessary to share the constituencies before the election so as to make it possible for the electors to give their votes in a block to the single candidate of the coalition. This necessitates a much more complete agreement than if the existence of a second ballot allowed a free candidature for the first: in the latter case it is the elector, in short, who shares out the seats among the allies; in the former it is the general staff of the parties who must do it themselves. The alliance is therefore more difficult to achieve, but, once concluded, it entails closer collaboration. Moreover the pressure of the electoral system which causes this alliance is much stronger: if there is no agreement the ballot will pitilessly tend to eliminate superfluous parties until finally dualism is restored. Several examples of this type of electoral collaboration could be given. That of the Danish Radicals and Socialists in 1910 has already been cited. This was very close since the two parties never, in any constituency, put up candidates in opposition to each other. Nearer to the present day there are the examples of the British coalitions in the 1918, 1931, and 1935 elections and the pact concluded in South Africa in 1924 between the Nationalist party (Hertzog) and the Labour party.

It is the very essence of proportional representation to isolate parties: it tends to confer on each party complete electoral autonomy. But as it very rarely gives an absolute majority to a single party it does nevertheless lead to parliamentary alliances. This contradiction between the electoral level and the governmental level is not the least of the defects of P.R.: it makes parties totally independent of each other at the first level and obliges them to collaborate at the second. Normally this makes the formation of parliamentary coalitions more difficult and the position of governmental majorities unstable. The example of Holland can be used to illustrate this point, for there government majorities seem to have been much weaker and shorter-lived under P.R. than under the simple-majority two-ballot system. But experience does not always confirm the conclusions reached by reason concerning the electoral independence of parties under P.R. It is indeed rare for the latter to be applied in its complete form, and the most frequent adulteration of it tends precisely to favour large parties and penalize small ones. Coalitions formed in order to draw up common lists, or 'agreements' for the distribution of remainders, can become quite fruitful. In Belgium there have been several attempts at coalitions between Socialists and Liberals so as to offer common lists. But the electors did not take kindly to them: the 1912 alliance turned many Liberal electors towards the Catholic party, which gained 130,000 votes. Nevertheless, at the 1946 elections a Liberal-Socialist cartel was formed in the provinces of Limburg and Luxembourg and in the arrondissements of Hasselt, Tongres, Arlon, and Neufchateau; it was not maintained in 1949, which resulted in both parties losing seats. Nevertheless it must not be forgotten that these alliances caused by P.R. are really the result of the alterations made in it. Integral proportional representation does not lead to alliances. Moreover the coalition has much less to gain from modified proportional representation than from a simple-majority ballot: in the latter case division may entail a complete reversal of electoral results; in the former it only modifies slightly the distribution of seats without making any very noticeable change in the balance of power. Unless, of course, there is a mixed system, in which case proportional representation is no longer in question. Western Germany provides some good examples of this. In general the electoral system is a compromise between the simple-majority single-ballot system and P.R. (seats obtained at the simple-majority ballot are definitely gained; a certain number of additional seats is then allotted according to proportional representation). In 1950, in the Länder elections, there was often an alliance between the Christian Democrats and the Liberals. In Westphalia–North Rhineland the C.D.U. did not present any candidates in twelve constituencies in which it campaigned for the Liberals, the opposite taking place in seventeen constituencies; thanks to this coalition Christian Democrats and Liberals obtained more than 53% of the seats with only 49% of the votes. The advantage of the alliance was even more considerable in Schleswig-Holstein, where the same coalition, joined by the German party, obtained nearly 45% of the seats with 36·4% of the votes. The French system between 1919 and 1924 tended to give the same result. First of all any candidate who had obtained an absolute majority was proclaimed elected, then seats were allotted to each list according to the quotient system, and all the remaining seats were given to the list which had the highest average. This clearly favoured the list which came top in the competition. It was therefore to the advantage of neighbouring parties to unite and present a common list; vote-splitting, moreover, made it easier to compile one. The parties of the Right understood this mechanism, created the 'National Bloc', and were rewarded with a great victory in the 1919 elections: they obtained 338 seats (if there had been integral P.R. the figure would have been 275).[1] The parties of the Left who had not united obtained only 197 seats (with integral P.R. the figure would have been 250). It is clear that this mixed proportional representation encourages coalitions: the 1951 system does so even more. Under it all seats are allotted to the list or group of allied lists obtaining the absolute majority, proportional representation remaining of subsidiary importance. The practice of alliances (although they were not national in character) made it possible for the Centre parties to gain 61% of the seats in metropolitan France with 51·4% of the votes, whereas the French People's Rally and the Communists, who fought in isolation, obtained only 39% of the seats with 48·2% of the votes.

Electoral, Parliamentary and Governmental Alliances. The classification of alliances is difficult: here we find ourselves on uncertain and shifting ground. First, we must distinguish between occasional short-lived coalitions and alliances proper which are more lasting. Right in theory, such a classification is not always very easy to apply: many alliances hailed with publicity and hope break up as quickly as coalitions; many coalitions are continually reconstructed and become true alliances. In France, for example, the left-wing parties have officially concluded alliances on only three occasions: in 1902, the Left-wing Bloc, in 1924 the Cartel, and in 1936 the Popular Front. In practice, 'Republican discipline' has however operated at almost every election in a spontaneous

[1] Cf. G. Lachapelle, *Elections législatives du 16 novembre 1919*, Paris, 1920.

coalition every four years. We shall therefore use both terms, coalition and alliance, it being understood that the former will be generally used of temporary agreements and the latter of lasting unions.

The fundamental classifications of alliances are based upon other criteria. In the vertical plane we may contrast electoral alliances, parliamentary alliances, and governmental alliances. The first occur at the level of the candidate, the second of the deputy, the third of the minister. All can coexist or may occur in isolation. Electoral alliances are themselves very varied, according to the ballot procedure and the closeness of the union: putting up joint candidates or joint lists at the first or at the only ballot, reciprocal standing down at the second ballot, agreements for the distribution of remainders or friendly arrangements in certain proportional systems, and so on. They may be either tacit or explicit, local or national. In the French system with a free second ballot the simple withdrawal of a candidate without his officially asking his voters to transfer their vote to a neighbouring candidate is often the result of a tacit alliance: each of the two parties avoids being compromised by its neighbour and none the less benefits from the advantages of union; an open alliance would be more effective but more embarrassing. In fact tacit alliances are fairly common in electoral systems with a second ballot; they are encountered in single-ballot systems if there are several parties (two of them avoiding putting up candidates against one another); in a proportional system, they are impossible. For similar reasons, moreover, electoral alliances seem to be more common locally than nationally. By officially leaving to their district committees the responsibility for coalitions, the parties seem less dependent than if they entered into a national alliance. The system thus permits Centre parties to employ very profitable see-saw tactics, benefiting from the support of the Right in some constituencies, of the Left in others: under the Third Republic, the Radical party extensively practised this art of straddling. Frequently there is contradiction between national and local alliances: in France, in spite of the Left Bloc, the Cartel, and the Popular Front, certain Radical candidates were always elected with the support of the Right. Obviously the extent to which the parties are centralized is an important factor here.

The electors however have a word to say sometimes: a distinction could be drawn between compulsory and optional alliances. In the first case the electors cannot veto the alliance unless he transfers his vote to a candidate entirely opposed to his own opinions. Take, for example, an agreement between the Socialists and the M.R.P. for an alliance of lists (*apparentement*) in order to distribute remainders or to obtain a majority premium (*une prime à la majorité*): the Socialist voter who does not accept the agreement is obliged to vote against his own party and for his worst enemies, the Communists or the Right. If there is only one list or one candidate put up by the allies the situation is the same (cf. the example of the C.D.U. and F.D.P. at the German Länder elections). On the other hand agreements to stand down before the second ballot leave the voter greater freedom. Take the case of the Radical party in France between the wars: in accordance with 'Republican discipline' its candidate would withdraw, inviting his electors to transfer their votes to the Socialist if he polled more votes. Many would not follow his advice and would abstain or even vote for the Centre candidate. By doing so they did not harm their party since it was in any case no longer involved: on the contrary they had done their best to ensure its success at the first ballot. Such independence on the part of voters is fairly common. At the 1928 elections the Radicals withdrew in many places in favour of Socialists, but 400,000 Radical votes were transferred at the second ballot to the Centre, in spite of the agreements between the parties. Conversely it happens that the voters effect a coalition in spite of discord between parties; until 1936 the French Communist party strictly applied the class-warfare technique and maintained its candidates at the second ballot; but a large number of Communist electors voted for Socialist candidates in spite of the instructions of the party, or else abstained, which indirectly favoured the Socialist candidates. In 1928 out of 425,751 electors voting Communist at the first ballot, in the 256 constituencies in which the party was involved in the second ballot, only 231,794 remained faithful to it, that is 59%. In 1932 the defection was more serious: in the 284 constituencies where a second ballot was held, out of 338,000 Communist voters only 185,000 voted for the party at the second vote that is 54%.

On the parliamentary level parties may unite in support of the government or against it. Every degree and kind of alliance is here encountered, from the fortuitous and exceptional coalition to organized union with common institutions, of which the most celebrated example is provided by the 1902 Left Delegation that was revived in 1924. The life of multi-party parliaments is dominate by alliances. So too in this case is the life of governments, which cannot be formed without agreements. Every governmental alliance which associates in office ministers from different parties is obviously complemented by a parliamentary alliance. The converse is not however true. Parliamentary alliances in opposition and parliamentary alliances in support are both encountered: a minority party may govern with the support of its own deputies and those of nearby groups who give it their votes without agreeing to share power with it. Since they are less involved in its activity they seem in the public eye to have less responsibility; they may therefore combine an affectation of pure disinterestedness with a much more demagogic attitude. Sometimes alternative support is utilized, reliance on the Right for help in passing conservative measures, reliance on the Left for help in securing progressive reforms. Simple abstention may also be adequate to provide support: the French Socialist party often behaved in this way towards left-wing ministries during the Third Republic. The parliamentary game consists entirely in the attempt to combine the advantages of power with the freedom of opposition; the internal structure of parties may help, so may the operation of alliances. From February 1934 until January 1936 the Radical party was represented in the French Government of National Union, centred on the Right (from Radicals to Conservatives), which it supported with its votes, and in the Left Delegation (and in the Popular Front Committee after July 1935), an opposition body centred on the Left (from Radicals to Communists). This is an example of what might be called the 'bat' technique carried to a very high pitch: 'I am a bird, look at my wings; I am a mouse, long live the rats!'

The relations between electoral alliances on the one hand and parliamentary and governmental alliances on the other are very complex. The second may exist without the first, as we have seen: in a system of proportional representation without agreement on lists, the parties face the electorate independently, but they are obliged to unite to form or to support a government if there is no absolute majority. Obviously the absence of solidarity at the electoral level diminishes solidarity in parliament and government. Each party tries to lay on its ally the responsibility for unpopular acts and to take the credit for popular ones. But when the voting system drives them to electoral alliances, these do not always coincide with the governmental alliances. It is easier to join forces to win seats than in order to exercise power: the former type of alliance only requires a negative agreement against an opponent, the latter a positive agreement upon a programme which demands a more deep-seated similarity. In some cases electoral alliances cannot be transposed to the parliamentary level because they are self-contradictory: the allies in each constituency are not identical. We have already quoted the example of the French Radical party making use of its central position to profit first from Right-wing withdrawals, then from withdrawals on the Left. At the 1907 elections in Austria, the Liberals were in general allied with the Christian Social party to fight the Socialists, but in Lower Austria there were Socialists united with Liberals against the Christian Social candidates, while in Upper Austria two Socialists were elected with Christian Social votes in opposition to the Liberals. Electoral agreements interwoven in this way, like the pattern of a ballet, obviously made it impossible to have any governmental alliance. Local coalitions are not alone in being drawn and quartered in this way: in France the major national alliances (Bloc, Cartel, Popular Front) never entirely prevented contradictory local combinations which greatly weakened the national alliance when it was translated into governmental terms; the breakdown of the Cartel in 1924 and that of the Popular Front in 1936 are partially explained by the behaviour of Radical deputies elected with the support of Centre voters.

Even if agreement at the electoral level does not involve similar contradictions it is always very difficult to prolong it into power. Divergences between the allies in doctrines and tendencies, differences in social sub-structure and the interests they safeguard very quickly show themselves. The chariot of state always bears some resemblance to the picture drawn in 1945 in the days of the three-party alliance by a French humorist—a vehicle drawn by three horses, one pulling to the Right, another to the Left, the third to the Centre. If the allies have reached agreement on a common programme their relations are much easier. Such a programme is however always vague, being made up of slogans and general headings more calculated to attract votes than to formulate a plan for positive action. In particular it generally defines aims rather than means: now government is a problem of means and the basic differences between allied parties generally concern means. We can go farther: there seems to be a natural difference between electoral alliances and governmental alliances. It could be formulated as follows: electoral alliances tend to be dominated by the most extreme party, governmental alliances by the most moderate party. The contrast is a reflection of the natural antipathy between governors and governed. Those who govern are compelled to take into account all the interests involved, which compels them to give no more than partial satisfaction to any; they are faced with facts which limit the scope of action. The governed never see more than their individual interests, which they try to defend with the utmost energy, knowing all the time that they will not obtain total satisfaction but must ask for more than they expect to get; they never know all the real facts about the problems facing the government and the narrow margin of possibilities left by them. Even in circles which consider themselves advanced, ignorance and prejudice are rife: in France the peasants pay scarcely any direct taxes and are convinced that the Treasury fleeces them; most Taxpayers' Associations are formed in social circles in which tax evasion and falsification are most widespread; the desire of the lower and upper middle classes in 1946–7 for free enterprise and the abolition of planning was evidence of a complete misunderstanding of the economic situation. By natural inclination many electors are therefore led into giving their votes to those who defend their point of view with the greatest energy, that is to the most extreme of the candidates inside their movement: at the electoral level coalitions are dominated therefore by the extremist wing. Once in power there is a complete change. The moderate section of the coalition is the most alive to the necessities of government: its moderation coincides with the limits imposed by facts. It is therefore the most capable of governing without straying too far from its electoral programme and promises. If the alliance is maintained at the governmental level it will of necessity be dominated by this section, since it is most in touch with reality.

The extremist party is therefore reduced to the alternative of either taking part in government and deviating from its doctrine or else breaking up the alliance. The attempt to find a compromise solution leads to unending fluctuations. Often the extremist ally takes refuge in support without participation, which makes it possible to maintain the coalition in weakened form whilst benefiting from the advantages of criticism and opposition. Such was the position adopted by the French Socialist party in the Left Bloc and the Cartel up to 1936; such too the position of the Communist party in the 1936 Popular Front. This position itself is however provisional. The practical difficulties of government gradually incline the party in office to greater moderation, and this draws it further from the common electoral programme and nearer to moderates on the other side; the disappointment of some voters increases and this leads the extremist party to adopt a more intransigent attitude, so that the distance between the allies increases. Overstretched, the rope one day breaks and the alliance is over. It is often reconstituted some time before the new elections. Developments in the French Legislature under the Third Republic provide a good illustration of the dynamics of alliances. A left-wing coalition basically composed of Radicals and Socialists won an electoral victory. As the Socialists would not join the government, it was basically made up of Radical elements. To begin with they kept some of the promises jointly made to the electorate. Then practical difficulties led them to call a 'halt', a 'breathing space' which separated them from the Socialists and brought them nearer to the Centre. About halfway through the life of the legislature the left-wing coalition broke up and there was a new governmental alliance—a union of Radicals with the Right Centre—different from the original electoral coalition. However, in order to retain adequate parliamentary backing this alliance was obliged gradually to extend towards the Conservatives. Beginning on the Left wing the legislature ended up on the Right. Not entirely, however, for the approaching elections sometimes caused a return to the initial alliance. This pattern was repeated in 1906–10, 1924–8, 1932–6. In 1936–40 the Communists played almost the same part as Socialists had done in preceding parliaments, while the Socialists played the Radical role, and they in turn took the place of the pre-1914 'Progressives'.

The pattern is not general. It is not peculiar to France, but nowhere else does it occur with the same perfection and the same regularity. Many countries have had lasting alliances thanks to the wisdom of the extremist party, to its absence of demagogy, and also to its strength. If it is definitely stronger than its moderate allies it must itself assume the responsibility of government; then the process of dissociation does not occur. This is no doubt the explanation for the stability of alliances in Scandinavian countries. There are many other factors also involved: party structure, social basis of parties, historical traditions, the ways in which opinion is formed, and so on. Finally the pattern illustrated is not applicable in a revolutionary period, in periods of national crisis, still awaiting analysis in depth, in which the need for change and for novelty temporarily overcomes the need for stability. The law of revolutionary government is the converse of that for normal government: realism urges full steam ahead, prudence and moderation become weaknesses when power is to be exercised. The government alliance itself becomes dominated by the most extreme party, whose doctrine and tendencies in this case are closer to the facts. The moderate ally is soon obliged to submit or else be destroyed. But the extremists of yesterday are the moderates of tomorrow, fated like them to be excluded from power until the day of counter-revolution or of stabilization. This new pattern is however no more absolute than its predecessor: both do no more than describe fundamental tendencies that may be modified or transformed by actual conditions, which are always special conditions.

Political Geography of Alliances. For greater precision this description of the relations between electoral and governmental alliances requires a definition of the second classification of alliances, that which considers from the horizontal point of view the different positions of parties on the political chessboard. Thus we can distinguish alliances of the Left and of the Right, union of Centre parties or concentration, the meeting of extremes and the various National unions. The first are the most common. In general they had their origins with the Socialist parties at the beginning of the century: the ending of the original two-party system drew the Conservatives and Liberals closer together in most countries, in some others it was Liberals and Socialists but more often the Socialists and the Radicals who had split off from the Liberals. This classic pattern has been approximately realized in varying forms in Sweden, Denmark, and Norway. But it is often complicated by social, religious, or political divisions. In Holland the religious question long separated the Catholic and Protestant Conservative parties: the Catholics were allied with the Liberal party against the Protestants until 1868: thereafter an alliance of Catholics and Protestants (Anti-Revolutionary) was formed against the Liberals and Radicals. At the beginning of the twentieth century the Radicals received the support of a Protestant fraction (it became the Christian Historical party in 1908) that later rejoined the Conservative alliance. This however broke up in 1925 over a religious issue, the embassy to the Vatican. Gradually a new alliance came into being, uniting all the Conservative parties (Catholic and Protestant) with the Liberals against the Socialists: this is somewhat similar to the situation obtaining in Switzerland at the same period.

In France the constitutional question linked with the religious question long determined alliances under the Third Republic: the clergy having long supported the opposition to the Republic and religion having served as the link between the various authoritarian and monarchist tendencies, the Republican party became identified with anti-clericalism. Whence the formation of two rival coalitions: 'Reactionaries' and 'Clericals' on the Right, Republicans and 'Anti-clericals' on the Left. In 1877 (on the occasion of the Sixteenth of May and of 'Moral Order') and in 1885 (with Boulangism) the two alliances were definitely sealed. Subsequently the link between the Right parties proved less close generally than that between those of the Left, and the gradual acceptance of the Republic by the Right changed the significance of the original cleavage. But until 1940 it never disappeared: on one side were the Left Bloc, the Cartel, and the Popular Front, on the other the National Bloc and the National Front. In some respects one might even hold that the Vichy episode was a right-wing victory and the Liberation a triumph for the Left. However, the appearance of Fascism and especially of Communism changed the nature of the problem.

If two rival coalitions, Left and Right, are set up and if they are sufficiently strong, a multi-party system may become very much like a two-party system. Thus from 1830 to 1925 Holland experienced an alternation very similar to that prevailing in Great Britain and other dualist countries. This forms a strange contrast with the stable distribution to be observed in the strength of the different parties considered individually (Fig. 41). It is similarly of interest to compare the alternation of the two great Danish coalitions, Socialists and Radicals on one side, Conservatives and Agrarians (*Venstre*) on the other, with the slight party variations. The two blocs here have not however the stability seen in Holland not being based on any electoral alliance because of proportional representation. It is significant that P.R. in Holland brought about as early as 1925 (that is after the second election in which the system was applied), a breakdown of the old Conservative coalition which had lasted since 1868. In any case a two-alliance system is not so sound as a two-party system. Within each bloc mutual rivalries may engender a demagogic attitude that bipartism tends to check the unity of view in the government is generally much weaker. In the last resort, however, all depends on the degree of cohesion manifested by the respective alliances or parties. The duality of Dutch alliances between 1868 and 1925 was more rigid than th duality of American parties. However, the two-alliance system allows a much greater variety of combinations than does the two-party system; without any modification of the electoral body and without any change in the strength of individual parties a reversal of alliances may bring about a considerable political upheaval. The

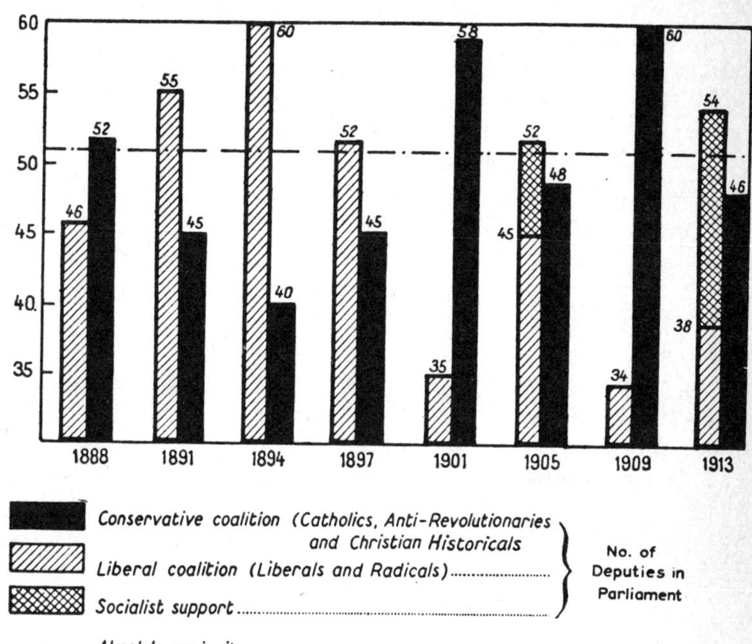

Fig. 41. Party alliances in Holland, 1888–1913.

best example is to be seen in Holland in 1868 when the Catholics, allied until then with the Liberals, made an alliance with the Protestants. The replacement of a system of dual alliances by another such system is however quite exceptional; more often reversals of alliances occur in countries where there is a three-fold division of opinion, and take the form of the shifting of the Centre party towards one or other extreme. The French Radical party acted in this way between 1919 and 1939. In Belgium, at the same period, the situation was somewhat different: it was the right-wing party (Catholic) which swung to and fro, allying itself first with the Centre party (Liberal), then with the left-wing party (Socialist). Between 1919 and 1940 there was no Socialist-Liberal ministry, as compared with two Catholic-Socialist and seven Catholic-Liberal ministries.[1]

The reversal of alliances sometimes has the effect of replacing two rival coalitions by a Centre alliance. In France the dislocation of the Left Bloc often found expression in an attempt at 'concentration' or 'the meeting of the Centres', as it used to be called at the beginning of the Third Republic. In 1905 the fall of Combes marked the end of the Left Bloc, and it was replaced on the formation of the Rouvier ministry by a concentration supported by the majority of Radicals, the Progressives and one-half of the Right, while the extreme Right, the Socialists and an important section of the Radicals formed the opposition. However, the approach of the elections put an end to the concentration and the Bloc was revived in 1906. Until 1909 it was active on the governmental level, although the Clemenceau ministry was often supported by a scratch majority, relying on the successive backing of the Right and the Left (see-saw tactics that represent the secret hope of all Centre parties). In 1909, under the banner of peace, Briand inaugurated a rejuvenated and subtle form of concentration which was to last until 1913, when it broke down over the question of military service (the three-year law). After the war the concentration was renewed in 1925, upon the speedy disintegration of the Left Cartel majority, and extended to the Right in 1926 under the title of National Union. In 1934 the process was reversed: the break-up of the Cartel after the events of the Sixth of February first brought about the formation of a National Union, under Doumergue, which then contracted into a concentration under Flandin.

During the Third Republic therefore concentration was often encountered at the level of government, but it was rarely extended to the electoral level. Only three such examples can be quoted: 1893, 1910, 1928. In 1893 however the only electoral evidence of concentration was the withdrawal of a few Catholics in favour of Progressives; its material influence was slight, not so its moral influence. In 1928 the Radicals generally pursued the tactics of the Union of the Left; concentration was brought about, in spite of the party's instructions, by the 400,000 Radical voters who transferred their votes to the Right at the second ballot. Only in 1910 was the experiment more conclusive; this was as a result of the circumstances which drove the Right and the Socialists into a

[1] To some extent this corresponds to the gradual shifting to the Right of the Belgian Liberal party, cf. the French Radical party after 1945.

'meeting of extremes' in order to obtain the passage of proportional representation. The impotence of concentration—so often practised on the parliamentary and governmental levels—to find its complement on the electoral level explains the distrust of the Popular Republican Movement for the simple-majority second-ballot system: being entirely dependent on the dream of a 'meeting of centres' (nowadays called the Third Force), it fears that the practices of the Third Republic will be renewed under the Fourth Republic. This fear takes no account however of the reality of Communism, which makes dualist alliances difficult. In any event the Fourth Republic lives under the banner of concentration since the breakdown of the three-party alliance with the eviction of the Communists on 6 May 1947; the same Centre majority, under a variety of forms, has since then tended to govern. Like the coalition of the Weimar Republic, which it resembles in more than one respect (save for the strength of the Socialist party), it is threatened on both Left and Right by the growth of powerful parties that are non-parliamentary in character: Communists and French People's Rally.

The French type of National Union, as it was practised under the leadership of Poincaré, Doumergue, and Daladier, must be clearly distinguished from the authentic National Union applied during the 1914 War in France and Great Britain, in several countries during the war of 1939, in Belgium between the wars, and so on. National Union of the Poincaré type is a coalition of all parties except the extreme Left; it is an anti-Socialist, or anti-Communist, alliance. Holland has put it into operation several times since 1925, Switzerland has applied it with some regularity since 1919. In France the three-party alliance of the Liberation represented a kind of reversed Poincarism, a coalition of all parties against the Right. True National Union is entirely different: it represents an association of all the major parties existing in the state, without exception. Such an obliteration of party differences is justified in exceptional periods of great national peril when concentration of effort is essential: it represents the normal form of war-time government in a democratic system. However, it sometimes occurs in peace-time: Belgium often had recourse to it between 1919 and 1939; of twenty successive ministries during that period, nine were cabinets of National Union. In South Africa the alliance of the only two parties between 1933 and 1941 produced the same kind of result. The system presupposes strong discipline in the parties as well as basic agreement upon political principles. It represents a transposition to the alliance level of the technique of the single party. But the single alliance does not present the same dangers, for its very structure safeguards it against the menace of totalitarianism and ensures a variety of tendencies and expressions of opinion. None the less the system corresponds to a profound crisis in the democratic regime.

Finally we must consider a form of alliance that is less common and more strange than the rest: the meeting of extremes. The coalition of the party farthest to the Right with the party farthest to the Left, for each of whom the other represents Public Enemy No 1, seems contrary to nature. But in nature everything is possible, and in fact such unions between carp and rabbit are not infrequent. For extreme parties always share a common opposition to moderate parties, and sometimes a common opposition to the regime. Under the Third Republic most attempts at concentration were vanquished by coalitions of extremists: it was to avoid this that concentration almost always disguised itself as National Union. Under the Fourth Republic the Communists and the French People's Rally have frequently joined in voting against the Third Force, just as Communists and Nazis had done in the Weimar Republic and, before then, Socialists and Fascists in the Parliament of Rome: the meeting of extremes is quite common in the form of an opposition alliance in parliament. It is much less common in the form of an electoral alliance, and particularly of a governmental alliance. The French elections of 1910 may be quoted as an example of the first case; the Right and the Socialists withdrew in favour of one another in some constituencies, as a result of reaching an understanding concerning the proportional representation reform that had been rejected by the Centre parties: here the extremes found common ground in a common programme. The same limited agreement may serve as a basis for a government supported by them. However, such a positive meeting often assumes a different significance: it corresponds to the tactics known as the 'policy of favouring the worst'. For a party of the extreme Left this involves favouring a right-wing policy to demonstrate its absurdity and to increase discontent, instead of supporting a moderate left-wing policy which would bring tranquillity but decrease its own chances. The aim is also to weaken its immediate rival, which is most dangerous because it is most similar, to the advantage of a distant opponent with whom no direct competition is involved. If a party of the extreme Right pursues a parallel policy there may result a real pact between the two extremes. If the 'policy of favouring the worst' is applied by one only of the parties, none the less a *de facto* reconciliation with the other party results. The Communist party followed these tactics in France and elsewhere up to 1935: thus it favoured the Right, especially in the 1928 elections, and this cost it a great many votes in 1932. But in this way it preserved its own purity and individuality throughout the period required for the building up of the party.

Relations between Allies. Formal relations between the allies are less important than the power relationship. The former, in any case, are limited to some few common institutions: Action committees in the case of the 1906 German Bloc, the Left Delegation of the 1902 French Bloc and the 1924 Cartel, the Committee of the People's Rally in 1936, and so on. These institutions may be situated at the electoral level, where they direct the propaganda of the allies and supervise the implementation of agreements, or at the parliamentary level, where they attempt to establish a common attitude and voting discipline amongst the participating groups. From this last point of view the Left Delegation was between 1902 and 1906 a model of the kind: Charles Benoist termed it 'a second ministry, extra-constitutional and irresponsible', Combes defended the 'concerted agreement upon the discussions to be undertaken and the resolutions to be taken: a system which safeguards the majority against ill-considered temptations'. All alliances do not include such institutions: unorganized coalitions are less rare than organized alliances. Nor are all based upon a common programme: each ally is anxious to preserve its freedom of action. The charters of alliances resemble propagandist statements rather than working plans; in consequence they are usually drawn up in terms that are deliberately vague and general. However, a distinction is to be made between purely governmental programmes drawn up by the parties on the occasion of the formation of a ministry of National Union, which are the most tenuous of all, and electoral programmes which may be a little less so if they awake any echo in public opinion and arouse any public enthusiasm: in that case one ally can exert a firm hold on the other by reminding it of the programme. For this reason electoral alliances are rarely based on any expressly defined charter; alternatively the charter is clearly limited in character, corresponding to the need of the more moderate ally to impose some limits on overbidding by the more extreme ally.

Common institutions and programmes are therefore, in the last resort, means for establishing a certain power relationship between the parties in coalition. In this connection one is tempted to make a distinction between equal and unequal alliances, but such a classification is only an intellectual abstraction. In fact every alliance is unequal, and the only worthwhile question is that of the degree of inequality. We may perhaps contrast relatively egalitarian alliances and pseudo-alliances in which domination is the rule; between the two stretches an infinite range of varieties and shades. Three principal elements have to be taken into account in defining the degree of inequality amongst the allies: their respective strength, their position on the political chessboard, and lastly their internal structure. The first is fundamental in electoral alliances under the simple-majority second-ballot system: the party which comes top of the coalition alone remains in the running at the second ballot, profiting from the standing down or withdrawal of its allies. The result is that an electoral coalition is never possible, under this system, except between parties that are not too disproportionate to one another, otherwise the weakest will be completely annihilated by the strongest. In practice local disparities generally correct the inequality of an alliance: one ally will be at the head of the poll in some constituencies, another elsewhere. But a major party may find it advantageous deliberately to forgo presenting candidates at the first ballot in some districts in order to allow a very weak ally to obtain at least some representation, and to profit from its withdrawal elsewhere where it might be in a position to hold the balance between two almost equal groups. Electoral agreements therefore very often assume a certain subtlety and flexibility, very different from the rigid and uniform character that seems to be implied by the operation of the simple-majority second-ballot system. Flexibility is even greater in the case of agreements under the single-ballot system in which the allies have to share out seats before the ballot in order to present in every constituency a single candidate or a single list. Alliances of this type are therefore more difficult but more binding. They are also more unequal: the largest party tends to dominate the smallest almost entirely, as is to be seen in the case of the National Liberals in Britain. Under the single-ballot system alliances tend generally to develop into fusion because of the degree of intimacy involved; but such fusion often takes the form of the absorption of the weakest by the strongest if the difference in size between them is very considerable

This emphasizes the vital part played by strength in the inequality of alliances.

At the governmental level the influence of strength is also obvious: the larger the allied party the more influence it exerts within the alliance. Until 1936 the Radical party exercised a veritable leadership within the Left Bloc because it was the largest party in the coalition. In 1936 the leadership passed into the hands of the Socialist party because it had advanced to first place. It will be noted that parliamentary strength clearly takes precedence over electoral strength, for the Radical party had lost the lead in the electoral field as early as 1932 with 1,836,000 votes as against the Socialist party's 1,956,000. Pre-eminence in an alliance is of considerable importance; it is often recognized that the party that heads the coalition must be responsible for presiding over the government. To justify their refusal to participate before 1936 and their change of mind at that date, the Socialists made a definite distinction between Socialist participation in a Radical ministry and Radical participation in a Socialist ministry. Leadership by the most numerous party has never of course been a general and absolute rule in governmental alliances; this basic tendency has had to compromise with many others., The extent of the difference between the allies plays some part in this respect; if it is very slight, control by the most numerous becomes a subject for discussion. The structure and nature of the strongest ally are also important: in 1946, for example, the Popular Republicans and the Socialists refused to take part in a ministry with Communist leadership inside a three-party alliance.

However, the greatest obstacle to the leadership of the strongest ally arises from the respective position of the allies. It has already been shown that electoral alliances tend to be dominated by the most extreme ally and governmental alliances by the most moderate: these tendencies naturally interfere with those produced by the respective strength of the parties in coalition. A smaller ally may sometimes be led to assume the responsibilities of government because of its more moderate position. In an approximate fashion curves of inequality within alliances can be drawn: in the periods preceding and following the election the extreme party is in command; the further one goes from the election, the more it loses influence to the advantage of the most moderate party, on account of the necessities of government. These inequality curves would correspond to the legislative cycles in a coalition system, demagogic at the beginning and end, more conservative in the middle period. It must be understood that the pattern is very general and that the interaction of special circumstances, both varied and numerous, often overlays it to the point of causing it completely to disappear. In the long run it seems that the alliance is finally dominated by the most moderate party: the extremist is compelled on the parliamentary level to support a certain number of measures in contradiction with its position, just as on the electoral level it gives support to a movement in contradiction with its own dynamics. If it refuses to do so the alliance breaks up; if it gives way it eventually assumes a fairly calm and dull complexion. This general tendency explains the gradual moderation of the French Socialist party under the Third and Fourth Republics; other European Socialist parties seem to have followed the same line of development under the influence of the same causes. Naturally the dialectic of alliances is not the only factor in this transformation. Many others have played their part, particularly changes in the social sub-structure of the party. The question still remains, however, whether the party became more moderate because it had 'gone middle-class' or whether it 'went middle-class' because it had become more moderate: the relationship is functional rather than causal. In any case the influence of alliances, in the sense described, seems undeniable.

The loss of spirit by extreme parties owing to the influence of elections is even more marked if their strength puts them in the position of being the official leaders of a coalition. For they must then take office and themselves adopt the prudent and moderate attitude that the exercise of power imposes. Their mass and governmental position make them lead the alliance, their activity brings them into line with their moderate colleague. Such a dialectic may help to explain the development of Scandinavian Social Democracy between 1919 and 1939. Consequently, whatever the position of the allies, alliances holding a majority end by adopting the manner and programme of the most moderate party: gradually the extremism of the other is worn down, smoothed away, dulled by the requirements of government to such an extent that it tends to march in step with its colleague. The 'rightism' of governmental alliances is consequently opposed to the leftism of public opinion and often cancels it eventually: the voters move towards the left-wing parties, but the left-wing parties themselves move towards the Centre, the two apparent movements lead to a real immobility

If the domination of the moderate is not to occur the alliance must remain in parliamentary opposition; minority coalitions remain subject to the authority of the most extreme party. They are not in any way torn between electoral demagogy and governmental moderation, since they are not subjected to the penalties of office: demagogy in opposition is a natural sequel to demagogy in elections, the advantage in both cases resting with the most violent party. The same reversal occurs in revolutionary periods, as we have seen: the most extreme party tends to dominate the alliance, whether it leads the government, participates in it, supports it or opposes it. For the law of revolutionary government is the exact converse of that of normal government: the problem is not to maintain an ever uneasy and compromise balance by attempting to reconcile the various conflicting interests, but to hasten the coming of the new order which alone can create a new balance as a result of the collapse of the old system. Here realism lies not in moderation but in intransigence. The result is that an extremist party intent on preserving its purity must remain in opposition and only quit it to take part in revolution or to help in bringing it about. However, the internal structure of parties may check the moderating tendency to be found in every governmental coalition.

The relations between allies are somewhat different in the case of a triangular coalition. The Centre party then acts the role of natural arbiter between the two extremes. The position of the Socialists in France was very strong in the days of the three-party alliance, although it was the weakest of the allies: its influence declined after the elimination of the Communists and the coming of the Third Force. But this tendency seems less definite and less general than the other: within the Third Force the influence of the M.R.P. continually declined between 1947 and 1951, to the advantage of the Radicals and the Right wing, in accordance with the 'rightist' trend of alliances. The basic political direction is not determined by the party at the centre of the coalition but by that at the centre of parliament: that is the one most to the Right in coalitions of the Left, the one most to the Left in coalitions of the Right. Generally speaking it is inaccurate to speak of the 'rightism' of governmental coalitions; the term is only applicable to coalitions of the Left, which tend to be more common because of social and political developments. It would be more exact to speak of the 'rightism' of coalitions of the Left and of the 'leftism' of coalitions of the Right. This twofold tendency explains why it is possible to describe with equal success French politics under the Third Republic as an alternation between Right and Left, between Authority and Progress, or as a general domination of the Centre, or else as a general trend to the Left. At first sight the three explanations are contradictory; in fact they are each based upon partial but complementary interpretations. Leftism results from the fact that the old Left parties gradually move to the Centre and to the Right, being replaced by new parties. The Right-Left beat is clearly perceptible if one studies the rhythm of elections or of parliamentary combinations, although the two do not always coincide. However, evolution inside alliances irresistibly impels towards the Centre: right-wing majorities lean to the Right-Centre and attempt to overlap the Left; left-wing majorities slide towards the Left-Centre and end by finding their support in the Centre and the Right. The Cartel Chamber ended with Poincaré, just like the Horizon-Blue Chamber; the Left Chamber of 1932 ended with Laval as did the Right Chamber of 1928.

A new element is however introduced into the problem by the intervention of Communist and Fascist parties, with their very strong organization and their Bund characteristics. Their totalitarian nature is hostile to all compromise, to any real agreement, to any real alliance. 'Whosoever is not with me is against me.' There is good reason for the fact that these words from the Gospel have been often quoted at Communist Congresses. None the less electoral, parliamentary, and governmental coalitions can prove a very effective means of action for such parties; all the more so because their very complicated and very sound organization safeguards them from contamination and disintegration, to which their allies are consequently vulnerable. The banal image of the iron pot and the earthenware pot gives a good description of the privileged position of parties of this type in an alliance: they represent the hard, impervious, iron pot that can break others but cannot be broken itself. They therefore make use of alliances in two different ways which may moreover be complementary: for camouflage and for colonization. The former aims at dispelling the cloud of fear and isolation which surrounds them. They want to show everyone that they are parties just like the rest, no more revolutionary and destructive than the others, just as democratic and respectful of institutions and liberties. The Communist parties adopted this attitude in Europe in 1935–6 with the formation of the 'Popular Fronts'. The hand held out to the Catholics by M. Thorez did something to banish the picture of the fellow with a knife between his teeth; collaboration with politicians as reassuring as M. Chautemps strengthened the impression, and so did acceptance of the reasonable and moderate programme of the People's Rally. The great electoral success of 1936, when the party doubled the number of its voters, showed that such tactics were profitable. Participation in power immediately after the Liberation was no more than a continuation, in more precise fashion, of the same general policy. The aim was to show that Communists could be as good, or even better, administrators than other men: the worthy middle classes were astonished to see that M. Thorez and M. Billoux did not behave like revolutionary, swaggering People's Commissars but conducted themselves correctly, gravely, like middle-class ministers. The backing of General de Gaulle and of the right-thinking members of the M.R.P. strengthened the conviction that the party had calmed down. Remembering that it had thought Léon Blum Satan incarnate in 1936, but had hailed him as the Messiah in 1946, the bourgeoisie was not far from thinking that Maurice Thorez would develop after the same reassuring pattern. The increase in Communist votes from 1945 to 1946, and still more the enormous rise in membership of the party, show how profitable the policy was.

Simultaneously the party put into operation within its alliances the technique of colonization which proved so successful in the Balkans. As early as 1936 signs of it were seen inside the various Popular Fronts. In France the re-establishment of Trade Union unity was also accompanied by systematic infiltration of the C.G.T. by the leading members of the former C.G.T.U.; in all the local committees of the Popular Front Communists made efforts to secure control: in mass action of this kind, demagogic by nature, their extremism conferred on them the natural leadership, in accordance with the general dialectic of alliances. Throughout Europe the Underground campaign offered the party a magnificent field for colonization: being the only party capable, thanks to its organization, of completely adapting itself to it, it sought to take control, aided in this moreover by the admirable courage of its militant members. It succeeded in part: all Resistance organizations were infiltrated from top to bottom by the Communists. At the Liberation their policy consisted in forming National or Patriotic Fronts, a kind of Popular Front extended to include the Right, inspired and controlled by the Communist party. Since it was very weak and its fellow allies were stronger in numbers it first undertook to secure the disintegration of the Socialist party in the name of working-class unity; working on the militants at the base through its cells, working upon the leaders at the summit by making use of rivalries, envy, and ambition, the Communists tried to attain total fusion, complete obedience. The 'Working-class party'—or the United Working class parties—could thus more effectively attack their bourgeois allies in the National Front: in this respect the breaking-up of the Hungarian Smallholders' party constitutes a model of the kind. Thus, thanks to its better organization, a quite small Communist party can dominate a much larger Working-class bloc, the Working-class bloc itself dominating an alliance of parties that is much more extensive. Furthermore, by demanding key-posts in coalition ministries (Justice, so as to be able to get rid of its enemies in purges, Interior and police, Information and propaganda, Army), the Communist party thus succeeded in attaining a completely unequal alliance in which its relationships with its allies resembled those of the mother country to its colonies. In this way, without excessive friction, it was able to prepare for the total seizure of power in Central European countries and the complete elimination of its former allies. It is to be noted that the Russian army had at no point to intervene directly in this transformation, which was the result of a very remarkable political strategy.

In Western European countries Communist tactics were identical. But the resistance of the other members of the coalition, particularly of the Socialists, and the difference in social and political conditions, prevented it from achieving the same success. In Italy, however, the strongest Socialist fraction (Italian Socialist party) united very closely with the Communist party. The alliance developed according to the general pattern just described. The Italian Socialist party followed its partner's line, gradually adopting its themes for propaganda and even its internal organization. In reaction against efforts towards independence amongst the Socialists which seemed to be making an appearance in 1950 the Communist party is even said to have developed a very well-organized system of infiltration, encouraging a section of its own leading strata (the figure of 10,000 tried and selected militants is mentioned) to enter the ranks of its ally in order to exert pressure upon the organizers and at the same time to urge the militants not to leave the party for other independent Socialist movements.

Although vouched for by reliable people[1] this fact naturally remains unverifiable. It is interesting to note, moreover, that the Italian Socialist party managed to regain its independence in 1956, thus proving that after all it is possible to resist Communist pressure and infiltration within an alliance. This example might possibly help to free Socialist parties from their feeling of inferiority to Communist parties, a phenomenon particularly marked in France and Italy.

We have paid particular attention to the process of domination of an alliance by Communist parties because it is the most complete and successful example. But Fascist parties have followed similar paths with much less flexibility and success. Out of the first thirty-five Fascist deputies who entered Montecitorio in 1921, thirty-four were elected from the lists of the National Bloc sponsored by the veteran Giolitti, who thought he could easily dominate the small party. When Mussolini assumed power in 1922 only three Fascists were at his side in the ministry: the other members of the cabinet were moderates, Democrats or Popular Christians. His allies thought to tame him in office, but he carried out the Fascist revolution and suppressed these allies. Hitler attained power with the help of Hugenberg's Nationalists and Seldte's *Stalhelm*, and his first ministry included beside himself only two other Nazis, Goering and Frick. Those who had helped him to power thought that he would wear himself out in office or that he would become more moderate. But he carried out the Nazi revolution and suppressed his allies. The patterns discussed above, which define the respective relationships of allies according to their strength and their political line, were here checkmated by the internal organization of the party, which, we have once again to recognize, is of fundamental importance.

[1] Special report of the Rome correspondent of *Le Monde*, Jean d'Hospital. Cf. *Le Monde*, 20 October 1950.

CHAPTER III

PARTIES AND POLITICAL REGIMES

THE development of parties has brought about a profound transformation in the structure of political regimes. Just as contemporary dictatorships, based on the single party, bear only a remote resemblance to personal or military tyrannies, so modern democracies, based on a system of several organized and disciplined parties, are very different from the individualist regimes of the nineteenth century, which depended on the personal interplay of members of parliament who were very independent of each other. It has become a commonplace in France to contrast the Fourth Republic, with its rigid 'monolithic' parties, with the Third Republic, which was characterized by the flexibility of its groups and the weakness of their organization. Certainly 1945 was an important landmark, with the adoption of proportional representation, the creation of the M.R.P., and the development of the Communist party, but an evolution in the same direction began in 1875. On the whole there is a greater difference between the 1939 regime and that of 1880 than between that of 1945 and that of 1939.

The substitution of a party regime for a regime without parties obliges one therefore to make a complete review of the traditional analyses of political systems. The classic distinction between the presidential system and the parliamentary system, for instance, is tending to become out of date: the British regime is just as different from the French as from the American, in spite of the external likeness between their institutions. The concepts of the ministerial Cabinet, the question of confidence, political responsibility and dissolution no longer mean the same in a two-party system as in a multi-party system. According to the 1936 Constitution, which was modified in 1946, Russia today has a parliamentary system, with a collective Head of State (the Praesidium) separate from the Cabinet and responsible to parliament (the Supreme Soviet): obviously the existence of a single party modifies all the data of the problem. To describe the U.S.S.R. in the classic terms of parliamentary government would be to place too much reliance on externals, but scarcely more so than when we talk in all seriousness of the balance of power between the British Parliament and Government, of the system of 'checks and balances', defined as the power of the first to 'overthrow' the second, and of the second to dissolve the first. In reality no conflict is conceivable between the House and the Cabinet in a two-party regime, unless there is schism within the government party, in which case the conflict no longer has the same meaning nor the same scope. Knowledge of classic constitutional law combined with ignorance of the part played by parties gives a false view of contemporary political regimes; acquaintance with the part played by parties combined with ignorance of classic constitutional law gives an incomplete but accurate view of contemporary political régimes.

I. PARTIES AND THE CHOICE OF RULERS

The simplest and most realistic definition of democracy is the following: a regime in which those who govern are chosen by those who are governed, by means of free and open elections. On the functioning of this selection lawyers have based a theory of representation, reminiscent of eighteenth-century thought, and according to which the elector gives the representative a mandate to speak and act in his name; in this way parliament, the mandatary of the nation, is the expression of national sovereignty. In practice elections, like the doctrine of representation, have been greatly changed by the development of parties. There is no longer a dialogue between the elector and the representative, the nation and parliament: a third party has come between them, radically modifying the nature of their relations. Before being chosen by his electors the deputy is chosen by the party: the electors only ratify this choice. This is obvious in single-party regimes where only one candidate is offered for popular approval. In multi-party regimes it is less obvious but no less real: the elector may choose between several candidates, but each of them is nominated by a party. If we wish to maintain the juridical theory of representation we must admit that the representative receives a double mandate: from the party and from his electors. The importance of each varies according to the country and the parties; on the whole the party mandate seems to carry more weight than that of the electors.

The idea of election (choice of those who govern by those who are governed) thus suffers a profound change. In regimes which desire to remain very close to classic democracy the real ballot is preceded by a pre-ballot, through which the party chooses the candidates who will later face the electors: the American technique of the primaries is the most successful example of this tendency. But the pre-ballot is never pure and the influence of party leaders is quite clearly shown in it; most often it is a ballot limited to a privileged category of citizens. The system of the double vote, so discredited under the French Restoration, comes to life again here in some curious forms. When there is no pre-ballot, candidates are nominated by party leaders according to a technique which is rather like co-option. In a multi-party system this is less important than the election which follows it; in a single-party regime it is much more important. In both cases the choice of those who are to govern takes place by a mixture of election and co-option, but the proportions of the mixture are different.

Parties and the Nomination of Candidates. American terminology distinguishes clearly between the 'nomination', the action of the party in appointing a candidate, and the 'election', the choice by the citizens between the candidates proposed by the different parties. In the U.S.A. the first operation is regulated in great detail: with the system of primaries and especially of 'open primaries', it has all the appearance of a real preliminary election, which explains the distinction. In other countries the nomination is more summarily organized; above all it has not the official and public character it is given on the other side of the Atlantic: it is a private act which takes place within the party. Often it is even secret, as parties do not like the odours of the electoral kitchen to spread to the outside world.

The degrees of intervention of parties in the nomination of candidates vary a great deal. The first question is that of monopoly or competition: must a candidate necessarily be put up by a party, or is he free to stand without the support of one? The problem arises both in the legal and the practical fields. In some countries the parties legally enjoy a monopoly: they alone can propose candidates; nobody can face the electoral body without them. Next to absolute monopolies, which are quite rare, we find relative monopolies: in the United States, and in many other countries, the electoral laws oblige candidates who offer themselves without party support to collect a certain number of signatures (2,000 in New York, for example). But the scope of a legal monopoly, absolute or relative, varies a great deal according to the regulations for the formation of a party established by the laws on associations: if, for example, all that is necessary is to make a declaration at the prefecture according to the very simple formalities of the French law of 1st July 1901, legal monopoly is quite an illusion. Generally countries establishing it make provision for a special procedure for setting up parties, and an administrative or jurisdictional inspection to recognize as 'parties' associations desiring to put up candidates. But the legal monopoly of parties is generally less important than the actual monopoly: no purpose is served by leaving complete liberty to non-party candidates if normally only party candidates have any chance of success. In France anyone may stand for the Presidency of the Republic: apart from freak candidates nobody ever takes advantage of this freedom except the few political personalities sponsored by parties or party alliances. In Britain anybody is at liberty to stand for the House of Commons, provided he pays a deposit: in practice nobody stands any chance of being elected without the support of a party. Often the practical monopoly is not so absolute in character; party candidates have simply more chance than the others, who are not, however, completely deprived of it. Here there might be found a varied range of situations, akin to those of isolated firms which try to resist combines and trusts.

But to distinguish merely between party candidates and non-party candidates is an over-simplification: in reality there are many intermediary positions. Sometimes the party intervenes to create a candidate *ex-nihilo*: his nomination alone makes him a suitable candidate to be offered to the electors and gives him the ability to achieve victory. This is the extreme case, and rare: it is met with in Communist parties and in some countries where there is a two-party system or proportional representation. Generally relations between parties and candidates are more subtle. Officially candidates are appointed by parties; in practice this appointment is something intermediate between pure nomination and mere ratification; it is a complicated negotiation in which the relative positions of the negotiators vary a great deal, as it is not always the parties that have the upper hand. Sometimes it is less a case of the party choosing the candidate than of the candidate choosing the party. Under the Third Republic it used to be said of such and such a candidate that he had 'received the investiture' of such and such a party. The terminology is interesting: it suggests that the initiative comes from the candidate rather than from the party, that the candidate has solicited the party, which has then granted its support. It coincides with a profoundly individualist ballot in which the personality of the candidates was of more importance than their political affiliations. An influential man desiring to gain the votes of his fellow citizens sought the investiture of the party to increase his chances: he even tried to combine several investitures. We cannot therefore speak of unilateral appointment, implying a relationship of subordination, but of a bilateral agreement leading to equality: this difference has a great influence on the dependence of the deputy on his party and the intervention of the party in the choice of the deputy.

The degree of party influence in the appointment of candidates depends on very many factors. The direct influence of legal factors and the part played by laws which can grant parties a monopoly or confer various advantages on them has already been pointed out. In the U.S.A. the development of the system of primaries is largely due to the intervention of the legislator who created them and made detailed rules for them. Besides these texts devoted to the appointment of candidates by the party electoral laws have a considerable influence in this domain: the ballot system is, together with party structure, the dominating element which determines the mechanism of candidatures. Naturally historical traditions and the general state of mind also play an important part. In Great Britain it is the custom for a candidate not to stand for election on his own but to be supported by a committee: party intervention is thus strengthened. In countries in which respect for the traditional social elites has been preserved the prestige of a name can make a candidate successful without party support: in the west of France the 'Republic of Dukes' long outlived its disappearance in parliament. Similarly the influence of parties on candidates is often less strong in country districts than in towns, in which individual personalities are less known to the electors. But these are secondary factors compared with the electoral regime and the internal party structure.

The influence of the electoral regime is very difficult to define. Each element in the electoral system which plays a part here must be examined separately: the size of the constituencies, whether voting is for a list or a single member, a simple-majority or a proportional system and whether or not there is a second ballot. The influences of these diverse factors sometimes work in opposite directions, so that their total action is weakened. The size of the electoral division is obviously very important. A mathematical type of formula might be suggested here: the influence of parties on candidatures varies in direct relation to the size of the constituencies. The larger the constituency, the greater is party influence; the smaller the constituency, the more restricted is party intervention. Obviously these axioms are not to be applied literally; they define roughly a general tendency of which, nevertheless, there can be no doubt. The smaller the constituency, the more possible is it for the electors to have individual knowledge of the candidate and the more does the campaign become a clash of personalities, between whom the elector chooses because of their personal qualities and not because of their political allegiance. When the electoral division becomes larger personal contact between candidates and electors decreases; the electors no longer know the candidates personally. The political label becomes the essential element in the voting, whereas it remains secondary in small constituencies. An analysis of the arrondissement ballot in France, as practised under the Third Republic, compared with the departmental ballot preferred by the Fourth, gives a perfect illustration of this general tendency. The loyalty of electors to certain candidates, in spite of their political evolution and changes of party, shows the predominance of the personal point of view: the case of Pierre Laval is typical. The 'parachuting' of candidates, so developed in the first proportional elections when some deputies had never set foot in their constituency before being elected, was radically impossible in the arrondissement system, except for personalities well known throughout the nation.

The possibility of direct contact between electors and candidates is not the only factor involved: the financial point of view cannot be neglected either. In a small constituency election expenses are not as high as in a large: it is not easy for candidates to stand without party support, but it remains possible. In a large constituency this is no longer possible: the expenses of the campaign can be borne only by parties or by collective organizations which tend to resemble parties. Moreover the size of constituencies must not be understood as referring only to the geographical size, the number of electors is equally important. In France the department is a large constituency when there is universal suffrage; it becomes a small constituency when suffrage is restricted, it being much easier for candidates and electors to know each other when there are few electors. Hence in democracies with a property-based suffrage the size of the constituencies increased the natural tendency for parties to play only an insignificant role. Similarly in the elections to the French Senate and the Council of the Republic personalities have more influence and parties less than in those to the Chamber of Deputies and the National Assembly.

The respective influences of list-ballot and single-member constituency usually work in the same direction, the first operating in large constituencies, the second in small ones. But the coincidence is not absolute: in the Third Republic municipal elections took place with lists and general elections were for single candidates. The size of the constituencies seems to be of greater importance than the nature of the ballot: the role of parties was smaller in municipal elections than in general elections. In municipal elections, moreover, it varied according to the communes: a classification of French communes according to size would no doubt show that the proportion of non-party candidates increases in inverse proportion to the size. It remains a fact that list-voting, through its collective character, naturally diminishes the influence of personalities, necessitates an agreement between several individuals, and gives their common ideas and tendencies predominance over the individual qualities of each, all points which naturally tend to increase the influence of parties. If cross-voting is allowed, the personal factor increases proportionately: it becomes possible to vote for a particular candidate in spite of the collective character of the ballot. The possibility of presenting incomplete lists even allows an individual to stand for election on his own. But cross-voting presupposes a certain initiative on the part of the elector, who must make modifications to the printed lists offered for his choice: experience proves that the force of inertia is a great obstacle to these modifications. Individual candidatures always have less chance of success than complete lists in a collective ballot. Nevertheless cross-voting is quite common, especially in small constituencies.

Proportional representation increases the influence of parties over candidates. We must distinguish between the result of proportional representation and the consequences of list-voting, which generally coincides with it (except in the transferable Irish vote). The result varies according to the type of proportional representation. When there is a national distribution of remainders party influence reaches its maximum: the candidates elected on the national supplementary lists, by means of the addition of the remaining votes throughout the country, are chosen directly by the party. Systems of agreed lists have results of the same nature, especially if the agreement is decided at the national level. Even when there is a local distribution of remainders and an absence of agreements the party's role remains important; the existence of cross-voting and of the preferential vote diminishes it slightly. But the general influence of parties on the constitution of the lists is so strong that the result both of cross-voting and of the preferential vote is much more to give the elector a greater freedom of choice between the candidates proposed by the parties than to make free candidatures possible. Experience proves that proportional representation results in an actual quasi-monopoly to the advantage of parties. The simple-majority system can have similar results if it has a single ballot and if it coincides with a two-party system following the general rule. Any dissident candidature seriously disturbs the system because of the dispersal of votes it provokes, and so electors generally turn from it and give their votes in a block to the two parties: the phenomenon of 'polarization' works against individual candidatures and tends to a party monopoly. In Great Britain non-party candidatures are even less frequent than in proportionalist regimes. To sum up, only the double-ballot simple-majority system makes a relative freedom of candidature possible if it coincides with small constituencies. Even then party candidates enjoy considerable advantages over the others.

Nevertheless the internal structure of parties may modify this state of affairs quite fundamentally. Cadre parties, which have no strong financial backing and live in perpetual money difficulties, are always soft-hearted towards candidates willing to cover the costs of the campaign, and in practice investiture is obtained without any great difficulty. Mass parties, which are generally parties of the Left, have less taste for this capitalist form of individual candidature. Moreover their constitutions often contain clauses intended to prevent an independent personality from receiving party support at the last moment: only those who have been party members for a certain amount of time can stand for election with party support. The system leads to a certain ageing of the upper strata, but maintains party influence. The degree of party centralization also exercises an influence over the freedom of candidates. In decentralized parties candidates are chosen at the local level by committees which are quite easily influenced by local personalities; in centralized parties, where it is the national ruling body which approves of the candidatures, party investiture is less easily obtained.

It is less a question, in these cases, of contrasting personal candidature and party candidature than of determining the degree of individual initiative left to the candidates. The contrasting of individual and party candidatures is oversimple; apart from a few eccentrics who have no chance of success nobody ever stands for election without support. Behind a candidate there is always an organization, at least in embryo, to support him in his campaign: an electoral committee, a newspaper, financial support, propagandists, and backers. The problem of non-party candidates consists in deciding how these various elements can come together outside any party. The absence of party monopoly does not mean that freedom to stand for election is within the reach of everybody, but simply that organizations other than parties can intervene in the electoral struggle, if we consider as 'organizations' the great private fortunes (whose direct role is becoming less important in this field). It is not certain that these organizations are any less closed than parties in the choice of their candidates; it is not certain that the limitation of the role of parties and the suppression of their monopoly increase the freedom of electors or the possibility of independent candidates standing for election.

Finally the problem of the techniques used by the parties in the choice of candidates is more important than the measure of their influence in this respect: it is a problem that arises, moreover, for all organizations which may appoint candidates. The procedure followed is generally very like that serving for the appointment of party leaders; as these are often the same as the members of parliament it is not easy to distinguish between the two investitures. In theory there are two main opposing systems: election by the body of members and nomination by ruling committees. In practice the difference between them is not as great as it seems because the meetings of members, at which the candidates are nominated, are subjected to the same manœuvring and pressure as the congresses where the leaders are elected. In cadre parties appointment is made by committees behind locked doors: they give themselves up to the delights of 'electoral cooking'. In America this system corresponded to the phase of the caucus, which was fundamentally a meeting of party leaders to appoint candidates for the elections. The only important problem then is the rivalry between local committees and central committees: in France the local committees win; American caucuses too were very local in character. In mass parties appointment by members is generally the rule, but it can be direct or indirect. Direct appointment is relatively rare: as an example, we may cite the appointment *polls* which function in Belgian parties. The system is very democratic in appearance, but in practice it is liable to considerable adulteration, as is shown by the criticism provoked in the Belgian Christian Social party by the appointment of candidates for the 1949 elections. Candidates could be proposed only by the National Committee, the arrondissement committees, any group of three local branches, or on a petition signed by 150 party members. Some candidates got themselves proposed by three minute branches, totalling in all a few dozen members. The final nomination and classing of candidates was done by a general poll of members on the rolls during the current year: in certain arrondissements 'candidates were known to have organized a member hunt and to have enrolled hundreds of members a few days before the closing date for participation in the poll. Some even tried to buy books of blank members' cards.'[1] To avoid these abuses it was suggested that a supplementary vote in the polls should go to members who had been on the rolls for more than a year.

The system of nomination polls can become one of the essential bases of the party community: membership of the party enables one to participate in the appointment of candidates for the elections. In fact the only real element of membership to be found in American parties consists in participation in the closed primaries, which can be compared with polls of the Belgian type. But this technique is relatively rare; when the nomination of candidates remains in the hands of members it is generally in an indirect fashion. Candidates are appointed by a congress or a conference composed of delegates elected by members in the branches: this is more or less the procedure followed in Swiss parties, for example, in which candidatures are decided by a delegate conference. The system was introduced into the U.S.A. in the first half of the nineteenth century, and it progressively replaced the technique of the caucus; the nomination was henceforth made by a 'Convention', composed of delegates appointed by district meetings. As there was no regular system of party membership the leaders themselves drew up the list of people summoned to these meetings at the base; voting took place amidst much manœuvring and pressure, so that

[1] Administrative report of M. Deghilage, General Secretary to the Congress, on 26 November 1949. *Bulletin d'information du Parti Chrétien Social*, December 1949, p. 660.

the Convention was much more representative of party leaders than of the mass of its electors and supporters; with all the appearance of democracy this was really not very different from the caucus. Moreover certain Conventions are officially meetings of delegates of executive committees and not of members' delegates: for example the National Convention, which deals with the nomination of the candidate for the Presidency. As a matter of fact many conferences and congresses in European parties are not very different in character: the committees of the branches play a preponderant role in the appointment of delegates. Nevertheless the system of formal membership, when it exists, does restrict to a certain degree the manipulations and interventions of the leaders.

Since the beginning of this century a new system of nomination has replaced the convention technique in the U.S.A., that of the primaries which is quite an original system, not really comparable with any other. It might be likened to the Belgian appointment poils, but these are based on a system of membership which does not exist in America. Instead of a selection of candidates by party members there is really a selection by its electors or supporters. It is moreover very difficult to describe primaries, for each state has its own regulations about them. In fact there is no one system of primaries, but there exist systems of primaries which are very varied and profoundly different one from the other. In principle a primary is a pre-ballot which serves to nominate party candidates for the real elections. Usually a whole group of candidates is appointed for various posts, not only political but administrative and judicial, since in the U.S.A. posts in local administration and justice are largely filled by election. The primary is generally organized by the public authorities, like the election itself; it generally takes place in the same polling booths, but for each party separately. Each elector chooses from among the candidates of his own party the one who is to defend the party colours at the elections.

According to the state we may distinguish between closed primaries and open primaries, both types being susceptible to numerous variations. In closed primaries only Republican electors can participate in the nomination of Republican candidates, only Democrats can participate in the nomination of Democratic candidates. But how is one to determine whether a particular elector is Republican or Democrat? The most customary method is that of enrolment. This may take place at the time of registration; the elector declares the party to which he wishes to belong for the primary; he cannot change until the next registration. On the other hand the enrolment may take place at the entrance to the polling booth, where the elector receives the 'ballot' of the chosen party; if he wishes to change his affiliation for the next primary he must obtain a certificate from the clerk some time before, the interval varying from six months to ten days according to the state. Some other states impose a test of loyalty to the party, commonly called a challenge. At the entrance to the polling booth the elector asks for a party 'ballot'. Before it is handed to him he is asked to declare that he supported the party candidates at the last elections and that he will support them at the next elections. In certain Southern states a personal undertaking to support the party candidate appointed by the primary is demanded. This is to ensure the defeat of independents. Thus the closed primaries take it for granted that voters admit their preference for a party. The candidates are nominated by supporters rather than by electors pure and simple. Enrolment, and even the challenge, come close to the European mechanism of membership; nevertheless there is not the regular subscription, nor the participation of members in the life of the party, in the establishment of its hierarchy, and in the appointment of its leaders. Enrolment and challenge only concern the primaries and have only a purely electoral significance.

They apply only to closed primaries. In open primaries the secret of each elector's political preferences is preserved; no party affiliation is shown. At the entrance to the polling booth the electors receive two 'ballots', one for each party; each ballot carries the list of the party's candidates; the elector marks with a cross those he prefers; but he has only the right to use one ballot. Alternatively each elector receives only one ballot, with two separate columns for each party; he has only the right to use one column, or else his vote does not count. In the State of Washington, nevertheless, the electors may vote for the 'colts' of either party according to the posts to be filled; on the ballot candidates are grouped by functions and not by parties. Finally, Minnesota and Nebraska have adopted for the State Legislature the system of 'non-party' primaries, which is used more generally for the election of judges: here no party affiliation appears beside the names of the candidates, the two receiving the most votes are the only ones to take part in the real election. Really this is no longer a primary but the first ballot of an election with limited cross-voting, after the pattern of the system which existed in Imperial Germany and in Belgium under the simple-majority system.

Thus some very varied techniques are included under the general name of primaries. Closed primaries correspond more or less to the nomination of the candidates of a party by its supporters; open primaries of the usual type to nomination by its electors. Both form the terms of a progression, of which the open primaries of the Washington type are the last stage in the direction of non-party primaries. They are no longer appointments of candidates but real elections. The whole system was established by degrees at the beginning of the twentieth century in order to break the influence of party leaders over the choice of candidates. To a fairly large extent it has succeeded; no doubt the present decline of the 'machines' must be partly attributed to it. Nevertheless the intervention of the leaders was modified rather than suppressed. Who can get his name on the party 'ballot' officially printed by the administration and handed to the elector in the primary? In general the member of a party who collects a certain number of signatures, which varies according to the size of the constituency. It is possible to oppose a dominant faction within a party by putting up a rival against its candidate; but this presupposes the existence of some embryonic organization, that is the creation of another faction. The primary system tends less to encourage the freedom of candidatures relative to the leaders than to develop internal factions and rivalries between groups of leaders. At the primaries the electors may judge between such rivalries, but the small number of electors taking part in the primaries takes away much of the significance from this choice (Fig. 42); moreover it seems scarcely more real than that available to European electors under the two-ballot system, for the candidates at the primary are in practice themselves selected by groups of leaders, as in Europe. The intervention of the leaders is only one stage further removed: it is no longer exerted for the nomination of candidates, but for the selection of 'candidates for nomination'. The vital question in American parties today is that of the *pre-primary*: the meetings of party committees for selecting candidates for the primary.

Parties and the Election Proper. Parties play the essential part in the first phase of the electoral operation, the appointment of candidates; but they are not absent from the second, choice *between* candidates, that is the election proper. In the first place they exer

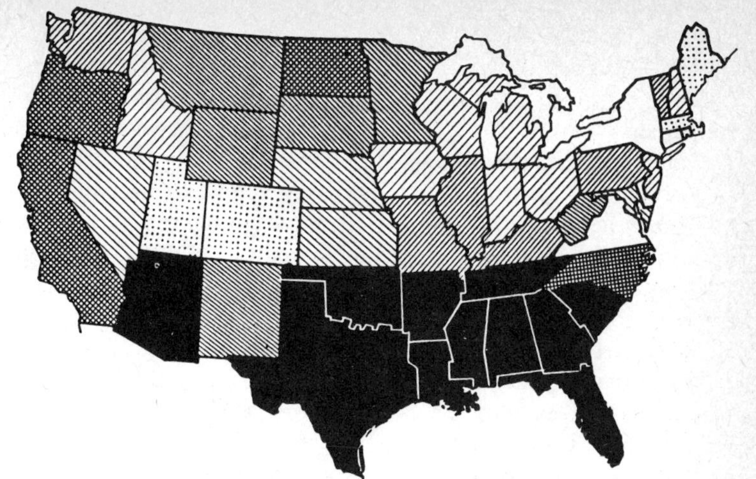

Fig. 42. Electoral participation in American 'Primaries'.

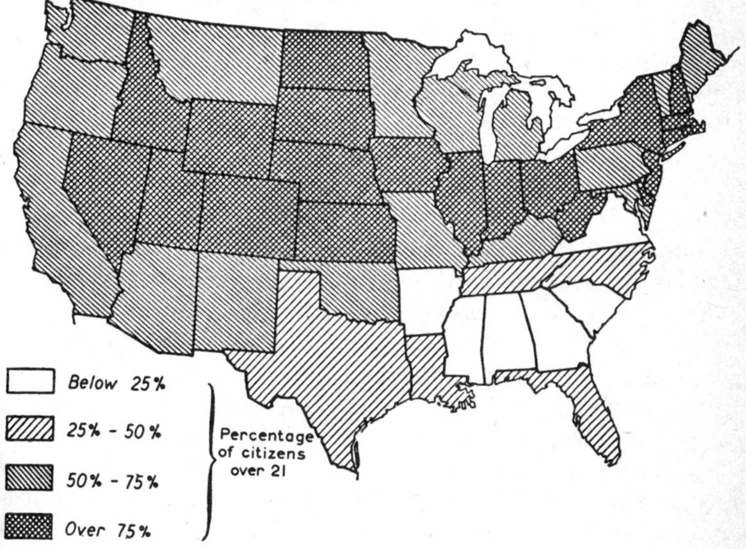

Fig. 43. Electoral participation in American Presidential Election, 1940.

on it a direct and vital influence by supporting the candidate in his electoral campaign. They provide the major part of the expenses for the campaign, except in cadre and caucus parties in which private financing remains predominant. Some countries have taken rigorous steps to control and to limit campaign expenses in order to prevent the power of money from weighing too heavily on propaganda and creating excessive inequality. But the development of mass parties has diminished the value of these precautions: the greatest sums for propaganda are today no longer expended by the Conservative parties who are backed by the 'financial powers', but by the mass parties which are backed by a crowd of members whose subscriptions provide a very large working capital. The German Social Democratic party was the first to demonstrate the superiority of semi-public finance based on a party tax over private finance based on donations from large firms. The British Labour party and the other Trade Union parties have achieved similar results; in France probably the greatest expenditure today is incurred by the Communist party. The intervention of parties in the campaign makes it possible moreover to by-pass the legal restrictions on propaganda and electoral expenses. In France, for example, no candidate has the right to fix posters elsewhere than on the reserved and limited official sites: but the parties post their own bills everywhere and these indirectly support their candidates. A modern electoral campaign might be likened to a concerto for solo instrument and orchestra: the candidate corresponds to the solo instrument, the sound of which tends to be more and more lost in the general din of the orchestra.

A distinction must be made furthermore between true electoral propaganda, carried out by the candidate in his attempt to secure election, and party propaganda at election time, which aims at spreading party doctrine, extending its influence and increasing its membership. In this respect a curious development has taken place which shows the transformation that has occurred in the nature and the role of parties. The first parties were purely electoral organizations, of which the prime function consisted in ensuring the success of their candidates: the election was the end and the party the means. Then the development of the functions peculiar to the party as an organization capable of directly influencing political life led to the election being used in the service of party propaganda. An electoral campaign offers exceptional opportunities of influencing opinion: in some countries candidates have a right to free use of meeting-rooms, to have their programme printed and distributed by official agencies, to use the national radio network, poster sites, and so on. Furthermore the public is in a particularly receptive mood as far as politics are concerned; at no time is the soil better prepared for increasing the virulence of party microbes. In pursuing electoral propaganda for its candidate the party has therefore gradually developed its own party propaganda. In the ultimate resort the initial situation is reversed: instead of using parties to ensure success at elections, elections are used to ensure the growth of parties; the party has become the end, the election the means.

This development finds expression in an increase in the number of candidatures and a change in their character. In the nineteenth century a party did not put up candidates in constituencies where it had no chance of success; today the practice is current: the Communist party has always systematically put up candidates everywhere. The electoral campaign thus takes on the character of a demonstration: the aim is not to be elected but to make the party known. This transformation has repercussions on electoral tactics. From 1924 to 1932 inclusive the tactics applied by the French Communist party (isolation and maintenance of candidates at the second ballot) was absurd from the point of view of electoral dividends: it decreased the chances of Communist candidates and turned voters away from them. But the tactics enabled the party to expound its propagandist themes in complete security, it preserved it from any compromise and surrender of principle, it strengthened its internal solidarity and deepened its influence; it paid in the long run. Generally speaking, in parties of the Communist or Fascist type, propaganda on behalf of the party always tends to take precedence over propaganda for the election; even if the latter occasionally takes first place and the party does seek primarily to increase its representation in parliament such an attitude is temporary. It represents a tactical move considered to be more effective than the other in a given set of circumstances; but reinforcement of its positions in parliament and success in elections are themselves judged to be only means for increasing the power of the party, which remains the essential element. Thus a dictinction could be made between electoral parties and parties of permanent agitation: the former alone are democratic and parliamentarian in policy, the latter make use of existing institutions in order to destroy them.

The indirect influence of parties upon elections by means of propaganda is always present. On the contrary direct intervention in the choice by voters exists only in some political systems. It is obvious in single-party systems where election is non-existent, the voters being restricted to approval of the party candidate. In this case the nomination of candidates becomes the real election: in so far as it is open, as it gives opportunity for rivalry and debate, there is a certain element of democracy present. In the Southern states of America the primaries thus assume fundamental importance: for this reason more voters take part than in the election proper (cf. Fig. 42 and Fig. 43); struggles between factions and rival candidates sometimes make the apparent unity of the Democratic party quite artificial. For Soviet Russia a similar study should be undertaken of the operation of the real living part of the electoral system: the preparatory meetings for elections held by Trade Unions, Youth Movements, Party units and all organizations that have the right to put up candidates; unfortunately precise and reliable information on this question is not available. In a two-party regime with one party dominant the results achieved are almost analogous: if the disparity between the two parties is such that one of them is practically certain of success, then its choosing of a candidate becomes the essential part of the election.

The direct influence of the party is seen in a second set of circumstances: in a proportional system with fixed lists and candidates ranked in a particular order which determines election. Take a constituency in which the Socialist party has had three seats in previous elections. Variations in its vote having been relatively slight from one election to another, the party may consider that the next election will give it a minimum of two seats and a maximum of four. The candidate entered at the head of the list is therefore sure of success, the second a little less so, the third much less, the fourth has only slight hopes, others have practically none; they are there for the honour, to make up the number; they are reduced to the role of electoral walkers-on. The respective chances of the candidates are therefore determined by the party; in the case of the No. 1 candidate they are as precise as in a single-party system. There is direct intervention in the election, which ceases to be a choice by the voters between the candidates: the voters merely fix on a quota within which the party exercises its power to nominate deputies. It is as if the electorate conferred on a particular party the right to choose 20% of the parliamentary representatives, to another the right to choose 15%, to a third 40%, and so on, the quota varying from one ballot to the next. In integral P.R. operating at the national level with a uniform quotient and overall distribution of remainders this description exactly corresponds to the facts. In less complete systems of P.R., which are more widespread, the pattern is slightly modified. But the right to nominate deputies remains entire so long as the system of fixed lists remains in operation, only the method of deciding the quota of deputies per party is changed.

If the preferential vote and cross-voting are allowed, the choice of deputies is restored, in part, to the voters: a kind of co-operation is established between them and the parties. In the system of complete preferential voting with no ranking order proposed by the parties, the latter lose all direct say in the election. In the pseudo-preferential vote system (French laws of 1946 and 1951) in which changes in list-order are allowed only if they command more than half the votes cast for the party, the latter retains its prerogatives intact: experience shows that variations never reach this proportion. As they do not occur in the same direction, they are moreover unable to change the order fixed by the party. In a proportional system with fixed lists the ranking of candidates is an act that therefore becomes as important as the selection of candidates. Normally the two should be carried out simultaneously; in practice, many parties allow their members to take part directly or indirectly in the selection, but in fact reserve ranking for their ruling committees, which thus retain a vital influence. The technique of lists with a ranking order imposed upon the voters also makes very astute moves possible: a candidate liked by the militants and not in favour with the leaders can be entered but ranked low, which appeases the militants and satisfies the leaders; in the same way if an outgoing deputy is demoted in the list his popularity with the voters will remain an advantage for the party, but he will be displaced by a more adaptable candidate. The threat of demotion is an admirable weapon in the hands of the party leaders for bringing deputies to heel.

These devices illustrate the general effect of the intervention of parties in the choice of deputies: a profound transformation of the machinery of election, an evolution towards a mixed system of election and co-option. The single party represents the extreme term of the development: election is nothing more than a sham, which scarcely veils the reality of almost unadulterated co-option. As compared with inheritance and election which have been frequently studied, co-option as a method of selecting rulers has been little investigated. Today however it is assuming an importance such as it has never had since the days of the Roman Empire. Traditionally all dictators have recourse to co-option to ensure the continuance of their power; practically very few succeeded in this until the twentieth century. Often co-option was rapidly transformed into inheritance. Today the single party is reviving the technique and regularizing it as never before; henceforth the co-option of the dictator is carried out within the party in the central nucleus which ensures his supreme power. In Germany Hitler personally appointed his successors in order of succession from amongst the small group of his companions; in Italy the nomination of Mussolini's heir was to be carried out inside the Grand Fascist Council; in Soviet Russia the appointment of a successor to the supreme leader is carried out in practice inside the Praesidium of the Communist party. The German system is more in conformity with the classic type of personal dictatorship; the Italian and Russian systems introduce a new type of collective co-option. In Soviet Russia it functioned in securing the replacement of Lenin by Stalin and in determining the succession to the latter; even the elimination of Trotsky produced no very serious crisis within the regime. It seems that the party has thus transformed the very notion of dictatorship: a regime, essentially ephemeral because it was linked with the life of an individual, is on the way to becoming a lasting regime because it is based upon a perpetually self-renewing institution, the party.

At the supreme leader or Central Committee level, the single party ensures pure co-option. At parliamentary representative level, co-option is tinged with an electoral hue. Although chosen by the party, deputies are submitted to popular vote, for which a grand parade of propaganda and ceremony is undertaken. The system is a revival of the plebiscite technique; instead of a persona plebiscite in favour of a man, it sets up a collective plebiscite in favour of an institution. The deputies are chosen by the party, bu ratification by the people with as many votes as possible remain very important. This resort to the rite of election gives the regim an appearance of democratic legitimacy. The personal plebiscit was used by Napoleon to reconcile the restoration of monarch with the official principles of the French Revolution; the collectiv plebiscite has the same significance. New religions transpose ol ceremonies and retain their places of pilgrimage. The rite has als a very real practical significance; it shows that all opposition efforts are vain, that a system which so efficiently commands unanimous obedience is omnipotent. The 99·9% majorities prove the efficiency of the system; they are obviously artificial, but so is the perfection of the machinery capable of producing this result. From another point of view the system makes possible, perhaps, some eventual introduction of democracy: the artificial vote does after all accustom to voting procedure peoples who have never known it: the external rites teach the outward behaviour of democracy. If the Turkish people had not practised these electoral gymnastics for twenty years in the abstract, as one learns the movements of swimming on dry land, lying flat on a stool, they would perhaps have experienced more difficulties in 1950 on plunging into democracy.

In a pluralist regime co-option is less entire and election regains some virtue. However, it is no longer a pure election but a kind of semi-co-option in which the part played by the voters is greater or less according to the party system. Co-option, of course, has never been entirely absent from election procedure: before there were parties serious candidates were generally sponsored by the outgoing members who had decided not to offer themselves for re-election. Here too the effect of party action has been to replace individual co-option by collective co-option. But it also extended the scope of 'patronage'. In practice, in a system with more than one party the voters' function is to choose between the candidates co-opted by the parties: co-option forms the first act in the electoral process, the election is only the second. The American system of primaries does not suppress this first term: it simply introduces an intermediate operation between the two terms. Proportional representation with fixed lists and fixed ranking order does not appreciably increase co-option; it merely transforms the process and makes it more obvious. In this case it is apparent that the voter does not choose the individual deputy and that he merely confers on the party a quota for co-option; but his choice is really no greater in the single-member voting system. He retains the appearance of choice because he votes for X or Y personally, but X and Y have been co-opted by the party, in just the same way as the candidates listed and ranked in order. Whether X or Y stand for election alone, or whether they are put at the head of a list accompanied by other candidates to make up the number makes no real difference. Fundamentally real personal choice exists only in a simple-majority system of voting for lists with cross-voting: even then it is limited to those named on the list, and they are always co-opted by the party.

II. PARTIES AND THE REPRESENTATION OF OPINION

The term representation is not here used in the legal sense. In this matter all that is worth saying has been said: the classic antitheses between imperative mandate and representative mandate, individual and collective mandates, revocable and irrevocable mandates are present in every manual if not in every mind. The intervention of the party which makes a third in this contractual relationship completely changes its nature however: the classic theory of representation no longer corresponds with the facts, supposing that it ever did and that it was ever anything more than an ingenious artifice for transforming national sovereignty into officially proclaimed parliamentary sovereignty. Here the word 'representation' is applied to a sociological phenomenon and not to a legal relationship: it signifies the resemblance between the political opinions of the nation and those of parliament. Deputies represent their electors not as a mandatary represents his mandator but as a photograph represents a landscape, a portrait its model. The fundamental problem consists in measuring the degree of accuracy of representation, that is the degree of correspondence between public opinion and its expression in parliament.

In this field the influence of parties is considerable. Every party system constitutes a frame imposed upon opinion, forming it as well as deforming it. The party system existing in a country is generally considered to be the result of the structure of its public opinion. But the converse is equally true: the structure of public opinion is to a large extent a consequence of the party system, as that is shaped by the circumstances of history, the evolution of politics, and a whole combination of complicated factors amongst which the electoral system plays a dominant part. The relations between opinion and parties are not unidirectional: they are a tissue of reciprocal actions and reactions, closely intermingled.

The Two Distortions of Opinion. Usually to measure the degree of representativeness a comparison is made between the percentage of votes obtained by parties in the country and its percentage of seats in parliament, that is between its electoral strength and its parliamentary strength. This is an incomplete assessment. The disparity between electoral and parliamentary strengths is no more than the second stage of distortion of public opinion. It is superimposed upon another distortion, less often remarked but perhaps more serious: the disparity between the distribution of votes and the true nature of opinion. For the distribution of votes is not public opinion itself but only one way, amongst many others, of expressing it, and one which always distorts it to some extent.

The second-stage distortion, defined as the disparity between the percentage of votes and the percentage of seats, can easily be measured. Here the electoral system plays the essential role. By very definition proportional representation leads to the least distortion: it is in fact based upon the idea of a perfect coincidence between the electoral strength and the parliamentary strength of parties. However, the practical modifications introduced in the operation of P.R. often diminish this coincidence. For it to be perfect, the country would have to form a single constituency or else distribution of remainders would have to be carried out nationally. Different political reasons generally lead to the rejection of both these methods and to a preference for less perfect techniques. A disparity then appears between the proportion of votes and the proportion of seats, varying according to the system adopted for the distribution of remainders, the electoral setting, the possibility of cross-voting, or agreed lists, and so on. In some countries the disparity is quite slight, in others quite large. The direction taken by the distortion depends on the type of P.R. in use. The highest average method favours the major parties, which tend to be over-represented, at the expense of the minor parties, which are fated to be under-represented: at the 1946 French elections the Radicals and their allies lost 27·2% of the votes which had been cast for them whereas the two stronger parties, Communists and M.R.P., lost respectively only 1·9% and 3·2%. On the other hand the system of highest remainders leads to over-representation of the minor parties. Agreed lists may introduce discrepancies into this general pattern. P.R. is not therefore as faithful a photograph of opinion as its supporters claim.

None the less it produces disparities infinitely less considerable than the simple-majority single-ballot system which in this respect achieves the maximum inaccuracy. Here we may note a constant tendency so long as there are only two parties: the majority party is over-represented and the minority party under-represented. The fact has no very serious consequences: it simply leads to an exaggeration of the variations in opinion of the electorate, as we have seen. But if the simple-majority system coincides with multi-partism the result may be a much more capricious representation, although it scarcely differs from the same general line: a party which has more votes than its nearest rival is in general over-represented by comparison with it (that is, either more 'over-represented' or less 'under-represented' than it). However, if the disparity in votes is very slight the representation may be completely distorted, the party having the smaller number of votes winning the larger number of seats, and vice versa. This situation occurred for example in Great Britain in January 1910, when the Liberals gained 275 seats with 43·1% of the poll and the Conservatives 273 with 47%. It recurred in 1929, when Labour won 289 seats with 37·5% of the votes and the Conservatives 262 with 37·97%; since 1948 the new arrangement of constituencies which gives Labour many seats with large majorities and the Conservatives many seats with small majorities makes the recurrence of this anomaly even more probable: if the two parties obtained an equal number of votes, the Conservatives would have approximately thirty seats more than Labour. In fact, at the 1951 elections the Conservatives obtained 321 seats with 47·96% of the poll against Labour's 295 with 48·78%. The same thing occurred in the Union of South Africa at the 1948 and 1953 elections, when the Nationalist party of Dr. Malan obtained the majority of seats in parliament although it had polled fewer votes than its opponent, the United party. A disparity may therefore occur even in a two-party system on account of the unequal size of constituencies. The opponents of the simple-majority single-ballot system do not fail to make great play with these examples to prove the absurdity of the system, but they forget generally to emphasize that they are very exceptional. In a multi-party system the inaccuracy of representation by the simple-majority ballot is obviously much more serious. But it must not be forgotten that it tends by nature to resolve itself since the phenomena of over-representation and under-representation involved provide in fact the principal impulse for a return to dualism.

It is generally held that the second ballot diminishes the inac

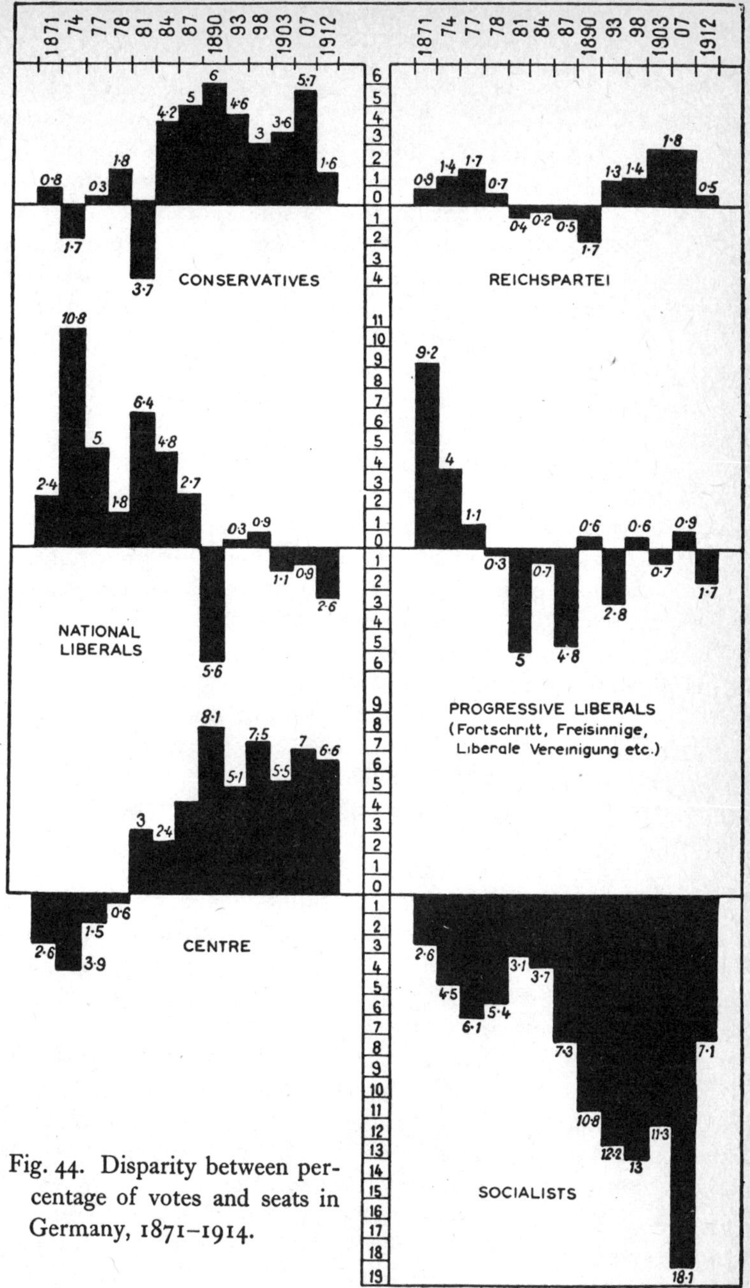

Fig. 44. Disparity between percentage of votes and seats in Germany, 1871–1914.

curacies of the majority system. From the purely numerical point of view this is not certain: a comparison between the number of votes obtained by parties in the first ballot and the total number of seats allotted to them after the second ballot reveals considerable disparities (Fig. 44). Of course, these generally remain much smaller than the exceptional anomalies sometimes involved in the simple-majority system, but they appear to be approximately equivalent to its average anomalies. They may even be considered more serious because of their direction, for the extent of a disparity is less important than the direction in which it occurs. In a single-ballot system combined with bipartism, however high the over-representation of the majority party and however great the under-representation of the minority party neither normally modifies the general pattern of the distribution of opinions. With the second ballot, on the contrary, the general pattern is completely distorted: what determines the direction taken by the disparities is not the respective number of votes obtained by the competing parties but their political positions and their alliances. Generally speaking, the second ballot is beneficial to the Centre and prejudicial to the extremes, that is the Centre is over-represented and the extremes under-represented. The political history of the French Third Republic gives a good illustration of this phenomenon, of which traces are to be seen in almost all two-ballot systems, e.g. Holland, Norway, Germany, and so on.

Obviously, if the final percentage of seats is compared with the percentage of votes obtained at the second ballot the disparity is notably diminished; that in fact is the justification of the system. It may then be claimed that it is an improvement on the accuracy of representation given by the single-ballot system, but this claim is based on a serious error of method. For only the first ballot gives a picture of the distribution of votes between the parties comparable with that presented by the single-ballot majority system or by proportional representation. The second ballot involves a compulsory regrouping of votes which makes it no longer possible to distinguish their true political complexion. To count as Radical votes in the 1936 French election the Communist votes transferred at the second ballot to the 'Valois' candidate because he was at the top of the Popular Front list is certainly to fail to take account of the real facts. Votes at the second ballot are grouped according to tendencies, not according to parties. Here then we pass from the second stage of distortion, measured by the disparity betwee electoral strength and parliamentary strength, to the first stage, defined as the disparity between the distribution of votes and the real nature of public opinion.

In so far as voting is free, secret, and not subject to pressure or manipulation which distort the result it is acknowledged to be a correct interpretation of public opinion. General though this belief is, it is not well founded: the electoral expression of opinion does not coincide with opinion itself but always distorts it in greater or less degree in varying directions according to the ballot procedure and the party system. The protagonists of any electoral reform always calculate the consequences of their system on the basis of the distribution of votes obtained by the parties under the old balloting procedure: such, for example, is the method used by Hermens to demonstrate that the majority system would have been less harmful to Weimar Germany than proportional representation. But such calculations are of necessity false, for the first effect of any electoral reform is to modify *not only the distribution of seats but also the distribution of votes.* The electors do not vote in the same way under the simple-majority system as under proportional representation, nor under the two-ballot as under the single-ballot, nor under list-voting as when voting for a single member. The phenomenon of 'polarization' provides a good example of the reaction of the ballot technique upon public opinion. It is difficult to analyse it in depth because electoral reforms have frequently coincided with an extension of the suffrage (universal suffrage, votes for women, etc.) or with major political events (1914 War, 1939 War, etc.). We can however study the influence of the abandonment of the majority system in favour of proportional representation in Switzerland, Denmark, and Norway. In these three countries the change led to elections within intervals of two or three years without significant changes in the franchise; in all three P.R. replaced a modified majority system (second ballot in Switzerland and Norway, some features of proportionalism in Denmark); finally all three are fairly tranquil countries in which opinion generally is marked by relative stability. The distribution of votes and not only of parliamentary seats amongst the different parties was profoundly altered by the electoral reform: the transformation is to some extent dependent on the entry into the political arena of new electors abandoning their earlier abstentionist attitude, but is considerably in excess of any effect they might have had (Fig. 45). In all three countries the adoption of proportional representation decreased the vote of the Centre party and increased the vote of the extremes.

We must then distinguish between formulated opinion and raw opinion. The first is the product of the kneading of the latter by party propaganda and of its moulding by the party system and the electoral system. Parties create public opinion as much as they express it; they form it rather than distort it; there is dialogue rather than echo. Without parties there would be only vague, instinctive, varying tendencies dependent on character, education, habit, social position, and so on. The Marxist theory itself which treats opinion as a reflection of social class holds that all classes are class-conscious; but class-consciousness does not exist unless a party exists to awaken and develop it. The minorities grouped inside parties according to the oligarchical and hierarchical organization that has been described engender the opinion of the masses. Naturally they could do nothing in the absence of the basis that we have termed raw opinion, but such an unleavened mass could do nothing either without the ferment of the parties. They give precision to individual opinion, enrich and develop it. They also strengthen it; before their action opinion is often unsure of itself; on seeing that it is shared by other men, stamped with official approval, taken in charge by an organization, it acquires authority and certitude. Parties also give opinion greater stability; without them it is changeable, versatile, fickle. In countries in which democracy has been newly implanted, in which parties have not yet taken strong roots, it is characteristic of elections that there are considerable variations from one ballot to the next, and this weakens the regime. Parties tend to crystallize opinion; they give skeletal articulation to a shapeless and jelly-like mass. Finally they cause similar opinions to coagulate: they minimize individual differences and smooth down personal idiosyncrasies to mould them into a few great spiritual families. The work of synthesis is not the least important side of party activity, for it alone makes possible the existence of elections and of some form of political representation, since both remain impossible in the inextricable welter of individual attitudes.

Public opinion being thus extricated from the mass of private opinions, the parties continue to keep it constantly informed, to guide and canalize it. The electoral campaign consists entirely in defining a 'platform' likely to attract the maximum number of electors by proposing particular aims to suit their interests. These

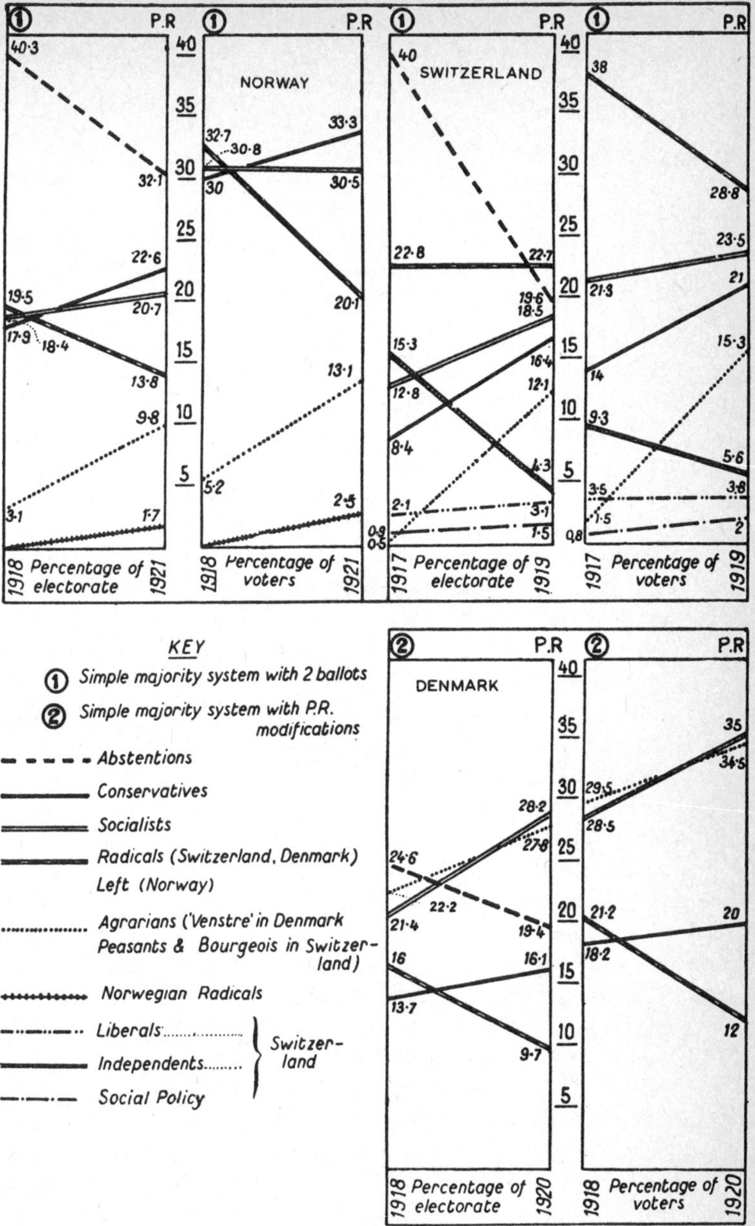

Fig. 45. Voting changes caused by an electoral reform.

particular aims, however, are no more than an isolated aspect, often superficial and secondary in importance, of the general activity of the party which will determine its attitude in parliament and to government. In consequence the very machinery of the election tends to distort opinion in accordance with a technique identical with that of certain ancillary movements: the question is how to make use of the coincidence of certain special objectives of the party with the wishes of the electorate in order to link the electorate with the general party policy which extends far beyond the particular aims. In this connection the French Communist party offers a very typical example. In 1956 more than 25% of French electors voted Communist, but only a very small fraction of the 25% really subscribed to the general policy of the party. The majority was composed of people fundamentally opposed to Communist doctrine but in agreement with the party on some particular issue: workers who considered it the only party capable of defending their class interests; minor landowners anxious to demonstrate their opposition to the great; smallholders and tenant farmers up in arms against their landlords; left-wingers traditionally wont to vote for the party farthest to the Left; patriots inspired by memories of the Resistance and the *maquis*, and so on. A detailed and methodical analysis, district by district, of the motives which led people to vote Communist would be extremely instructive. It would confirm the divorce between public opinion and its electoral representation, for Communist strength in the country and the basis for its representation in parliament are determined by this 25% of the electorate voting Communist. The example of the Communist party has been chosen because it is particularly typical, but the disparity between raw opinion and formed opinion exists for all parties. It is greater in proportion as the party is more centralized, better organized, more firmly based on a complete and coherent doctrine which enables it to act upon opinion instead of registering it and to organize the masses instead of following them.

All who vilify the party system denounce such distortion without comprehending that it is inevitable and really is much less deformation than formation. They fail to realize that raw opinion is elusive, that formed opinion alone can be expressed, and that the method of expression necessarily imposes on it a frame which modifies it. Different methods of approach may perhaps make it possible to come closer to opinion in the raw: the public opinion survey, field studies, special investigations, for example. On the political planes the referendum may also lead to less distorted knowledge upon a particular question; moreover it is to be noted that its results rarely match those obtained in elections, even on purely governmental questions, as witness the typical example of the Belgian referendum and elections in 1949. In any case every method of investigation imposes its own form upon opinion. Every party system constitutes a different frame for the expression of opinion, and produces therefore a different type of political representation. Public opinion is one of the factors in the system, but the system, which is dependent upon other factors, particularly ballot procedure, is conversely one of the factors in public opinion. Public opinion, electoral system, and party system thus form three interdependent terms which are not unidirectional in the influence of each upon the other in spite of current belief. Often the action of the latter two upon public opinion cannot be separated out. Every modification of the electoral system tends to a corresponding modification in the party system. And, in turn, any such modification of the party system has a direct impact on the expression of opinion. It may therefore be said that any modification of the electoral system exerts an indirect influence over the expression of opinion. But certain changes in the party system are independent of the electoral system, and their effect upon the representation of opinion is therefore exerted in isolation.

A typical example is provided by the breakdown of the French three-party alliance in 1947. Up till then the collaboration of the Communist party with the Socialists and the M.R.P. had established a left-wing government majority and guided French opinion in a progressive direction; the alliance was no more than a revival of the 1936 Popular Front in which the participation of the Communists had had the same consequences. In 1947 the Communist ministers were driven from the government and the agreement between the three parties was broken; it was not prolonged with Communist support; on the contrary a profound breach occurred between the former allies. Since then the expression of public opinion has assumed a different form: the *cordon sanitaire* round the Communist party modifies it without any transfer of votes, even without any election. It turns towards the Centre and slides to the Right: the Socialist party inclines towards an increasingly moderate reformist policy, reflecting its necessary participation in Centre governments, the M.R.P. tones down its social programme and gives precedence to the conservatism of its voters over the progressive views of its militants; the Radical party and the moderates recover an influence they had lost. These party modifications are not purely internal phenomena, they entail corresponding modifications of formed opinion and perhaps, by reaction, of raw opinion. A simple separating line between the parties is sufficient to change the general complexion of opinion. Interesting comparisons might be made here with the experiments which are the basis of Gestalt psychology.

Party Systems and the Distortion of Opinion. Here it is impossible to apply the method used to assess the distortion involved in the parliamentary expression of opinion as compared with its electoral expression: both are clearly distinct and measurable, which makes it possible to determine the disparity between them with considerable preciseness. But raw opinion and opinion formed by the party system do not present the same characteristics: the duality is moreover formal rather than real. In fact raw opinion does not exist, at least it is not ascertainable. We can only apprehend various types of formal opinion: opinion formed by field study, by Gallup poll, by proportional election or by majority election, by the two-party system or by the multi-party system, and so on. Some are nearer than others to the raw truth but we cannot know it; on this point we can have only beliefs or intuitions. The only possible method for assessing the influence of party systems on the distortion of opinion consists in comparing opinions formed by each system: it is thus possible to define the different trends of each of the different distortions, but not the extent to which they distort.

The influence of party systems, and of the electoral systems which produce them, upon the geographical localization of opinions is very marked. The problem assumes several aspects. One of them has already been alluded to in the course of studying the existence of local parties under the simple-majority single-ballot system. Since the tendency towards bipartism engendered by this electoral system manifests itself especially within constituencies, the result is that several parties may coexist in the country as a whole so long as they fight only in twos in each constituency. In consequence minor parties may subsist at the national level because they are major parties in certain districts. They may be autonomist or regional parties (e.g. Irish Nationalists, Slovak party in Czechoslovakia, etc.), future major national parties which are beginning to arise in districts where the population is particularly favourable to them (e.g. Socialist parties in industrial towns), or even former major national parties demoted to the local level by the merciless process of elimination already described (e.g. Liberal party in Great Britain today). Generalizations can however be based upon these results, for the very technique of the simple-majority ballot entails entrusting the task of representing the entirety of a region to the candidate who is placed above his rivals, without taking into account the votes cast for the others: minorities can then only be represented nationally because they are majorities in particular constituencies. The result is that the simple-majority system accentuates the geographical localization of opinions: one might even say that it tends to transform a national opinion (that is, one actually to be found throughout the country) into a local opinion by allowing it to be represented only in the sections of the country in which it is strongest. The case of the United States is particularly striking; it is too well known to require elaboration here.

On the other hand proportional representation works in the opposite direction: opinions strongly entrenched locally tend to be broadened on to the national plane by the possibility of being represented in districts where they are in a small minority. The more perfect the system of proportional representation, the more marked the tendency: distribution of remainders at the national level favours it, as do all systems of which the practical consequence is to treat the whole country as a single constituency. Thus it is noticeable that in countries which have adopted P.R. after the simple-majority system there is a kind of gradual 'nationalization' of opinions and of parties. This has already been pointed out for Holland; it is equally striking in Switzerland, Belgium, etc. It is difficult to say which of the two tendencies—'nationalization' resultant upon P.R. or localization brought about by the simple-majority system—more exactly interprets public opinion. In fact they each distort it in a different direction, the former by diminishing the local characteristics of an opinion, the latter by emphasizing them. The political significance of the process is clear: proportional representation tends to strengthen national unity (or, to be more precise, national uniformity); the simple-majority system accentuates local differences. The consequences are fortunate or unfortunate according to the particular situation in each country. In France P.R. seems to have accentuated the tendency to centralization and uniformity, which is to be regretted. In Belgium, on the contrary, it diminishes the rivalry between Flemings and Walloons, which might become inflamed by the restoration of the simple-majority system which tends to accentuate the Flemish aspect of the Catholic party and the Walloon aspect of the Socialists and to transform them both into autonomist parties. In the United States the majority system increases antagonism between North and South and particularist organization in the South.

The problem of the geographical localization of opinions also presents another aspect not to be confused with the preceding one. In the political attitude to be adopted by the citizen there are at work two categories of factors: specific, local factors and general factors. They might equally well be termed personal and ideological factors, though the two antitheses are far from coinciding exactly. Distinction between the two categories is not easy, for they are often closely bound up together in the unconscious, so to speak; some kind of sociological psycho-analysis would be required to separate them. In any case our problem is to determine the influence exerted by party systems and electoral machinery upon each of them, some encouraging the development of the local factors in opinion at the expense of national factors and vice versa. The practical importance of the question is evident: the policy of a parliament varies profoundly according as the members were elected for essentially local reasons or for their attitude on major national interests. Here the antithesis lies not between proportional representation and the majority ballot, but between voting for a single member and list-voting, the former being compatible with P.R. (use of the transferable vote) and the second often operative under the simple-majority system. In fact single-member voting presupposes a small constituency in which 'parish-pump politics' naturally predominate, while list-voting operates in a wider setting in which local points of view are restrictive of one another and allow general questions to assume a fair degree of importance. It must also be added that the single-member system, granted its personal character, gives greater scope for the making of personal promises and renders the local ties of the candidate very important; he is therefore naturally inclined to restrict his thoughts to the narrow circle to which he owes his election. The list-ballot on the other hand diminishes personal influence (which completely disappears in the case of the fixed list) and obliges the elector to vote for a party rather than for individuals, that is for an ideology and a national organization rather than for the protector of local interests.

Observation confirms the results of this analysis. It is certain that list-voting in the setting of the department (which in France replaced single-member voting in the arrondissement in 1945) has contributed a great deal to the broadening of the political horizons of members of parliament and governments. By contrast the very markedly local character of the preoccupations of Congress in America—so often unheeding of the world-wide responsibilities America must face—arises in large measure from the smallness of the electoral districts and the voting for a single member which goes with this. Other factors however are at work and may considerably alter the overall results, notably the extent to which the parties are centralized. It is to be noted that Great Britain, in spite of her attachment to the single-member system and the small constituency, does not display the usual defects of localism. The exception may perhaps be explained by the combination of the two-party system and centralization of parties: the former makes it extremely difficult for a candidate to fight as an independent outside the traditional major armies; the latter submits the selection of candidates to the close control of the central authorities of the party. This tends to give candidates a wider field of vision. This second factor is no doubt more important than the former, as is demonstrated by the example of America where, in spite of the two-party system, the decentralization of parties preserves their local bias.

The geographical distribution of opinion largely depends therefore on the party and electoral systems, whether these act in concert or in isolation; the same may be said of its political distribution. Some aspects of the distortion of public opinion have already been discussed in our investigations of the phenomenon of polarization, of the changes in the parliamentary strength of parties, and in particular of the influence of electoral systems on the distribution of votes. Here we shall only add a few complementary remarks. The first concerns abstentions: except in single-party dictatorships where the poll may attain a figure of nearly 100% of the electorate the number of abstentions is always considerable. The figure normally reaches more than 10% of the electorate and very frequently more than 20%. In the United States it is very much higher, being generally between 40% and 50% of the citizens of voting age in the Presidential election, the poll being even lower in some states. In some Southern states the abstentions have been over 80%; in Carolina they exceeded 90% (Fig. 43). Thus the distribution of votes never coincides with the distribution of opinions:

between the two exists a void corresponding to the abstentions. Now these vary in number according to the party system. They seem to reach a maximum in two-party systems with one party dominant where the election is semi-automatic: herein lies the explanation for the low polling figures in the Southern states of America. On the other hand they seem to reach a minimum in two-party systems where the two parties are in balance, for every vote is then of great importance. In a multi-party system modified by electoral alliances, as it operates under the second-ballot simple-majority system, results are approximately the same at the second ballot as under the single-ballot system; at the first ballot the number of abstentions is generally higher. If one of the parties is clearly dominant and if its victory is a foregone conclusion, the percentage of voters becomes very low, as in the single-ballot system. On this point pre-1919 Switzerland may be compared with the Southern states of America; from 1902 to 1911 the figure for abstentions lay between 43·2% and 47·5%; in 1914 it even reached 53·6%. Under a proportional system the results seem to lie between the two; it is in any case difficult to draw conclusions, for the adoption of P.R. has generally coincided with the establishment of universal suffrage or of the vote for women, a fact which prevents comparison within the same country. Only in Switzerland, Norway, and Denmark is comparison at all possible (Fig. 45).

A much more important question is that of the divisions of public opinion. Our analysis of the number of parties has shown that divisions arise not only from natural differences between citizens but also from external factors, of which the most potent is the electoral system. To that extent political divisions represent a pattern imposed on public opinion from without rather than a reflection of differences existing within public opinion. Bipartism resultant upon the single-ballot simple-majority system has the effect of suppressing secondary divisions of opinion and causing it to coagulate around two rival major tendencies, whereas multi-partism encourages the development of shades of opinion by enabling each to find expression in a separate party. It is generally concluded therefore that multi-partism ensures more faithful representation. The truth is possibly not so simple. It is by no means certain that the complexity of opinions which results from P.R., both because of its multiplying effect and because of the individual independence it confers on parties, corresponds more exactly to the facts than the simplification produced by bipartism and the majority system. It has already been noted that public opinion seems to manifest a deep-seated tendency to divide into two rival major fractions within which are to be found many shades of opinion but which have relatively clear external limits. The disadvantage of a dualist system would thus be its tendency to abolish the secondary differences which exist within each 'spiritual family', but it would appear none the less to have the essential merit of correctly expressing their general antagonism. On the other hand a system of multiple, independent parties, such as P.R. produces, would have the serious defect of completely obliterating the basic cleavage in opinion and over-emphasizing divisions on points of detail. Finally a multi-party system corrected by alliances, such as is produced by the second-ballot majority system, would offer the advantage of simultaneously allowing—thanks to the give and take of second-ballot agreements—the expression of the basic cleavage as well as of the secondary antagonisms within each group. It is to be noted moreover that a two-party system would achieve the same result in so far as each party preserved some flexibility of structure, allowing the growth and coexistence of different 'fractions' within it.

Another aspect of the problem concerns the extent of differences of opinion, and here similar confusions are encountered. It is currently maintained that multi-partism has the advantage of diminishing the extent by dissolving major antagonisms into several fractions, whereas the straightforward two-party system leads to the two blocs situation, that is to maximum antagonism. This is a confusion of the numerical differences in representation within parliament with the depth of political differences. In reality the respective consequences of multi-partism and dualism are diametrically opposite to the current notion. In his article in the *Encyclopaedia of Social Sciences*, Holcombe has rightly noted that parties tend to resemble one another in a dualist system, though he has given no reasons for the similarity. They can be easily defined. Let us take a precise example, that of contemporary Britain, neglecting the Liberal party which is no longer important. Who decides whether the Conservative or the Labour party shall win the election? Not their fanatical partisans who, being unable to cast their vote for any party further to the Right or to the Left, will naturally vote for them whatever they do, but the two or three million moderate Englishmen, politically situated at the Centre, who vote sometimes Conservative, sometimes Labour. To win their votes the Conservative party is forced to attenuate its Conservatism and Labour its Socialism, both of them adopting a calm tone, a reassuring aspect. Both will have to draw up policies clearly aimed at the Centre and therefore profoundly similar. We arrive at the paradoxical situation that the Centre influences the whole of parliamentary life in the very country in which the electoral system prevents the formation of a Centre party. The result is an obvious decrease in the extent of political divisions. The 'two blocs' myth which is so prevalent in France does not correspond with the facts. However, some distinction should perhaps be made between the propaganda put out by a party at election time and its action when in office: the former is relatively moderate in order to win over the 'floating' voters situated at the Centre, the latter is less so in order to satisfy the militants who are more extremist. Here there would appear to be an obvious exception to the general tendency of parties to be more temperate in the exercise of power than in their electoral campaign: there would appear to be a kind of reversed demagogy, of which the Communist parties provide further examples in their propaganda. None the less the majority bent of each of the parties naturally decreases the gap between promises and deeds and restricts its demagogy, of whatever kind it be.

In a system with many independent parties, corresponding to proportional representation, the results are reversed. Each party can normally increase its representation only at the expense of its immediate neighbours: in France, for example, the Communists at the expense of the Socialists, the Popular Republicans at that of the Moderates, Radicals or French People's Rally, and so on. Each therefore tries to emphasize the differences of detail which distinguish it from its nearest rivals, instead of drawing attention to their profound similarities. The result is an aggravation of political divisions and an intensification of differences. The exacerbation of rivalry between neighbouring parties seems to coincide with a general 'extremization' of opinion, Left parties being attracted more to the Left, Right parties more to the Right. Inside every group each tries to outbid his neighbours. Under the Third Republic this phenomenon was more marked on the Left than on the Right, because the Right had a guilty conscience, being composed of former opponents of the regime or else of former left-wingers driven into conservatism as a result of Leftism: the desire of all Centre parties to appear 'Left-wing' is very significant in this respect. 'Extremization' shows itself none the less on the

Right: its moderates and converts are always vilified; after 1934 it obviously felt the attraction of Fascism; in 1945–6 the demagogic call for 'A free economy' weighed heavily on the Radical party and even on a section of the M.R.P. 'Extremization' of opinion seems to have been less developed in other countries, though there appears to be a general tendency of this kind. In so far as it is operative, opinion finds itself led in the opposite direction to that which it follows in a two-party system: the pressure exerted on it is centrifugal instead of centripetal. The exigencies of government naturally limit the centrifugal impulse but also enable extremist parties, which have no share in power, to maintain an intransigent and demagogic attitude that seriously embarrasses the Centre parties because of the threat of election day. The government is therefore always handicapped by the 'extremization' process.

Even if alliances for the second ballot intervene to correct the effect of multi-partism the process does not vanish: electoral alliances always tend to be dominated by the most extreme party. However, the see-saw movement of Centre parties makes for some decrease in rivalries by toning down the general antagonism of the two blocs. This sedative action is accompanied by some confusion however: among those elected from the Centre some win thanks to the support of the Right, others thanks to the support of the Left. Because of this Janus-like attitude, Centre parties tend perpetually to be torn between two contradictory forces: qualms of conscience amongst their diverging deputies lead them to adopt now a conservative, now a progressive policy; the process is well illustrated by the example of the Radical party under the Third French Republic. In short, rivalries are not so much toned down as made much less stable: antagonisms take on an alternating character which corresponds to no real variation in public opinion. In what way can such composite deputies, who do no more than mark the points at which contraries meet, be said to be representative? For representation to be less distorted, the Centre party would need to remain very flexible, divided into opposing fractions which correspond to the distribution of the votes cast for it; otherwise its cohesion introduces an element of artificial unity into the electoral body; the extent of divisions is not diminished but perverted. Moreover, it will be observed that the second ballot and alliances present no obstacle to the aggravation of political differences between neighbouring parties which seek to accentuate their divergences in order to attract the voters floating between them; on the contrary the device of standing-down, which enables that ally who heads the poll to monopolize representation, makes differences more remunerative.

The internal structure of parties also exerts a profound influence upon the extent of divisions. Homogeneous, centralized, and totalitarian parties introduce into public opinion irreducible cleavages which are not to be found in real life. In France, for example, the nature of the Communist party sets it completely apart from all others, but Communist electors are not so different from their fellow-citizens. When Communism is referred to as a 'separatist' movement, a distinction must be made between the party and the section of opinion that it represents: the term is accurate for the former but not for the latter. The isolation of the party therefore distorts the representation of French opinion. In fact, the majority of French opinion today now inclines to the Left as in 1936: the addition of Communist voters, Socialist voters, and those Radical and M.R.P. voters who are really progressive gives a total of more than half the country. But the nature of the Communist party, which prevents it from collaborating with the others, and which compels the 1947 breach in the three-party alliance to be maintained, does not permit this progressive majority opinion to find expression on the parliamentary and governmental plane.[1] This characteristic of the party introduces a radical divorce within the ranks of the Left and so completely paralyses it. As a result of this internal 'iron curtain', the whole of French politics leans to the Right, and this does not correspond with public opinion. It is as though the left-wing votes cast for the Communist party were nullified, for the Communist deputies are out of the game. They can disturb the game but not join in, with a few exceptions: representation of national opinion is therefore completely distorted. The re-establishment of the three-party alliance or the birth of a new Popular Front would not render it more accurate, for the revolutionary and disintegrating attitude of the Communist party would not represent the reformism and fidelity to the regime of the electors of such an alliance. Opinion would be distorted in another way, but it would still be distorted.

This example leads us to examine the fundamental question of

[1] The 1951 electoral system had ended the three-party group's majority in parliament, though it retained it in the country with 53·3% of the votes. As a result of the 1956 elections the Left again had a majority in Parliament either on the 1936 Popular Front Pattern or on the 1945 three-party pattern. Owing to the isolation of the Communist party, however, this majority could not form a government.

the coincidence between public opinion and the government majority, which is the essence of the democratic system. Here a distinction must be made between imposed and free majorities. When the distribution of seats among the parties is such that there can be no doubt about the majority, with the result that it is independent of the activity of deputies and of parliamentary intrigues, there is an imposed majority. On the other hand when several parties have an almost equal number of seats, no one of them being able to govern alone, the formation of a majority depends largely on the will of the deputies and the party organizers, and public opinion plays no direct part in the matter: the majority is then a 'free' majority. The first case corresponds to the traditional conception of democracy; the second leads to a mixture of democracy and oligarchy in which the electorate is called upon to determine by its vote only the percentage of influence to be accorded to the respective party organizations. The party system in this connection plays an all-important part which may be expressed in the following formula: the two-party system tends to a majority imposed by public opinion, the system of many independent parties to a free majority, the system of many dependent parties to a semi-free majority.

Take the case of a British election: the day after the poll, it is known who will take office, the majority is known with certainty: one party forms the government, the other the opposition. The process was inoperative only during the 1918–35 period as a result of the temporary three-party system which the electoral regime itself destroyed, or during war-time as a result of governments of national union: both are exceptional cases. Under normal conditions, in every country in which the simple-majority ballot has given rise to bipartism the government majority is imposed on parliament by public opinion. The system slightly distorts opinion by artificially amplifying it but it does not pervert it. The party system plays something of the role of a magnifying glass which makes possible a clearer distinction between the majority and the opposition. Compare this with the system of many independent parties resulting from proportional representation, pre-1951 France, for instance: all kinds of majority are possible, or almost. In the 1946–51 Assembly there could have been (1) a Centre majority (Socialists, M.R.P., Radicals, and a few moderates) which did in fact govern from 6 May 1947 under various names; (2) a three-party majority similar to that which existed in the two Constituent Assemblies (Communists, Socialists, and M.R.P.) which governed until 6 May

1947; (3) a majority on the pattern of the 1936 Popular Front (Communists, Socialists, and a few 'progressive' Radicals and Popular Republicans); (4) a moderate majority stretching from the extreme Right to the Socialist party (including even a few Ramadier-type Socialists); (5) an anti-Communist National Union majority including all parties except the Communist; (6) finally, a majority on the pattern of the 1914 'Union sacrée' comprising the unanimous Assembly. As the choice between these six combinations did not depend on the electorate but only on activities inside parliament, the role of the people consisted only in fixing the number of combinations and the degree of probability of certain amongst them, according to the percentage of seats allotted to each party. Similar happenings are to be seen in most proportionalist states save in the exceptional case when a party obtains an absolute majority of the seats.

In a system with many dependent parties produced by the two-ballot regime the determination of the majority is less free because of the electoral alliances that the parties are obliged to contract. But these are not necessarily transposed on to the governmental plane; they tend even to be loosed at that level by natural divergences. The example of France between 1928 and 1939 shows that the number of possible parliamentary combinations remains high. Although in most countries which operated the two-ballot system before the 1914 War majorities were generally more stable and more in conformity with the indications of the poll, it is none the less a fact that voting itself is always strongly influenced by the interplay of alliances which remains quite free: for example, the end of the isolation of the Communist party in France in 1936 and its entry into the Left coalition profoundly altered the balance of the majority; its eviction from the three-party alliance had the same effect in 1947. We are here far removed from the 'imposed majority' system produced by bipartism and can speak only of 'semi-free' majorities.

III. PARTIES AND THE STRUCTURE OF GOVERNMENT

The development of parties has burst the bonds of the old political categories inspired by Aristotle or Montesquieu. The classic contrast between parliamentary, presidential, and National Convention regimes can henceforth no longer serve as the pivot for modern constitutional law. Kemalist Turkey, Soviet Russia, and Hitler Germany were profoundly similar because each was a single-party state, although the first practised the National Convention regime, the second a semi-parliamentary regime, and the third a semi-presidential regime. In spite of their common attachment to the parliamentary regime, Great Britain and the Dominions, under a two-party system, are profoundly dissimilar from Continental countries under a multi-partist system, and in certain respects are much closer to the United States in spite of its presidential regime. In fact the distinction between single-party, two-party, and multi-party systems tends to become the fundamental mode of classifying contemporary regimes.

Its importance however threatens to cause a certain amount of confusion. Although the number of parties is a vital element in the structure of government, other factors must not be neglected in its favour. Comparison between Great Britain and the United States offers an excellent illustration of the importance of the internal organization of parties, British centralization clearly contrasting with American decentralization. In the same way the purely political differences between Soviet Russia and pre-1950 Turkey are essentially based upon the totalitarian and homogeneous nature of the Communist party and the heterogeneous and restricted nature of the People's Republican party. The contrast between the rigid parties of the Fourth French Republic and the flexible parties of the Third is too often quoted to need further emphasis. The respective power of parties exerts no less an influence: the existence of a dominant party may transform the nature of a regime, as can be seen in some American states and in pre-1914 Switzerland. Further, a simple change in majority sometimes produces the same effects. If the majority in Congress and the Presidency of the United States are in the hands of the same party, the official 'separation of powers' is much diminished; if they are held by different parties, separation is much increased. The influence exerted by parties leads to the conclusion that governmental structure is relative and can be modified by a simple change in the relationship of political forces within the country. This is very different from the rigidity of the classic constitutional definitions.

Parties and the Separation of Powers. The degree of separation of powers is much more dependent on the party system than on the provisions of the Constitution. Thus the single party brings in its train a very close concentration of powers, even if the Constitution officially prescribes a marked separation: the party binds very closely together the various organs of government. Its role is no different in a pluralist system, but simply less marked. Rivalry between parties weakens the links that each of them could establish between parliament and government: the constitutional separation of powers regains therefore some measure of effectiveness; it may even be paralleled by a party separation arising from the specialization of each party in a given task. The two party and the multi-party systems here produce entirely opposite results. The influence of parties on the separation of powers depends not only on their number but also on their internal structure and even on their respective strengths: weak, decentralized organization generally increases separation, with some exceptions; changes in majority may, under some circumstances, profoundly affect it. Each of these factors operates in a different way in the different systems—parliamentary, presidential, and National Convention. Real separation of powers is therefore the product of a combination of party system and constitutional setting.

On the whole the two-party system tends towards concentration of powers. One party holds an absolute majority in parliament; one party holds all the offices of government: the party therefore forms a powerful link between the two. Officially Great Britain has a parliamentary system, that is a system with modified separation of powers, Cabinet and Parliament each specializing in a particular function (executive power for the Cabinet, legislative power for Parliament), but disposing of means for reciprocal action enabling them to influence one another (Commissions of inquiry, question-time, vote of censure, and vote of no-confidence for Parliament; power of dissolution for the Government). In practice the existence of a majority governing party transforms this constitutional pattern from top to bottom. The party holds in its own hands the essential prerogatives of the Legislature and the Executive. Government posts are in the hands of its leaders, who apply its doctrine and its programme as expressed in its electoral 'platform'; draft Bills are prepared by the party's research groups, tabled in its name by a party representative in the House, voted by the party parliamentary group, and applied by the party Government. Parliament and Government are like two machines driven by the same motor, the party. The regime is not so very different, in this respect, from the single-party system. In this, Executive and Legislative, Government and Parliament, are constitutional façades: in reality the party alone exercises power. In the two-party system the artificiality of the official bodies is not as great; in particular the existence of an opposition party confers great importance on parliamentary debates. Their issue is not, of course, in doubt: if the majority party wants its point of view carried, it can, by reason of its majority, always win; but the obligation to face the running fire of opposition criticism may lead it to reflect and to modify the rigour of its plans, because of the effect on the electorate of the debates which are well publicized. There is more artificiality about the Government: the Cabinet is based more or less on the General Staff of the victorious party; often the respective influence of the various ministers upon decisions made in common is determined by their position in the party rather than by the importance of the task they are allotted in the Government (as in single-party regimes). The single-party and the two-party systems differ radically on the limitation of power and the existence of an opposition; they are very close as far as concerns the separation of powers, or rather their concentration.

However, the extent of this concentration and its very existence depend to a considerable degree on constitutional structure; parliamentary and presidential regimes are here quite clearly opposed. The former officially establishes a much diminished separation of powers; the latter on the contrary produces the total isolation of government and parliament, each confined to its own sphere of duties and incapable of effectively influencing the other. Thus the parliamentary regime superimposes some concentration of powers upon the concentration produced by the two-party system; the presidential regime contrasts with it by establishing a rigid separation of powers. In the former case the constitutional system and the party system converge to some extent, in the latter they clearly diverge. The concentration produced by the two-party system will therefore be naturally greater in a parliamentary regime in which it is encouraged than under the presidential regime in which it is checked. This formal analysis is however too rigid; the reality is much more subtle. Under the presidential regime the relationships between the powers are entirely different when the parliamentary majority and the presidency are both held by the same party from what they are when each is held by a different party. If dates of election and terms of office coincide it is obviously more common for one party to hold both; it would be extraordinary for the electors to vote simultaneously for one party for parliament and for its rival for the presidency. The personality of the presidential candidate and his personal prestige might exceptionally bring about this result, especially if the organization of the parties and their doctrinal cohesion were not strong: in the United States electors sometimes vote Democrat for the State legislature and governorship while voting Republican for Congress and the Presidency, or vice versa. Disparity between the latter two votes would not therefore be absurd. Two examples can be found, moreover, 1876 and 1916, though neither is very definite. In 1876 the elections for the House of Representatives confirmed the 1874 Democratic majority, whereas the Presidency fell to the Republican, Hayes, but he owed his success to a technical point in the electoral law, having polled 250,000 votes fewer than his rival, Tilden; furthermore the majority in the Senate remained Republican. In 1916 the Senate majority remained Democrat, like the Presidency; in the House of Representatives the Democrats lost the majority, without the Republicans recovering it, as a result of minor parties holding the balance. Most frequently the disparity between President and Congress arises from the elections being held at different dates: the President being elected every four years, the House of Representatives and one-third of the Senate every two years, the majority may alter in an intermediate election during the course of the President's term of office. In fact this situation has occurred thirteen times in the history of the United States: in 1838, 1846, 1850, 1854, 1874, 1882, 1890, 1910, 1918, 1930 and 1946.

If the same party holds simultaneously both the Presidency and the majority in both Chambers it almost entirely does away with the constitutional separation of powers. The difference between the presidential and the parliamentary regimes becomes blurred in fact although they are distinct constitutionally. There is a strong resemblance to the British system or, at least, there would be if the flexible organization of American parties did not diminish the concentration of powers attained by the majority party. By contrast if the Presidency and the Congress are each controlled by a different party, the official separation of powers is heightened by rivalry between the two parties, and this superimposes a second separation. Here the two-party system increases division between the powers instead of decreasing it; if American parties were centralized and hierarchical like British parties the separation would be so great that it would bring about almost complete paralysis of the regime. A simple change in the relative strength of parties leads to a complete transformation of the very nature of the political regime. Discussion in the abstract of the separation of powers in the United

States and of the extent of the separation is pointless. In reality the United States is subject to two different political regimes, according to the distribution of seats in Congress: if the Presidency and the majority in Congress are on the same side then there is a high concentration of powers; otherwise there is a marked separation of powers. However the contrast is attenuated by lack of homogeneity in the parties: were the structure of American parties to be transformed in the direction of stronger organization and greater centralization, as many experienced observers demand, it would undoubtedly be unecessary to alter the system of partially renewing Congress and to ensure that terms of office were concurrent, otherwise very serious governmental crises might arise.

The very mechanism of the parliamentary regime prevents it from suffering this tug-of-war between majority and government, since in it government is of necessity a reflection of the majority. It leaves it vulnerable however to another division which may also occur in the presidential regime, viz. opposing majorities in the two chambers. Of fairly frequent occurrence in the United States (e.g. in 1875–9, 1883–9, 1891–3, 1911–13), it is even more frequent in European parliamentary regimes. Indeed the upper House was originally conceived as a means of moderating the democratic tendency of the lower House. The initial conception has been slowly fading in almost all cases as a result of general changes; none the less differences in methods of recruitment and in periods of office frequently bring about a political difference between the two chambers. This diminishes the concentration of powers achieved by the majority party, either by compelling it to come to an agreement with its rival in order to form a government acceptable to both Houses, or by limiting its liberty of action because of the opposition of the upper House in which it is in the minority. A new type of separation of powers tends to be set up with the line of demarcation running, not between parliament and government, but through the middle of parliament, so that one chamber forms with the government a true political unit in opposition to the other chamber. There are very many examples of such a situation: in Scandinavia the rivalry between the aristocratic Chamber and the popular Chamber coincided with the progressive establishment of the parliamentary regime at the end of the nineteenth century; in Great Britain the great struggle of 1906–11 ended with the pre-eminence of the House of Commons. Nearer in time there is a typical example in the fight between the French Senate and the Popular Front majority in the Chamber of Deputies between 1936 and 1938; comparable rivalry between the Australian Senate and Chamber of Representatives led to the dissolution of 1951. Generally the division of power which results from this difference between the two Houses is much less serious than that produced by the conflict between President and parliamentary majority, for usually the Constitution makes provision for resolving the difference, and this most often ends in the victory of the popular chamber. Moreover the powers of the upper House are tending to decrease in parliamentary regimes: in almost all cases it retains no more than the power of delaying the decisions of the lower House, not the power of completely blocking them. Under the American presidential regime, however, conflicts between the two assemblies might be insoluble if the decentralization and heterogeneity of the parties did not decrease opposition between the two majorities.

The internal structure of parties therefore exercises a fundamental influence on the degree of separation or concentration of powers. In a parliamentary regime cohesion and discipline in the majority party obviously increase concentration. If voting discipline is strict, if the internal fractions are reduced to impotence or obedience, parliament's function is reduced to rubber-stamping government decisions, which are in fact identical with party decisions. The act of rubber-stamping gives rise to very free discussion in which the minority party can express its opposition, but it is no more than platonic. By contrast if voting discipline is less strict the government majority is less certain; the party in office must take account of rivalries between its own factions which may compromise its parliamentary position; the prestige of parliament is raised and separation of powers is to some extent restored. Here too a simple change of majority may modify the nature of the regime. In Great Britain, for example, discipline, centralization and cohesion are more developed in the Labour party than in the Conservative party; in consequence, there is greater concentration of powers when Labour has a majority than when the Conservatives are in the majority. In the nineteenth century, when the organization of British parties was less strong than it is today, the separation of powers was less diminished by the two-party system. This explains the classic descriptions of the British parliamentary system as a system of balance between Legislative and Executive, as a system of 'checks and balances'. Such views are still current today as a result of a misunderstanding of the development of party structure

In a presidential regime the internal organization of the parties plays an almost similar part, but its influence varies considerably according to whether the same party holds both the presidency and the majority in parliament or whether they are in separate hands. Strong, centralized and disciplined organization obviously suppresses any separation of powers in the case of presidency and parliamentary majority being held by the same party; on the contrary it aggravates separation to the point of insoluble conflict and paralysis of government when the two are at loggerheads. On the other hand, weak and decentralized organization expressed as an absence of voting discipline weakens concentration of powers in the first hypothesis and makes their separation less serious in the second hypothesis. The idea of a United States President supported by a majority party in Congress ruling with the same freedom as a British Prime Minister is quite erroneous: the President must always reckon with the divisions in his own party. Each Senator and each Representative remains very free in his relations with the parliamentary group; voting is as variegated in American parties as in the French Radical Socialist party under the Third Republic. A Democratic President always has a few Democratic members against him; in the same way no Republican President is ever supported by every Republican member of Congress. By way of compensation each can find support inside the opposite camp. The result is that in practice there is not such a clear-cut distinction between cases where presidency and parliamentary majority are at one and cases of disparity: in the former hypothesis the decentralization and heterogeneity of the majority party decrease presidential authority and the concentration of powers, in the latter they diminish antagonism between President and Congress and prevent the paralysis of the machinery of government. The American system is thus situated in an intermediate zone between separation and concentration, tending to the former in the exceptional periods when Congress and Presidency are in the hands of opposing parties, tending strongly to the latter in normal circumstances; in both cases the personal prestige of the President affects the degree of separation or concentration.

In presidential and in parliamentary regimes, though more in the latter than in the former, the size of the majority at the disposition of the party in office also has an influence upon the separation of powers. If it is great the authority of the party in parliament is great; it is not embarrassed by the opposition; it can claim to represent the will of the country. If, on the other hand, it only disposes of a small margin over its rival (like the Labour party in the House of Commons after the 1950 elections), its moral position in the country is less assured, and so is its material position in the House; it only needs several of its deputies to be absent for the opposition to defeat it in a vote. Parliament therefore regains all its importance, and the separation of powers is restored. An excellent example of this situation is to be seen in the exhaustion tactics initiated by the Conservative party in March 1951; they forced a succession of late night-sittings in order to tire the Labour members, who were compelled to be always in attendance for fear of a snap vote. However, the adoption of the French technique of the *boîtier*, allowing the votes of members to be cast in their absence, would be adequate to strengthen the parliamentary position of a party with a weak majority, and re-establish in its favour strong concentration of powers. It does not indeed seem that its prerogatives are restricted by the narrowness of its majority in the country: the nationalization of steel carried out by the Labour party after the 1950 election is a proof of this. Parliamentary strength is always much more important than real strength in the country: the fact that the Labour party had obtained only 48·7% of the poll in 1945 was completely obliterated by the fact that it controlled 390 votes in the Commons; public opinion itself considered Labour as having a strong majority.

The effects of multi-partism are concordant. In general it tends towards separation of powers. In the first place it allows free play to constitutional separation. In the parliamentary regime the government must find support from a coalition of associated parties: their alliance is always uneasy and intrigues are perpetually being hatched in the lobbies of parliament to break up the existing combination and replace it by a new one. It is here that the 'parliamentary game', almost non-existent under the two-party system, flourishes and assumes full significance: the chambers recover their freedom with regard to the government; they are no longer restricted to the role of rubber-stamping amidst platonic protests from the opposition. The means of interaction between parliament and government, artificial in the two-party system, here become significant again. One can rightly talk of a balance of powers and of a system of checks and balances, symbolized by the parallelism between the vote of no-confidence, which enables parliament to overthrow the government, and the right of dissolution, which enables the government to send parliament to face its electors. Of these means of action some moreover are subject to the direct influence of the party system. In relations with the government multi-party parliaments prefer to use the interpellation technique, whereas two-party parliaments tend to make use of the question: the difference is revealing. In a two-party regime the vote of confidence is almost automatic and loses any real significance: the assembly is reduced to asking questions that carry no sanctions in order to exercise control. In a multi-party system the vote of confidence threatens at any moment to endanger the existence of the government, whence the importance of interpellation followed by a vote.

Multi-partism tends on occasion to superimpose a second separation of powers upon that resulting from the Constitution or the nature of the institutions. The classic separation of powers rests upon a distinction between the functions of the state defined according to their legal nature: parliament makes the laws, which are acts of general import; the government applies them by means of individual measures. Over against this separation there can be conceived a separation of powers based upon a distinction between the material duties of the state: financial, economic, social, police, judicial, educational, military, diplomatic, and so on. By regrouping the different ministries in homogeneous sectors a horizontal classification of state activities can be established; thus there would be the Economic sector (industry, commerce, agriculture, merchant shipping, public finance), the Social sector (responsibility for social welfare, depressed classes, poor persons—the 'egalitarian' sector), the Public Safety sector (police and justice), the Ideological sector (instruction, education, censorship of arts and literature, etc.), the Diplomatic sector (foreign affairs and army). In a multi-party parliamentary system such a horizontal separation of powers is sometimes added to the traditional vertical separation. Each party associated in the government tends to demand a well-defined sector of activity which has some affinity with its electoral support or which will enable it to develop its political strategy.

Such specialization does not always exist. On the contrary some governmental combinations practise neutralization tactics: complementary departments are entrusted to rival parties so as to tone down the policy of each Minister by that of his neighbour who is an opponent; or else a Minister is given an Under-Secretary of State, chosen from another party, who watches and keeps a check on him. Sometimes specialization is no more than embryonic: under the Third Republic the Radical party generally claimed the Ministry of the Interior and, less frequently, Education. It may however be taken very far: during the three-party alliance period in France each ally controlled one homogeneous sector of national affairs. Rigid party discipline and electoral isolation led furthermore to a definite predominance of party solidarity over government solidarity. In these circumstances the Council of Ministers resembled a Diet in which the ambassadors of the various parties sought to aehieve a compromise: often important Councils were preceded by separate meetings of the ministers in each party to decide on the common line to be followed. Horizontal separation of powers has rarely been pushed so far. It is clear that it depends a good deal on the internal structure of the associated parties: under a system of decentralized and flexible parties with little discipline, the individualism of deputies finds its reflection in the individualism of ministers and is hostile to the division into sectors. A system of rigid or centralized parties, however, is better adapted to it: in France the relaxation of discipline in the M.R.P. and the Socialist party after 1947, coupled with the admission to the majority bloc of the Radical party with its weak structure, greatly diminished horizontal separation. The respective strength of the allies is also very important: a true separation into sectors presupposes some equality between the parties. Horizontal separation of powers is one of the forms of coalition government in a multi-party system, but not the only form; by contrast an aggravation of the classic vertical separation is a general phenomenon.

Obviously in a presidential regime only the latter can occur since the government does not reflect divisions within the assemblies. Parliament and Executive are not linked by any majority party which bridges the gap of isolation resultant upon the nature of the institutions. The authority of the President over his own party is insufficient to bring the Chambers into line with his policy, for the party remains in a minority. However, the separation of powers is less complete than under the two-party system in cases where presidency and parliamentary majority are not held by the same party. For the President is no longer faced by a homogeneous parliamentary majority opposed to his policy, but by a heterogeneous majority composed of several parties that he may attempt to break up. The difference in the position is even more marked from the point of view of government authority than from the point of view of separation of powers.

Parties and Government Authority. Party unity obviously increases government authority: the Assemblies turn into a Rump-Parliament in which well-ordered applause replaces debate: at the most, discussion is limited to technical criticism on points of detail formulated by deputies against particular ministers and never questioning the general policy of the government (this system is well developed in Soviet Russia). In practice an appearance of democracy and parliamentarianism cloaks strict dictatorship. Accounts must also be taken of the structure of the single party and of its true position in the state. A non-totalitarian party may allow the development of limited opposition and thus introduce a degree of flexibility into dictatorship. A party that is not completely integrated with the state may itself constitute an opposition force: sometimes Fascist single parties have risen against the conservatism of the regime and have had to suffer severe purges and much *capitis diminutio.* Furthermore some are outside the government and in practice impotent, like the Portuguese National Union whose activity is slight. With these reserves the single party has certainly been the means employed to conserve the external forms of a democratic regime with balance of powers and limited government while an authoritarian regime with an omnipotent government was substituted for it. It represents the contemporary political incarnation of the hermit-crab technique, consisting in emptying a political regime of all reality and substance, preserving only the externals like an empty shell in which an entirely different system is installed: thus in the eighteenth and nineteenth centuries the progressive separation of king and cabinet enabled the old absolute monarchies to transform themselves into parliamentary democracies.

Although it has not carried out so radical a transformation, the two-party system too has strengthened the authority of the government but without destroying the apparatus of democracy. We have seen that it tends to substitute concentration of powers for their formal separation, but this concentration operates to the advantage of government and to the detriment of parliament. The party becomes a means of ensuring the domination of parliament by government, for the latter is controlled by the party leaders, whose subordinates are the deputies who form the majority in parliament.

The internal hierarchy of the party is, in a sense, projected on to the organization of state institutions. Inside the government party solidarity becomes the reinforcement and the cement of ministerial solidarity; in relations between cabinet and House the authority of the supreme leaders of the party over the elected representatives establishes the subordination of parliament to government. Thus a Liberal writer, Mr. Ramsay Muir, could write of 'cabinet dictatorship'. The internal hierarchy of the party is moreover not the only means of increasing the prestige and authority of the government: the two-party system also entails a radical transformation of those means by which each of the powers influences the other which are characteristic of the parliamentary regime. The ways in which parliament can influence government lose their importance or their individual significance. The vote of censure or that of no-confidence, which in theory enable parliament to overthrow the cabinet, can no longer achieve this result, except for snap votes if the margin between majority and minority is slight, but these are always the exception. With this one reserve only weakness or relaxation of discipline within the government party can make it possible for parliament to recover its prerogatives and overthrow the cabinet. Of course the exercise of power always creates divisions within the party in office; it heightens the conflicts between internal fractions and the contrast between moderates and extremists, but these dissensions rarely go so deep as to cause a split. At most, some deputies of the majority party will be found abstaining (and more rarely voting against the party) on a motion of confidence in order to show their disagreement with the leading fraction, so long as the margin between majority and minority is adequate for the display of bad temper to cause no damage. The government often uses the vote of confidence as a weapon to restore discipline within its party: it compels the internal opposition to surrender by challenging it and threatening it with expulsion.

The right of dissolution makes this weapon highly effective. If the government sends deputies to face the electorate as a consequence of a split in the majority party the dissidents will be in grave danger of being defeated at the new elections; by setting up against them orthodox candidates the leaders of the government party will in a single-ballot system put them in an awkward position. Thus the traditional means for interaction between parliament and government are transformed into means for action by the government on its own party. A kind of 'general post' is produced: the internal hierarchy of the party becomes a link between public institutions; the official links between public institutions strengthen the internal hierarchy of the majority party. The modification is however one-sided: only the means by which parliament can influence government are deprived of efficacy or completely diverted from their original purpose, to the extent of becoming weapons enabling the cabinet to make recalcitrant representatives toe the line. The means by which government influences parliament are modified in operation but not in result; they remain devices for exerting pressure on parliament. The use of dissolution just described remains true to its original aim: to strengthen government stability by limiting ministerial crises by the threat of new elections; to ensure that the electorate shall be the judge in cases of deep-seated conflict between Executive and Legislative. Whether the cabinet puts the question of confidence in order to bring to repentance the dissidents in its own party or to keep several parties inside a government coalition, it always starts from the same idea: to strengthen its parliamentary position. Whether it proclaims dissolution in an endeavour to secure the electoral defeat of dissidents expelled from its own party or of former allies who have left the coalition, its aim is always a kind of crude surgery: to lance the abscess which interferes with efficient government.

Thus the two-party system upsets the balance of powers provided for in parliamentary theory not only by creating for the government a new and most efficient weapon for influencing parliament based upon the internal hierarchy of the majority party, but also by paralysing or by transforming to the advantage of the cabinet the classic weapon with which parliament influences the government, whilst at the same time preserving with little modification the means for government to influence parliament. This description is only valid in so far as the majority party possesses sufficient cohesion. If it is no more than an agglomeration of individuals relatively independent of one another the power of the party leaders is weakened, and so is the power of ministers over their parliamentary majority. If voting discipline is enforced in the majority party the government lives a quiet life, its sole preoccupation being to prevent internal divisions and the threat of schism from arising; if there is no such discipline the devices described do not operate: party hierarchization becomes more theoretical than practical, and consequently incapable of conferring on the government any real authority over the Chamber. Within this body the opposition can hope to break up the majority by playing the game of individual seduction; backstairs intrigues and parliamentary prestige alike recover their importance. The minority party is no longer restricted to waging a purely propagandist campaign with an eye to future elections, and no chance of earlier success owing to the solidarity of the government; the government in this case is not so solid and the hope of a change in majority no longer illusory. However, the general development of parties as well as the logic of the simple-majority electoral system (which serves as the basis of bipartism) seems in fact to tend towards a strengthening of party structure and therefore of government authority.

To some extent this increase is compensated for by the dependence of the government on the militant members of the majority party and the bodies which express their will. A Labour cabinet is more dependent on the Trade Union Congress than on the House of Commons. In a two-party regime the ministry cannot in practice be overthrown by parliament, whereas it can be by a meeting of party members. The facts are accurate but exaggerated conclusions are often drawn from them, for the development of parties tends progressively to restrict internal democracy and the freedom of action of militants, as we have seen. The leaders command increasingly effective means of influencing Congresses, and these generally make it possible for them to retain the leadership without too much difficulty. When they are in office moreover such means are greatly reinforced by the prestige of power, by the favours that can then be shared amongst the recalcitrants to help convince them, by the threat of seeing the party's majority in jeopardy. Were the party Congress to disown the leaders they would be compelled to withdraw from the government; such a withdrawal would make it difficult to reconstitute a cabinet supported by the same party; this difficulty would lead the way to dissolution; dissolution occurring under such circumstances, when the majority party would be obliged to confess its incapacity to govern because of its internal divisions, would in all likelihood bring about defeat. The argument is a powerful one; repeated in various guises by the party leaders it generally suffices to ensure them a majority in party Congresses. These end at very most with partial reconstructions of the ministry; the fall of a government as a result of a party Congress is extremely rare under the two-party system. Real though it may be, the sapping of government authority by the activity of party militants is limited.

Under the presidential regime the foregoing schema is somewhat altered if presidency and parliamentary majority are held by the same party; in the contrary event, it is completely upset. In the former case the party establishes a link between the government and the assemblies as in the parliamentary regime; the President's leadership of the majority party gives him authority over parliament: party hierarchy reinforces government authority. But since the classic means for reciprocal action between Executive and Legislative do not exist in such a regime, they cannot be affected by dualism of parties; we do not therefore find any diminution in the prerogatives of parliament over government combined with maintenance of the prerogatives of government over parliament; the effect of dualism is more restricted. If parliamentary majority and presidency are controlled by different parties the effect is completely reversed: dualism ensures a homogeneous parliamentary majority which makes it possible for the assemblies to make an effective stand against the power of the President and to limit it in considerable measure. Separation of powers coincides with a decrease in the prerogatives of the government. The extent to which they are decreased depends on the extent of cohesion in the majority party and on its internal discipline, these factors both operating in the opposite direction to that described above: the more disciplined the majority party the greater its capacity to oppose the President and the weaker the authority of the government. On the other hand a heterogeneous and undisciplined majority party offering its opponents greater liberty of manœuvre and opportunity for intrigues strengthens the position of the presidency when this is controlled by the adversary and weakens it in the opposite case, as the example of America shows.

Weak internal party structure thus brings dualism nearer to multi-partism. The consequences of the latter system vary greatly according to the kind of political institution: multi-partism weakens the government in a parliamentary regime but tends to strengthen it under the presidential regime. The example of France compared with Great Britain provides a good illustration of the first case. The absence of a majority party makes it necessary to form heterogeneous French cabinets based upon a coalition, or else minority cabinets relying on the parliamentary support of neighbouring parties. The former are perpetually torn between the contradictory tendencies of their members, for here party solidarity operates against government solidarity instead of strengthening it. The division exists within the heart of the government: each allied party has to be on its guard not only against its declared enemies but also against its allies. Furthermore the latter represent its most dangerous enemies at election time, as we have seen, since the electoral campaign in a multi-party system is necessarily directed against nearest neighbours. A programme of government action is therefore possible only for a very short period, for limited objectives and very lukewarm measures. In fact the multi-party system leads to the rule of half-measures and a perpetual preoccupation with current affairs. Minority cabinets can scarcely function in any other way: they have the advantage of homogeneity but the disadvantage of less-assured parliamentary support; for these reasons they are as a general rule less common. It is more profitable to take allies on board the ship of state where they will share the responsibilities and the natural unpopularity of office than to let them take refuge in parliamentary support which is less obvious and less compromising in the eyes of the electorate. Except in Scandinavia minority ministries are generally transitional cabinets destined to open the way for a reversal of alliances or to show the impossibility of such a change.

Internally weak, multi-party governments are also weak in their relations with parliament. The separation of powers which here recovers reality and vigour is primarily of advantage to parliament: the upsetting of the balance works clearly in its favour. The means for action by the Legislative on the Executive again become completely effective, whereas the prerogatives of the ministry over the assembly entirely lose effect. Cabinet collapses which are exceptional and rare under the two-party system become normal and frequent and are scarcely mitigated by the fact that the same men are often to be found in different ministerial combinations. Interpellation, usually replaced by questions in the two-party system, becomes an essential means of controlling the government and further of endangering its existence; it always appears to be used politically rather than technically, generally rather than specifically. Finally, on the occasion of the voting of any motion the opposition tries to put the government in a minority without overthrowing it: parliament paralyses its initiative and is hostile to its wishes. In two-party systems the hold the cabinet has over the majority party allows it to obtain without serious difficulty the passage of the principal items of legislation and of the budget; in multi-party systems the coalition of majority parties hardly ever attains such a degree of discipline. Even when the government remains in power it generally remains impotent to secure the passage of its projects without considerable amendment, especially on questions that are electorally important.

Subject to very considerable pressure from parliament, the government disposes of no really effective power over it. Its basic weapon, the right of dissolution, loses any practical significance and turns into a cardboard sword. Here we must beware of a common confusion. Some observers view the absence of dissolution as the real source of the impotence of French ministries as compared with the authority of British cabinets; they see the parliamentary regime as a system of balance between Executive and Legislative in which dissolution is the parallel to the vote of no-confidence; the disappearance of the former coinciding with the preservation of the latter is, in their eyes, a tipping of the balance in favour of parliament, and has caused a weakening of government. This reasoning is much too abstract: the failure to use dissolution is less a cause than a consequence of ministerial weakness in a multi-party system. Under the Third Republic the right of dissolution existed; the cabinet did not use it because it did not dare, because it lacked the necessary energy to use it. In Weimar Germany the use of the right of dissolution did not strengthen the authority of the government; on the contrary, it ended simply by precipitating the collapse of the regime by ordaining its impotence. Dissolution ceases to be effective because it does not allow the electorate to give a clear expression of opinion and to designate the majority that conforms to its wishes. In a system with many independent parties, engendered by proportional representation, shifts in voting are too slight to alter appreciably the balance of forces inside parliament; the same ministerial combinations remain possible before and after dissolution, and no problem is solved. In an alliance system, engendered by the second ballot, less indefinite results may be achieved, but the see-saw tactics of the Centre party muffle the expression of the national will and lessen the significance of the election. In brief the right of dissolution is really effective only in a two-party system, and there it becomes useless for judging between parliament and government in proportion as party discipline and cohesion make such conflicts less probable; in fact dissolution tends here to serve as a method of shortening the life of parliaments with a view to avoiding 'final-year demagogy', and to causing elections at the moment judged most favourable by the party in power, which thus tries to compensate for the natural handicap under which the government labours, compared with the opposition, in the winning of votes.

The structure of parties and their respective strengths and alliances also have a bearing on the authority of government, but it is difficult to reach definite conclusions on these different points. The existence of a dominant party produces the most marked transformation. It strengthens the government and weakens the influence of parliament; if the dominant party is exceptionally in possession of an absolute majority, as has occurred in Norway and Sweden, there is a close similarity to the two-party system. However, the unusual and unstable character of this situation generally leads the governing party to show prudence: it often forgoes constituting a homogeneous ministry and prefers to share power with allies, not only in order to extend its parliamentary support and to share responsibility, but also in order to give the alliance a normal and habitual appearance which will allow it to retain power should it lose its absolute majority. The mentality of coalition ministries peculiar to multi-partism even persists in the exceptional cases where such a coalition is no longer necessary. If the dominant party is reduced to a minority by the alliance of all its rivals, the situation of the government is on the other hand much weakened, the majority being ill-assorted, heterogeneous, and undisciplined compared with a compact, powerful, and unified minority. Moreover the general public which has come to consider the presence in power of the dominant party as 'quasi-legitimate' is always somewhat disturbed by such coalitions, and this decreases still further the prestige of the government.

A system of close and stable alliances may also transform the foregoing schemas and reduce the gap between multi-partism and bipartism; in so far as a true dualism of alliances is established the situation resembles a dualism of parties. None the less homogeneity and discipline are always much less developed within an alliance than inside a unified party; the authority of the government is therefore less considerable and the liberty of action of parliament consequently greater. If one of the allied groups assumes a dominant position with respect to the other, because of disproportion in strength or in structure, the cohesion of the alliances may be more developed and the similarity to bipartism more marked. Centralization and party discipline have less definite consequences. On the one hand they render government coalitions more difficult and more superficial, because of the strength of party ties which prevent the individuals coming from different parties from collaborating effectively in a common task; on the other hand they increase their stability by diminishing the influence of intrigues and changes of individual attitude amongst the parliamentary representatives. It might almost be said that in a multi-party system disciplined and centralized parties produce relatively stable but impotent governments and that undisciplined and decentralized parties produce less impotent and less stable governments. A comparison between the Third Republic and the early years of the Fourth will illustrate this contrast. Before 1939 the weakness of parties allowed of relatively homogeneous cabinets in which individuals from different political groups were willing to accept the authority of a common leader because of his personal prestige, (e.g. Waldeck-Rousseau, Clemenceau, Briand, Poincaré); some ministries enjoyed real unity of outlook and quite considerable power; but lack of discipline among the parties in coalition and the perpetual interplay of personal intrigues condemned them to a marked degree of instability. In the period 1945–7, on the contrary, the rigid discipline of parties forbade any ministerial homogeneity, any real authority for the head of the government, and condemned ministries to impotence; but the same discipline ensured the cohesion of the majority and tended to stability of government; a vote of no-confidence was inconceivable. Nevertheless the preceding formulae are too exact and too rigid to give a true interpretation of a state of affairs that is fluid and ill-defined.

In a presidential regime multi-partism tends rather to increase the authority of government and to decrease that of parliament. If there is opposition in parliament between the presidential party and the majority party the increase in authority is very marked by comparison with bipartism: instead of finding itself confronted in parliament with a homogeneous and coherent majority the Executive finds only a heterogeneous coalition, and this gives scope for dividing and destroying tactics. The situation is even more favourable to it than in the case when dualism is accompanied by an absence of internal party discipline; rivalries are more pronounced between different parties than between individuals within the same party (in the U.S.A., however, the lack of party homogeneity is so marked that the difference is not appreciable). If presidency and parliamentary majority are controlled by the same party multi-partism gives the government less authority than does bipartism, since the President cannot use his power as leader of the majority party to bring pressure to bear on parliament. None the less the government is infinitely stronger than in a parliamentary regime. It retains the two features of which multi-partism deprives it under the parliamentary regime: homogeneity and stability. Parliament may oppose its plans for legislation but it cannot overthrow it or break it up; the government on the other hand can foster parliamentary intrigues with the aid of the deputies who support it in order to break up the coalition of parties embarrassing it, to reconstitute them after its own desire and especially to encourage temporary alliances for each particular Bill.

Multi-partism causes an even deeper transformation in the structure of the presidential regime: it increases its personal character. In a two-party system the parties are big enough to dwarf the President who appears to be more the leader of one of them than an independent personality. In a multi-party system, on the other hand, the tall figure of the President stands out alone from a mass of parties: his membership of one of them gives him no prestige because it is a minority party unable to govern by itself. The popular majority cast for him takes on a personal character. No party can claim to be the representative of the nation, the President alone may do so. Parliamentary majorities are the result of alliances between parties in which the wishes of party organizers play as great a part as the indications of the ballot-box; in contrast the President may validly claim that a popular majority has found clear expression in his person. The natural impotence of multi-partism emphasizes with even greater clarity the privileged position of the President, who is alone able to act effectively and with continuity. It is the natural course for multi-party presidential regimes to tend to personal power; much strength of character is required in the holders of the Presidency to resist a temptation that is made almost irresistible by the nature of the system. The term 'temptation' suggests that personal power is considered as an evil but the evolution of power inside parties has shown that this idea is gradually losing ground.

Parties and the Function of the Opposition. A distinction has already been made between a horizontal separation of powers based upon a classification of the activities of the state into sectors and the old traditional separation of Legislature from Executive. Even upon the vertical plane itself the latter separation is gradually losing importance in favour of a new distinction between the functions of government and the functions of opposition. The existence of an organized opposition is an essential feature of 'Western' democracy, its absence a feature of 'Eastern' democracy. Many indications might be discovered in the course of history of such a separate organization of the opposition: in the time of the Republic of Rome the creation of the tribunes of the *plebs* provided with the right of *intercessio* would correspond exactly to the notion, in the beginning at least; later the Church played this kind of role towards the feudal monarchs of the Middle Ages. From the eighteenth century onwards the functions of the opposition were no longer separately organized; instead of creating within the state separate institutions in opposition to the true institutions of government, rivalry was established within the ranks of the latter: the same general aim was pursued by 'limiting power by power', by creating an opposition within the government instead of outside it. The separation of the Legislative from the Executive was originally due to this idea; alongside the king, an assembly was established to limit him. The subtle distinction between legislative actions and executive actions had the sole aim of legitimizing the distinction by a technical division of functions: the separation of powers has come to be considered as a consequence of the division of labour. Once the monarch had disappeared, the Jacobin experiment having shown the dangers of a concentration of powers in the hands of the Convention, new embodiments of the functions of opposition were sought, always in the form of internal rivalry between different organs of government. The two-chamber system corresponds to the same idea. The contemporary development of political parties, while simultaneously modifying the classic separation of powers, has transformed the function of the opposition by giving it once again expression external to the government in a separate body: minority parties are the heirs of the tribunes of the *plebs*.

In a single-party system, however, external opposition does not exist. In the Supreme Soviet in Moscow there are indeed 'non-party' deputies just as there were 'independent' deputies in the Ankara National Assembly after the failure of Fethi Bey, but both are elected on the party lists and chosen by the party. The real opposition, in a single-party system, is found inside the party. It here takes the form of dissident groups, of minority tendencies which criticize the government at party meetings with varying degrees of freedom; they may even find expression on the parliamentary level as we have seen in Turkey. In Soviet Russia organized fractions continued to exist inside the Communist party until about 1934; they played quite an important role in the days of Lenin and the early years of Stalinism. In Italy the Fascist party always displayed a clear division into Left, Right, and Centre. In Germany there were quite serious differences in the Nazi party before 1934. The present-day Russian Communist party is developing a quite original system of internal opposition in the form of 'self-criticism': the members and leaders of the party at all levels are continually invited to undertake personal criticism of their own actions and to realize their own shortcomings. Properly speaking this technique is more akin to public confession than to the function of the opposition; its aim is less to give form to any resistance to the regime than to overcome such resistance. Self-criticism seems to be used chiefly to secure orthodoxy and strict obedience at all levels; it is complementary to the system of purges and expulsions: the act of self-criticism consists in recognizing one's errors in relation to the party leaders and in obtaining the right to remain within the party community. In the nature of things therefore an analysis of the influence of parties upon the function of the opposition must primarily deal with systems of more than one party.

Multi-partism and bipartism give rise to quite different structures. The two-party system tends to make the opposition into a real institution. To the division of functions between government and opposition there corresponds an equally definite distinction in the organizational sphere between majority party and minority party; the coexistence of the two distinctions brings about a real separation of powers in the technical sense attributed by lawyers to that term. In Great Britain the allocation to the leader of the minority party of a salary paid by the state together with the official title of 'Leader of the Opposition to Her Majesty's Government' really gives the opposition the status of an official body. In a multi-party system this institutional form is eschewed because the line of demarcation between opposition and government is not clear. Some governments are supported by shifting majorities leaning on the Right to secure the passage of some measures, on the Left for others: in such cases any distinction between government and opposition disappears. Even when the government is supported by a more clearly defined majority, this is not so distinct and stable as under the two-party system: individuals or small groups pass from one side to the other of the line of demarcation; there are incessant intrigues to alter or overthrow alliances. Finally the opposition is composed of heterogeneous elements, often even more heterogeneous than those of the majority: it is easier to secure agreement *in opposition* to a policy than *in support* of a policy; it is even possible for individuals to gather together in opposition without any real agreement, as occurs in the case of a 'meeting of extremes'. Here no real organization assumes the function of opposition.

In a two-party system the unified opposition remains however a moderate opposition; the very conditions of political warfare which imply a certain alternation between the parties, and the possibility that today's opposition will tomorrow assume the sole responsibility of office, preserve it from any exaggerated demagogy which might react to its disadvantage. The tendency to court the Centre in electoral campaigns operates in the same direction. On the other hand in a multi-party system the oppositions tend naturally to be demagogic as a result of a converse process: not being threatened with the possibility of having to make good their words, opposition parties can indulge in unlimited criticisms and promises. The very tendency of the electoral conflict, which leads each to fight against its nearest neighbour, encourages the opponents to outbid each other, and favours domination by the extremes. This violent opposition remains however a confused opposition. The differences among the parties who form it and their mutual rivalries prevent any clear alternatives being offered to public opinion for it to express its will. The fact that the line of demarcation between opposition and government is often difficult to draw, and the frequent existence of two oppositions, poles apart, adds further to the confusion. By contrast the opposition under a two-party system remains distinct in spite of its moderation, that is to say that public opinion can grasp with some accuracy the difference between the points of view of the majority and of the minority and so can choose with full knowledge of the facts. In parliamentary debates and in electoral campaigns two major solutions are face to face, simplified and generalized no doubt, but allowing both deputies and electors a definite choice. The definiteness of the opposition seems to constitute an essential factor for its effectiveness as well as for the strength of the democratic regime.

In a multi-party system confusion is increased by the fact that a distinction has to be made between an external opposition provided by the parties of the minority and an internal opposition existing amongst the majority parties themselves. Government decisions are the result of a compromise between the parties associated in office, but each of them reserves the right to defend its own point of view to its militants and its electors and consequently to criticize the compromise reached by the government by making its allies responsible for the shortcomings; each of the government allies acts in opposition to its own government. The whole technique of such internal opposition consists in differentiating between immediate practical necessities and the long-term structural reforms that are part of the party's doctrine; the former provide an excuse for taking part in the government which is criticized in the name of the latter. Consequently internal opposition is easier and more effective the more coherent and truly revolutionary the party's doctrine, so that opposition does not appear to the electorate as a pretext designed to excuse co-operation in the ministry. This is the explanation for the mastery displayed by Communist parties in the matter of opposition from within that was so evident in the 1945 coalitions in France, Italy, and elsewhere: their organization, leadership, and doctrine banished the suspicion that they might be turning 'bourgeois' and abandoning their primary aims for the sake of the immediate advantages of a share of power. They remained somewhat alien inside 'Bourgeois' and Social Democratic governments, and this enabled them to break away easily. The use of ancillary organizations (Trade Unions, Fronts, and so on) which remain outside the ranks of government, increases the effectiveness of internal opposition.

The number of parties is not alone in affecting the nature and form of the oppposition: alliances, party strength, internal organization also play their part. The role of opposition is not exercised in the same way by a major party, which groups many diverse and often contradictory interests, as by a minor party which groups only a few individuals of intractable temperament or a few interests that are particularly well defined: the second category is naturally more demagogic and extravagant than the first. The social heterogeneity of a party is perhaps more important than its strength: a party representing a single social class and relatively homogeneous may adopt a more clear-cut and uncompromising attitude than a party representing several classes with divergent interests, or a heterogeneous class (like the 'bourgeoisie' or the 'middle classes'). However the parties have invented a technique which enables them to avoid the disadvantages of heterogeneity: it might be termed 'sectional opposition'. The aim is to support separately the claims of each social group by means of strictly differentiated campaigns, ensuring as complete a separation as possible between them: campaigns are simultaneously waged in support of farm workers' demands for increased agricultural prices and in support of industrial workers' demands for keeping down food prices; in support of the desire of tradesmen and industrialists for 'private enterprise' and of the desire of wage-earners for 'controls'. A study of the specialized journals of the parties (for industrial workers, farm workers, etc.) would demonstrate the increasing development of these sectional campaigns.

The existence of a dominant party seems also to produce certain effects upon opposition. If domination is prolonged the opposition is reduced to impotence; such a situation occurs chiefly under the two-party system, which it modifies considerably. It sometimes happens that the opposition, being kept long out of office, assumes a more violent and extravagant attitude. What particularly happens is that the country gradually loses interest in political campaigns and elections, because they are ineffective. In this respect, a comparison between the Southern states of America and Switzerland before the introduction of P.R. is most instructive. In Switzerland from 1874 onwards the Radical party enjoyed uncontested domination; holding an absolute majority in spite of multi-partism it ruled alone with no fear of being overthrown. In the Southern states the Democratic party has been predominant since the Civil War (in some states the Republican party is so weak that they might almost be said to have a single-party regime). In both cases the existence of a dominant party is the result of a civil war; but the Swiss Radical party prolonged the federal domination of the victor (as did the Republican party in America until 1912 except for two short periods); on the other hand the American Democratic party represents the reaction of the defeated states (as does the Catholic party in the Sonderbund Cantons). In any case the same state of indifference has occurred in both countries: the number of abstentions was higher in Switzerland before P.R. than in any other European country, attaining more than 50% of the electorate in 1914; it is even higher in some Southern states of the U.S.A. where it exceeds 90% of the citizens of voting age. In Switzerland the development of the referendum and of popular initiative had to some extent palliated these disadvantages and restored to the opposition an effectiveness of which long-term domination was depriving it. In America the system of primaries, facilitating the growth of factions inside the Democratic party and the rise of internal oppositions works in the same direction but with much less efficiency, Southern primaries not being counted amongst the most regular and well attended.

Solid and homogeneous coalitions may give a multi-party system a close resemblance to a two-party system and make the opposition more coherent, more moderate, and more distinct. Conversely a two-party system in which the parties are lacking in discipline, centralisation, and organization may have an opposition often nearer in its operation to the multi-party than to the two-party pattern. In the United States, at the parliamentary level, the opposition works more like that in France than that in Britain. At the electoral level things are somewhat different, for the struggle remains restricted to two opponents, one supporting the government, the other criticizing it. The campaign for the Presidency remains moderate, clearly defined, and not very demagogic because it is possible that either candidate may be entrusted with the responsibility of government. Campaigns for the Senate and the House of Representatives are quite different.

Finally the nature of the opposition is bound up with the general context of the party conflict. Here three different types can be discerned: a conflict without principles, a conflict over subsidiary principles, a conflict over basic principles. In the United States the first type is the rule: the two parties are rival teams, one occupying office, the other seeking to dislodge it. It is a struggle between the *ins* and the *outs*, which never becomes fanatical, and creates no deep cleavage in the country. It may be criticized for depriving the opposition of any real significance, for diminishing its role in the state, for decreasing democracy by taking from the elections any validity as a choice between policies. American elections interpret public opinion very poorly: the very machinery of party conflict prevents opinion from forming itself clearly and adopting an attitude on the major problems which overshadow the existence and the future of the greatest nation in the world. The 'parochialism' of American politics is not only the result of having small single-member constituencies (after all, Senators are elected by states which are sometimes immense constituencies), but even more of the total absence of doctrine and principle amongst the political parties, which gives pride of place to interests and quite naturally to particular local interests which are closer at hand and clearer. In presidential elections the absence of principle emphasizes the personal nature of the campaign.

Great Britain and Northern Europe (including Western Germany) come into the second category. The division between parties corresponds to a doctrinal and social division. Conservative and Labour, for example, each hold different views on production and the distribution of wealth, on the distribution of incomes, on the organization and promotion of the elite, and they represent two opposed groups: the party division coincides approximately with the stratification of society. None the less these parties remain in agreement on the basic principles of the political regime; they do not question the democratic set-up, the right of each man to freedom of speech, the need for free and open elections implying the existence of more than one party. Each party accepts the rules of the game and this allows all to exist. The difference in doctrines and social sub-structure does not prevent them living side by side: the opposition assumes a solidity and a definiteness that it cannot attain in the United States, but does not endanger its own existence. No party yearns after monopoly and totality, and this ensures the strength of the regime.

In France and Italy political warfare is quite different in appearance. It is not concerned with subsidiary principles but with the very foundations of the state and the nature of the regime. The Communist parties do not accept Western democracy, do not agree with pluralism of parties, which they would replace by a single party, and do not recognize any right of opposition or of freedom of speech for all. The non-Communist parties refuse to countenance the single-party system, the totalitarian view of the state, the destruction of the opposition and the suppression of political liberties. Between these two groups rivalry assumes the character, not of a sporting fight between two rival teams but of a struggle to the death, with the difference that the fatal blow can only come from one side: the seizure of power by the Communists would entail the suppression of the other parties; government by the latter would on the contrary mean toleration of the Communist party by them unless they were to forswear their principles. This third type of party struggle is not restricted to those states which have a strong Communist party; it is common to all that have a totalitarian party organized like a *Bund*, as soon as such a party acquires a certain power; 1920 Italy belonged to this category although it had no Communist party. Division over basic principles is much more a party issue than an issue between voters. In France, for example, Communist voters are undoubtedly just as attached as others to freedom of speech, to respect for the opposition and the political forms of democracy. In Italy the middle classes who bore Fascism to power probably had no desire for a dictatorship. But the very nature and techniques of organization of totalitarian parties enable them to neglect such internal opposition when they are in office. It is superfluous to emphasize the brittleness of this third type; by definition it only remains viable so long as the totalitarian party remains in opposition or so long as it only collaborates to a very slight extent in government. If it is in office alone, it suppresses its rivals; if it collaborates extensively in government, it makes a start on the process of disintegrating its rivals which we have described.

Such a political regime is therefore possible only with a multi-party system. The two-party system is inconceivable as soon as one of the parties becomes totalitarian in nature, for alternation would sooner or later bring it to power and simultaneously wreck the two-party system. The establishment of a two-party system is conceivable in Germany as a result of the operation of the law for simple-majority elections, but not in France or Italy, for there one of the two rivals would be the Communist party. Of course the natural tendency towards moderation that is produced by the operation of the two-party system would end by slowly destroying the totalitarian nature of the Communist party and ending its *Bund*-like character, *if the party agreed to observe the rules*. But its nature and character do in fact exclude such a possibility; at the very first electoral victory of the Communists the two-party arrangement would be suppressed. In a multi-party system, on the contrary, the presence of a totalitarian party may be prolonged in so far as it is restricted to opposition or to very slight participation in the government: the normal functioning of the system prohibits its obtaining an absolute majority and claiming office in isolation. It is enough for the other parties to have realized the dominating and disintegrating role that it plays in every alliance because of its structure for it to be isolated and any serious threat to the regime warded off. However, the life of the regime will be much more difficult, since the totalitarian party is naturally more intransigent and more implacable in opposition than the others, as well as being more efficient (on account of its structure, of which the technical superiority has been described).

The political situation which results favours the growth of opposition totalitarian parties, and herein lies the gravest peril for the regime. Fascist propaganda finds extremely fruitful material in exploiting the fundamental inequalities between the Communist party and its democratic rivals. The latter are prevented by their principles from destroying it as it would in their place destroy them; their less developed structure makes them vulnerable to its propaganda, whereas it is much less sensitive to theirs; government responsibilities lose them popularity whereas its attitude of permanent opposition allows it full scope for demagogy. By harping on these themes, Fascist parties increase the natural fear of Communism among its opponents and gradually attract their supporters away from the democratic parties; the corresponding weakening of these gives Fascist propaganda added force and this accelerates the process: caught between two rival totalitarian parties the non-totalitarian parties are threatened with collapse. This Fascist dialectic is today checked by memories of the war: their collaboration with the occupying Power and their share in crimes against humanity have caused the banning of Fascist parties created before 1945; the cloud which hangs over them alienates also their possible imitators. Time however is slowly breaking down these barriers. If the democratic regimes do not succeed in stabilizing and weakening their Communist parties, not by police measures, which would be contrary to their principles, but by a transformation of their economic and social sub-structure, they will be as helpless in the face of Neo-Fascism as Weimar Germany was in the face of Hitlerism. They will not long escape the infection of Fascism if they allow the conditions for Fascism to develop.

CONCLUSION

It is not perhaps unnecessary to remind readers here that the descriptions given in this work are provisional and hypothetical in character, often being based on documentation too restricted and cursory to permit of definite conclusions. Frequently we have had to draw imaginary lines to link the few shining points scattered in the dark: the resultant patterns can give only a very approximate idea of reality. The development of the science of political parties (it could perhaps be called *stasiology*) will no doubt lead to the revision of many of the patterns we have traced. None the less some general phenomena seem more or less established, and from them some general conclusions can be drawn.

The opponents of 'party systems' will find much ammunition in this book. The organization of political parties is certainly not in conformity with orthodox notions of democracy. Their internal structure is essentially autocratic and oligarchic: their leaders are not really appointed by the members, in spite of appearances, but co-opted or nominated by the central body; they tend to form a ruling class, isolated from the militants, a caste that is more or less exclusive. In so far as they are elected, the party oligarchy is widened without ever becoming a democracy, for the election is carried out by the members, who are a minority in comparison with those who give their votes to the party in general elections. Parliamentary representatives are increasingly subject to the authority of the party inner circle: this means that the mass of electors is dominated by the small group of members and militants, itself subordinate to the ruling bodies of the party. The argument must be carried further: even supposing that parties were ruled by parliamentary representatives it would be an illusion to think them democratic. For elections themselves ill-interpret the true state of opinion. Parties create opinion as much as they represent it; they form it by propaganda; they impose a prefabricated mould upon it: the party system is not only the reflection of public opinion but also the result of external technical factors (like ballot procedure) which are imposed upon opinion.

The party system is less a photograph of opinion than opinion is a projection of the party system.

The general development of parties tends to emphasize their deviation from the democratic regime. Growing centralization is increasingly diminishing the influence of members over leaders, while on the other hand strengthening the influence of leaders upon members. Electoral processes are gradually losing ground in the appointment of leaders: co-option or nomination from above, which used to be modestly veiled, are now partially acknowledged in constitutions and sometimes loudly proclaimed as a sign of progress (in Fascist parties). The development of vertical linking and the watertight compartments which are the result restrict the freedom of action of the base and increase the sphere of influence of the apex; they make possible a close regimentation of party members that can prevent any move towards independence of the centre and can preserve strict orthodoxy. Discipline among members is tightened both by these material means and by an even greater effort of propaganda and persuasion which leads them to venerate the Party and its leaders and to believe in their infallibility: the critical attitude gives way to an attitude of adoration. Parliamentary representatives themselves are compelled to an obedience which transforms them into voting machines controlled by the leaders of the party. Thus there arise closed, disciplined, mechanized bodies, monolithic parties whose organization outwardly resembles that of an army, but whose methods of regimentation are infinitely more adaptable and efficient, being based on a training of minds rather than of bodies. Their hold over men is strengthened: parties become totalitarian. They require of their members closer adherence; they provide complete and final philosophies of the universe. Zeal, faith, enthusiasm, and intolerance are the rule in these modern churches: party struggles turn into religious wars.

But would a system without parties be more satisfactory? That is the real question. Would opinion be better represented if candidates were to present themselves individually before the electorate without it being able really to know their attitudes? Would liberty be better preserved if the government found itself faced with only a scattering of individuals not grouped in political formations?

We are living on a completely artificial notion of democracy forged by lawyers on the basis of eighteenth-century philosophical ideas. 'Government of the people by the people', 'Government of the nation by its representatives', these are fine phrases for arousing enthusiasm and fashioning eloquent perorations. Fine phrases with an empty ring. No people has ever been known to govern itself and none ever will. All government is oligarchic: it necessarily implies the domination of the many by a few. Rousseau, whom his commentators have forgotten to read, was well aware of this: 'In the strict sense of the term, no true democracy has ever existed and none will ever exist. It is contrary to the natural order for the majority to rule and the minority to be ruled.'[1] The will of the people is profoundly anarchic: it wants to do as it pleases. It vaguely considers government as a necessary evil: its instinctive attitude towards it is hostility. Alain has given a remarkable analysis of the natural conflict between the governors and the governed. All government implies discipline. All discipline is imposed from without: 'self-discipline' is itself the result of education, which implies a prior external discipline, and is always very limited. Government and constraint are inseparable, but by definition constraint is external to the constrained. A people does not constrain itself; it is constrained. It does not govern itself; it is governed. To proclaim the identity of governors and governed, of constrainers and constrained is an admirable way of justifying the obedience of the latter to the former. It is pure abstraction and verbal juggling.

True democracy is something different, more modest but more real. It is defined in the first place as liberty 'for the people and for all sections of the people', as the 1793 Constituents put it. Not only liberty for those privileged by birth, fortune, position, or education, but real liberty for all, and this implies a certain standard of living, a certain basic education, some kind of social equality, some kind of political equilibrium. The Marxist distinction between nominal liberties and real liberties is only partly correct; it is true that the political liberties recognized by Western regimes remain a formality for a large section of the masses for lack of an adequate standard of living, of adequate education, of social equality or of an adequate political equilibrium. Yet they may become real liberties: there is no point in beginning by suppressing them. Now the study of contemporary political phenomena reveals one obvious fact: in countries which have attained a certain degree of material civilization and a certain standard of living (Europe, North America, Great Britain and the white Dominions), liberty and the party system

[1] *Social Contract*, Book III, Ch. IV.

coincide. In the nineteenth century, when economic and financial powers alone disposed of the Press, of techniques of information and propaganda and of a means of organizing the electorate, democracy did not exist: the rise of parties and especially of working-class parties has alone made possible any real and active co-operation by the whole people in political affairs. Even totalitarian parties, like the Communist party, make a contribution in some countries to the existence of democracy: their suppression in France and Italy would threaten to strengthen (for a time at least) the conservative elements, and so to upset the equilibrium which ensures a minimum of liberty to every 'section of the people': the existence of more than one party is both the cause and the reflection of this equilibrium.

In countries where the standard of living and education of the people are still much inferior (Asia, Africa, South America) the coincidence no longer occurs. Here parties are formal in character: rival factions struggle for power, using the voters as a soft dough to be kneaded as they will; corruption develops and the privileged classes take advantage of the situation to prolong their control. Under certain circumstances, the single party may provide a first organization of the masses, enabling them gradually to acquire some political training; the authoritarian regime it produces may suppress feudal systems of all kinds and conditions and create the economic and social conditions required for the future development of political liberty. The structure of the transitional regime must however be such that it will not destroy all hope of later liberal developments.

At the same time the system makes it possible to form a ruling class, sprung from the people, to replace the old. On this question, pluralist and single-party regimes are at one. The deepest significance of political parties is that they tend to the creation of new elites, and this restores to the notion of representation its true meaning, the only real one. All government is by nature oligarchic but the origins and the training of the oligarchs may be very different and these determine their actions. The formula 'Government of the people by the people' must be replaced by this formula 'Government of the people *by an elite sprung from the people*'. A regime without parties ensures the permanence of ruling elites chosen by birth, wealth, or position: to secure admission to the governing oligarchy a man of the people must accomplish a considerable effort to rise above his initial position; he must also work his way up the ladder of middle-class education and lose contact with the class in which he was born. A regime without parties is of necessity a conservative regime. It corresponds to the property franchise or else to an attempt to cripple universal suffrage by imposing on the people leaders who do not come from their ranks; it is further removed from democracy than the party regime. Historically speaking parties were born when the masses of the people really made their entrance into political life; they provided the necessary framework enabling the masses to recruit from among themselves their own elites. Parties are always more developed on the Left than on the Right because they are always more necessary on the Left than on the Right. To suppress them would be an admirable way for the Right to paralyse the Left. The classic protests against their interference in political life, against the domination exercised by militants over deputies, by Congresses and committees over parliament take no account of the capital developments of the last fifty years which have accentuated the formal character of ministers and parliaments. Whereas they were once exclusively the instruments of private, financial and economic interests, they have today become instruments in the hands of the parties, amongst which the place of mass parties is becoming increasingly important. This transformation represents an advance of democracy, not a retreat. From this point of view the single party itself represents a progress if it is not compared with pluralist systems but considered within the framework proper to it, dictatorship. A dictatorship with a single people's party tending to create a new ruling class is nearer to democracy than party-less dictatorships of the personal or military type which strengthen the feudal powers in their control.

Democracy is not threatened by the party regime but by present-day trends in party internal organization: the danger does not lie in the existence of parties but in the military, religious, and totalitarian form they sometimes assume. Two further facts of importance must be emphasized in this connection. All parties have not adopted the same kind of organization. In Great Britain, Canada Australia, Northern Europe, the only groups to display this tendency are small and uninfluential. The same is true of the United States where the development of primaries has had the result of weakening party organization rather than strengthening it. Closed totalitarian parties of the *Bund* type still remain the exception throughout the world: if evolution is to lead towards them, it has scarcely yet begun and many factors may check it or deflect it.

From another point of view certain features in these new party structures ensure an admirable training of the political leading strata as well as closer and more faithful contact between the mass of the people and their ruling elites; isolated from their context, these features might increase the democratic nature of parties instead of destroying it. The real way of protecting democracy against the toxins that it secretes within itself in the course of its development does not lie in cutting it off from modern techniques for organizing the masses and recruiting leaders—such an operation would make of it an empty vessel, a vain show—but in diverting these to its use, for they are in the last resort mere tools, capable no doubt of being used for good as well as for evil. To refuse to use them is to refuse to act. If it were true that democracy is incompatible with them, this would no doubt mean that democracy is incompatible with the conditions of the present day. All the speeches upon the benefits of craftsmanship and the evils of industrialization do not alter the fact that the artisan's day is done and that we live in an age of mass-production; regrets for the individualist and decentralized cadre parties of the nineteenth century and imprecations against the vast centralized and disciplined parties of today do not alter the fact that the latter alone suit the structure of contemporary societies.

BIBLIOGRAPHICAL NOTE

MOST works devoted to parties deal chiefly with the development of their doctrines and their social composition: very few treat of their internal organization and of their influence on the political system which are the subject of this study. This book is based primarily upon first-hand documentation: the statistics, constitutions, and pamphlets of various political parties, information communicated by their secretariats, personal investigation amongst their leaders and members. The bibliography proper is made up primarily of the following works:

BOOK I

PARTY ORGANIZATION

BAILEY, S. D. (ed.), *The British Party System*, London, 1952.

BRAYANCE, A., *Anatomie du parti communiste français*, Paris, 1953.

BULMER-THOMAS, I., *The Party System in Great Britain*, London, 1953.

BRYCE, J., *Modern Democracies*, revd., New York, 1921.

The American Commonwealth, Vol. III, London, 1888.

DUVERGER, M. (*et al.*), *Partis politiques et classes sociales*, Paris, 1955.

EINAUDI, M. and GOGUEL, F., *Christian Democracy in Italy and France*, Notre Dame, Indiana, 1952.

EINAUDI, M., DOMENACH, J. M. and GAROSCI, A., *Communism in Western Europe*, Ithaca, New York, 1951.

FAUVET, J., *Les forces politiques en France*, Paris, 1951.

FUSILIER, R., *Le parti ouvrier social-democrate suédois*, Paris, 1954.

GOGUEL, F., *La vie politique de la société française contemporaine* (Cours de l'Institut d'Etudes Politiques de Paris, 1948–9).

La vie politique et les partis en France (Id., 1950–1).

HARTMANN, *Die politische Partei*, Brünn, 1931.

HESNARD, O., *Les partis politiques en Allemagne*, Paris, 1923.

HEYDRE, F. VON DER and SACHERL, K., *Soziologie der deutschen Parteien*, Munich, 1955.

HOFFMANN, S., *Le Mouvement Poujade*, Paris, 1956.

LIPSET, S. M., *Agrarian Socialism* (*The C.C.F. in Saskatchewan*), Los Angeles, 1950.

LONGUET, J., *Le mouvement socialiste international* (Encyclopédie socialiste, syndicale et coopérative de l'Internationale ouvrière), Paris, 1913.

LOUIS, P., *Le Parti socialiste en France* (Encyclopédie socialiste, syndicale et coopérative de l'Internationale ouvrière), Paris, 1912.

LAWRENCE LOWELL, A., *Governments and Parties in Continental Europe*, 2 vols., London, 1896.

MACKENZIE, R. T., *British Political Parties*, 1954.

MCHENRY, D. E., *The Labour Party in Transition*, London, 1938.

MENDIETA Y NUNEZ, L., *Los partidos politicos*, Mexico, 1947.

MICHELS, R., *Political Parties*, (Eng. trans. 1st ed.) London, 1915; *Zur Soziologie des Parteienwesens in der modernen Demokratie*, 2nd ed., Leipzig, 1925.

MILHAUD, E., *La Démocratie socialiste allemande*, Paris, 1913.

MONNEROT, J., *Sociology of Communism*, London, 1953.

MOSS, W., *Political Parties in the Irish Free State*, New York, 1933.

NAPOLITANO, *Il Partito Communista dell' U.R.S.S.*, Rome, 1945.

OSTROGORSKI, M., *Democracy and the Organization of Political Partis*, 2 vols., London, 1902.

OVERACKER, L., *The Australian Party System*, New Haven, 1952.

PELLOUX, R., *Le Parti national-socialiste et ses rapports avec l'Etat*, Paris, 1936.

PRÉLOT, M., *L'évolution politique du socialisme français*, Paris, 1939.

REZETTE, R., *Les partis politiques marocains*, Paris, 1954.

ROSSI, A., *Physiologie du Parti communiste français*, Paris, 1948.

SEURIN, J. L., *La structure interne des partis politiques américains*, Paris, 1953.

WALTER, G., *Histoire du Parti communiste français, Paris*, 1948.

To these may be added the many American publications describing American parties, especially:

BONE, H. A., *American Politics and the Party System*, New York, 1949.

COUSENS, T. W., *Politics and Political Organization in America*, New York, 1948.

HERRING, P., *The Politics of Democracy*, New York, 1940.

HOLCOMBE, A. N., *Political Parties of Today*, New York, 1924.

KEY, V. O., *Politics, Parties and Pressure Groups*, New York, 1950.
Southern Politics, New York, 1950.

MERRIAM, C. E. and GOSNELL, H. F., *The American Party System*, 4th ed., New York, 1949.

OVERACKER, L., *Money in Elections*, New York, 1932.

Parties and Politics (Annals of the Academy of Political and Social Science, September 1948).

POLLOCK, J. K., *Money and Politics Abroad*, New York, 1932.

RAPNEY, A., *The Doctrine of Responsible Party Government*, Urbana, 1954.

SAIT, E. M., *American Parties and Elections*, 3rd ed., New York, 1942 (bibliography).

SCHATTSCHNEIDER, E. E., *Party Government*, New York, 1942 (bibliography).

Towards a More Responsible Two-party System. Report of the Committee on Political Parties of American Political Science Association (supplement to the *American Political Science Review*, September, 1950).

BOOK II—PARTY SYSTEMS

ASSOCIATION FRANÇAISE DE SCIENCE POLITIQUE, *Les élections du 2 janvier* 1956, Paris, 1957.

ARRIGHI, P., *Le statut des partis politiques*, Paris, 1948.

BUTLER, D. E., *The British General Election*, London, 1952.

CADART, J., *Régime électoral et régime parlementaire en Angleterre*, Paris, 1948.

DURANT, H. W., *Political Opinion*, London, 1948.

DUVERGER, M., *L'influence des systèmes électoraux sur la vie politique* (with F. Goguel, J. Cadart, G. de Loÿs, S. Mastellone, A. Soulier, A. Vlachos), Paris, 1950.

GOGUEL, F., *La politique des partis sous la Troisième République*, Paris, 1946.

GOSNELL, H. F., *Why Europe Votes*, Chicago, 1930.

GUÉRIN, D., *Fascisme et grand capital*, 2nd ed., Paris, 1945.

HAMMER, *Regierung, Parlament, politische Partei und ihre Wechselbeziehungen*, 1929.

HERMENS, F. A., *Democracy or Anarchy?*, 1941.

HOGAN, J., *Election and Representation*, Oxford, 1945.

KOELLREUTTER, O., *Die politischen Parteien im modernen Staat* Breslau, 1926.

—— *Der Deutsche Staat als Bundesstaat und als Parteienstaat*, 1927.
LACHENAL, F., *Le parti politique, sa fonction en droit public*, Bâle, 1944.
LAVAU, G. E., *Paris politiques et réalités sociales*, Paris, 1953.
LIÑARES QUINTANA, S., *Los partidos políticos, instrumentos de gobierno*, Buenos Aires, 1945.
MANOÏLESCO, M., *Le Parti unique*, Paris, 1936.
MABILEAU, A., *Le parti libéral dans le système constitutionnel britannique*, Paris, 1953.
MCCALLUM, R. B. and READMAN, A., *The British General Election of 1945*, London, 1947.
NAWIASKY, H., *Die Zukunft der politischen Parteien*, 1924.
NICHOLAS, H. G., *The British General Election of 1950*, London, 1951.
PRÉLOT, M., *L'Empire fasciste*, Paris, 1936.
ROHDEN, P. R., ed., *Demokratie und partei*, Vienna, 1932.
ROSS, J. F. S., *Parliamentary Representation*, 2nd ed., London, 1948.
SCHREIBER, W., *Die geltenden Wahlrechtsgründsätze und die Frage der Splitterparteien*, 1931.
SIEGFRIED, A., *L'évolution politique de la France de l'Ouest sous la Troisième République*, Paris, 1913.
Tableau des partis en France, Paris, 1931.
Géographie électorale du département de l'Ardèche, Paris, 1950.
SOULIER, A., *L'instabilité ministérielle sous la Troisième République (1871–1938)*, Paris, 1939.
STELLING-MICHAUD, J., *Les Partis politiques et la guerre*, Geneva, 1945.
TINGSTEN, H., *Majoritetsval och proportionalism* (Riksdagen protokoll bihange), Stockholm, 1932.
Political Behaviour, London, 1937.
TRIEPEL, H., *Die Staatsverfassung und die politischen Parteien*, Berlin, 1927.
VEDEL, G., *Les démocraties marxistes* (Cours de l'Institut d'Etudes Politiques de Paris, 1950–1).
VIRGA, P., *Il partito nell' ordinamento giuridico*, Milan, 1948.
WALINE, M., *Les partis contre la République*, Paris, 1948.

A general bibliography of political parties is not yet available. A preliminary list is appended to the article 'Political Parties' in the *Encyclopaedia of Social Sciences*, Vol. II, pp. 636 et seq. and contains some 400 titles, classified by countries. It stops at 1933, however, and is very incomplete, including few Review articles and scarcely any of the pamphlets and documents published by parties. These are of prime importance but are listed fully nowhere to my knowledge. (G. D. H. Cole gives a list for the British Labour Party from 1914 to 1947 in his *History of the Labour Party from 1914*, London, 1948, pp. 488–500.)

A recent basic bibliography is to be found in the volume of studies published under the direction of S. Neumann, *Modern Political Parties*, Chicago, 1956, pp. 425–46.

INDEX

(Names in bold type refer to parties.)

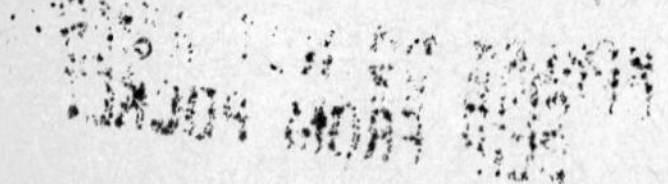